MW00800226

"*It Goes Without Saying* guides rea⟨ of Ned Hall, one of the twentieth c⟨...⟩y ⟨ ...⟩ prominent theorists of space and perception. Combining Hall's timeless insights with Jack Condon's incisive observations on human connection and communication, this book is guaranteed to stimulate new experiences of the different worlds that surround us all. Condon's skillful prose leads us through Hall's life and beyond, to places of enchantment, wonder, discovery, and human understanding."

—*Matthew Liebmann,*
Peabody Professor of American Archaeology and Ethnology,
and Chair of the Department of Anthropology, Harvard University

"*It Goes Without Saying* is a treasure trove for anyone interested in cross-cultural communication. John Condon's discussion of the work of Edward T. Hall is eye-opening even for those of us who were familiar with it, and the many insights gleaned from his own lifelong work, especially in Japan, as well as the classic and recent work of many others, enrich our understanding of the themes and perspectives that Hall pioneered. I filled the margins of my copy with asterisks, and made notes of many page numbers with material I want to follow up. This book is an invaluable resource for those who teach related courses, regularly communicate across cultures, or simply engage in human communication."

—*Deborah Tannen,*
Distinguished University Professor, Georgetown University,
and author of many books including
You Just Don't Understand: Women and Men in Conversation

"Professor and humanist, Jack Condon has written one of the most significant books of this decade about the nuances and subtleties of culture and communication—what is overt and covert, explicit and tacit, visible and invisible. Armed with a keen eye, open heart, and scalpel pen, Condon takes the readers on a breathtaking journey of insight and wonderment on how humans make meaning in interactions with others through sensing and sense-making. This is an exceptional book, scholarly and erudite, wrapped in a highly engaging and accessible narrative that will take readers to destinations that are both familiar and unknown."

—*Arvind Singhal,*
the Samuel and Edna Marston Endowed Professor of Communication,
The University of Texas at El Paso,
and the William J. Clinton Distinguished Fellow,
Clinton School of Public Service, University of Arkansas

"*It Goes Without Saying* is a delight to read and is a long-awaited contribution to the field of Intercultural Communication. John Condon is a skillful storyteller who masterfully weaves together a tapestry of knowledge through vibrant anecdotes and examples. Reading this book feels like a private conversation with the legendary and erudite interculturalist, John Condon, who explains with delight how various fields converge to deepen our understanding of mankind. Every sentence a delight, each word to be savored, each example to be digested."

—*Tomoko Yoshida,*
Professor, Faculty of Business & Commerce,
Keio University, Tokyo, Japan

"In an era of globalization, rapidly fueling connections without context, hence heightened misunderstandings across national and cultural boundaries, there could not be a more timely, insightful exploration of Culture as Communication. John Condon's in-depth and wide-ranging work provides a rich and critical resource for understanding confusing and often dangerous misperceptions within and across national boundaries."

—*Joe Lurie,*
Executive Director Emeritus International House,
University of California, Berkeley

"Lyrical, inviting and incisive, *It Goes Without Saying* shows us familiar territory through new eyes, and through ears attuned to nuance and distinctions that matter. As the chapter on "Rhythm and Synchrony" exemplifies, the book interweaves neuroscience with the universal givens of music and movement, yielding both culture-specific revelations and insights into kindredness across cultures. In tapping his experiences and his decades-long friendship with Edward T. Hall, Condon has created a work both compelling and human, a work that deserves to be read by every student of communication, conflict resolution and leadership."

—*Michelle LeBaron,*
Professor, and dispute resolution scholar,
Peter A. Allard School of Law,
The University of British Columbia, Vancouver, Canada

"Edward T. Hall's work is timeless, yet it seems that it has fallen out of favor in today's fast-paced information age. Thankfully, this book expertly weaves together a myriad of characters, stories, and disciplines to help us understand how intercultural communication came into being and its relevance for now and beyond. John Condon is our gifted bard who devotedly transmits this wisdom for future generations."

—*Kevin Gore,*
Senior Lecturer in Marketing and Intercultural Communication,
Haaga-Helia University of Applied Sciences, Helsinki, Finland

"Unclutter. Sit in your favorite spot. As Jack urges, use all the senses in your body to immerse yourself in this compelling, layered, and nuanced narrative on culture and sense-making. The gentle and powerfully woven stories keep you reflecting and learning long after you put down the heavily-thumbed book."

—*Nagesh Rao,*
Professor, Department of Social Medicine,
Ohio University, Athens, Ohio

"*It Goes Without Saying: Culture* as *Communication* provides insight and perspective critical to the relationships we have today with others and the world we live in."

—*Chad Goeden,*
Associate Director for International Students Programs,
International Students and Scholars Office, Columbia University

"If you thought you knew about Edward T. Hall, then read this . . . Jack Condon masterfully shares impressions, anecdotes, and pictures that draw us into the many culture-thought-and-pattern domains that E. T. Hall elucidated. An invaluable guide that expands us both as cultural persons and researchers!"

—*Steve Kulich,*
Past President, International Academy of Intercultural Research;
Founder SISU Intercultural Institute,
Shanghai International Studies University

"This is a hitchhiker's guide to intercultural awareness."

—*Michael Twomey Valdes,*
ConArte, Mexico City

It Goes
Without Saying

Other Books by the Author

Semantics and Communication
In Search of What's Japanese about Japan
(with Keisuke Kurata)

An Introduction to Intercultural Communication
(with Fathi Yousef)

Buenos Vecinos: Comunicándose Con Los Mexicanos
(translated by Carmen DeNeve)

With Respect to the Japanese

With Respect to the Japanese: Going to Work in Japan
(with Tomoko Masumoto)

Intercultural Encounters with Japan
(edited, with Mitsuko Saito)

Intercultural Communication for What?
(edited, with Mitsuko Saito)

異文化間コミュニケーション: カルチャー・ギャップの理解

It Goes Without Saying

Culture *as* Communication

JOHN CONDON

Random Mouse Press
Jemez Springs, New Mexico 87025 USA

For more information:
Random Mouse Press PO Box 90 Jemez Springs, New Mexico 87025

Cover Designer: Lina Biel
Interior Design: Creative Publishing Book Design

Published in 2025

ISBN Paperback: 979-8-218-37138-8

For David Warren and Rina Swentzell

The two friends to whom the book is dedicated, Dave Warren and the late Rina Swentzell (1939-2015), both from Santa Clara Pueblo, have informed and inspired me for decades, as they have for so many.

Sixty-some years ago I met Dave in Mexico City when we were both doing very different kinds of doctoral research in Mexico. Even then I recognized him as perhaps the most eloquent person I'd ever met—and one of the funniest. A wise historian and educator, Dave was the first Native American to serve on the President's Committee on the Arts and Humanities, was Acting President of the Institute of American Indian Arts (IAIA), the founding Deputy Director of the Smithsonian National Museum of the American Indian (NMAI), and consultant with Indigenous cultural preservation organizations in Tibet, Australia, and China. Dr. Warren's legacy includes influencing the repatriation of human remains and artifacts from universities and museums, and he has had an enduring impact on respect for cultural integrity and for intercultural understanding. When he was named a Santa Fe "Living Treasure," Dave said, "Well, that's better than being a buried treasure."

Rina Swentzell was a gentle, soft-spoken, cultural scholar, artist, author, architect, historian, and guide to many within in the Pueblo Indian communities and to non-Indigenous people (including E. T. Hall) who sought her knowledge and insights. She walked a delicate line in sharing much about her cultural history, values, and practices, but not sharing so much that she risked disapproval by the community elders. Dr. Swentzell was part of a four-generation family of distinguished artists, including her siblings, children, and grandchildren. Though self-effacing, Rina was a fierce advocate for the rights of all people, within her tribe and beyond, and spoke out about how federal policies and values were often at odds with tribal values in education, architecture, and sovereignty.

Contents

Foreword

I met John (Jack) Condon at the Summer Institute for Intercultural Communication in Portland, Oregon, in the summer of 1990. I had just completed my first year of the MA program in Whole Systems Design at Antioch University in Seattle. Part of my role as a student in this self-directed program was to find resources and learning opportunities in my chosen area of focus—intercultural communication. Through word of mouth, I learned about the Summer Institute, immediately applied for the internship program, and found a home. Kindred spirits shared similar experiences, grappled with ways of navigating cultural contradictions and ambiguities, and discussed how to balance conceptual tools with real world application—all critical capacities for my life path in intercultural communication.

Serving as a senior faculty member and faculty fellows coordinator at the Institute, Jack Condon anchored and catalyzed my learning that summer as he has continued to do for more than thirty years. He has been pivotal in my arrivals, departures, and centering in intercultural communication for many decades, just as he has been for so many people around the world. When I think of Jack, I think of poetry in motion—words, people, colors, actions, images, ways of being and seeing, carefully constellated in ways that create new meanings, rhythms, and possibilities. Jack is a designer, a curator of experiences, relationships, learning, and spaces. And like poetry, he juxtaposes elements, musical and cacophonous, creating art—the art of living and being fully human.

Jack's latest creation—this wonderful book, *It Goes Without Saying: Culture as Communication*, about his engagement with Edward T. Hall (Ned) as a person, a practitioner, and illuminator—is a stunning illustration of poetry in motion. "Chapter One: The House on Astor Street," which chronicles Jack's first meeting with Ned, as he asked to be called, reveals so much about Ned and about Jack. Ned's enthusiasm for learning, his excitement in sharing his work, his ability to illuminate new ways of seeing, and new language for meaning-making—Ned's "metaphorical crafting"—is reflected and amplified through Jack's insightful and lyrical telling.

Having had the pleasure of meeting Ned at the Summer Institute in 1994, taking a class from him and later co-teaching a class with him on *Tacit Culture* at the University of New Mexico in the late 1990s, I can personally attest to Ned's sharp inquisitiveness, his brilliant analogic and metaphoric mind, and his love of storytelling. As an octogenarian, Ned, retired for many years, spent hours in our class and even more hours at weekly potlucks with our PhD cohort telling stories. Stories of his life, stories embodying and elucidating the concepts he developed and named, and stories grounding his way of knowing in the senses, in context, and in relationships.

These many years later as I head toward retirement myself, I reflect fondly and gratefully on the experience of knowing Ned, learning from him, teaching his work, and now encountering Ned anew through Jack's eyes. Throughout my twenty-five years of teaching in Los Angeles at one of the most diverse universities in the US, I've started my upper division general education course on Intercultural Communication with Edward T. Hall and Mildred Reed Hall's concise and informing chapter, "Key Concepts: Underling Structures of Culture." This allows me to begin the semester with ideas foundational to intercultural communication, introduce Edward T. Hall as an initiator of the field, and pass along many of the stories Ned shared to illustrate his work. Each year, I'm struck by students' comments about the power of Ned's work to explain their everyday life experiences.

As Jack demonstrates throughout the book, Hall's genius and contribution is in making visible what is hidden and taken for granted in our everyday lives, and naming the cultural patterns regarding key dimensions of human experience such as time, space, and context. Students who commute, literally, between multiple cultural contexts in one day—from immigrant homes, to diverse universities, to corporate workplaces—frequently say, "learning about monochronic and poly-chronic orientations to time just blows me away because it explains so much." Other students comment, "the concept of high and low context helps me understand how much I have to switch the way I do things, how I talk and even how I think when I leave and then return home." Ned's critical work is enlivened through Jack's stories, his insightful commentary and sublime connections. Jack's sense of humor, beauty, and irony expand and illuminate Ned's profound teaching. Now, with the gift of Jack's book, I can only imagine how students of all ages and disciplines will resonate with and benefit from Hall's work.

As I read this book, I'm reminded fondly of being a student in Jack's graduate seminars. In the book and in his classroom, which was most often his kitchen or living room, city streets and rural villages, or in local homes and border towns, Jack always contextualizes concepts and theories in space and time; he shares backgrounds and biographies and traces influences from past, contemporary, and future thinkers; he provides stories that not only illustrate but embody the concepts and ideas he's presenting; and, as much as possible, Jack invites readers/learners into situations to gain multi-sensory, multi-model, and multi-dimensional experiences, which can, through reflection and practice, become learning and knowledge.

For example, Jack shares how Ned, forced to enroll as a teen by his father in an impressionist art class, learned much that impressed him (pun I'm sure intended on Jack's part and certainly mine) about perception, art, and learning; the ways Ned's understanding of culture was forged in his early years as an outsider working with Navajo and Hopi communities in the Southwest; and how Ned's deep appreciation and awe of the land of enchantment was enhanced through his friendship with photographer Ansel Adams. Through the stories, places, and encounters Jack shares, the reader experiences the embodied physicality of culture, the attentive decoding of cultural experiences through inquiry and intuition, as well as the ways the body is used as an instrument of knowing—all foundational to Ned's epistemology and methodology of intercultural communication.

Jack, in this book and in the classroom, also encourages reflection on the limitations of theories and concepts. What's missing or what may be obscured? What's not addressed and what are the implications? If Hall's concepts are reduced to pairs of opposites instead of insisting on understanding them on a continuum, they can lead to dichotomous thinking, overgeneralizations, and, if mishandled, can even reinforce hierarchies of difference, where, for example, low context communication or monochronic orientations to time are viewed as preferable or superior. Jack notes in the book that Ned's concepts and theorizing did not address structural hierarchies, such as systemic racism that privileges certain groups while disadvantaging others. While Hall directed his students in a study about race and race relations in Denver, Colorado, in the 1940s, his work and contributions focused primarily on micro-level interpersonal interactions and pragmatic approaches to cultural differences without delving into broader social, historical, and political contexts.

Ironically, the intercultural field emerged from the privileged positions of educated white, American, middle- and upper-class men in the midst of global decolonial movements and struggles to dismantle systemic racism in the 1950s and 1960s. Hall stood out in his time and place pragmatically and conceptually opposing prevailing racist, ethnocentric, and Eurocentric attitudes; but he was also part of his time and place, where his social location, upbringing, and access all shaped his experience, perception, and understanding of reality. How can we recognize the limits and partiality of Ned's and all knowledge construction while also benefiting from the foundational insights Hall provided? I advocate a "both/and" approach, highlighting what is useful while also pointing to what is or can be limiting and problematic.

To read Ned through Jack's eyes is to enhance and deepen our understanding about what it means to be human. Jack's perspicacious and poetic assemblage of Ned's work, a medley of sources, experiences, and impressions, a connection of dots that adds depth and dimension, allows us, readers and co-experiencers, to feel, sense, experience, and know Ned and Ned's work more deeply. It also opens up new terrain of discovery and possibilities enlivening Ned's work for a new generation. The challenge for Ned, and now for Jack in his writing about Ned's work, is to communicate about the analogic realm—the relational, embodied, and sensorial realm—through digital means, words and written texts. Jack rises to the challenge with this stunning tour de force. The book is an intertextual kaleidoscope of stories, histories, a layered mind map of ideas from mathematicians, artists, philosophers, popular culturists, neuroscientists, and linguists—to name just a few. Imagine meandering through a mashup of all the cultural bazaars you've ever experienced. May the smells, thoughts, sights, sounds, feelings, theories, tastes, rhythms, believable and beyond imagination, envelop and uplift you.

Kathryn Sorrells
Los Angeles, California

Departures

A departure is a beginning, starting out on the path toward the desired destination. And a departure can also be stepping away from that path. By considering culture as communication, and by looking at the *inter,* Edward T. Hall departed from what most others were concerned with. By focusing on "intercultural communication," a term he coined, Hall inadvertently launched an academic field and its application as a consulting profession that now spans the globe. Hall gives us ways to look more closely at what has become an increasingly more familiar experience of people whose backgrounds are significantly different trying to work together. I am fortunate to have known Edward T. (Ned) Hall for forty years, through his writing, then as a colleague at Northwestern University, and later in northern New Mexico as a neighbor and friend.

Although some concepts and words Hall introduced became part of a vocabulary known throughout the world, many of his ideas and insights that never attracted much attention now seem even more relevant today. Advances in research, including neuroscience research, unavailable when Hall was writing, now sharpens, often affirms, and sometimes casts doubt on what he could only speculate. His principal method of research was the same way all of us try to make sense of confusing situations: simple everyday observation and occasionally asking questions. And that's just about what *we* notice as one part of the *inter.* We are less conscious of what is often the more important part of the communication that Hall urged us to pay attention to: our own everyday culturally influenced behavior.

Years ago, at the Summer Institute for Intercultural Communication in Portland, Oregon, for four decades an annual gathering place that attracted thousands of participants in dozens of professions from all over the world, where I was a founding faculty member, I once offered a three-day workshop about Hall's ideas and his influence. Unlike most other workshops, this one did not imply it would be "practical," so when quite a few people joined the workshop I wondered aloud: "Why are you here?" Several said, "I never took a course in 'intercultural communication,' so this looked like a chance to learn from the beginning."

But there are always "beginnings," rarely an agreement about "*the* beginning." Opinions about the starting point, destination, and how to get there vary. My intent is to call attention to some of the concepts or categories that largely have gone unnoticed, and to elaborate and update others that are well known but applied simplistically. Indeed, one of the pleasures in writing the book has been discovering the richness in almost every concept; what here is treated in a few paragraphs or a chapter, could be elaborated. Moreover, research and discoveries in neuroscience and in artificial intelligence make even more clear how "culture" and "communication" are inextricable. So here, Hall's ideas are points of departure, as he himself departed from well-trod paths. Assuming few people will have read all of his books, this book attempts to bring many of his major themes together along with relevant research and implications for today. Variations on themes by E. T. Hall.

This is not a book to encompass all of what might be included in a basic course in intercultural communication. It leaves out much that is crucial to understanding many intercultural tensions, including topics and arguments Hall would have wholeheartedly endorsed, but seen as outside of his focus on observed interaction. Nor is this book intended as a textbook. I've written a few of those, including what was apparently the first dedicated textbook for students of intercultural communication when publishers said there was no market for such a book because there were very few classes on intercultural communication. Today that topic is among the most popular at colleges and universities.

Now, freed from expectations that specific topics must be included, I hope this book might invite further explorations about guideposts rediscovered. I'd like readers to think of this book as more like a conversation as we move along a path shaped by Hall's insights, but then explore these further and in new ways.

Into our conversation I've invited the voices of friends and colleagues from whom I've learned, often while teaching together. They are here not because they write as researchers or scholars, though several are, but because they all speak from experience and from the heart, and what they share is informative, interesting, and thought provoking. Like psychologist Carl Rogers, I'd rather be a learner than a teacher. Teachers know it's impossible to separate the two.

This book is the most personal I've written. My own interests, friendships, and the experience of living abroad, in Latin America, East Africa, and Asia for over twenty years will be apparent because sharing what I've learned was part of the motivation for writing the book. Some readers may find too many references to Japan or Mexico or maybe the Pueblo Indian communities in New Mexico.

One challenge in writing any book is dividing it into chapters when everything is connected to most everything else. Many authors must feel this way. Life doesn't present itself in discrete chapters. Sometimes I wondered if the book might more appropriately be printed as a deck of cards to be sorted and re-sorted, with the potential of new insights that result from new combinations. C. Wright Mills suggested something like that in his book *The Sociological Imagination* (Oxford: Oxford University Press, 1959), published the same year as Hall's *The Silent Language.*

I love books. This book, my twentieth, is my first that is "self-published." It lacks the feel of a proper print publication, and lacks the sniff of authority that comes with the imprimatur of a venerable publishing house. "Self-publishing" is an option that is part of the ongoing digital and media evolution, in photography, movies, music, and other media that in some ways democratizes what can be created and shared as never before. The very idea of publishing a *print book* today may seem anachronistic when e-books and audiobooks, appeal to more people today than a book in print. Here it is in this form, with the advantage to being able to revise, correct, improve, update quickly, and at a lower cost, though missing a bibliophile's aesthetic and a publisher's gravitas.

My wish is that you find something of interest, maybe of value in your work or everyday life, and—so important in Hall's hopes—a mirror for self-reflection.

Jack Condon

Acknowledgements, with Thanks

W hen I think of all of the people who have influenced me, directly and indirectly, and so also helped shape this book, my thoughts go in all directions, a kind of free association of ideas and people who go way back in time. I thought of Diego Rivera's majestic mural *"Sueño de una tarde dominical en la Alameda Central,"* or "Dream of a Sunday Afternoon in Alameda Park." Arrayed across this enormous mural (52 feet/15.7 meters by 15 feet/4.7 meters) are figures from throughout Mexican history, heroes and villains, from ancient indigenous empires to the modern era that appeared in Rivera's "dream." Most of the people who form the background in the mural are facing forward, as if gathered for fanciful a group portrait. Maybe they came together in a stream of consciousness answer to Rivera's wondering, "How did we get here?" Rivera himself, not a modest man, is front and center, but here he presents himself as a ten-year-old child, holding hands with the skeletal *"la Catrina," profundamente Mexicana.* Towering over Rivera is his wife, Frida Kahlo, today more famous than her husband and sometime lover.

But in the foreground, we see ordinary people of the time when the mural was painted, anonymous people, not posing for their portraiture but shown actively involved in a context that reveals the tensions of ethnic, social class, and economic power inequities, issues so important to Rivera and Kahlo. Here on the right, we see a policeman scowling at an Indigenous family, ordering them to leave the park because people of their social class don't belong here. To the left we see an element of the underground economy and in resistance to the racial and social class inequality that Rivera depicted in much of his work, a kid picking the pocket of a wealthy visitor.

Academics and attorneys cite precedent, answers to how others helped bring us to where we are, but front and center should be on the now. I guess this book is my personal "Sunday Dream" where past and present intermingle as they often do in dreams.

Here are some people I want to acknowledge and thank:

Let me first thank Karin Bergh Hall, artist and widow of "Ned" Hall, and Professor Hall's son, retired attorney, Eric Reed Hall, for their friendship of many years, and for sharing stories that fill in some of what was not included in Hall's autobiography. And special appreciation to Gladys Levis Pilz who was Hall's Teaching Assistant and dissertation advisee, and Arie Pilz who also knew Hall as a lifelong friend and mentor, both of whom shared information and personal stories about a person who so influenced their lives, professionally and personally.

An unsung hero in earliest years of the intercultural communication field, David Hoopes founded the Intercultural Press to share ideas, concepts, theories, and illustrative experiences. His graduate studies were in "American culture," and he said that almost nothing he had studied could answer questions that visitors from abroad would ask. The entire intercultural communication field is indebted to Hoopes for his pioneering publications.

I want to thank those I've learned from by way of many long friendships and often through working together. Some offered more help, especially those whose names and words appear in this book, and others whose influence has been more subtle—some might be surprised to see their names here. In no particular order, I want to thank: Carmen DeNeve, Muneo Yoshikawa, Sherwood Smith, Richard Harris, Nagesh Rao, Deborah Tannen, Sheila Ramsey, Miguel Gandert, Matthew Liebmann, Glen Fukushima, Patti Digh, Leslie Weigl, Marcia Warren, Lauren Mark, Claudia Chapa Cortés, Cheryl Forster, Keith Terry, Tomoko Masumoto, Sharon Waller, Ted Dale, Susan Carter, Dorianne Galarnyk, Bibiana Arcos, Frank Perez, Marie Sheffield, Adrian Sandia, Bruce La Brack, Clifford Clarke, Ernie Gundling, Chenoa Bah Stillwell-Jensen, Kenichi Saito, Monserrat Hernandez, Porter Swentzell, Roxanna Springer, Marilyn Fabe, Christina Kennedy, Michael Condon, Tatyana Fertelmeyster, Jean Mavrelis, Thomas Kochman, and Jack Parsons.

Finally, *mil gracias* to two Kathryns.

Kathryn Sorrells, who kindly wrote the Foreword to this book, has been a close friend and colleague for many years, is a creative and gifted artist in many genres, an award-winning educator in one of the most culturally diverse universities in the US, and an influential author. As a doctoral candidate at the University of New Mexico, Kathryn persuaded Professor Hall to come out of retirement and, for two years teach a special graduate seminar with her, the final classes Hall taught. Kathryn advanced the study of intercultural communication by bringing into the field a concern for social justice, one of the desired outcomes of more effective communication across cultural groups. She does so in her book *Intercultural Communication: Globalization and Social Justice*, and also through her students' actions.

Kathryn Stillings, a dear friend who has edited the work of several of the best-known writers in the field, generously offered to edit this book. I believe anyone who writes anything to be viewed by the public benefits from an editor. With an editor who is also a friend, questions and suggestions often venture off into long conversations (departures!), stories shared, and with Kathryn, not infrequent laughter. I've never enjoyed collaborating with, and benefiting from, an editor as much as with Kathryn. Now, I'm a little sad that the book is published because we enjoyed working together so much—but without Kathryn's editorial experience, skill, and sensitivity, the book might never have been published. If you enjoy this book, you must thank Kathryn. If you didn't enjoy the book, blame Kathryn.

It Goes
Without Saying

Sketch by Robert Caslin

CHAPTER ONE

The House on Astor Street

The task is . . . not so much to see what no one
has yet seen; but to think what nobody has yet
thought, about that which everybody sees.
—*Erwin Schrödinger*

I t was, as I recall, a crisp autumn afternoon in 1963 when I
knocked on a door at 1218 North Astor Street, in the high-end
neighborhood in the near north side of Chicago, Illinois, where
Edward T. Hall then lived with his wife, life partner, and collaborator,
Mildred, and their two children, Ellen and Eric. I was twenty-four
years old, shy because I looked like I was nineteen, and had only
recently been invited to join the faculty of the department now called
"Communication Studies" at Northwestern University, in Evanston,
just north of Chicago.

Approaching the home of a famous professor I had never met, I
worried that maybe I would just be bothering a person who surely
had better things to do than to talk to me. I was a little nervous.
Four years earlier, just months before completing my undergraduate

studies, I had read Hall's seminal book, *The Silent Language*, when it was first published. One of my professors told me he thought I might find it interesting. Indeed, I did. It helped me make sense of my first year of college as a kid, first time abroad, in Mexico City, and again in Mexico when in my doctoral research I was trying to make sense of Mexican-US communication in everyday life. I knew it had to be more than our dismal political history.

Now, as a college teacher I could encourage—require—such reading for my students. Hall's book was one I wanted to include, even though the course "Language and Thought" was centered on words. What about the unspoken that Hall called the silent languages? What goes without saying?

That summer I was about to travel for two months, visiting countries in Central and South America for the first time, which gave me a sincere excuse to write a letter to Professor Hall, then resident anthropologist at the Illinois Institute of Technology (IIT) in Chicago, requesting to visit him at his office to ask his advice about what I might observe during my travels that I might not otherwise recognize. To my surprise he replied immediately, and suggested I visit him not at his office, but at his home.

And here I was in one of Chicago's most fashionable nineteenth-century neighborhoods. A few years earlier in 1959, residents in the area were scandalized when Hugh Hefner, editor of the new *Playboy* magazine, moved into another old house just a few blocks away and established what would become the first "Playboy Mansion." I wasn't thinking about that then, but now, looking back, it comes to mind, and helps mark an era that two generations later would be vicariously experienced through a popular TV series "Mad Men."

That first meeting remains vivid. Professor Hall greeted me at the door, invited me in, and when I addressed him as "Professor Hall," he asked me to call him "Ned." The discomfort that international students who come to the US feel when asked to call their professors by their first names was what I felt then. It would be years before I could call him "Ned." I had friends who even called their parents by their "first names," but I wasn't raised that way, so it was a "cultural thing" though I wouldn't have been able to describe it that way then. What is intended as welcoming, and an ambiguous status-reducing offer, can feel like a well-intentioned burden to anyone who values status differences through which we would show respect. But that's getting ahead of the story.

Professor Hall invited me back to his office, gesturing toward the light coming from a room down the hall. Walking through that corridor I passed several brightly lit, very large paintings. Only later would I learn how much Hall drew from the arts in his work, including borrowing a vocabulary he learned when, as a teenager, he was forced to take a class on "Impressionist Art" instead of working as part of a road crew as many teenage boys would want to join. In my limited vocabulary about art, the paintings were "abstract" or "modern art," what I'd seen at museums like Chicago's Art Institute, located not so far from the Hall residence. Now I believe they were abstract impressionist paintings, but the experience was like passing through an intimate art gallery, with each painting highlighted by a beam of light. I paused and stepped back to look more carefully at one, and Professor Hall took that moment to remark not about the painting, but to point out the source of the illumination—a tiny spotlight mounted on the opposite wall. He had devised these lights that I hadn't even noticed until he pointed them out.

The office was spacious and brightly lit. There were stacks of papers and books all over the room, but it did not feel chaotic, just impressive in trying to imagine what information and insights these small towers of papers and books might hold. Later I would appreciate what an organized man he was, reading his notes and correspondence and talking with some of the students he advised. Hall's academic papers and correspondence are now archived at the University of Arizona where he received his MA in anthropology.

We sat down and made small talk, an interval that must have seemed a longer time to Professor Hall than to me, though when one is nervous, time can feel like those melting watches in Dalí's famous painting, "The Persistence of Memory." Psychological time.

I asked what he was working on now. "Space," or something similar and in a tone that indicated "I'm glad you asked." With a new enthusiasm, he talked about big questions: about how we experience space, and how we shape spaces that affect and become a part of that experience. In his book—then his only book—he called attention to how we feel and learn to act and interpret a kind of language of space. "Space Speaks" was the catch phrase, and that part of *The Silent Language* was then, and for many still, one of those, "I'd never realized that until now!" moments of discovery, and for decades would become a feature in presentations about intercultural communication, a term Hall introduced.

Most impressive that afternoon was the range of subjects and areas of study that he mentioned, and his enthusiasm for each, especially in his excitement that these were all connected. He spoke of research that seemed to come from areas of study I never had heard one person talk about as if they were part of his specialization. It didn't feel like he was showing off to someone who knew nothing about any of this. Rather, it had the quality of a child's enthusiasm of discovery but with insights few parents bring together. Almost giddy, so different from other professors I have been privileged to learn from but whose reflective tone was of sentences that would begin with: "We have found that . . . ." Hall's voice came from a place of unbridled curiosity and excitement about how our categorical vocabularies limit our full appreciation. At that time, for me, that was a revelation.

He talked in terms of physiology and psychology about how we see—and don't see—and something similar about hearing, and about our skin, our largest organ for sensing. And how our experience of space involves so many senses, and what the brain does in this process.

About the importance of acoustical space, how we know where we are in part because of how we hear. About psychological studies of how schizophrenics perceive their personal space bubble being enclosed upon. He mentioned the findings of sociologists concerned with urban density, and stress, and about architects, urban planners, and he mentioned photographers and other visual artists. In my memory now, it was a kind of stream of consciousness of wonder, as each thing he mentioned connected to the next.

He credited the help of research assistants (IIT grad students, I imagined) for what they were uncovering when they explored as he had urged: to learn everything they could about how we experience space. Thinking back on that visit, it is possible that Professor Hall, whom I worried about bothering, may have enjoyed having an audience of one with whom he could share his enthusiasm for what he was in the midst of without being obliged to mentor. All this that Hall told me was part of what would appear two years later in *The Hidden Dimension*, a book that firmly established his reputation, a book now considered a classic.

At some point, Hall asked me to remind him what I had come to ask him about, and even then, as now, for both of us it was the least important part of the visit. Of course, I could not have imagined this conversation would be the beginning of what would be friendship spanning four decades. It was not long after that first meeting that we would be colleagues, in different departments, at Northwestern University, and, many years later, I would find myself living in northern New Mexico where Hall had grown up, and then returned to the land and people he loved. This is also where I have lived for over forty years, during which time we were neighbors and friends.

Two things I have come to realize that were present that afternoon, and that have become more apparent and more meaningful since. One was that the view from his hallway, a short passageway rich in artwork, was my entry into his space and a glimpse of how he looked at the world. It was not the art displayed, but Hall's ingenuity in crafting ways to cast light on what we look at but may not see so clearly, even when it is right before our eyes. Hall loved the art but he was not the artist; rather, he was one who helped to illuminate the wonder that is before us.

It was not just the physical crafting of lights and lenses, but the metaphorical crafting that would come to give us novel points of view, including direct guidance on how to perceive, and often a new, ordinary language vocabulary that could be easily learned to help us look at things in a different light. This would be a reason he would come to have such a wide reach and, indeed, bring together people from different fields and traditions to shape a new field: intercultural communication. It would also provoke his critics.

The other realization is about the excitement and significance of centering our attention on life as experienced, without being constrained by the conventional cultural and academic categories that often limit understanding. As with other features of language, learning a new word helps us recognize something that may not have been quite in focus; paradoxically, attraction to particular words can lead us to stop seeing. This is also a theme in Hall's work.

"Multi-disciplinary" is what some would call such an approach, but that seven-syllable term accepts the imposed boundaries of institutions that create categories and draw distinctions that many perpetuate and defend as "reality." My friend, David Warren, Native American historian and scholar who knew and admired Hall, calls him "an epistemologist" who appreciated that there are many kinds of truths and ways of knowing.

"Culture hides more than it reveals
 and strangely enough what it hides,
it hides most effectively from its own participants.

Years of study have convinced me
that the real job is not to understand foreign culture
but to understand our own."

Edward T. Hall

*Edward T. Hall, at age 83, talking with doctoral students
from the Department of Communication, University
of New Mexico, at the author's home in 1997.*

Photo by Miguel Gandert

CHAPTER TWO

An Anthropologist
of Everyday Life

Ned Hall lives anthropology—
one of those rare people who lived it before
he even knew the word.
—*Paul Bohannan*

Neither the life of an individual nor the history
of a society can be understood
without understanding both.
—*C. Wright Mills*

E dward Twitchell Hall was born on May 16, 1914, in Webster
Groves, Missouri, and he died on July 20, 2009, at his home
in Santa Fe, New Mexico, at the age of 95. His was a remarkable life
that spanned most of the last century, and continues to influence our
thinking about who we are in this twenty-first century, and maybe
helps us get along in the world where consideration of "intercultural
relations" demands more respect than historic power relationships.

Hall recounts the first-half of his life story in his autobiography, *An Anthropology of Everyday Life*, so if you seek details about his biography and insights he drew from his life, that's where to look.[1] Hall wrote a second part of his autobiography; that latter part of his interrupted story remains in draft form on a shelf in a shed, I learned from Gladys Pilz, for whom Ned was a mentor, and later, a close friend.[2] His long-time publisher, Doubleday, concluded that the market for E. T. Hall's story was shrinking as the twentieth century was coming to an end. Still, his published autobiography makes for rewarding reading, and not a few feel it may be his most interesting book.

Nothing Means Anything Without Context

Born in a prosperous suburb of St. Louis, Missouri, young Ned's life was never that of a boy who enjoyed a carefree childhood. At age five, Hall's mother decided to pack up and move a thousand miles west, first to El Paso, Texas, and then further north to Santa Fe, the remote capital of New Mexico, which had become a state just nine years earlier. Not long after settling in, his mother decided that the family should return to Missouri, where Hall attended a private school in which he was not happy, in part because he was dyslexic. And then, seven years later, young Ned returned to Santa Fe, this time with his father but without his mother. His parents divorced when he was 13, and his effort to come to terms with that separation was something he would struggle with for rest of his life. His life-long interest in psychology would be as much personal as later it was also professional.

It is hard to imagine a place more different from Webster Groves, Missouri, than Santa Fe, New Mexico, in the early decades of the twentieth century. At that time, St. Louis was the fourth-largest city in the US and had recently hosted both a World's Fair and the Summer Olympics. In stark contrast, small, rural, remote Santa Fe must have seemed a nothing town, in the middle of nowhere, in an alien land. Visitors mocked it as "Prairie Dog Town," comparing the adobe buildings to rodent mounds. Ironically, these days, "real adobe homes" sell for millions of dollars. Many are the second or third homes of the wealthy who visit only once or twice a year. This is not where Ned Hall grew up.

Nuevo Mexico, as the region was named when it was a province of Mexico, was the northernmost part of the *Virreinato de la Nueva España*, the Viceroyalty of New Spain, which lasted from 1521 until Mexico declared its independence from Spain in 1821. This region of New Spain, then the colony's most remote area, was devoid of the gold and silver that the Spaniards sought, and absent the formidable and magnificent aboriginal cities found in other parts of Mesoamerica and in South

America. This far-off province of *Nuevo Mexico* was distant and of little value to the centralized government. Its culture evolved and survived as a separate place, a *patria chica*, a small and distinct version of the nation, like a vernacular of a language, and a marginal place for

John Gast, American Progress, 1872

Mexican authorities that would become a cultural puzzlement in the path of "manifest destiny," the exhortation of a nineteenth-century journalist that the United States reach coast-to-coast.[3]

A decade before the Puritans landed on the Atlantic shore of North America in 1620, the Spanish had established an outpost in Santa Fe, where the governor's palace was built and functioning at a time when Shakespeare was still writing. That building, now the oldest public building in the US, would be home to the provincial governors sent from Mexico City. Until, in 1680, the colonized and much-abused Indigenous "Pueblo Indians" (as the Spanish had named them because they lived in villages, *pueblos*) rose up against these alien rulers, and the Spanish were routed and chased hundreds of miles from their colonial headquarters to the current location of the US/Mexico border. Many Native Americans celebrate this as "the first American Revolution," the only time in the Americas when a confederation of Indigenous leaders successfully revolted and drove the colonizers—who had steel armor and weapons and Arabian horses—from their land.

Twelve years later, the Spanish returned and reasserted their authority, but with concessions to those who had vanquished them. Importantly, the Pueblo languages and their spiritual beliefs and practices were formally allowed along with those imposed by the colonizers: two languages, individuals with two names, and two spiritual practices. This remains today, with a range of feelings about it. In 1811, with Mexican Independence, the territory became part of Mexico. Not long afterwards, US President Polk provoked a war with the newly independent and struggling Mexico in order to acquire more land in which to extend the slavery of the South. The US extracted nearly half the land of Mexico, including the Mexican state of *Nuevo Mexico* which was split three ways, the US Territories of New Mexico, Arizona, and a small area of Colorado. In 1912, New Mexico became the next-to-last contiguous state, just two years before Ned Hall was born.

Perhaps the most famous of the territorial governors sent from Washington was Lewis "Lew" Wallace who served from 1878-1881, and who, while at the state capitol, wrote much of the novel, *Ben-Hur*, published in 1880. Wallace, a Civil War general, sent to be governor of the territory to help quell outlaw skirmishes, famously summarized his judgment about the territory: "All calculations based on experience elsewhere, fail in New Mexico."

"New Mexico exceptionalism," we might say—a feeling during Hall's early years that later became a boast to encourage writers, artists, and more recently, celebrities and tourists, to this curious place. This history is important in appreciating the world in which the young Ned Hall lived.

The history that students have been taught in our schools is from an English colonial perspective, largely ignoring the pre-contact Indigenous history, and mostly ignoring the presence of the rival Spanish on this land, which preceded the English by a century, and made a cultural impact that not only continues today, but is markedly altering US national culture. Especially in the first decades of the twentieth century, when racist and ethnic prejudices became law, the land where Hall grew up seemed as if it were a foreign country, as indeed it was then—geographically, historically, and culturally.

Now we know this place as part of "the Southwest," an apt description on a US national, geo-political map, but one that belies the cultural history that still endures. The region is a northern extension of the land and peoples of today's Mexico and Central America, *el norte.* For millennia, long before the Spanish settled in the region, the area was connected by trade and a variety of other reasons, and was home to more than two thousand indigenous, spiritually centered, agricultural communities that the Spanish would later identify as people who lived in pueblos, which were often raided by the Comanche, Diné (Navajo), and Apaches. When the Spanish arrived, there were perhaps one hundred pueblos, maybe more. Today, there are just nineteen pueblo tribes in the place marked off as New Mexico, but, if we ignore these artificial boundaries, there are many more, including the Hopi in Arizona, and even more in what is now south of the international border, in Mexico.

In 1610, the Spanish colonizers established their modest regional capital, *La Villa Real de la Santa Fe de San Francisco de Assisi*, or "The Royal City of the Holy Faith of Saint Francis of Assisi." While local boosters now call Santa Fe "The City Different," it—and the whole region—really were different from most US Indigenous cultures. Especially the languages were a magnet attracting European scholars— German linguists, in particular—to come to the US so they could study languages that were "uncorrupted" by European languages.

Writers, as well as painters from abroad, were drawn to this place. D. H. Lawrence with his wife Frieda lived here off and on between 1922 and 1925, and Lawrence wrote parts of his novels *Sons and Lovers* and *The Plumed Serpent* here. Before his death in Venice in 1930, he told friends he hoped to return, in part because the high desert was a more hospitable setting for one suffering from tuberculosis. Later, some of his ashes were returned and encased in a building on the ranch that Frieda deeded to the University of New Mexico.

The English writer Aldous Huxley briefly lived in New Mexico and visited the Lawrences at their ranch. In one of the most famous dystopian novels of the twentieth century, *Brave New World*, Huxley would describe this place as an island of undisturbed tradition, a veritable theme park. Hall's son, Eric, describes Santa Fe in the 1920s as a "Bohemian art center" and internationally known as "gay friendly" where even the conservative Catholic community outwardly maintained a live-and-let-live tolerance of these radical outsiders. This is where Hall grew up.

As noted, New Mexico and Arizona and a portion of Colorado are part of a contiguous region, geographically and culturally, which the US acquired as a result of the Mexican-American War (1846-1848) and would later arbitrarily divide into separate territories in the nineteenth century. Perhaps there were too many Indians, too many "Spanish"—historic rivals of the English speakers—and far too many "racially mixed" people for a country where, in some states, interracial marriage was legally prohibited until 1967. And surely also, in the land where power and its history were largely Protestant, there were too many Catholics. And so, for these reasons, in addition to others, New Spain's northern-most province of Nuevo Mexico was split up into parts of three states.

To urge the US Congress to admit the acquired Territory of New Mexico to statehood, there emerged a useful myth of "the three cultures": Indian, Spanish, and "Anglo"—a term that meant "neither of those other two" but mostly meant "white." People whose place of origin was Africa, though, one of whom, "Esteban," arrived in the region even before the first Spaniard, would presumably be "Anglo" by that three-part designation.[4] The "three cultures" trope was also an implicit reassurance to the men in Washington that there was no miscegenation, "inter-racial marriage," in this place, so distant and alien in almost every respect. Of course, the "three cultures" was misleading, as architectural historian at the University of New Mexico, Chris Wilson, has explained in his excellent book, *The Myth of Santa Fe*, and is part of what Wilson calls "invented tradition."[5]

Today, there is an upside to the "otherness" of the region: it gives a distinct identity—some now might say "branding"—of the state that appeals to tourists.

The television series, "Breaking Bad," (2008-2013) set in Albuquerque, the state's largest city, an hour to the south of Santa Fe, probably didn't do much to dispel the image of this land as a kind of "other" place. Even now, some postal clerks in the US tell customers mailing something to New Mexico that they will need additional postage. The state license plates indicate "New Mexico, USA" as if to remind visitors that this place really is part of these United States.

The land and peoples of New Mexico exerted an enormous influence on Hall's life, and also on his appreciation of communication and culture. As he would often tell his students, "nothing means anything without 'context,'" and it is difficult to appreciate how Hall came to see the world without appreciating the influence of this regional, geographical, and cultural context. New Mexico would be his home, and yet at the same time it was a place that also seemed far away from the home he left behind when his mother decided to move. He grew up in a place that people he would later meet would imagine as the Wild West. Even in the 1930s, Hall described this land as ". . . the last gasp of the nineteenth century."[6]

Sweet Are the Uses of Adversity

Hearing and reading Hall's recollections of his childhood, the words "dysfunctional family," a term not yet available when he was growing up, comes to mind, in addition to "abandonment." Rina Swentzell, from Santa Clara Pueblo, whom I was fortunate to know as a friend, and to whom this book is dedicated along with her cousin David Warren, recalled conversations with Ned even after he had retired and returned to his beloved Santa Fe.[7] "We talked about so many things, and we argued about many things." She says that one thing that stands out for her is how often Hall would speak of his childhood. "He felt he was an orphan, abandoned by his mother." It was a feeling that ran deep.

Hall's feelings of childhood abandonment and emotional family struggles as a child may well have sharpened a sensitivity that shaped his life's work. Marilyn Fabe, psycho-biographer and film scholar at the University of California, Berkeley, remarked about the potential effects of such childhood experiences:

> Children in troubled families have to become more sensitive and observant to verbal and non-verbal behavior to survive. Feeling like an orphan, moreover, is feeling like you don't have a home, which might have given him particular insight into the experience of strangers in a strange land because, possibly, he always felt like one. His feeling abandoned by his mother (not having sufficient closeness with her) might also be related to his interest in proxemics.[8]

Hall's parents divorced when he was living far from his mother, and yet he also traveled to Europe with her and her new husband, a German-American sculptor. There is a not too subtle edge in Hall's writing when he describes the German-Americans he knew as a youth. He credits his mother for his early sensitivity to aesthetics, and also the sense of wonder she evoked in telling him European folk fairy tales of the brothers Grimm and Anderson, so different from the stories that many of his neighbors' children would be told.

In Santa Fe, Ned's neighbors were "Spanish," the ethnic category of choice in the regional vernacular then—even today in some villages—and Indians—still a proper term—from the nearby Pueblo Indian communities. Ned credits a woman who worked as a maid and caretaker for the family when he was young with his earliest realization that one's background affects how we experience our different realities. This personal history shaped an outlook on life reflected in all of his work, his profession and his values, and his attention to the natural and built environments.

The Natural Environment

"Not of human scale," University of New Mexico journalism professor who later became best known as a novelist, Tony Hillerman, said of the region's physical landscape. A feeling expressed powerfully, without words, by Ansel Adams, whose photography helped millions feel the awe that the land and sky inspires. Adams and Hall were friends. Hall appreciated Adams's art, and also was intrigued by the potential of photography for his research. Arie Pilz, an intercultural consultant working closely with native communities for many years, believes Adams and Hall exerted a mutual influence on each other. Indeed, Hall and Adams spent many hours together when they were developing their photos in the darkroom at the Museum of Anthropology in Santa Fe, Hall's son Eric recalls. We might imagine their conversations about the land and people of the region, Adams with his grand images of the land, and Hall with his close-up images of the people.

From personal experience and anthropological work, Hall respected the majesty of the land. He saw it as a gift to those who appreciated it, and would eloquently present it that way to the world. He also knew that for the land-based cultures of Native Americans its meaning went far deeper, down to their core—their place of origin and sustenance, their identity—protected by hills that hold the stories, and the more distant sacred mountains that embrace the tribal community, and all that that extends beyond. What may be an aesthetic "landscape" to visitors is but an outsider's glimpse of a part of those whose identity is rooted in that land where the spirits of those who have gone before still reside. It's not "real estate," "property," a "commodity," nor virgin land nor widowed land. Pueblo communities are, as David Warren has pointed out, "theocratic states" in the midst of a secular nation that is ill-prepared to appreciate or comprehend what that means.[9]

The physical environment was an enormous influence on Hall, as on so many people. Yet, Hall gives little attention in most of his writings to the natural landscape; it was the built- and social-environments that would become a defining feature of his work. How houses are aligned in a community, how rooms are laid out and used: this was what he wrote about and helped others see. Were he alive now, I imagine he would expand or redirect his attention to the physical environment that holds us, and how we need to work together to keep this human enterprise continuing.

Young Ned Hall was an outsider where he grew up and studied and worked. The history of insights into intercultural understanding is a history of outsiders, or those who are or feel they are marginalized, and then have the privilege of telling others what they have felt and what they think they have learned. Although Hall's references and anecdotes that intercultural communication practitioners might cite are more likely to be international, his discovery and appreciation of the "cultural" and "intercultural" were home-grown in his own early life. Today we have learned that these are the years that shape each of our lives.

The Los Alamos Ranch School for Boys

When he was twelve, Ned's father enrolled him in the progressive and expensive Los Alamos Ranch School for Boys. It was one among several of the nation's most prestigious "ranch schools" that appeared between the First and Second World Wars, the only one in New Mexico, with others in Arizona, Wyoming, and California. The school's location in the Jemez Mountains west of Santa Fe was, itself, a crucial part of the curriculum. In the Jemez Mountains, the school buildings would have been most visible of human structures on that forested plateau, which offered breathtaking views of the valleys below and the other mountain ranges in the distance. At about 7500 feet/2300 meters above sea level, where winter snows later made this ski country, the Los Alamos school was physically challenging. A strenuous life in nature resonated with many of the students' fathers who were, or claimed to be, inspired by the life of Teddy Roosevelt.

The teachers were largely graduates of Ivy League schools, the curriculum was serious and intense, with the grander goal of helping to shape moral character and to inspire and foster a sense of commitment to the betterment of society, no less than to maintaining high academic standards. Only 40 students were enrolled each year.

At each table in the Ranch School dining hall a teacher or counselor sat with the students to engage them in conversation at every meal.

The boys wore Boy Scout uniforms, with short pants worn year-round; there was no heat in the screened-in porches where they slept. The school assigned to each boy a horse and taught him how to care for it and how to ride it well. Considered "luxurious" then, but affirmed today in many rehabilitation programs that see the value of forming a link between people and animals they must care for. Hall developed a life-long love of horses, deepened by his practical skill on horseback years later during the Great Depression. Hall often talked about his research work traveling on horseback; "grounded research" has a different meaning when going from place-to-place on horseback rather than by car or pickup truck.

Even at the school Hall was, in many ways, an outsider; he was local, while his classmates were far from home, many from wealthy families on the East Coast. His family was neither famous nor wealthy. He had nothing in common with the experience and privilege of his classmates, yet he did have the sense of place that his classmates needed to find.

In a fascinating book, *Prep School Cowboys: Ranch Schools in the American West*, Melissa Bingmann characterizes many of the students of these schools in

Young Ned on Frisk, his Ranch School horse

her telling chapter, "The Problem of the Rich Man's Son."[10] In it she describes the felt responsibility to inculcate in the sons of the wealthy and powerful a strong moral character and responsibility for the greater good. Bingmann writes at length about "the West" as seen—not just then and at those schools, but later in the popular culture of Western movies, and in ways that would spread far beyond the US. She writes that "No place has been so consistently identified with maleness as the region as the American West."[11]

Of the students at these exclusive between-wars prep-schools, their surnames read, as Bingmann writes, like the Social Register. Parents included: William Randolph Hearst, the Governors of Maine and New Hampshire, Mrs. Fred Astaire, Albert L. Deane of the General Motors Holding Corporation, Dr. Robert Hutchins of the University of Chicago, and journalist Dorothy Thompson and her husband, Sinclair Lewis. Bingmann goes on to name families whose sons attended just one of these prestigious schools, the Evans School in Arizona: Saltonstall, Roosevelt, Vanderbilt, DuPont, Sperry, Cabot, Heinz, Pulitzer, Lowell.

Among the boys who attended the Los Alamos Ranch School were sons of the Colgate (toothpaste) family, a boy whose family was part of the Sears Roebuck extended family—he would later build "the Sears Tower" in Chicago, for a time the tallest building in the world; and a boy whose father was president of the Chicago Cubs baseball team, and who himself would become the colorful and innovative manager of three major league baseball teams, Bill Veeck. His autobiography, *Veeck as in Wreck*, is considered classic baseball lore.

Another of Hall's classmates was William S. Burroughs, scion of the Burroughs family of the then-prominent office machine company that bears that name. Hall and Burroughs, whose classmates called "Bugs" because he was interested in biology, were friends and the same age. Decades later he would achieve fame (or notoriety) through his novel, *Naked Lunch*, a defining part of the Beat Generation, the period in the '60s when Hall's books introduced his take on culture to millions, while Burroughs became part of that era's counter-culture. Their respective books that brought fame to each were published in the same year, 1959. Years later, another prominent writer, Gore Vidal, attended the Los Alamos school, but just for one year, perhaps anticipating his lifetime work of wit and cynicism about authority. He was not happy at the school, and apparently the feeling was mutual.

It was just one early teenage year (before "teenager" was a term) that Ned Hall was able to be at the Los Alamos Ranch School, but in conversation and in his writing, he credits that year as among the most important in his life:

> The principles the school got across in everything it did, particularly outside the classroom, were of importance: 1) doing things right, 2) having and maintaining good equipment; 3) impeccable planning and organization. To me, that's a lot. What is more, little was said about these three principles, but everyone from the gardener [to the headmaster] practiced them 24 hours a day. The message was a powerful one.[12]

Years later, this exclusive boys' school would gain international and historic significance, though in a way unimaginable when Ned Hall was a student there. The Manhattan Project, the ambitious undertaking in research and development to design and make an atomic bomb, needed a secret location, and, at J. Robert Oppenheimer's suggestion, the Los Alamos Ranch School's location seemed perfect for this secretive work. The land was taken, with compensation, by the government, the school rushed its last term, and "Project Y," which would come to be called the Manhattan Project, had its home.[13] The former Ranch School buildings were where the lead scientists in the project lived and where social events occurred, but the laboratories and test sites required an estimated 54,000 acres (219 square kilometers). Much of this was already government Forest Service land, but there were also Hispano homesteaders who were compensated for the seizure of their lands at a rate far lower than their Anglo neighbors. Disputes and lawsuits related to lands seized, as well as compensation for cancers that resulted from the effects of the nuclear "gadget" tested at Trinity Site, are ongoing.[14]

Now this area is part of the Manhattan Project National Historical Park, in partnership with two other key sites: Oak Ridge, Tennessee, and Hanford, Washington, where uranium was processed. Almost all of the buildings quickly constructed at this "secret site" in New Mexico have long since been destroyed—though the Los Alamos National Laboratory is bigger than ever nearby—and what remains of the historic buildings are those substantial buildings of that remote but esteemed prep school. Where fourteen-year-old Ned Hall learned to work a lathe in "shop class" later became Enrico Fermi's home; where he may have visited the infirmary is now the Los Alamos History Museum.

Hall attended the Los Alamos Ranch School his freshman year and summer camp before and after that year. Apart from short stays at the main ranch, most of the summer was spent on horseback exploring the Valle Grande, a large caldera that is now part of the Valles Caldera National Preserve. Hall writes that this time, the end of the 1920s, was therapeutic in the vast and beautiful landscape of the high desert after the feeling of being orphaned. But at the end of that summer, Hall was shocked to be told by school's headmaster that he would no longer be attending the Los Alamos Ranch School, but instead be transferred to a different school, the Aspen Ranch School in Santa Fe.

The Aspen Ranch School was run by a man named Appleton whom Hall described as "a nut" playing cowboy. Nevertheless, Appleton turned out to be perhaps the most effective teacher he ever had.[15] It was at this time that Hall experienced yet a second "abandonment" when his father told him he would be living with Theresa Dorman and Joe Bakos, people he barely knew. At their home he was given a room off their kitchen that had been used as a storage area.

Hall's mother, now divorced from his father, had visited Santa Fe again in the 1920s with her second husband-to-be, a sculptor, Heinz Warneke. Apparently, Hall's mother had become friends with

Theresa, whom she introduced to her former husband. Hall's father was persuaded by Theresa to leave his son in her care in Santa Fe, and save "all that tuition money" by having young Hall attend the public, and thus free, Santa Fe High School. In an unpublished work, Hall describes this woman, Theresa, and his fate in her hands:

> Theresa wormed her way into the life of our family the summer of 1926, first, as a "friend" of my mother and later of my father . . . . I had been exploited as an object more like someone who had been kidnapped and held for ransom and in the process moved around to suit her purposes.
>
> At this point, I should say something about my father; On the matter of status he was a divided soul. A descendent of the original colony of Puritan settlers of modest means, who had pulled himself up by his own boot straps, to become a successful businessman: vice president of the Ralston Purina Co working for Donald Danforth as Danforth's chief of advertising. Dad wore the most expensive tailored suits and alternated between throwing out his chest as he twisted the waxed ends of his mustache, and saying, "I'm nothing but a simple New England lad." He never did settle on who he really was—only on the impression he felt he should make and later talked about when he was in big business. When mother left him for Heinz, he was devastated and even took up painting as well as an interest in art.
>
> Theresa was what people used to call an adventuress. At some point along the way she teamed up with a confidence man named Dorman who specialized in a variety of scams to relieve wealthy people of their money. Her story was that she was an Italian Countess whose husband had taken her money and lost it gambling. Of course, there were other stories about Theresa, some of them more plausible than others, such as

that she and a blond worked on the first-class passengers on the trans-Atlantic ocean liners.

When Dad arrived, Theresa wasted no time getting the information she needed which was, how much it [tuition] was costing him. . . . "My goodness. You could give us the money, he could stay with us where he would have a home and go to Santa Fe high school for nothing." No sooner said than done, and I found myself living in Santa Fe with Theresa Dorman, adventuress . . .[16]

Hall writes of being excited to get a real job in the summer of 1929, after his junior year—his first chance to get a paycheck at the end of the week. Ned wanted to work as part of the state road crew. He would be "a rodman," the job he formally applied for at the government office, because the rodman's only requisite skill was to hold a surveyor's rod upright so that the surveyor down the road can look through the transept and calculate the distance. But it was not to be. Theresa, recognizing she would lose the room and board money if he moved away for the summer, instead enrolled Ned in a summer art class taught by Cyril Kay-Scott, who Hall described as an Englishman of some note who had emigrated to Santa Fe with his two wives, and who later would become Dean of the School of Art at the University of Denver, and later still, director of the Denver Art Museum. (Cyril Kay-Scott's story is actually even more interesting than that.[17])

The Impressionist art class was attended mostly by middle-aged women, except for Ned, and it turned out to be among the most important experiences in this young man's intellectual life. Right now, I think of how Steve Jobs, the visionary who reshaped cultures with his Apple computer, would credit his enrolling in a course in calligraphy at Reed College in Portland, Oregon, after formally dropping out, for the inspiration that would later shape his professional life. He describes this in his commencement address at Stanford University in 2005.[18]

This was not an art history class, though Professor Kay-Scott would refer to some artists but apparently not show any of their works because he did not want his students to be influenced by ghosts of the originals. It was mostly about the students doing the paintings. Hall was astonished by how different the paintings were that each student, looking at the same scene, created each time, and he remembers each time better than the previous. In his autobiography Hall writes, "[Cyril Kay-Scott] really knew what Impressionism was all about. Ever since then, art has run like a golden thread throughout the fabric of my life."[19]

Though he doesn't say this directly in his autobiography, Hall's experience anticipates his later belief, philosophy perhaps, that experience, the "doing," precedes and is necessary for the understanding of anything. That includes, importantly, making mistakes. Until you make a mistake you can't recognize what you need to learn and know, he believed.

"Impressionism"—he devotes a chapter to this in his telling of his story—would become an implicit part of his outlook and insight, perspectives, and connectives. "One might say that the Impressionists' gift to the Western world was that they taught us to look at that world in a more intelligent and perceptive way. No longer could the visual perception be taken for granted."[20]

Today we may think of the Impressionists as the artist's response to the invention of the camera and its increasing refinements. Why return to brush and pallet of paint to present what one sees when a photographer can "capture" more efficiently the same scene or portrait? Ned would set aside the brush that was his mother's choice of expression and the tools of his sculptor step-father in favor of the camera in this era in which photography became an art form. But that summer's Impressionism art class made a lasting impression on him, one that he would appropriate and re-purpose: "With a minimum of fuss Cyril taught us the vocabulary and the grammar on which the Impressionists' system of painting was based; the isolates, sets, and patterns, an analytic method and classification system that I was to explain thirty years later in my first book, *The Silent Language*."

"Isolates," "sets," and "patterns" have a correspondence in linguistics, and, while Hall was attracted to the elegance of linguistics as a possible model for studying nonverbal behavior, he sought a separate vocabulary for his contributions to semiotics, notably his proxemics. But this is getting way ahead of the story.

Coming of Age in the Great Depression

After graduating from Santa Fe High School at age 16, Hall entered college—Pomona College, his first year—just as the nation, indeed the whole world, found itself in what would become the Great Depression. Dissatisfied with the school in California, Ned enrolled at the University of Colorado where he took his first class in anthropology, one of those life-changing experiences that many college students can relate to. He was attracted to archaeology, a fascination seemingly distinct from the cultural anthropology with which he would become recognized. For more than a decade, he maintained his research on Pueblo III Culture indented-ware ceramics.

With his college plans disrupted by the growing economic depression, Hall left school and looked for work through one of the alphabet-soup agencies that the Roosevelt administration created to resuscitate the economy and create work for the millions of unemployed. Hall was only nineteen-years old when he obtained a job with the Indian Emergency Conservation Work (IECW) program, a government agency established to provide work for Native Americans during the Depression years.

Around the same time, Hall married Elizabeth Boyd, an artist and anthropologist ten years his senior, who also joined the ranks of the WPA (Works Progress Administration). Fiercely independent like Ned, she remains known as "E. Boyd," not using a name that would reveal she was a woman at a time when women artists received less respect, and keeping her family name because, as she later said, "I was in and out of so many marriages it was easier to keep one name." A painting made when she and Ned were together is featured on the cover of Ned's book about that era, *West of the Thirties.* The marriage ended a few years later.

For four years, Hall worked on the Hopi and Navajo/Diné reservations.[21] Geographically adjacent, these communities are linguistically and culturally dissimilar—and historically mutually hostile. Today we might look to the Middle East for a comparable analogy. In *An Anthropology of Everyday Life*, Hall remarks that he was one of very few white people who thought that if this new IECW program and its organizers were going to work with Native Americans, they ought to learn something about them. His disdain for the racist, ethnocentric attitudes of the time stands in stark contrast to the Eurocentric "deficit view of culture"—talk of what "they" lacked or "have yet to learn" that was prevalent then—and is still heard when some politicians speak.

Decades later, Hall wrote about those most important years in *West of the Thirties: Discoveries Among the Navajo and Hopi.* Perhaps the least-read of all of Hall's books, but maybe among the most important as it reveals—as recalled in his later years—a very young man, hired at a distance to manage a project fraught with contested (an understatement) intercultural relationships.

The very title, *West of the Thirties,* frames in words of place and time that together must be appreciated for the context of the story to be told. The "West" conjures up, for many readers, romantic images of wide-open spaces and sunsets, "the last frontier," a bygone place much as others might imagine "the Indian" as "the vanishing American." "The Thirties" evokes black-and-white photos of breadlines in cities and destitute farmers, hobo songs of irony ("Big Rock Candy Mountain"), and later, Woody Guthrie songs of national affirmation such as "This land is your land . . ." that many Native Americans find offensive. These years would become among the most important in Hall's professional development. His best teachers were the Hopi, Navajo/Diné people he worked with and lived with, and the Spanish-speaking people whose family roots dated back hundreds of years.

Anthropologist Bruce La Brack calls *West of the Thirties* a model intercultural case study looking at Hall's time working among and with these two very different tribal groups, the Hopi and the Navajo/Diné, and the bureaucracy of a government agency. La Brack writes:

What set his early observations apart from other social scientists of that era was that Hall combined unusually keen and sensitive observation skills with a respectful understanding of how different cultural systems approached practical, everyday problems. The Diné and Hopi experiences provided maximal contrast sets for comparing cultural patterns, which Hall not only intuitively recognized, but came to deeply appreciate. Moreover, he was also able to clearly articulate those meaningful differences to others without jargon or judgment.

He not only directed multi-cultural work crews, but simultaneously functioned as a cultural translator, behavioral interpreter, and systems analyst. He provided invaluable insights and explanations about how deeply culture pervades our everyday lives, and was especially attuned to how difficulties that are encountered when communicating interculturally are inevitably grounded in those differing perspectives.

He was not the first anthropologist to recognize how culture could be a significant impediment to successful interaction across social boundaries, but he was the very first to propose and describe many of the "cultural general" categories that today facilitate and encourage cultural comparisons more broadly. His work was deeply rooted in his direct exposure to cultural differences as a very young man trying to make sense of the varieties of human experience he was encountering as part of daily life on and off the reservations of the Southwest. [22]

Hall dedicates *West of the Thirties* to Lorenzo Hubble, a "second-generation Indian trader, friend and mentor, who grew up as Spanish, Navajo, Hopi, and Anglo-American. Sharing the real-life experience of four cultures, he set me straight as to the true meaning of accommodation and understanding."[23] Hubbell, now legendary, an American original, was a polyglot working in four languages (Spanish, Diné, Hopi, English), and was a kind of institution himself when young Ned Hall met him. Hubble is credited with convincing the Navajo weavers that their work was art—not a separate word then in the Diné language—that their weavings (dismissively "blankets") could be sold not by the pound, as they had been, but individually for their beauty. He was an early influence on Hall's growing awareness of intercultural communication, through both observing Hubble's interactions and the advice he offered this kid tasked to be the foreman of an interculturally challenging team.

Hubble's Trading Post is still functioning, but since 1960, it carries the cachet of a National Historic Landmark, and another cultural category—"tourists"—now step inside enroute to or from Canyon de Chelly, Arizona. If a trading post sounds like a category from the nineteenth century, this one is, begun in 1878. There are many other still important trading posts in the southwest, even in towns where a WalMart might be not so far away. A combination of general store, pawn shop, bank, and local service center including, at some, like the Ellis Tanner Trading Post in Gallup, New Mexico, assistance with tax preparation, and as the name suggests, a place experienced in the barter economy. In Gallup and elsewhere, some car and truck dealers, furniture shops, and other local enterprises sometimes accept as payment for purchases wool, sheep, and other items—local commodities—in lieu of cash. They also have a history, not always savory, but not as

This painting of a trading post by E. Boyd appears
on the cover of West of the Thirties.

impersonal and alienating as pay-day lenders (loan sharks) and banks. For readers who are familiar with Hall's theory of context, the trading post is way up on the "high context" end of that scale. More on this later, but briefly, the distinction has to do with shared knowledge that "goes without saying" (high context) and at the other end of that continuum: assume nothing, spell out everything. Trading posts, for better or worse, were personalized; banks required forms to be filled out irrespective of any personal history with the bank (low context).

Those years with the government IECW program may have been the most important years of Ned Hall's education, not to be confused with schooling, a distinction he would later describe as "informal learning" in contrast to "formal learning." He left the Depression-era program in 1935 for schooling, majoring in anthropology. In the span of six short years, he completed his BA at the University of Denver, his MA at the University of Arizona (where he would later donate his correspondence and research notes), and a PhD at Columbia University, the school of Boas and Sapir and others whose work would shape the field and mentor a generation of anthropologists who influenced a nation.

After the US entered World War II, Hall enlisted in the army. A physical condition prevented him from being drafted, but motivated by the national spirit of patriotism of that time, and also because he wanted to learn more about "the culture of a bureaucracy" such as he had encountered in his years with the IECW, he says he talked his way into the army. He was curious to learn how a massive organization can train young people from diverse regional, class, and educational backgrounds to quickly become proficient in skills that could mean life or death. Hall's interest in cultural approaches to teaching and learning was keen throughout his work, though it has received less attention than other topics he addressed.

With the European theatre ending, Hall was transferred to the Philippines during last days of the war in Asia. In his autobiography he contrasts the leadership styles of Eisenhower in Europe and MacArthur in Asia, much to the disparagement of MacArthur, a feeling I would hear from other friends who were vets from that time. A colleague and friend when I taught at International Christian University (ICU) in Japan, Holloway Brown, had been with MacArthur when he famously returned to the Philippines. He told me about MacArthur's several "takes" on wading ashore so that the staff photographer would get just the right image; his vanity was well-known. Hall writes: "Eisenhower simply would not have tolerated the multiple indignities and outrages against Black troops that were common in the Philippines."[24]

By his own account, his four years of military experience totally changed him, and he credits that experience for the insight that behavior precedes perception, contrary to the conventional wisdom of the time. Hall also credits his war experience for his important realization about the distinctions between "informal," "formal," and "technical" aspects of culture that would be part of his whole way of thinking about culture, communication, and also learning and learning how-to-learn. It was the realization of the "technical" learning—impersonal by design: if you follow the instructions, you will learn what you need to know or do.

Though the Army was not known for always making rational assignments, Hall was able to demonstrate the necessary physical and mental strengths to be assigned to the Officer Corps, and he was placed in Officer Candidate School and became an engineer. He asked to be assigned to a "Negro" unit, the official term in the still-segregated military, and served for two-and-a-half years as a junior officer with that unit in two theaters of war. After the surrender of Italy and Germany, he was based in Paris for a time, before being deployed as a junior officer to the Philippines until the war ended in 1945. In the post-War era, he also served in an administrative post in Micronesia, a time he remembered fondly. Four decades later, during a visit to the Summer Institute for Intercultural Communication, Hall and the institute director, Janet Bennett, who had been a Peace Corps volunteer on the island of Truk, shared memories of Truk and other Micronesian islands. Bennett remarked that she was impressed with Hall's detailed recollection of places and even the people they had known three decades apart.

Those who identify as or know something about "Third Culture Kids" (TCKs), children who grew up in a diversity of countries and languages and cultural identities, may be familiar with sociologists John and Ruth Useem who coined the TCK term. TCKs include "military brats," the children of foreign service personnel, and children of international corporate executives, among others. Regarded as a socially and culturally distinct kind of person when the sociologists began their research, in today's globalized world TCKs are legion. The Useems identified a number of characteristics of TCKs, including learning to make friends quickly and say good-bye to friends more easily than those for whom a single place shapes one's identity.

John Useem played an important role in Ned Hall's life. They had known each other from Hall's days at Columbia when Hall was invited to give a talk in one of John Useem's classes at Barnard. They met again during Hall's time in Micronesia. And most importantly, again later, when Hall was reassigned to Honolulu in order to write a report on his administrative experiences in Micronesia. John Useem had also been posted to Honolulu, and when Ned mentioned that he was looking for someone who could assist him in writing up his field notes, Useem suggested one of his former students, Mildred Ellis Reed, who had degrees in both sociology and anthropology, and who happened to be vacationing in Hawaii with her family. They met, hit it off, and four months later were married. "Mildy" was a refined New Englander; Ned was a rougher South Westerner: a marriage made in heaven. Until her untimely death from cancer in 1994, they were life-partners, colleagues, and co-authors.

After being discharged from the army, Hall wrote of his experiences in an article called "Race, Prejudice, and Negro-White Relations in the Army," published in the *American Journal of Sociology*.[25] His article begins, "Even a professional army cannot divorce itself from the culture patterns and attitudes of the civilian population from which it is derived." Most of what he writes is about relations with and between the units, and the crucial importance of competent leadership, which often trumps racial attitudes. But he also compares the experiences of the soldiers, Black and white, in different parts of the world. For example, Black officers received more respect in France and in England than in the US, generally because consideration of rank counted for more than race in those countries. Enlisted Black soldiers were also more welcomed, especially by many women in those countries, than they were in the US. The article was published just as Hall joined the faculty at the University of Denver.

The Academic Life

Decommissioned Officer Hall returned to the US to pursue his academic career, and was invited to join the faculty at University of Denver to head up the anthropology department where he had completed his undergraduate studies just years before. He joined as Assistant Professor, with an informal understanding that he would be appointed as head of that department the following year.

Soon after he began teaching, he was invited to join the Denver Mayor's Committee on Human Relations, which pledged to assay the condition of race relations in the city of Denver. Hall was the lone social scientist on a committee largely comprised of representatives from civic and local political organizations. He later said that it was in the process of his investigation that he came to appreciate the difference between what Clyde Kluckhohn and Hall's former mentor, Ralph Linton, called "manifest culture" in contrast to "latent culture," which Hall believed was the deeper culture. In part, it is the difference between what we present as representing our values and our imagined reality, and what is experienced in daily life. For example, the organizational chart that indicates the company's management structure and areas of responsibility may not be a reliable guide to how information flows and decisions are made.

Hall discovered that many people, especially those in privileged positions, give value to opinion surveys and formal statements by officials. It is not just about public relations, though that is surely a piece of it, but about what one part of a community experiences and believes, in contrast to what goes on every day: the actual behavior that is observable if one knows where and how to look for it. This distinction was not new, and what appears in today's news and commentary, especially with the use of charts and other graphics, suggests that even more credence is given to statistics today than in the past.

Figuring out how one can discover and learn from this was a realization that Hall credits with reshaping his future work as a researcher and teacher. He was the esteemed professor, but his students were the experts about what was really going on in Denver. And so, his students became his teachers, and he became the eager student. He coached his students to be the researchers, for they knew more about everyday life than he, as an outsider and detached academic, would ever experience.

It was during this brief period that Hall changed his way of teaching from the posture where the professor is the authority, to a modest and eager role in a classroom that would facilitate a student-centered and collaborative approach to teaching and learning. It marked a change from a top-down relationship that was part of anthropology's history, to a "folklorist" approach toward learning that inverts the relationship of "the researcher" and the "subjects" of research. That this does not sound at all radical today, at least at many institutions, is a small triumph of ethics in research. It is also the result of an increased social and political influence of those communities regarded as "objects of study."

The committee's very critical 400-page report, largely written by Hall, about the condition of Denver's inter-racial, inter-ethnic relations had one immediate impact: his university contract was not renewed.

The following year, he left the mountain west and moved east, joining the faculty at Bennington College in Vermont. Warm and socially comfortable in eastern society where Mildy had grown up, she and Ned were, by all accounts, a delightful couple much sought after as dinner guests. She took on the role of manager, reining in her husband's pursuit of so many topics that excited him. She was also her husband's schedule manager, a competence he recognized immediately when she first began to work for him in Hawaii, and which would become increasingly valued especially as he began to receive more speaking and writing requests, and, later, as she co-authored three books with Ned.

Moving to the academic communities in New England brought Hall into contact with scholars and writers from many disciplines. One of the people he met at Bennington College and formed a close friendship with was Erich Fromm. In the era when he and Hall came to know and learn from and with each other, Fromm was among the best-known psychologists and writers in the US. Breaking with Freudian theory, Fromm helped form a new, humanistic grounding of psychology that, in retrospect, remarkably reflects Hall's beliefs and values.

Fromm was, and remains, a major figure internationally in psychology and in what became known as the Frankfurt School of Sociology and the social sciences broadly. A neo-Freudian (today we may not always realize what an influence Freud, his followers and detractors, exerted in that era), Fromm's 1941 book, *Escape from Freedom* (in the UK published as *Fear of Freedom*), became an immediate classic and remains on the required-reading lists on many a syllabus. Fromm had left Europe with the rise of Nazism, and Bennington College was home to this much-sought-after émigré intellectual from 1941-1949. There are themes in Fromm's writing about political psychology that may have influenced Hall's later writing about "the grip of culture."

The attraction of similar questions, insights, and research findings among those that are defined differently by disciplines is, in part, because of a shared vision that transcended those labels. Hall's attraction to psychology was both general, as it offered other perspectives on what most interested him, but also personal. He sought the guidance of therapists for much of his life. Hall and Fromm became very close, and it was Fromm who encouraged Hall to accept the invitation to go to Washington and try to apply his experience and insights in a post-war, colonial-dissolving world that both envisioned. Can you prepare engineers, health workers, and educators to be more effective in a new world of newly independent nations?

As coincidence or kismet would have it, the independent school of psychology that Fromm had founded would be housed in the same building that was to become the Foreign Service Institute. So Hall and Fromm would meet again, and, after he was appointed as director of the Point Four Program at the Foreign Service Institute, Hall also became a Fellow in Fromm's Washington School of Psychology.

The Foreign Service Institute

With nations of Europe and Asia beginning to recover from the devastation of World War II, and, as after every war, a moment of hope for something better, a new wave of demands for independence in Western colonies swept across the globe. Emerging from the war without the destruction experienced elsewhere, with a cultural value system that encouraged change, and with a secularized missionary spirit to spread the good news of democracy and material development, the US was energized for a new international role that would last into the next century. Today it is easy to view this period with the US ascendant as an opportunity for a new colonialism, *Pax Americana*, with a smiling face. At the time it was seen as a new hope for the spread of independence and democracy—but with fears well founded that it would soon also be exploited.

The post-war years into the 1960s were a heady time for those who committed to social and political change across the globe, and

Hall was very much a part of that era. In 1946, Congress established the Foreign Service Institute (FSI) with the purpose of training Foreign Service Officers and staff. The goal was to provide language instruction and other skills and information deemed necessary for the thousands of people who would soon be sent to embassies, consulates, and aid programs about which most had little, if any, experience or knowledge. Wendy Leeds-Hurwitz, in an excellent review of Hall's work at the Foreign Service Institute, points out that prior to 1946, the US Foreign Service was known to give less attention to language qualifications for entry than any other nation's foreign service.[26]

In President Harry S. Truman's 1949 inaugural address, he laid out four themes, point-by-point, with point number four a plan to offer technical assistance to the "developing nations" of Asia, Africa, the Middle East, and Latin America.[27] This was different from the Marshall Plan that offered financial assistance to rebuild war-torn Europe; rather, it was to send engineers, health administrators and medical doctors, educators and others for direct assistance. Thus, it became known as the Point Four Program, a name that was dropped four years later under President Eisenhower and simply called "a technical assistance" program. It was to head this program that Ned Hall joined the Foreign Service Institute. His challenge was to better prepare individuals to work more effectively with people in lands far away and in cultural environments these technical assistance personnel knew nothing about. A dozen years later, the newly created US Peace Corps directors faced a similar challenge, and again, years later in the era of "globalization," so did corporations, NGOs, university study-abroad programs for tens of thousands of students leaving the US, and international student offices trying to ease the transition faced by students coming to the US.

This was a challenge that Hall relished. He was one of many anthropologists who were in the program, along with linguists with an anthropology background, and vice versa. Participants complained about the classes taught by anthropologists as too theoretical or illustrated with examples from cultures unrelated to where they would soon be sent. What they wanted to learn was anything that they saw as practical, and something they could relate to as they imagined their everyday interactions with the people they would soon be meeting and attempting to work with. Hall used the term "micro-analysis" to describe what his experience told him was most important and least appreciated, including those themes for which he would become best known: matters of time and timing, and interpersonal spatial relations. Many other of his approaches to intercultural relations were also taking shape at this period when culture and communication were central to the study of future Foreign Service personnel, and obviously—to him—inseparable. A still radical notion at that time.

Ray L. Birdwhistell, whose pioneering work helped establish "non-verbal communication" as a field of study, was at the FSI in the summer of 1952, pursuing his work in "kinesics," a term he coined for the systematic study of nonverbal communication comparable to and modeled on linguistics.[28] Two of the most influential linguists of that time had joined the Foreign Service Institute: Henry Lee Smith and George Trager, whom Smith brought in and who would become an especially close colleague of Ned. Like Hall, Trager appreciated that communication involved much more than speech. Terms he suggested included "meta-linguistics" and "paralanguage." Today these inventive ways to characterize and legitimize a new area of study still lack a term that crosses disciplines as, of course, the subject must. "Semiotics" is prominent; for undergraduates in communication programs, probably "non-verbal communication" is the user-friendlier term.

Hall worked closely with George Trager, not only to integrate the cultural and language training program, but in other respects as well. For Hall, the applied linguistics that Smith and Trager brought to the project affirmed anthropologist Hall's understanding of culture, and suggested a model for "teaching culture." Trager was excited by Hall's expansive view of cultural themes that could be seen in new ways. On a blackboard, the two men began a list of human activities that shape "a culture," and this evolved into a 10 x 10 matrix (included in *The Silent Language* and Chapter Three of this book). Hall describes the afternoon when he went to the board and wrote five pairs of terms: language and technology, social organizations and all defensive activities, work and play, the two sexes and what they learn, and time and space, viewed by Hall as "the entire structure as a unified whole."[29]

But this was emblematic of Hall: an openness, or maybe a desire, to go beyond what he felt was the canonical in his field, to see connections across disciplines and to see that as exciting, and to imagine how to present this in ways that could benefit non-specialists and non-academics in words most people could understand. Maybe it was also influenced by his respect for what he would call "technical learning"—assuming that those who seek to learn have no relevant experience.

Linguistics, which at that time had been a discipline within anthropology, provided one model for the assignment Hall was given at the FSI. If foreign languages can be taught in a relatively short time to adults, why can't the "languages" of intercultural behavior also be taught? Linguistics is considered a "social science," often said to be the closest to the natural sciences. Hall and his colleagues were looking for elements of "culture," the "building blocks," to use a metaphor of the time, which could be identified and taught in some way comparable to the teaching of language.

While that was the goal then, later it would be the model for Hall's study of how we experience our spatial environment, and how we use "space" as a kind of language to indicate status, attitudes toward others, aggression, and much more. "Proxemics" was the word Hall would coin for that study, loosely modeled on linguistics, and it remains a defining contribution to the fields of communication and anthropology. It is interesting that this all started with his charge to figure out ways to better prepare technical assistance personnel during his ten years at the State Department.

At the end of his tenure at the FSI, Hall's efforts were, at best, a limited success. When Hall left, a State Department official would say: "Let's not have another anthropologist here."

It is not unusual that in the pursuit of one goal, even those deemed successful, the ancillary discoveries during the process may be regarded as more important than the original purpose that they were to serve. Today's micro-technologies, which are part of our personal and social environments, for example, were developed to launch astronauts to the moon. One may question whether Hall's mission at the Foreign Service Institute was successful, but in the process, he developed a perspective and concepts and, inadvertently, a new academic discipline, and applied areas of training that are now recognized throughout the world.

In 1955, *Scientific American* published Hall's article, "The Anthropology of Manners," which included some of what he had worked on at the FSI. Encouraged by its reception, he expanded the range and audience when he wrote his first and still best-known book, *The Silent Language*, published in 1959. It was into the beginning of what would be a decade of fleeting optimism, international tensions and conflict that would split nations and generations, and social change, not least in academic: programs in which Hall's *Silent Language* appeared. It inspired and helped justify a new area of study in one discipline and anticipated what became a global profession.

This was also the time of McCarthyism and the reactionary House Un-American Activities Committee in the north, and the emergence of the brave and searing struggles of the civil rights era in the South. It was when the oldest president, Eisenhower, would be replaced by the youngest, Kennedy. It was when two new states would join the union beginning with Alaska, the first state not contiguous with the other 48 but on the same continent, and then finally, Hawaii.

Appropriately, the year before *The Silent Language* was published, a novel, *The Ugly American*, by Eugene Burdick and William Lederer—a story of "technical assistance" abroad—became a best seller and its title a national trope, a theme in the Democratic presidential campaign, and even an entry in the Merriam-Webster dictionary ("an American in a foreign country whose behavior is offensive to the people in that country"). The title actually refers to a character in the novel who was sent to a Southeast Asian country to offer technical assistance, a dedicated US engineer who lives among and identifies with the people in the village where he works. The early editions of Hall's book included on the jacket blurb "Why are we ugly Americans . . . ?"

Personal story: Years after Hall had retired and returned to New Mexico, and several years after I began teaching at the University of New Mexico, I wrote to Hall and confessed that I had been suffering from clinical depression. I don't remember what prompted me to share that—we were not the closest of friends—but I do remember what he wrote back. He said that he, too, had experienced depression after leaving Washington and the Foreign Service Institute, and with the familiar symptoms, including inability to sleep. And so, he told me, "I got up an hour or two early each morning . . . and I wrote *The Silent Language.*" If you are looking for a motivation to write a book, I don't recommend this approach. I responded to my depression by refusing to take meds, like "Prozac," as family and friends advised. Instead, I got a rescue dog, whom I named "Prozac," and he rescued me.

The Silent Language was a book that made people notice what they had not thought about, and called for self-reflection—culturally and also individually—in a mirror reflecting contrasts mostly from societies abroad, but also using stories from his experience with Native Americans and to some extent local "Spanish." ("Hispanic" had not yet been invented by the US Census Bureau; "Latino," a word chosen by the editor of the *Los Angeles Times*, never did catch on in New

Mexico. Imagine visiting New Mexico from Latin America and being assumed to relate to any of these terms.)

Note that Indian lands have a status as sovereign nations and communities with legal rights comparable to those of foreign governments. The US government has treaties—so many violated in the past—with sovereign Indian tribes, though few people in the US learn this in their history classes. So, "culturally," and not just legally, Hall's references to the "first Americans," "American Indians," are, and remain, as "foreign" in contrast to the mostly European, "Western," "white man's" cultures. It's also notable that in all of the wars in which the US was involved, beginning with World War I, a greater percentage of Native Americans have served in the US military than any other ethnic group.

Left out of Hall's work and its early impact were contrasts within the nation, where the issues were not "just cultural," but also historic, and not easily glossed over as mainly the result of ignorance. Hall was progressive in his time, much as his mentors and, later, colleagues, like Melville Herskovits at Northwestern, had been. Apart from his work regarding racism in Denver and one article in *Sociology* centered on racial relations in the US, Hall wrote little about Black/white relations.

Hall resisted many methods of social science. Neither the quantification through surveys, a hallmark of sociology, that gave value to what people said how they acted or what made sense to the options offered by the questioner, nor experimental studies, contrived or just compared . . . rich sources of information, especially for comparisons. "The lone cowboy," as one article about Hall described him, he was an observer and story-teller of individuals acting with other individuals. Though sensitive to social systems and deeply invested in wanting to change them, I believe he saw his contribution to understanding and guidance to be in a smaller frame, simplified as "nonverbal communication," but also deeper into evolutionary roots, and also broader.

Hall was not the first anthropologist to write a book that attracted a popular audience and provoke reactions within the academy. More famous before were books by Hall's contemporaries, Ruth Benedict's *Patterns of Culture* (1934), and Clyde Kluckhohn's *Mirror for Man* (1949). Benedict had done important work in New Mexico, and Harvard University's Kluckhohn so loved the land that his remains are buried where he guided the country's first inter-disciplinary and first multi-year, five-culture "values study" centered at Ramah, New Mexico. Of several publications on this research, the most comprehensive is *People of Rimrock: A Study of Values in Five Cultures.*[29] Florence Kluckhohn, Clyde's wife, colleague, and professor in her own right, who was also part of the research team, developed a theory of "value orientations" that would also shape the early years of the emergent intercultural communication field. Her method combined traditional qualitative research methods of anthropology—observation and interviews—with the quantitative methods of sociology—questionnaire surveys—that could yield statistical data. Years later, Kathryn Sorrells asked Hall about those studies conducted not all that far from Hall's beloved Santa Fe. Of course, Hall was dismissive of that approach, saying something on the order of: "They usually find what they are looking for."

It was the popular appeal of *The Silent Language* that provoked some in the venerable American Anthropological Association, the discipline's most important professional association, to convene a panel at their annual conference, to critique his newly popular book. Ned talked about that experience more than once with me; I think it hurt him. He told me, "When I came into that room to see the chairs lined up and where I would sit, I knew what they had planned."

"They nearly rode me out of the AAA," he said. Naively I asked, "Was it because your book was so easy to understand?" I wasn't intending to be sarcastic. "No!" he said, "it was because I didn't write about kinship and . . ." other canons of the field he believed his colleagues expected to be acknowledged. And maybe also because he crossed the line between an in-group of serious researchers and scholars, and anyone else who might be interested. But then, like the fabled horseman, Ned hopped on his horse and rode off in all directions in his anger about how he was treated. Of course, Hall believed that he had something to share that would be of value to everyone, not just other academics. Probably most academics believe something similar.

Deborah Tannen, Distinguished University Professor at Georgetown University, whose research and publications on communication between women and men (*You Just Don't Understand: Women and Men in Conversation*), and mothers and daughters (*You're Wearing That? Understanding Mothers and Daughters in Conversation*), among many others, have found a wide and appreciative audience, tells me that at home her parents had *The Silent Language*, and she had read it long before she became a scholar. She said that she believes that book gave her the encouragement to write books to reach a wider readership than just other academics.[31]

The Impact of *The Silent Language*

While Hall's first book inadvertently launched what became a field of study for academics wanting to expand what we'd been offered, and evolved into a profession, now globally, there were many people from many backgrounds around the same time who were looking for something that the available disciplines and professions didn't seem to offer. Coming together were language teachers and interpreters; missionaries; a rare business person; academics in communication, sociology, political science—a collection of people who otherwise might seem to have nothing in common but who were itching to find a missing something that brought us all together. Hall's *Silent Language* gave us something with which to scratch that itch.

And it seems not surprising that this field of intercultural communication emerged in the US—with its history of cultural values and an "attitude" to convert others, the post-war wealth and power lacking in much of the world devastated by the war, and an idealism that often follows revolutions and wars. It was part of what led to the founding of the UN and the Marshall Plan; it was part of that Point Four Program that Hall headed for a decade; it was part of what gave rise to the US Peace Corps at that same time; it was part of the appeal of what Kennedy proclaimed in his inaugural address, "A torch has been passed to a new generation . . ."; and it was in that zeitgeist Alaska and Hawaii were admitted into the US as states outside of the contiguous forty-eight.

Like so many other social changes in the 1960s, the traditionally conservative educational institutions were changing, including what would become departments of communication. Indeed, at the beginning of the decade of the sixties, today's communication departments were then mostly departments of speech. The study of rhetoric in its many forms, with its history dating over two thousand years and as one of the first "liberal arts," centered the curriculum. In the US, graduate dissertations largely examined the texts of speeches of political figures, nearly all from the US. It was a very parochial field, a study of the speeches of "dead white men," as today's critics might say.

Public Speaking was often a required course not only within those departments, but often required of almost all students following a liberal arts program, just as it had been at Harvard University when it was founded. To be a "required course" is often a kiss of death, but not a few students would later credit their public speaking class as one of the most important courses in their college experience. In the twenty-first century, employers rank the ability to communicate effectively as an essential competency they seek in new hires.

In the decade of the sixties, many young scholars were redefining the field more broadly, giving greater attention to group processes, appreciating the "non-verbal" (then a novel term), and the rising influence of the social sciences with new approaches and wider perspectives, in contrast to the humanities that had centered the discipline in the past. In a way, it echoed the changing US political culture of the era, from attention to the humanities to that of the social sciences. Some college departments experienced a schism between the rhetoric people and the social science people at the time *The Silent Language* appeared, providing the impetus for "intercultural communication" becoming a field of study.

Departments were beginning to expand the scope of offerings and so there was a gradual shift in what they wished to be called, eventually leading to "Communication," or some variant of that. There were fierce battles, within and across fields—academics are famously territorial. New courses appeared: Interpersonal Communication, Group Communication, Nonverbal Communication, and in the 1970s, Intercultural Communication. Full disclosure: when I queried publishers about a proposed college textbook on "intercultural communication" at the beginning of the 1970s, only two expressed a mild interest; others declined, saying that there was no market, meaning no courses, for such a book.[32] Today these are among the most popular communication courses.

Part of the motivation to expand the scope of research and teaching beyond rhetoric and speech was the desire to expand the frames of reference—both beyond speeches to a wider scope of communication, and beyond a white-US and Anglophile view—to consider other cultural perspectives, particularly from other parts of the world, reflecting those who were most responsive to Hall's influential book. Mostly absent in Hall's writing was attention to the diversity of cultural communities in the US. Apart from his article about Black soldiers during WW II, his focus returned to the Hispanos and Indigenous communities in New Mexico with which he was most familiar, and later his books were about international relations. At a time when Black/white relations in the US were drawing national attention, boosted by a trove of work by African American authors who wrote from a depth of history and pain and calls for justice, Hall had little to offer. Black comedians were more often the storytellers, using humor to contrast Black and white communication styles, and much more. Popular television series, *All in the Family* (1971-1979) and *The Jeffersons* (1975-1985), both inspired and produced by Norman

Lear, used comedy to draw attention to some of what academic researchers were exploring, and some themes more often identified with a history of reinforcing stereotypes and bigotry. At this time, its intent was positive and commercially successful as well, without ever using the stuffy term "intercultural communication."

Linguistics professor Thomas Kochman's important book, *Black and White Styles in Conflict,* published in 1981, described Black communication styles as they often contrast with "white styles" that added to the intercultural tensions.[33] Hall wrote about this in general, but never in these new terms from a different intercultural environment that Kochman provided. Kochman's book received more attention than other books on "intercultural communication" did at that time—he appeared on the popular television *Oprah Winfrey Show,* rare for the author of a book on intercultural communication that described interaction. It was probably not until decades later when another linguistics professor, Deborah Tannen, appeared on television to talk about intercultural miscommunication and conflicts—not regarding race or ethnicity, but between women and men in intimate relationships—that another important revelation about intercultural communication was offered to a wide audience. Wide, indeed: her important book on intercultural communication, *You Just Don't Understand: Women and Men in Conversation,* was on *The New York Times* best-seller list for three years and was translated into 31 languages.

A Bauhaus Environment:
Illinois Institute of Technology

Chicago was Hall's home during his last fifteen years as an anthropology professor, first at the Illinois Institute of Technology (IIT) in Chicago, and later, moving up Lake Shore Drive to Evanston, just north of Chicago, where he joined one of the major anthropology programs in the US at Northwestern University. It was in these schools that he elaborated and refined work he had begun at the Foreign Service Institute.

Hall's early years shaped his fascination with and respect for the natural environment; this was balanced later with his very serious interest in architecture and urban design, and how these affect human behavior. It seems predestined that after growing up in the mountain west, completing his doctoral work and teaching in New York, and then taking his position in the Foreign Service Institute in Washington, DC, that Hall found himself doing perhaps his most detailed research and most exciting teaching in and near the city that the American Institute of Architects called "the city with the finest architecture in the nation," and which many regard as America's most architecturally significant city. Hall's lifelong passion for architecture was well-served by living in Chicago with its historic buildings of Louis Sullivan, Dankmar Adler, Daniel Burnham, and perhaps best-known of those whose work dated from the nineteenth century, Frank Lloyd Wright.

Among the innovative and influential twentieth-century architects, perhaps no one exerted an influence as great as Ludwig Mies van der Rohe, whose Bauhaus-born modernist structures of glass and steel came to shape the skylines of cities everywhere. Like Hall's friend Fromm, Mies escaped Nazi Germany to come to the US. He was appointed head of the architecture school at Illinois Institute of Technology (formerly the Armour Institute of Technology), and designed the master plan for the campus and the buildings for which the school is internationally known. Crown Hall, home of IIT's School of Architecture, is considered Mies's finest work, even more honored than his better-known buildings such as Manhattan's classic Seagram Building.

It was at IIT that Hall did his pioneering work on his theory of proxemics, grounded in an evolutionary history and demonstrated in ethology (the study of animal behavior), human physiology and sensory awareness, and the influences of culture that culminated in the publication of *The Hidden Dimension* in 1962. This was Hall's most detailed social science work, with a context deep and wide. His lesser-known *Handbook for Proxemic Behavior*, now long out-of-print, guided others on how to conduct such studies. Like the precise geometry of Miesian architecture, Hall's research, presentation, and guidance in the study of what he named "proxemics" draws attention to the structure of space, and especially our perception of and reactions to the ways that our spatial sensitivity affects us. His research and the resulting book were deeper and more detailed than the broad view of culture and communication in his previous book, *The Silent Language*, and his later, more evocative work that draws upon metaphor more than the precision in this book. *The Hidden Dimension* had a significant impact on designers, city planners, other "applied anthropologists," and photographers and other artists.

Photographer Miguel Gandert describes the influence that *The Hidden Dimension* had on him as he was beginning to find his way to becoming an internationally recognized photo documentarian. Years later, Gandert and Hall came to know each other through the graduate seminar on intercultural communication that Miguel and I taught. Of that early influence on his photography Gandert says:

> During my college years, I remember I enrolled in an anthropology class and discovered that one of the required readings on the syllabus was Edward T. Hall's *The Hidden Dimension*. As an aspiring photographer, I absorbed many of his reflections on culture and composition and began to realize the profound influence he would have on me as a photographer and a filmmaker.
>
> Hall's ideas gave me a new approach to thinking about the way I photograph, how I interact with my subjects, and how I understand and negotiate physical space. He gave me insight into spatial and compositional ideas, such as what to include and what to leave out of a frame and I developed this concept into a strategy I have used for over forty years.

His conceptual writings on proxemics exposed me to new interpretations concerning the camera, its placement, and how that influenced a personal and cultural relationship to my subject. Did I want to be an active or passive agent in the art of making an image?

This approach helped me to orient my camera and affected my choice of lenses—I found that using a wide-angle lens enabled me to work in close proximity with those I photograph and incorporate more information that way as well. I believe this method of recording culture has helped me create a sense of intimacy for my viewers, allowing me to be a more active participant in what Hall would describe as "the dance of life."[34]

Culture as Communication

Northwestern's anthropology department attracted Hall not long after his breakout book on the spatial dimension of communication was published, as the department enjoyed an international reputation. Hall struck a deal: he would teach just one, three-month academic term ("the quarter system") each year. It would be Winter Quarter, often bitterly cold on the campus that hugged Lake Michigan, but Hall enjoyed a large office at the top of the building where the department was housed, with broad windows with grand views that let in the sunshine. And his office even had an outer office, too. For this radical anthropologist who maintained such a limited schedule, this was a space destined to provoke the jealousy of some of his colleagues—echoes of the American Anthropology Association's conference critique when *The Silent Language* was published.

Hall's much-sought-after undergraduate class, "Culture as Communication," which attracted students from across the university, was limited to 60 students. Gladys Pilz, his Teaching Assistant (TA), had never heard of E. T. Hall when she responded to his note about the job posted on the departmental bulletin board, which would lead to a lifetime of friendship and professional guidance. She was the class gatekeeper for who got in, the TA who read all 60 assignments each week and recommended those papers she found most interesting and what seemed to be patterns or trends in the themes in what the students wrote. (This was not an unusual TA role in that era; today's TAs, usually graduate students working on their degrees, are often teaching the classes.) Gladys Pilz remembers: "It was magic! Students always seemed to arrive excited, eager for the class. Smiling! I'd never known any university class like this. They loved him!"

What the students wrote about in their assignments, their perceptions and interpretations, were the focus of each class. Hall rarely came with a prepared lecture; from the students' responses to his assignments, he made connections and comparisons and asked more questions. It was a design that he credited to what he said he learned years earlier in Denver when he was asked to study "race relations," and he realized that his students were the ones who should be his teachers. This, as noted, transformed his ideas about teaching. Hall's class might now be called "a student-centered class," echoing the ideas of another prominent Chicagoan, Carl Rogers, whose "Rogerian" client-centered therapy upended ideas about psychological counseling during this same era. Did they ever meet? Seems likely, given their mutual interests and personalities, and at that time when Chicago, then the nation's "Second City," was a center of creativity and the two were at the peak of their professions, but maybe not.

During his time at Northwestern, Hall also taught a graduate seminar with several students who were first to test his ideas, and at the time that he also wrote what became his most influential book, *Beyond Culture*, published the year he retired, 1976. That was the book in which he introduced his concept of "context"—higher and lower—which devolved into a simple dichotomy of "high context" and "low context." This was also the book in which Hall's described in some detail the work of William Condon (no relation) on how our speech and physical movements are synchronized.[35]

After Hall Retired

Through the 1970s, I taught at the innovative, bi-lingual, and relatively international university in Japan, International Christian University (ICU), located in Mitaka, a suburb of Tokyo.[36] ICU had offered a course in intercultural communication from the 1960s, long before such a course appeared in curricula elsewhere. It was also one of a dozen universities in the world to offer a program in conference interpreting, preparing those most important but largely anonymous people whose role in intercultural communication remains unheralded. I've never known more creative and dedicated undergraduates, as they sensed they were at the beginning of a new field, not usually encouraged in the conservative Asian culture. In 1972, we hosted a radical six-day intercultural communication conference that matched each participant coming to Japan with a Japanese undergraduate student. During the one-day break, each student was the guest's guide and interpreter to explore areas of interest in Tokyo.

One scholar attending was Clifford Clarke who grew up in Kyoto and had just arrived as a grad student and international student advisor at Stanford University. Clarke's presence, along with others who would become prominent in the intercultural field, presaged the Stanford Institute for Intercultural Communication, that later evolved into the Summer Institute for Intercultural Communication (SIIC) in Portland, Oregon, that endured as a venerable institution for four decades, and influenced thousands of participants from all over the world.

In 1976, ICU hosted a symposium that brought together some of the best-known scholars and writers, principally from Japan and the US, this time including Edward Hall who had just retired.[37] An enthusiastic presenter, his well-received talk centered on the human need to feel a sense of autonomy and active involvement rather than just accepting what is given. Hall compared public housing—where future tenants had no physical or emotional investment in where they lived—with government housing where tenants were required to provide sweat equity. He also spoke about cars that demand little and are too comfortable. He also compared the automation and comfort of new cars with "lowrider," family-customized cars in Chicano/Hispano New Mexico. "Folk art," he called these. Hall would be surprised to find that the center of the Chicano-identified low-rider cars and its culture in 1976 had moved, twenty years later, from Española, New Mexico, to Tokyo and Osaka.[38]

The 1976 conference was also where Hall introduced his newly published book, *Beyond Culture,* which of all of his books, apart from *The Silent Language,* was the one most often recommended to anyone who asked which of his books would be most interesting to someone curious about intercultural communication.

Interest in Japan was on the rise at that time, reaching its peak in the next decade when, in the US, Japanese cars and many things Japanese—foods, schooling, business management—were more than just trendy. There was also "Japan bashing"—backlash—with Japanese automobiles publicly smashed in anger because they were outselling Detroit-built cars, threatening jobs and a legacy. There were fears of Japan buying up US real estate and iconic US buildings and art, but at the same time, joint-ventures with businesses from both countries were taking shape, and in popular culture, *sushi* appeared as an option at baseball stadiums.[39]

As the US looked west to "the East"—retaining the metaphor from that nineteenth-century London compass and map—it was also returning to issues at home, born and festering from the nation's founding. Matters intercultural, not previously described that way, were local, homegrown, and deeply rooted, and were recognized as far more important than remote, seemingly abstract, international or "culture general" examples and theories that characterized much of Hall's work. As courses in the field grew in popularity, the emphasis in college courses shifted from across boundaries that divided nations to those that divided neighborhoods and neighbors. Social justice, a concern largely absent from intercultural communication, found its place in this field along with its overdue attention in literature, arts, histories, and in the social sciences. Just two decades earlier, "Race Relations" was among the least popular courses in Sociology.

Where interest in international relationships was recognized as more important than ever in the US, apart from political science, was in business. This would be the field of research, education, training, and with the digital revolution, innovative ways of diagnostic screening of potential candidates for overseas assignments, and measures of the impact of their experience.

The Global Is Local

Hall's "dream contract," teaching and inspiring undergraduate and graduate students during one term each year, meant teaching three 50-minute classes per week over a ten-week period, plus time for preparation and grading. This arrangement permitted the Halls considerable time to be away from the university. A good deal of this time was spent abroad, interviewing corporate CEOs and lower-level managers in this area that was emerging and immediate in the "real world," with academic interest and professional involvement of academics not far behind.

"Globalization" was a term that surfaced and became a watchword in the 1980s, like an approaching front to prepare for in a weather forecast. Globalization was the cultural context to which the Halls applied their insights. This was the domain in which intercultural communication was central. With the increased prestige of Schools of Management and their MBA degrees, more than a few people were taking intercultural communication seriously. Failures were recorded in the bottom line—this was when "the bottom line" escaped the corporate idiom and entered the national vernacular. Expats sent abroad sometimes felt so inadequate in their new setting that they returned home even before their contracts had run out, to be replaced by others who would try again. A close friend, the late George Renwick, regarded by many as a dean of intercultural communication consultants, reminded me that academics can study intercultural communication issues they find interesting, but businesspeople have to make decisions and take action. Businesspeople meant business.

After retirement, Hall published four books, two of which were reflections on his life and insights he had wanted to share for many years: *An Anthropology of Everyday Life* and *West of the Thirties: Discoveries Among the Navajo and Hopi*. Bookending these were books based on his research in the business contexts to which he applied the concepts and theories he had developed. These books were explicitly international—also multinational—and centered on business culture in four different countries. Moreover, now the "inter-" was beginning to be both face-to-face, and increasingly mediated by technologies, and so not confined within the space of a single conference room. More parties would be involved, and with multinational corporations, a more complex management structure than when a corporation had a single home office. These two new books, one centered on Japan, the other in Europe, differed from his other books not only because they were "culture specific," but also because they were based mainly on interviews that the Hall team conducted in Europe, the US, and Japan, and relied less on his personal experience.

By 1990, when the Halls published *Hidden Differences: Doing Business with Japan*, the interest in "intercultural communication with Japan" had passed the peak of its trendiness, as had some of the earlier joint-ventures in business and also in academics in that risk-averse land. The Halls were not the first westerners in awe of Japanese aesthetics, technology, and the resilience witnessed in the postwar era. And they were enamored with Japanese subtle "high context" communication that is more apparent to visitors than in contexts where subtlety is absent. Their book appeared a little late to the party. Founding figures in most fields are respected by the Japanese, but *Hidden Differences* (in translation) received less attention than his earlier work that was not Japan-specific.

Hall presented his work in a qualitative form—stories, experiences, what often is regarded as "soft" in the formal cultures of the business world—rather than the "hard data" of numbers that result from surveys and questionnaires. For that quantitative authority of the time, the late Dutch researcher Geert Hofstede's book, *Culture's Consequences: International Differences in Work-Related Values*, in two editions, has been considered the go-to source, with data from branch offices around the world of a single corporation, IBM.[40] Hofstede had been an executive before stepping out so that he could manage this ambitious research project. His work has been influential, less now because "hard data," quantitative and comparative, have a short shelf-life, but more because of his conceptualizing "dimensions" of how we view relationships. Among the most often mentioned are "Power Distance" and "Uncertainty Avoidance," the former about how involved employees feel they should be in decisions that affect them, and the latter as the category indicates, tolerance of ambiguities and surprises. Hofstede's "dimensions" had polar terms—high/low, close/distant, etc.—needed in making questions that will yield "scores" and statistical results that count as "hard data." Hofstede's quantitative research, however, remains relevant—and dated—because it's "hard data."

Saved in Translation

Understanding Intercultural Differences: Germans, French, and Americans, a more ambitious book, based on research conducted over the previous decade, also appeared in 1990. In the contexts of business management, this in some ways, is the most interesting because it includes national cultural descriptions that the authors consider relevant in the context of business, and particular intercultural issues in each of the combinations: US-German, US-French, German-French, etc.

Most interesting to me and from conversations with Hall, it was a matter of pride that he wrote three different versions of *Understanding Intercultural Differences* in English, with one to be translated into French, another in German, assuming that the French and the Germans and the US would approach this work differently.[41] Both Halls had traveled and briefly lived in Europe. Knowing that the French and the Germans and the US wouldn't view anything the same way (so many contexts!), Hall decided that if there were to be translations of his book it should also be presented in three different versions—not just translations from one original. And he was able to do just that, a remarkable feat. Whether or not successful, it is a testament to the Hall's respect for cultural perspectives, and who gets to tell the story.

Who might comment on this book? Christa Uehlinger is a Swiss friend who knows Hall's work well, and who has worked professionally in France, Germany, and in the US. She also is an attorney and a university professor teaching courses on international business, and is an intercultural consultant. Christa's extensive review appears as an appendix; following are a few of her observations of the Hall and Hall book.

Noting that the book appeared the year that the Berlin Wall came down (1990) and that political cultures have changed, she picks up on US cultural perceptions in some ways in which the Germans and French are viewed. Nevertheless, she finds the book rich in insights and the application of familiar concepts by the authors, including matters of time and space, which she notes as a major source of intercultural friction.

Germany, France, and the US are monochronic cultures, with Germany far more so than the US. "This shows in punctuality in sticking to plans and in defined procedures. . . . Once a decision is taken it will not be altered. The American approach of sometimes changing plans or decisions at the last minute is seen as distracting," a point she extends to other European cultures. This Swiss reviewer believes that the authors overstate the American "M-time" compared to the other cultures explored.

Centralization is a pervasive feature of French cultural space, both in the built environment and also metaphorically in matters of status and social circles. "In the 30 years since this book was written, it has not been possible to integrate migrants from former colonies into the elite. Everyone moves in his or her circle and these are hardly permeable," Uehlinger writes. She also confides "a faint suspicion that the culture of the country under study also influences the researchers." Indeed, Ned and Mildy were life-long Francophiles.

Many of us who were excited, and in some way guided by Hall's earlier work, embarked on paths that did not begin in the business world. Academics regarded schools of management or business as lacking an appreciation of the more subtle and deeper values of human culture, the fine arts, the sensitivities of intercultural engagements for their own sake and moments and memories. The classroom, not the conference room. The friendship forged in a college dorm, not so much negotiation arranged at a formal face-to-face meeting, preceded by countless email and phone exchanges, legal teams. . . .and more that Ned Hall never told us about. It was simpler then.

A Sudden Loss, Newfound Joy, and then a Voice Silenced

It was also at this time, in 1994, that Mildy was diagnosed with cancer. Death was impatient; she died later that year. At a memorial service in Santa Fe, tributes were voiced from many, including novelist Tom Wolfe, and local Tewa friend, Tito Naranjo, who offered a Tewa prayer. A similar memorial fifteen years later, a "celebration of life," would be held in the historic St. Francis Auditorium within the Museum of Art.

A decade after Mildred's death, Hall remarried. Karin Bergh, a ceramic artist, had known the Halls because her stepfather, a retired anthropologist living in Santa Fe, was a friend, and the two families sometimes joined for picnics and other get-togethers. Exploring her Swedish roots—Karin's father was Swedish—she moved to Sweden and married a Swede, but after 20 years in Stockholm and a divorce, she returned to Santa Fe and settled in the same neighborhood where Hall lived. Karin recalls that her neighbor was one of the first people in Santa Fe to go jogging. "He was so energetic and good looking!" Hall also took an interest in her and, Karin says, helped her readjust to "the American way of life, not to mention the Santa Fe way of life." A decade later they were married. In a few short years, Karin experienced the joys and the sadness that one affirms in a traditional marriage vow: in sickness and in health, 'til death do us part.

Well into his mid-80s, Hall remained active, even being coaxed out of his retirement to collaborate in teaching seminars organized by Kathryn Sorrells, then completing her doctoral work at the University of New Mexico. These would be the last courses Hall would teach.

In 2000, Hall suffered from the first of what would become a series of strokes. It was shortly after we had returned from a conference on cultural values in Seattle where Hall was at his best. When I visited him in the hospital after his stroke, he seemed as alert and upbeat as ever. The couple moved to a new home with all the rooms on the same floor, anticipating possible additional strokes when Hall might need a wheel chair. And soon his physical movement was limited, and soon his voice was muted. His face showed he was alert and his gestures were still expressive, as when he would offer a guest a toast with a glass of wine. But in a cruel irony, now his language was silent.

The year 2009 was the 50th anniversary of the publication of *The Silent Language* and the 150th anniversary of the publication of Darwin's *On the Origin of Species*, an influence on Hall's thinking about ethology and the evolution of the human brain, and seeing culture as a part of the evolutionary process—a grand vision. To me it seemed appropriate to offer a special anniversary one-day session on Hall's life and legacy at the Summer Institute for Intercultural Communication in Portland, Oregon. After all, the Institute bore the name he is credited with coining, and Hall had sometimes visited for evening gatherings years before, and had donated many of his books to an impressive library that he maybe didn't fully realize he inspired.

With the enthusiastic agreement of Karin, I proposed a late afternoon phone call from Portland so that everyone who had joined our session could congratulate him on that anniversary, thank him for his work, wish him well, maybe also sing a belated "Happy Birthday," as his 95th was just weeks before—knowing that he would not be able to speak to us.

Among the participants who joined that workshop there were several people in their early twenties who were just learning about this field, so new and exciting to them. They knew little about Hall, other than having heard his name. I was touched that along with the usual academics, professional trainers, and other "interculturalists," were some from a whole new generation who would be making contact with the person credited with getting it all started.

At their home in Santa Fe, Karin wheeled Ned to the kitchen table and, with the phone at the ready, we called and began our brief words of thanks and our well wishes. About halfway during our passing the phone from person-to-person, each expressing thanks, it seemed for a moment that the call had been dropped. Terry Ash, a participant who had the phone at that moment, said, "Oh, I hope we didn't get disconnected! Ned, are you still there?" "Yes," came a voice I had not heard for a long time. I was shocked and teary. We completed our round of congratulations and good wishes, and said goodbye.

The next morning, I received news that Edward T. Hall had died during the night. A memorial service was held at the historic St. Francis Auditorium in Santa Fe, on August 17, 2009, heralded by drummers and chanters from the Pueblo community.[42]

Notes

1. Edward T. Hall, *An Anthropology of Everyday Life: An Autobiography* (New York: Doubleday, 1992).

2. Gladys Pilz signed up to serve as Professor Hall's Teaching Assistant at Northwestern University, though at the time she did not know him or about his work. She read all of the papers his undergraduate students wrote, and came to know him through attending his classes, and, later, asked him to direct her doctoral research and dissertation. This evolved into a close, life-long friendship, shared with her husband, Arie, who credits Hall with influencing everything in the work with Native American communities that he and Gladys undertook for decades. This author, also a friend, is deeply grateful for the insights of Gladys and Arie Pilz that appear in many parts of this book.

3. John Gast's "American Progress" depicts "Manifest Destiny," the belief that the United States should expand from the Atlantic Ocean to the Pacific Ocean in the name of God. In 1872, Gast's painting, also called "Spirit of the Frontier," sold as an engraving. It shows a scene of people moving west that captured the view of white Americans in the post-Civil War era. Guided and protected by a blonde goddess-like figure, aided by the technology (railways, the telegraphs), Native Americans and bison are driven off their lands. Note that the "angel" is bringing the "light" (as witnessed on the eastern side of the country) as she travels towards the darkened west.

4. Esteban de Dorantes was an enslaved African man who was part of a Spanish expedition when it was shipwrecked in 1527. He is the first known non-native person to reach the present-day states of New Mexico and Arizona.

5. Chris Wilson, *The Myth of Santa Fe: Creating a Modern Regional Tradition* (Albuquerque: University of New Mexico Press, 1997). Richard Harris kindly pointed out to me that Eric Hobsbawn and Terrence Ranger wrote about the "invention of tradition," predating Wilson's use of the term.

6. Personal conversation with the author.

7. Rina (Naranjo) Swentzell (1939-2015) was a potter and scholar, receiving an MA in Architecture and a PhD in American Studies from the University of New Mexico, one of the first Pueblo women to receive a doctorate. Her husband, Ralph Swentzell, was a professor at St. John's College in Santa Fe. She was also the matriarch of noted artists and scholars, including her

daughter, sculptor Roxanne Swentzell; granddaughter Rose Simpson, an artist working across a range of genres; and grandson, Porter Swentzell, a professor at the Institute of American Indian Art. She shared much of her knowledge of Pueblo architecture and cosmology with non-native scholars and researchers, managing to be helpful without revealing more than would be allowed. Also see Joseph H. Suina, "Pueblo Secrecy, the Result of Intrusions," *New Mexico Magazine* (January, 1992).

8.   Personal correspondence with author.

9.   A beautiful appreciation of this is Rina Swentzell's telling of a Pueblo cosmology, that life exists in and flows through all that surrounds us, animate and inanimate: https://www.youtube.com/watch?v=8zHAiOKN6Vo

10.   Melissa Bingmann, *Prep School Cowboys: Ranch Schools in the American West* (Albuquerque: University of New Mexico Press, 2015), and John D. Wirth and Linda Harvey Aldrich, *Los Alamos: The Ranch School Years, 1917-1943* (Albuquerque: University of New Mexico Press, 2003)

11.   Bingmann, *Prep School Cowboys.*

12.   Hall, unpublished notes.

13.   Kai Bird and Martin Sherwin, *American Prometheus: The Triumph and Tragedy of J. Robert Oppenheimer* (New York: Vintage Books, 2006), 69-70, 205-207.

As the storm clouds of what would become WW II spread across Europe in the 1930s, Hitler invaded Poland in 1939 and proceeded across the continent. The majority of people in the US were opposed to entering the conflict until, on December 7, 1941, the Japanese attacked Pearl Harbor, Hawaii, and President Roosevelt declared war on Japan, and then, four days later, declared war on Germany.

Back in 1939 Albert Einstein had written a letter to FDR warning that the Germans were embarking on developing a nuclear weapon, a letter that later, after the US bombed Hiroshima and Nagasaki in Japan, Einstein said he most regretted writing. Fearing Nazi Germany could develop the ability to create a weapon of massive destruction, a race was begun to create such a weapon before Germany where the best physicists in the world worked and taught others. Among the best-known today is Werner Heisenberg. A most ambitious, massive, project was begun in Manhattan, but involving the efforts of laboratories in three states: the Manhattan Project. But who should be asked to head up such a project under the supervision of the War Department? The choice of the head physicist was a lanky, brilliant polymath—he taught himself languages, giving an impressive speech in Dutch just six weeks after arriving in the Netherlands—and the somewhat controversial physicist, J. Robert Oppenheimer from the University of California, Berkeley. Oppenheimer had studied with Heisenberg. "By all accounts Oppenheimer admired Heisenberg and respected his work. He could not have known then that in the years ahead they would become shadowy rivals." (Bird & Sherwin, *American Prometheus*, 65).

But the research and development for this endeavor, involving thousands of scientists and engineers, would have to be as secret and protected as possible, somewhere off the map. Oppenheimer had an idea of a place. In New Mexico. Oppenheimer had fallen in love with New Mexico many years earlier where he and his brother, Frank, had spent some of their happiest summers. He had even written a poem about his feelings or the place, "Crossings," which was published in the Harvard literary magazine, *Hound and Horn*, in 1928.

That same year, he and his brother persuaded their father to lease a 154-acre ranch in the high desert, which, after the war, Robert Oppenheimer purchased as his sanctuary for many years. So he was well aware of the Los Alamos Ranch School on its 800-acre campus, just 40 miles by horseback from a place he loved, when he proposed the site to General Leslie Groves as a possible location for the secret laboratory.

On a snowy November afternoon in 1942, they visited the site together, and Groves, surveying the vast land that Oppenheimer loved, declared "this is the place." "Oppenheimer got what he wanted—a spectacular view of the Sangre de Cristo Mountains—and General Groves got a site so isolated that there was only a winding gravel road and one phone line into the place." Four days later, Washington drafted the paperwork to purchase the school, and the school cancelled Christmas and New Year's break so that students could finish the term and graduate at the beginning of 1943.

A major film, *Oppenheimer*, directed by Christopher Nolan, appeared in 2023, based largely on the book *American Prometheus,* which won a 2006 Pulitzer Prize in the biography category. Oppenheimer has been the subject of other literary works, dramas, and an opera by John Adams.

14. Jim Yardley, "Land for Los Alamos Lab Taken Unfairly, Heirs Say," *The New York Times*, August 27, 2001. See also Myrriah Gómez, *Nuclear Nuevo México: Colonialism and the Effects of the Nuclear Industrial Complex.* (Tucson: University of Arizona Press, 2023).

15. Hall, unpublished notes.

16. Hall, unpublished notes.

17. Gladys Pilz writes: "As a personal project I researched the life of Cyril Kay-Scott, partly because I knew Phyllis Crawford, his fourth wife, very well when I lived in Santa Fe. His real name was Frederick Creighton Wellman; he was the father of Paul Wellman and Manly Wade Wellman, both well-known authors. He abandoned his first family and married a woman who was an accomplished concert pianist. Then, leaving her, he 'ran away' to South America with a young woman from New Orleans, at which time they decided to use false names, presumably to escape being traced by her family."

18. Steve Jobs's commencement address to Stanford University, June 14, 2005, can be found at https://news.stanford.edu/2005/06/14/jobs-061505/

19. Hall, *Anthropology of Everyday Life*, 59.

20. Hall, *Anthropology of Everyday Life*, 57.

21. Diné is the preferred name for the Navajo tribe.

22. Personal correspondence with author.

23. Edward T. Hall, *West of the Thirties: Discoveries among the Navajo and Hopi* (New York: Doubleday, 1993), Dedication.

24. Hall, *Anthropology of Everyday Life*, 156.

25. Edward T. Hall, "Race, Prejudice, and Negro-White Relations in the Army," *American Journal of Sociology*, Vol. LII, no 5 (March, 1947): 401-409.

26. Wendy Leeds-Hurwitz, "Notes on the History of Intercultural Communication: The Foreign Service Institute and the Mandate for Intercultural Communication Training," *Quarterly Journal of Speech,* 05, June, 2009, 264.

27. The term "developing nations," while at the time an improvement in a semantic progression throughout the years—"backward nations," "undeveloped nations," "underdeveloped nations," "developing nations"—is no longer used by the United Nations and the World Bank. Though most of the classifications originated on a Western, capitalist, economic model (though "overdeveloped nations" is not part of the set), all of the terms are fraught with cultural assumptions and judgments of inferiority compared to those in positions of power.

28. Ray L. Birdwhistell, *Kinesics and Context: Essays on Body Motion Communication* (Philadelphia: University of Pennsylvania Press, 1970).

29. Hall, *Anthropology of Everyday Life*, 214.

30. Evon Vogt and Ethel Albert, eds., *People of Rimrock: A Study of Values in Five Cultures* (Cambridge: Harvard University Press, 1966).

31. Personal correspondence with the author. In many ways, Deborah Tannen's detailed presentation of social interaction comes closer to Hall's interests than many identified with intercultural communication.

32. The proposed book, *An Introduction to Intercultural Communication*, was published in 1975, and is widely considered the first dedicated textbook in the field. Today, instructors have a large choice of textbooks with a focus more on diversity within the US and a diversity of voices that were not heard when intercultural communication became "a thing."

33. Thomas Kochman, *Black and White Styles in Conflict* (University of Chicago Press,1981).

34. Personal correspondence with author.

35. We met in Professor Hall's office. Condon, W. S., and L. W. Sander, "Neonate Movement Synchronized with Adult Speech: Interactive Participation and Language Acquisition," *Science* 18, no. 4120, 1974.

36. In many ways it resembled the small, liberal arts colleges in the US with a broad, mostly Protestant affiliation, though no intent to proselytize. It's *honkan*, main building, had been part of the Nakajima Aircraft Company that was active during WWII. Now engines for Subaru automobiles, which evolved from the Nakajima company, are manufactured next to the campus that itself is one of the largest in Japan. It was a rare university where many members of the faculty lived on campus, as did the president; the library had open stacks, and there were other amenities that in Japan were innovations.

37. The 1972 conference featured presentations by leading Japanese scholars in the social sciences, including anthropologist Chie Nakane, sociologist Hidetoshi Kato, and psychologist Takeo Doi, as well as Japanese film director Kaneto Shindo, and film scholar Donald Ritchie, among others. Dean Barnlund, Clifford Clarke, Mitsuko Saito, and I were among the those who brought perspectives from the emerging field of intercultural communication. The proceedings appear in: John Condon and Mitsuko Saito, eds., *Intercultural Encounters with Japan: Communication—Contact and Conflict* (Tokyo: Simul Press, 1974).

The 1976 conference in which Hall participated also included mass media scholar Wilbur Schramm, Y.V. Lachsmana Rao, Yasumasa Tanaka, Arifin Bey, Edward C. Stewart, and many others including Sadako Ogata, who later became the UN High Commissioner for Refugees. The proceedings appear in: John Condon and Mitsuko Saito, eds., *Communication Across Cultures for What? A Symposium on Humane Responsibility in Intercultural Communication*, with a Foreword by Kenneth Boulding (Tokyo: Simul Press, 1976).

38. Originating in post-war Mexican American communities in the southwestern and western states of the US, and later identified with Chicano culture, a "lowrider" refers both to a customized car and also those who design and customize the car, often including across generations of a single family. With extra batteries and hydraulics, the car can ride low to the ground, and also rise high, sometimes "jump," and perform acrobatics. Lowriders' custom paint jobs often include Roman Catholic iconography, sometimes as murals. Even the entire underside of the car may appear in chrome; when exhibited, mirrors are placed under the engine for viewers to appreciate the work.

    Española, New Mexico, located not far from Santa Fe, has claimed to be the "Lowrider Capital of the World," and was also where a monthly magazine, *Lowrider*, was originally published. A poster promoting the city proclaimed: "I've seen the Taj Mahal and the Great Wall of China, but I'd never seen anything until I saw the mating dance of the lowriders in Española, NM." In the 1980s, lowriders attracted a following in Japan where annual shows are held, and some of the classic lowrider cars are now in Japan. Japan also publishes the largest monthly *Lowrider* magazine. One of the best-known lowrider cars, "Dave's Dream," is owned by The Smithsonian National Museum of American History in Washington, DC.

39. A dictionary's acceptance of words borrowed from foreign languages is a lagging indicator of intercultural influence. *The Third Edition of the Oxford English Dictionary* (2024) included 23 new words from Japanese, half of them related to food.

40. Geert Hofstede, *Culture's Consequences: International Differences in Work-Related Values*. Thousand Oaks, CA: 1984

41. Edward T. Hall and Mildred Reed Hall, *Guide du comportement dns les affaires internationales: Allemagne, Etats-Unis, France [Guidelines for conduct in international affairs: Germany, United States, France]* (Editions Du Seuil, 1990).

    Edward T. Hall and Mildred Reed Hall, *Verborgene Signale: Studien zur internationalen Kommunikation – Über den Umgang mit Amerikanern*

[Hidden signals: Study on international communication – On interacting with Americans] (Gruner & Jahr, 1983).

Edward T. Hall and Mildred Reed Hall, *Verborgene Signale: Studien zur internationalen Kommunikation – Über den Umgang mit Franzosen [Hidden signals: Study on international communication – On interacting with the French]* (Stern/Gruner & Jahr, 1984).

Edward T. Hall and Mildred Reed Hall, *Une étude de la communication internationale – comment communiquer avec les Allemands [A Study of International Communication – How to Communicate with Germans]* (Gruner & Jahr, 1984).

42. One of the few speakers Ned requested that Karin ask to speak at his memorial service was Ernst Rothe, his psychotherapist during his last years in Santa Fe. Gladys Levis-Pilz gave the eulogy. Also speaking were his son Eric Reed Hall who welcomed the guests, and his grandson, E. T. Hall III; Malcolm Collier, son of John Collier, noted for his work in the southwest and inspiring the field of Visual Anthropology; John Talley and Greg Cajete from Santa Clara Pueblo; and myself.

Calligraphy by Amy Jones

CHAPTER THREE

Mapping the Territory

About Ned Hall, it seems to me he was slightly
too intellectual for the total popular audience
and too popular for the academics—
seems to me a good place to be.
—*Jack Parsons*

A modest request: take a minute or two to scan the "word cloud" on the facing page, about the time needed to read a page of text.

It's a non-linear organization, so words that your eyes connect, and how you connect them, provide a fleeting personal grammar. As your eyes roam across these words, do you react differently to words you recognize than to some that may be new? Do you pass by the unfamiliar or do those words make you more curious? And the familiar words—most are part of ordinary speech—in the context of this book, do they invite more attention? Each of these concepts connects with the others. Drawing from memory and sensory experience, imagine how these are related. Selective perception? All perception is selective.

These words, with the exceptions of "neuroscience," "implicit bias," and "colonialism," represent some of Hall's best-known topics that we explore in this book, but how to present these key concepts as a constellation of ideas before considering them separately? I mentioned to a friend, art historian Robert Caslin, that I thought maybe a "word cloud" could be a way to give a non-linear overview of topics, and immediately he reacted: "Good idea—students like those." Of course! Good teachers always learn from their students.

Arranging topics in alphabetical order complicates seeing connections, overlap, even inseparability. In *Orality and Literacy: The Technologizing of the Word,* Walter Ong observed that writing introduces a hierarchy.[1] Just ask Aaron Aaronson and Zbigniew Zybertowicz. Arranging chronologically is no better.

At least two generations have grown up in a largely non-linear, visual and aural media environment, and with the desire and ability to express themselves in the same way. Pictures and iconic graphs, emoticons or emojis, nudge out words—perhaps seeming a lazy choice for those in my generation, but expressing attitudes and imprecise feelings that make up most of everyday communication that digital technology has given us. I recall a college senior in Japan telling me that she felt uncomfortable receiving messages that didn't include an emoji, which made her feel closer to the sender. Because she was about to graduate and was applying for a job, I worried she might include a smiley face or that she would insert into her application that she would ❤ to work there. Then I realized it was another example of an intercultural communication challenge, and I shouldn't be dismissive.[2]

Studies of the creative process among scientists, as well as artists, indicate that the visual or even the aural is part of some of their best thinking. There is a risk of valuing the representation more than what it represents, the word for the thing, the map for the territory. The stream of consciousness of James Joyce's *Ulysses* mirrors our own associative thinking, how we connect one idea or concept with another in a manner we don't ordinarily give voice to, or write. Richard Dettering called the connections that hold meanings others might not understand as following a "psycho-logic."[3]

Picasso had already moved through his cubist period, presenting three dimensions on a two-dimensional canvas, upsetting a public who wanted things to "look like reality." He was attacked for painting unrealistic portraits with facial parts not in their normal positions. One time a stranger pulled Picasso aside and taking a photograph of his wife from his wallet, "*This* is how a woman looks." Picasso studied it and then observed: "She's rather small. And flat."

When Stravinsky's *Rite of Spring* was first performed in Paris, the audience famously rioted because what they heard was dissonance, not music. Freud's writings intrigued as they disturbed, and influenced Hall's generation in ways we can't appreciate today. Albert Einstein upset the idea that space and time were separate, and "relativity" became a watchword that influenced our thinking about how our languages map our realities, and that maybe the verbs matter more than the nouns. Process. Buckminster Fuller, a friend of Hall, whose worlds they recognized as similar, expressed that when he said: "I live on Earth at present, and I don't know what I am. I know that I am not a category. I am not a thing—a noun. I seem to be a verb, an evolutionary process—an integral function of the universe."[4]

"Culture is Communication," popularly attributed to Hall, was expressed a century ago by that towering figure in anthropology, Franz Boas, a man who called out the ethnocentrism and racism in the scholarship of his time. Boas retired from Columbia University just before Hall entered their graduate program. Inextricably linked, "culture" and "communication" are not the same but each is both process and product for the other. Which invites a comparison to the chicken-and-egg puzzle. I like a version by Samuel Butler: is a hen the egg's way of making another egg? Or, is the egg the chicken's way of making another chicken?

Regarding the relationship of culture to communication we might ask: Is communication the way culture reproduces itself, or is culture what we call the reproduction (with variations) of the systems and processes of communication? Hall sought to describe "culture" *as* "communication," and that is what this book invites you to think about.

A Map of Culture

Along with his linguist colleague George Trager, with whom he shared an office at the Foreign Service Institute, Hall believed there were relatively few behaviors that run through evolution, and they are specific enough to be described and compared across cultural categories. These would also be much easier to talk about than the complex of behavior that is called "culture"—to say nothing about values, assumptions, and beliefs that arose only as the brain evolved to be self-reflective and create philosophies, and later conduct experiments to try to explain our behavior to ourselves.

With the goal to interpret culture as communication, Hall and Trager constructed a 10 by 10 grid of "Primary Message Systems" that would encompass the range of activities identified as integral to culture. Hall included this chart, which he called "A Map of Culture," as an appendix in The Silent Language. Although some of the names for topics he used then have other meanings today (for example, "bi-sexual," by which he meant the binary gendered distinction), his "map" may be likened to cartographers' early maps of continents and seas that, with further research, proved incomplete and inaccurate.

To call it a "map" seems a misnomer, if by "map" one thinks of geo-political maps that emphasize regions and boundaries, the way that word "culture" is most often used when viewed from a distance, but when viewed from within, culture, is a dynamic of interdependent, often mutually supporting activities, where any change in one thing affects others. Viewed from within, it is a bee's experience, not just the hive seen from without.

Hall thought "culture" was best described by the activities, routines, and assumptions that might characterize it; "culture" is most obvious when a new technology appears and disrupts old patterns of relationships. No matter how many other categories those defining "culture" add or highlight, if they are presented as a list—we love lists—and not seen as part of systems, indeed, a system of systems, we miss the significance that Hall emphasized. Hall wanted the technical assistance volunteers, teachers, medical personnel, and others to anticipate possible consequences as they came to appreciate what for many was a fuzzy idea of "culture." He wanted these professionals who were about to go abroad and share their knowledge and experience, to appreciate that their contributions, especially if considered successful, might affect the very cultural community they wanted to help and ideally improve, often without foreseeing the full range of their impact. Today we might use the term "unanticipated consequences."

A MAP OF CULTURE

Primary Message Systems	Interactional	Organizational	Economic	Sexual
	0	1	2	3
Interaction 0	Communication Vocal qualifiers Kinesics Language 00	Status and Role 01	Exchange 02	How the sexes interact 03
Association 1	Community 10	Society Class Caste Government 11	Economic roles 12	Sexual roles 13
Subsistence 2	Ecological community 20	Occupational groupings 21	Work Formal work Maintenance Occupations 22	Sexual division of labor 23
Bisexuality 3	Sex community (class, sibs) 30	Marriage groupings 31	Family 32	The Sexes Masc. vs. Fem. Sex (biological) Sex (technical) 33
Territoriality 4	Community territory 40	Group territory 41	Economic areas 42	Men's and women's territories 43
Temporality 5	Community cycles 50	Group cycles 51	Economic cycles 52	Men's and women's cyclical activities 53
Learning 6	Community lore—what gets taught and learned 60	Learning groups— educational institutions 61	Reward for teaching and learning 62	What the sexes are taught 63
Play 7	Community play—the arts and sports 70	Play groups— teams and troupes 71	Professional sports and entertainment 72	Men's and women's play, fun, and games 73
Defense 8	Community defenses— structured defense systems 80	Defense groups —armies, police, public health, organized religion 81	Economic patterns of defense 82	What the sexes defend (home, honor, etc.) 83
Exploitation 9	Communication networks 90	Organizational networks (cities, building groups, etc.) 91	Food, resources, and industrial equipment 92	What men and women are concerned with and own 93

| Territorial | Temporal | Instructional | Recreational | Protective | Exploitational |
4	5	6	7	8	9
Places of interaction 04	Times of interaction 05	Teaching and learning 06	Participation in the arts and sports (active and passive) 07	Protecting and being protected 08	Use of telephones, signals, writing, etc. 09
Local group roles 14	Age group roles 15	Teachers and learners 16	Entertainers and athletes 17	Protectors (doctors, clergy, soldiers, police, etc.) 18	Use of group property 19
Where the individual eats, cooks, etc. 24	When the individual eats, cooks, etc. 25	Learning from working 26	Pleasure from working 27	Care of health, protection of livelihood 28	Use of foods, resources, and equipment 29
Areas assigned to individuals by virtue of sex 34	Periods assigned to individuals by virtue of sex 35	Teaching and learning sex roles 36	Participation in recreation by sex 37	Protection of sex and fertility 38	Use of sex differentiating decoration and adornment 39
Space Formal space Informal space Boundaries 44	Scheduling of space 45	Teaching and learning individual space assignments 46	Fun, playing games, etc., in terms of space 47	Privacy 48	Use of fences and markers 49
Territorially determined cycles 54	Time Sequences Cycles Calendar 55	When the individual learns 56	When the individual plays 57	Rest, vacations, holidays 58	Use of time-telling devices, etc. 59
Places for learning 64	Scheduling of learning (group) 65	Enculturation Rearing Informal learning Education 66	Making learning fun 67	Learning self-defense and to stay healthy 68	Use of training aids 69
Recreational areas 74	Play seasons 75	Instructional play 76	Recreation Fun Playing Games 77	Exercise 78	Use of recreational materials (playthings) 79
What places are defended 84	The When of defense 85	Scientific, religious, and military training 86	Mass exercises and military games 87	Protection Formal defenses Informal defenses Technical defenses 88	Use of materials for protection 89
Property— what is enclosed, counted, and measured 94	What periods are measured and recorded 95	School buildings, training aids, etc. 96	Amusement and sporting goods and their industries 97	Fortifications, armaments, medical equipment, safety devices 98	Material, Systems, Contact with environment Motor habits Technology 99

Notes

1. Walter Ong, *Orality and Literacy: The Technologizing of the Word* (London: Methuen & Co. Ltd., 1982).

2. Japanese popular culture has exerted a considerable influence globally on culture as communication, including the "emoji" by the Japanese internet communication company, Docomo, in 1999. (Docomo's i-mode phone was also the precursor of the smart phone.) Shigetaka Kurita was only 25 when he developed the original 176 emoji, now acquired by the Museum of Modern Art in New York City. In 2023, around 3,000 are on the official Unicode list. Kurita has said, "Both emoji and *kanji* [characters] are ideograms, but I did not find inspiration for designing emoji in the *kanji*. I found inspiration in pictograms, manga, and all sorts of other sources." The original intention was to provide images that could be used to convey the meaning of something or an emotion more quickly than written text. The word "emoji" is a portmanteau word combining "e" (pronounced "eh," meaning picture) and "*moji,*" with "*ji,*" being the Japanese term for "written character." Graphic novels gained popularity in Japan where "manga" and "anime" were more prominent and taken more seriously than "comics" and "animated movies, cartoons" were in "the West"—France, a notable exception. Today, emojis face some of the same challenges of words, especially as used in most of the world, including ambiguity and interpretations across cultures and languages.

3. Richard Dettering, "Toward A Psycho-Logics of Human Behavior," *ETC: A Review of General Semantics* Vol. 15, No. 3 (Spring, 1958), 181-189, Institute of General Semantics.

4. R. Buckminster Fuller, *I Seem to Be a Verb: Environment and Man's Future* (New York: Bantom Books, 1970).

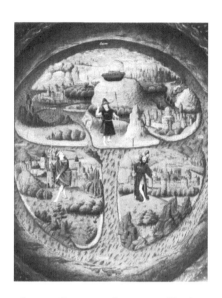

Regarding the Analogs Called Maps

This map from 1440 CE is in the tradition of "T-O maps" dating from 700 years earlier, where the "T" represents the waters of the Mediterranean Sea and the Nile River, and the "O" the oceans surrounding the earth. Unlike today's convention of making the top of the map North, the earlier top of European maps was East, the direction from which we see the sun rise, and literally the orientation. The continent on the top half of this map is Asia, and the other two continents in the lower half are Europe on the left, and Africa on the right. Noah's Ark is visible on the top, along with other religious iconography. The three human figures represent Noah's three sons. The implicit center of the map is Jerusalem. This map was not made for navigating—there were better maps for that purpose then.

Today's commercial map makers center their world maps on the country in which the map is made, and political decisions influence where borders are shown; sometimes even entire countries are left out. All maps are abstractions, incomplete, made for a particular purpose, and reflect assumptions and values of the mapmaker. So, too, with Hall's "map."

Neural networks of the human brain
Photo by Yurchanka Siarhei

CHAPTER FOUR

The Evolutionary Brain

We don't come from primates, we are primates. We are not a
race, we are a species. We are animals. We are mammals. We are
a product of nature. We belong to it and we are a part of it.
—*David Attenborough*

The real problem of humanity is the following: we have paleo-
lithic emotions; medieval institutions; and godlike technology.
—*E. O. Wilson*

I t was exactly a century before Hall's *The Silent Language* that
Charles Darwin's *On the Origin of Species by Means of Natural
Selection* displaced *homo sapiens* from their biological egocentrism,
much as Galileo had displaced the earth as at the center of the universe.
We are an evolved species, and, over time, Hall would come to regard
"culture" as a stage in our continuing human evolution.[1] Today,
however, those working in the field of intercultural communication
as educators, advisors, or consultants who put culture as a central
theme in their profession are not likely to consider, let alone mention,
evolution. A buzzword, "evolution" is not.

During his years in New Mexico, Hall learned from Indigenous communities how creatures that preceded and outnumber us are shown respect. "We are the five-fingered ones," say the Diné (Navajo), noting a distinguishing feature of the human variety of animals.[2] This is markedly different from the view in "the white man's world," to use the Indigenous vernacular during Hall's era. In a "Western" perspective, as proclaimed in some holy books, we are apart from and have dominion over the lesser animals. If only Adam had realized how much we are all related, and that the base of his brain was reptilian. And don't even think about that rib.

At the Los Alamos Ranch School, young Ned's appreciation of ethology (the study of animal behavior) was especially influenced by his bonding with the horse he was given to care for and learned to respect. As an adult, Hall's respect and affection for horses increased as he would travel great distances on horseback for his work at remote locations, inaccessible by motor vehicles. He often spoke about those experiences and what he learned not only about equine-human communication, but also about ways of knowing the land with his horse as his teacher, a sensitivity to the land not possible by car or truck.[3]

In *Animals in Translation,* by Temple Grandin and Catherine Johnson, Grandin talks about animal behavior that few people understand, including communication between humans and the animals they live with, whether at home or on ranches or livestock lots.[4] Grandin says that it is because she is on the autistic spectrum that she is better able to appreciate and "translate" how animals perceive and think:

> . . . I am a visual thinker. . . . During my thinking process I have no words in my head at all, just pictures.[5]
>
> Visual thinkers of any species, animal or human, are detail-oriented. . . . I think this is probably the hardest part of an animal's existence for normal people to relate to. Verbal

people can't just turn themselves into visual people because they want to, and vice versa.[6]

The reason we've managed to live with animals for all these years without noticing many of their special talents is simple: we can't see those talents. Normal people never have the special talents animals have, so normal people don't know what to look for. . . . But now that I've seen the connection between autistic savantry and animal genius at least I have an idea what I'm looking for: I'm looking for ways animals can use their amazing ability to perceive things humans can't perceive, and to remember highly detailed information we can't remember.[7]

Had Grandin's or similar work appeared earlier, I believe Hall would have been an eager reader, underlining many parts of her books that would have informed and implicitly affirmed his life-long belief of the value that ethological research offers to our understanding of human behavior.

The "Monkey Trial"

Evolution was a hot topic in the US when Hall was growing up. He was eleven years old at the time of the Scopes Monkey Trial, as journalist and author H. L. Mencken called the 1925 state of Tennessee prosecution of a high school teacher, John T. Scopes. His crime: teaching about evolution. Tennessee's Butler Act prohibited the teaching of evolution in public schools. The Scopes Monkey Trial was among the most sensationalized trials of the early-twentieth century, in a near-circus-like atmosphere as reporters from the press and from the nascent radio and movie media descended on the courthouse. The trial pitted the wily progressive attorney Clarence Darrow, now a folk hero, who represented Scopes, opposing William Jennings

Bryan for the prosecution. Bryan was a three-time Democratic Party presidential candidate. He was also one of the most famous orators in the country at a time when "orator" was a term of distinction, and his was a voice opposed to teaching evolution.[8]

The trial was dramatized in a 1955 play, *Inherit the Wind*, later a movie, and presented in several television performances.[9] The play continues to be performed by high school drama groups, even in Tennessee. Since 2000, fourteen states have passed laws that challenge the teaching of evolution in public schools. Today evolutionary theory is still challenged, primarily by those who, like Bryan, are voices of faith-based conservatives who reject anything that appears to contradict what the Bible says. In most countries, the theory of evolution is taught without incident, the exceptions being parts of the US and in Turkey where Darwinian theory conflicts with some Muslim teachings. Many people would agree with Nobel Prize physicist Richard Feynman's words: "I prefer questions that can't be answered, to answers that can't be questioned."

Few scientific theories have been more extensively studied and consistently affirmed than the theory of evolution. Whenever I see a roadrunner bird, New Mexico's official state bird and almost as common here as in a Chuck Jones cartoon, I see that birds are our closest living relative to the dinosaurs. Apart from those still fighting against evolution.

The relevance of Hall's work is mostly about the pragmatics of everyday life—how we sense and make sense of the behavior of others, in the workplace, school, and intimate relationships including marriage. And how we regard demographic changes in the makeup of regions and communities. It is at the interpersonal level that Hall's contributions are best known and applied, especially nonverbal behavior, which is fitting. Overlooked is Hall's interest in relating our behavior to our evolutionary history. A goal, and implicit throughout his work, was to offer a "bio-based theory" of culture bolstered by ethological, neurological, and psychological studies. He often asked Darwinian questions like: what is the survival value of "culture"?

In several of his books, Hall devoted many pages to ethology, writing in some detail to suggest that our pre-human ancestors are relevant to understanding human behavior. That there is much to learn from other species, either by way of analogy or because of our own evolutionary history, never drew much attention by those in the field of intercultural communication. Hall's interests included territoriality and its defense, the effects of crowding, and other spatially related matters, and especially those sequences of interactive behavior that can provoke or reduce the possibility of conflict that he called "adumbration," or foreshadowing what behavior to anticipate. We have much to learn from other species. For example, how do two dogs react when encountering each other for the first time? There may be signals of curiosity, of defending territory, of dominance and deference, of challenge, or an invitation to play. What can we learn from our best friends of the four-legged variety?

The Triune Brain

It is not surprising that Hall took a special interest in the influential work of the pioneering neuroscientist, Paul D. MacLean, who was then chairman of Yale University's Laboratory of Brain Evolution and Behavior. It was there that MacLean developed his theory of "the Triune Brain": that the human brain is a living record of our evolutionary history, as evidenced in the brain's three successively evolved and layered parts.

Starting from a reptilian brain, estimated to date back 250,000 years, this "old brain" is responsible for our basic motor functions for survival. Also called "the brainstem," the oldest part of the brain controls what is essential to life: breathing, blood pressure, body temperature, and other functions outside of our consciousness. "If you get a small area of damage in your brainstem (from an injury, tumor, or stroke) you could be rendered comatose . . . extensive damage to the brainstem is almost always fatal."[10]

In an unpublished piece, Hall enumerates some 25 behaviors that we share with snakes and lizards and other reptiles. He mused that it was fortunate that evolution produced legs so young ones could move fast, since reptiles may eat their young.

The fight or flight mechanism is centered in the reptilian brain, its sensing range is limited, and there is no capacity for learning. Hall would joke that a bureaucracy, including the army and the parts of government administration that he experienced working in Washington, seemed to rely on the reptilian brain.

The Limbic Brain, the "Feeling Brain"

Onto this, there evolved 180,000 years ago "the limbic brain" (MacLean introduced the term "limbic"), which is sometimes called "the feeling brain," and it was to this Hall would give most attention. Hall characterized the limbic system as pattern-sensitive, "feeling oriented," that also allowed for the acquisition of behavior that Hall estimated to be 80 per cent of what we do non-consciously. He believed the limbic complex was at the heart of what we call "culture," and which gets us in trouble when we interact with others whose lived experience is different.

Now more often called the "limbic complex," this area of the brain evolved to give us emotions, memory, learning, time perception, spatial memory, and even perception of faces to discern what and whom to trust. Little wonder that Hall was most interested in the limbic complex, believing that it deserved special attention if we are to understand ourselves and our everyday communication, rather than placing so much emphasis on the subsequently evolved cognitive region, which is what is most celebrated when we differentiate ourselves from "mere animals."

The limbic system also connects the old brain's autonomic and reflexive behavior with the conscious awareness linked to the cognitive forebrain. Central, literally and functionally, to the limbic system are the *amygdala* and the *hippocampus* that "appears to have a special role in laying down the memory traces for facts and events."[11]

During the televised hearing of a US Senate Judiciary committee in 2020 that would eventually vote to confirm Brett Kavanaugh as a justice of the US Supreme Court, a key witness who spoke in opposition was Dr. Blasey Ford, a psychologist at Stanford University. Ford accused Kavanaugh of a sexual assault at a party, decades earlier, when both were high school students. She described in neurological terms her memories of the trauma she said was inflicted by the nominee, and as a psychologist she introduced to many who were following the internationally televised hearing the term "hippocampus," embedded in the limbic system, and its primacy in our memory.

"Indelible in the hippocampus is the laughter. The uproarious laughter between the two [boys who she testified had her trapped in a room and pinned her down on a bed], and their having fun at my expense," she said, referring to Kavanaugh and his friend, Mark Judge.

Memories, however imperfect they may be, play an important part in our lives and how we perceive and react to people we've just met but who stir those memories. Imagine a boy in elementary school who, in one class, has a new teacher, a young woman with long blonde hair, wearing distinctive glasses, and speaking in a voice quite different from how his mother or aunt talked. One day when the teacher asks the class to answer a simple question that he misunderstood and boldly answered, all his classmates laughed at him. He felt that the teacher embarrassed him in front of everyone, and he never forgot that moment. Many years later, he meets someone, perhaps a co-worker or perhaps his supervisor, whose appearance and voice reminds him of that teacher, and he feels as if that experience from long before is happening all over again. The poor woman can't understand his hostility. It is likely that even he can't explain his reactions.

This is another form of PTSD that, while more often identified with the re-experienced emotional trauma from war, can also be triggered by other experiences including those that others present barely notice and forget moments later. Such a deep emotional impact affects a lifetime of feelings about oneself and the other, and may alter patterns of action and reaction throughout life. In his book, *Brain and Culture*, Yale University professor of psychiatry, Bruce E. Wexler, says this in another way: the limbic system "provide[s] the basis for familial and social behaviors and for preverbal visual and vocal displays of emotion. Emotion is an inter-individual process that alters the moment-to-moment functional organization and activation patterns of the brain in the individuals who are interacting."[12]

It is through the limbic system that we feel and hold those feelings, so very important in all our relationships and, ultimately, in our sense of who we are and what we value. Asked on her 75th birthday what she had learned in her life, poet Maya Angelou said, "People will forget the things you do, and people will forget the things you say. But people will never forget how you made them feel."

The Cerebral Neocortex

In Hall's interpretation, each area of the brain with its own structure and chemistry meant that each experienced a different reality, and that these are not always in concert. Our brains sometimes don't agree with each other, causing us confusion as they fight it out, he said. The "feeling brain" connected our different ways of sensing, but it took the neocortex or forebrain, "the thinking brain," to give us love and hate. The youngest part of the brain, which evolved an estimated 40,000 years ago, is the neocortex that allows for cognition and symbol systems including language. This is the largest part of the brain, the "gray matter" that most people imagine when they think of a brain, with its curves and swirls that we are most likely to visualize as "the brain." (A friend, Patti Digh, says that whenever she sees a brussels sprout, she imagines a little brain.) This forebrain, neocortex, is what makes possible language and logic and mathematics: symbol systems. Adeptness in these systems comprises much of what is socially rewarded. It is often also equated with a popular notion of "culture"— music, architecture, speech, and literature—topics that might be seen in the "Culture" section of a newspaper, and what people take pride in, often with nationalistic associations, and historically, used as a standard to judge and often disparage others. Of course, the ability to imagine and examine our brain is possible only because of the neocortex, that uppermost third in MacLean's triune brain theory.

Less emphasized in the triune brain theory is the hemisphere division of the forebrain. As MacLean called our attention to the evolution described vertically, later our attention became directed to the horizontal and asymmetrical "divided brain," the right- and left-brain hemispheres as explained by neuroscientist and psychiatrist Iain McGilchrist. He describes the right hemisphere as "presenting" our sensed experience of the external world, and the left hemisphere as *re*-presenting (or representing) that experience in symbolic form; in McGilchrist's judgment, too little attention is given to the right hemisphere and too much to the left. That would have appealed to Hall who, like McGilchrist, believed we give too much attention to the cognitive and too little to "the feeling brain," the pre-conscious, pre-cognitive side.

MacLean's Triune Brain theory was a significant advancement in the study of the brain at the leading edge of the emergent field of neuroscience we know today. MacLean's work impressed not only Hall but other serious writers who brought MacLean's triune brain theory to the general public. Among these were Carl Sagan in *The Dragons of Eden* (1977), and essayist and novelist Arthur Koestler in his *The Ghost in the Machine* (1967).

David Linden, a neuroscientist at Johns Hopkins University who writes with clarity and wit, likens the evolved triune brain to an ice cream cone:

The brain is built like an ice cream cone (and you are the top scoop): through evolutionary time, as higher functions were added, a new scoop was placed on top, but the lower scoops were left largely unchanged. In this way our human cerebellum, and the midbrain are not very different in overall plan from that of a frog. It's just that a frog has only rudimentary higher areas in addition (barely more than one scoop). All those structures plus the hypothalamus, thalamus, and limbic system are not that different in humans and rats (two scoops), which have a small and simple cortex, while we humans have all that plus and hugely elaborated cortex (three scoops). When new, higher functions were added, this did not result in a redesign of the whole brain from the ground up; a new scoop was just added on top. Hence, in true kludge fashion, our brains contain regions, like the midbrain visual center, that are functional remnants of our evolutionary past.[13]

Hall wrote relatively little about the brain, its structure and functions, and how these inform any discussion of culture and communication and intercultural communication. The evolutionary perspective of the brain, and insights from ethological researchers might receive less attention, not because they are less important but because so much more is known about and continues to be discovered through neuroscience research. If Hall were twenty years younger, his writing would have reported the research and its implications for intercultural communication, like the article "Your Brain on Culture" that appeared in *Psychology Today* the year after Hall died.[14]

As the field of neuroscience evolved and expanded, books about the brain written for the general audience multiplied accordingly. In addition to the few cited in this book, my modest bookshelf includes an array of books about the human brain, each with a different focus: *Mind Wide Open: Your Brain and the Neuroscience of Everyday Life;*

The Emotional Life of Your Brain; *Incognito: The Secret Lives of the Brain*; *The Teenage Brain: A Neuroscientist's Survival Guide to Raising Adolescents and Young Adults*; *The Secret Life of the Grown-Up Brain: The Surprising Talents of the Middle-Aged Mind*; *The Female Brain*; *The Japanese Brain: Uniqueness and Universality*; *The Brain that Changes Itself: Stories of Personal Triumph from the Frontiers of Brain Science.*

One theme in marketing some of these books is a word that rarely appears in the research reported by neuroscientists: secret. The real secret is that today there is so much information about the brain accessible to the ordinary reader that it can feel overwhelming. Yet, as we continue to learn more about our brains and how they function in everyday communication, more and more we can talk in terms previously only in the province of specialists: "brain plasticity," "mirror neurons," and even "amygdala" and "hippocampus." Like all discoveries and realizations, the full applications and implications are themselves, let us say, still evolving.

Hall's life spans the same era, almost exactly, as MacLean's, though the pioneering brain specialist didn't publish his triune brain theory until 1990, late in his life. Hall mentions the triune brain briefly in *Beyond Culture*, in his discussion of "Cultural and Primate Behavior in Education," but in his classes and in subsequent presentations he liked to talk about this triune brain and evolution. "MacLean . . . has demonstrated that man has not one but three brains and therefore three natures, which may not always be in step with each other."[15]

The Major Triad

Years before he learned about "the triune brain," Hall had introduced a three-part perspective on culture, as we experience "it" and how we talk about "it": *formal, informal,* and *technical.* He called this "the major triad." Among the least known and utilized of Hall's lenses, he applied this three-part distinction in perspectives not only to cultural communities, varying by region and generation, but also to

approaches to learning and teaching, and attitudes toward change—
crucial issues in preparing technical-assistance professionals who were
about to offer their expertise to more traditional communities. It is
a sweeping perspective described in a scant few pages presented in
everyday language. It also draws upon his appreciation of psychology
and art, and his gift for anecdote and story. It is with regard to how
one approaches the understanding of "culture" and "learning," that
informal, formal, and technical remain important and under-utilized.

This triad matched well with the triune brain theory, as Hall
saw it, though not in an evolutionary order. It was the "informal,"
including all we acquire or figure out on our own, that he connected
to limbic system, that "feeling brain." The formal, he believed fit
the old brain, hierarchical, rule-based/right or wrong, and in Hall's
application, characteristic of bureaucracy. The "technical" was a good
fit for the forebrain, the cognitive, whole systems understandable
within themselves.

I'm thinking of my own frustrations of trying to understand instructions about some computer software that I know makes sense. I'm
thinking of the title of an Edgar Dale essay, "Clear Only if Known."[16]

Notes

1. E. T. Hall, *Axioms* (unpublished).
2. Thank you, Chenoa Bah Stillwell-Jensen.
3. In Hall's copy of *The Man Who Listens to Horses: The Story of a Real-Life Horse Whisperer* (Random House, 1997), the book by Monty Roberts that inspired the movie *The Horse Whisperer*, Hall underlined many sentences about the crucial communication between human and equine species that affirmed his experience with horses decades earlier.
4. Temple Grandin and Catherine Johnson, *Animals in Translation: Using the Mysteries of Autism to Decode Animal Behavior* (Scribner, 2010).
5. Grandin and Johnson, *Animals in Translation*, 16.
6. Grandin and Johnson, *Animals in Translation*, 26.
7. Grandin and Johnson, *Animals in Translation*, 8.
8. Bryan graduated from Northwestern University with a B.O. (Bachelor of Oratory degree). Years later, Hall (and this author) also taught there, long after the university had scrubbed the embarrassing B.O.
9. The drama, written by Jerome Lawrence and Robert Edwin Lee in 1955, was also commentary on the demonization of writers and politicians by the later disgraced Senator Joseph McCarthy. In 1960, the film, *Inherit the Wind*, directed by Stanley Kramer with an all-star cast, was released. The drama was again remade for television in well received versions presented in 1965, 1988, and 1999, a testimony to the attraction of the power of abuse of orthodoxy against those who would challenge it. Arthur Miller's now-classic 1953 drama, *The Crucible*, was also an allegory and commentary on "McCarthyism," drawing on trials from an earlier time in US history, the late-seventeenth-century Salem witch trials.
10. David Linden, *The Accidental Mind: How Brain Evolution Has Given Us Love, Memory, Dreams, and God* (Cambridge, MA: Belknap Press of Harvard University Press, 2007), 9.
11. Linden, *Accidental Mind*, 17.
12. Bruce E. Wexler, *Brain and Culture*, Cambridge, MA: MIT Press, 2008, 32.
13. Linden, *Accidental Mind*, 21-22.
14. Beth Azar, "This is Your Brain on Culture," *Psychology Today*, August 31, 2010.
15. Hall, unpublished work.
16. Edgar Dale, "Clear Only If Known," *ETC.*, XV (Summer, 1958), 290-293.

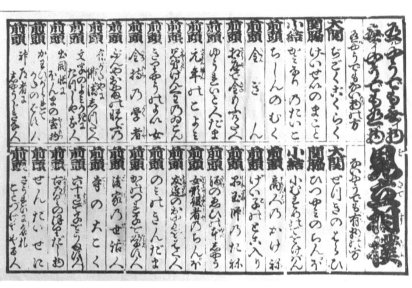

Late-eighteenth century Japanese satirical banzuke-hyo chart

Things that Seem to Exist but Don't, and Things that Don't Seem to Exist but Do: About Culture

O n my wall is a late-eighteenth century Japanese satirical print that presents two lists: *"Things That Seem to Exist but Don't,"* and *"Things That Don't Seem to Exist but Do."* It's printed in a Japanese calligraphy and format similar to that used even today to announce the names and ranks of sumo wrestlers, which is part of what makes people smile at it. In this particular document, the list of *Things That Seem to Exist but Don't* includes *heaven, hell,* ranking highest, and much lower, *wealthy scholars.* The list of *Things That Don't Seem to Exist but Do* includes *"bargains at second-hand stores"* and lower ranked, *"the balls of a flea."*

The word "culture," it has seemed to me, deserves a place in such a registry, but under which heading would "culture" be better placed? Is culture something that seems to exist but really doesn't, or is it something that doesn't seem to exist, but actually does? Getting people to take "culture" seriously as something real continues to be a challenge. In the context of anthropology—despite a history of 150

95

years—the culture concept remains one of the most contested in the social sciences. An informal survey by Bruce La Brack of anthropology textbooks revealed that the word "culture" was missing in the index of most new books, though it appears respectable as a modifier, "cultural" as in "cultural history." As if "butter" were banned, but "butter flavored" is allowed.

In terms of that old Japanese satiric chart, the culture concept, foundational in the last century, has moved in this century from heading B to heading A—something believed to exist but now in doubt, at least to those anthropologists who have abandoned the word "culture" altogether. Readers who may appreciate a brief overview of the history of the culture concept in anthropology should refer to the endnote summary of this history by La Brack, one of the first anthropologists who appreciated what the field of intercultural communication had to offer that he didn't find in anthropology.[1]

How to define this most basic of concepts in anthropology has itself become a subject of study. A few years before Hall's first book appeared, two prominent anthropologists, Alfred Kroeber and Clyde Kluckhohn, prepared a report titled *Culture: A Critical Review of Concepts and Definitions*, in which they compiled and evaluated over 150 definitions organized under six generic headings.[2] Disagreements and proposed definitions have not abated, sometimes seeming as if there were at least as many definitions for the culture concept as there were anthropologists doing the defining. Frustration with defining "culture" calls to mind US Supreme Court Justice Potter Stewart's struggle with defining pornography: "I can't define it but I know it when I see it."

To stimulate discussion about the relevance of the culture concept today, the former chair of Harvard's anthropology department posed two questions to his colleagues: *"What's the use of culture? And can the culture concept serve as a unifying paradigm for anthropology at Harvard in the 21ˢᵗ century?"* In response, Matthew Liebmann, currently Chair of the Department of Anthropology at Harvard, and also a friend, wrote a thoughtful reply that is included in this book as an Appendix.

Liebmann notes some of the criticism: "the culture concept is widely critiqued as abstract, essentializing, ahistorical, homogenizing, primordial, bounded, discrete, and totalizing, among other complaints." He notes the dissatisfaction with the term is signaled by the "lexical avoidance behavior . . . " that is, just not using the word "culture." He continues:

> Yet to me, reports of culture's death seem a bit exaggerated. It is one of those zombie terms that keeps dragging itself back from the grave. Try as we might to kill it, culture simply won't give up the *geist*.
>
> While some anthropologists may no longer find the culture concept worthwhile, seemingly everyone else does. I, for one, find this heartening for the future of our discipline. The culture concept opens avenues for discussion between ourselves and non-anthropologists in ways that [substitutes such as] *habitus* and *discursive formations* just can't. Regrettably few other anthropological concepts enjoy such widespread popularity. Notions of culture are regularly employed in business, in law, in politics, in other academic disciplines, and in everyday life. As [Marshall] Sahlins notes, "people want culture, and they often want it in the bounded, reified, essentialized and timeless fashion that most of us do now reject."

What Liebmann and Sahlins remind us is that "culture" as a concept has escaped their discipline and found a place closer to "everyone else" who "wants culture." Liebmann concludes his commentary: "The fact that we can still debate the cornerstone of our [anthropology] discipline after more than a century is something anthropology should embrace and celebrate." He concludes, "Or maybe culture isn't the true cornerstone of anthropology after all—arguing about culture is."

Hall's work did exactly what some anthropologists regret and what Liebmann defends: making a connection between the work in anthropology where "culture" was central and the worlds of non-specialists who can benefit by considering cultural influences in their lives. "The best reason for the layperson to spend time studying culture is to learn something useful and enlightening," Hall wrote. "One of the most effective ways to learn about oneself is by taking seriously the cultures of others. It forces you to pay attention to those details of life which differentiate them from you."[3]

Hall resisted offering a concise definition of "culture," including those included in that famous Kroeber and Kluckhohn report, but he identified four features that most definitions have in common as they apply to his focus on internalized, "subjective culture." First, subjective culture is primarily about what is socially *acquired*. That is, what is internalized largely without conscious awareness. The first language (or languages—a monolingual environment is not the norm globally, or even in the United States) one is exposed to as a child is *acquired* as if by osmosis, and largely without much awareness. Within their first year, children have acquired the sensitivity to what sounds and rhythms of speech are relevant, indeed essential, for the child's future survival, and a vital predisposition is etched in the brain. A language taught in the classroom is *learned,* a very different process, often with explicit grammatical rules to help the learner understand language patterns. That's why someone who has learned a foreign language often can explain it more clearly than native speakers can themselves, and yet rarely speak it like a native speaker. Culture is also *learned* socially (learning to drive or to type, or to prepare favorite foods), abilities that become habitual behavior.

Second, as socially acquired and learned, culture is also a shared experience and process. It is part of our connection with others. Though each person is unique, which Hall also emphasized and urged be respected, "cultural" is not the word to describe individual uniqueness.

Third, unless or until one encounters someone whose cultural assumptions and behavior are noticeably different from what seems "normal" by one's own experience and expectations, one is unlikely to be conscious of what has been acquired and learned. This is expressed in one of Hall's best-known quotes: "Culture conceals more than it reveals," adding that, "the culture we've internalized conceals most from ourselves."

And fourth, a change in any fundamental aspect of the complex systems of the assumptions, behavior, and expectations that make up culture will affect other aspects. Any new technology of significance, like the birth control pill in the middle of the last century or the cell phone around the beginning of this century, has altered patterns of relationships and so also the shared culture.

Regarding Hall's fourth characteristic, consider how the pandemic of this century disrupted and altered all kinds of relationships among friends and strangers, relationships about and at work and play and home, and the use of space and its design. When health conditions for enough people allowed for quarantines and other restrictions to be removed, a time to go back to normal, two things became apparent. What would have been ordinary behavior a year earlier was, if briefly, awkward behavior. And, after a year of isolation, remote learning or working (for those privileged enough to be able to do their work from home or other remote location), "normal" wasn't always what people wanted to go back to. "*The* office" and "*the* classroom" took on new meanings and altered functions and significance.

Climate change is today's most profound force, affecting everyone and everything including how we envision ourselves and our future. Other systems that we may have thought of as separate—systems of economics, politics, identification with a region, especially land-based cultures where faith and identity are intimately connected with place—can change external conditions with which we contend and inevitably change our internalized culture.

This interconnectedness feature of culture was crucial for the professional technical, medical, and educational specialists who attended the crash courses at the post-WWII Foreign Service Institute. Even to a greater degree today this is true for everyone, with globalization in its many forms and increased interaction in increasingly multicultural nations, cities, organizations, families, and individuals. What's more, cultural change, for better or worse, arrives not from some aid from abroad but by global forces already present.

There is another crucial feature of culture that some might find implicit in Hall's description, but that I believe will benefit by calling attention to it: the human capacity to assign meanings to aspects of otherwise "natural" experience. This includes two topics for which Hall is best known: meanings assigned to spatial distances, and social meanings assigned and assumed about time. What we learn is a "comfortable distance," and what is too close or too far for comfort. In a potential romantic relationship, coming too close too soon may be going too far too fast. Similarly with time, there are norms regarding what is an appropriate interval between a message received and a reply. And when the return message arrives so late that it says more about that person replying or how that person regards the relationship. These are part of those "silent languages" Hall called our attention to before the Internet and long after "time talked." What he wrote about how we give meanings to space and time may have been the part of his seminal book that readers paid most attention to, as we like stories we can relate to. Theories—they take more effort.

In a wonderful little book, *Food is Culture,* by Massimo Montanari, Professor of Medieval History and History of Food at the University of Bologna—don't you love that title!—expresses a similar argument about the meanings we give to what we consider "food," because our (human) food is never "natural."[4] And so, to extoll "natural food," he says, is an oxymoron because our food ways are part of culture, meanings we have assigned, and therefore not "natural." "The dominant values of the food system in human experience are, to be precise, not defined in terms of 'naturalness,' but result from and represent cultural processes dependent upon the taming, transformation, and reinterpretation of Nature."[5]

The bounty of nature becomes "food" only as it is transformed physically or just symbolically into what we regard as appropriate as "food" and how and when it should be consumed. Montanari's discussion of food makes a general case about "culture," that food is about how a people—community, region, tradition even through a diaspora—perceive, treat, give, and acquire particular meanings, perform, and share.

Writing about the adoption of agriculture (the term long precedes but is not unrelated to the anthropological term "culture") some six to eight thousand years ago, Montanari describes how plants selected for cultivation were those that were most nutritious, particularly grains that benefited from care and attention. "Each area of the world had its grain of choice: wheat spread in the Mediterranean regions, sorghum on the African continent, rice in Asia, corn in America."[6] What Montanari writes about food can be said about almost every other aspect of our lives, including clothing and shelter.

A friend, Professor Kevin Gore, pointed out to me how much information about culture and interpersonal relationships one can learn just by asking about a particular food a guest might be served when visiting in a different cultural community.[7] In the spirit of the aphorism that "the way to a man's heart is through his stomach," Gore, who is also a gourmet chef, observes that one way into the heart of a family-culture is taking a real interest in the special foods one is served as a guest at the table. Asking questions that provide context about when and where and prepared by whom can reveal a great deal about general cultural background, and often of personal and relationship significance. For example, subsistence, including food, as it relates to territory and the temporal—not just what, but who prepares and serves the food, and who takes care of the dishes afterwards, and where and when people eat, what might be affected if or when the place and timing is thrown off some enculturated schedule? Who should be and should not be present? Do men and women eat together? Adults and children at the same table? If not, who dines first? You might be surprised at what you can discover from asking, even friends, such questions about routines and changes in their lifetimes.

Gregory Bateson remarked that "food is love," something I try to remember as a guest and as a host. All those mostly "W" questions of journalists that parallel those of the culturally curious—who, when, where, why, and how—can lead a guest to express appreciation and at the same time gain even more appreciation of the gifts on the plate.

The Culture Concept as a Metaphor

You might hear someone say: *"If you leave home to work or study abroad you also leave your culture and enter another, but you can't just leave your culture behind because it is the lens through which you see things and the scale by which you pass judgment."*

Such a sentence might sound like a truism about culture and intercultural encounters. But such a mixed metaphor! A careful listener might think, "Let me get this straight: You say that culture is a place you can leave and go to another. But then you say it's a possession, like baggage that one carries? Yet you emphasize it's something within us, and it influences how we perceive, judge, act, and react? I don't get it." "Exactly!" critics of the concept might reply.

Though Hall's emphasis was on that last part, he also used "culture" in those other ways, too. Trying to understand this concept by paying attention to how it is used metaphorically can add to our confusion. And saying, "well, it's all of those things" is not a good start if one is looking for a simple definition.

Three Levels of Culture[8]

"Culture" encompasses three different levels in Hall's view, and when these are mixed together what results is confusion.

The primary level: " . . . rules are known to all, obeyed by all, but seldom if ever stated. Its rules are implicit, taken for granted, almost impossible for the average person to state as a system, and generally out of awareness." This is the landscape that Hall explored and urged others to visit, too.

The second level: "though in awareness is largely hidden from outsiders . . . [that] can . . . be the special culture of virtually any group or society." Stories we don't share, what must not be revealed. Hall may have recognized this during the time he grew up in New Mexico, especially among Pueblo Indian communities, as he realized what stories, information, not to be shared from outsiders is part of every family.[9]

Third is the explicit, manifest culture " . . . what we all see and share with each other. It is the façade presented to the world at large. Because it is so easily manipulated, it is the least stable and least dependable for purpose of decision making . . . Most social sciences and political science . . . [are] directed at strategies for penetrating the screen separating manifest culture from secondary level culture." A public face, often what is presented, marketed, in the commodified forms in the tourism industry.

It doesn't take gall to divide something into three. Indeed, it is a favored division in western philosophy, religion, and psychology and other social sciences. Among Hall's several "threes," this succinct tripartite presentation he thought was maybe the most important—but it was largely ignored or forgotten.

Culture is Communication. Life is Communication!

With communication as the framework, Hall, with linguist colleague George Trager, sought to describe culture in terms that arose from a biological base so that they could be compared and presented in a way that would be understandable to the layperson with no particular background in anthropology. An ambitious undertaking. But in communication terms these would not be "variables," or categories of assumptions, values, and beliefs, but regarded as "message systems"—ways in which each person connects with others, and collectively descriptive of whole societies.

Instead of calling these "building blocks," a metaphor he often employed, Hall chose the abstract term "isolates" that he likened to the notes on a musical score and that he elaborated elsewhere. Hall and Trager identified ten—does that number reflect a cultural bias?—which were framed in communication terms: *primary message systems* that they saw as biologically based and suggested were universal, though Hall avoids that loaded term. These are:

- Interaction (today, "interpersonal communication")
- Association
- Subsistence
- Bisexuality (a binary division of gender; today, the distinction between sex and gender is widely recognized, but the binary division runs deeply embedded in many cultural practices)
- Territoriality
- Temporality
- Learning
- Play
- Defense
- Exploitation (use of materials)

Devoting many pages to these ten "primary message systems," Hall discussed how these were expressed in terms of his "major triad," the formal, informal, and technical lenses, and offered a 10 x 10 grid of each message system intersecting with others (included in *The Silent Language* and Chapter Three of this book).

Hall's contemporary and far better-known anthropologist Margaret Mead commented on a still perennial topic—how to define and confine with names for "generations"—a useful gift inflicted on us as technologies mess with Hall's primary message systems.[11] In mid-twentieth century US, a "generation gap" was taken to be a serious social issue. "Gap" was also a buzz word then, and in this case, concern about what was seen as a new separation between parents and their children. Mead blamed, in part, the automatic dishwasher, then a relatively recent technology inserted into the modern US kitchen. Before that, efficiently doing dishes in middle-class homes meant one person washes and the other dries. There was also a democratic spirit: I dried last night; you dry tonight. Not that such a practical social practice no longer exists. This practice also reenforced values of "fairness," taking turns. Managing the routine dishwashing activity would include conversation and so, re: Professor Mead, less of a gap, but the automatic dishwasher disrupted patterns and changed what was somewhat social into individualized tasks. For Hall, such an inquiry revealed much about an underlying culture.

Play and the organizational category in these basic message schemes would include play groups and teams. These intersections provide topics and questions for deeper inquiry. For example, taking US society as a whole, the intersection of play and economics is one of the most significant features of the culture, and one that affects other categories or areas of interest such as "Learning." At this writing, there is attention to the question: should college athletes be paid? State legislatures pass laws prohibiting transexuals from competing on gendered teams that don't match what was assigned at birth. These are intercultural issues every bit as much as any that flare up between people who have grown up in different countries, speaking different languages, and with different worldviews. Or they may feel worse within the same country and language as some resist these cultural changes even as they accept others—technological, seemingly impersonal and with no agenda, notably—that may affect changes at least as profoundly.

The aspects of everyday life that Hall and Trager came up with as barely latent "message systems" are at least as relevant today as they were when they were introduced as a way to show the technical professionals going abroad what they needed to consider—the culture part—when they try to understand their new environment and appreciate how whatever they are bringing might alter patterns of behavior and human interaction that could date back a thousand years.

My impression is that attention to these "message systems" has mostly been ignored by many involved in intercultural relations. Or maybe they are addressed by others, whose professions speak in terms in the parlance of urban planning or in tech transfer. It's not surprising that in his time Hall was most appreciated by those who identified with "applied anthropology."

This conceptualization of "primary message systems" mostly disappeared from Hall's subsequent writings, with the two notable exceptions: "territoriality," in *The Hidden Dimension,* the theme of his subsequent book on the built environment and interpersonal proximity and his guidebook for those who would pursue that cultural message system; and "temporality," in *The Dance of Life: The Other Dimension of Time.*[11]

These themes of space and time were the ones featured in Hall's first book, in the first chapter and two that conclude the book. I suspect that these were the most interesting and relatable parts of the book that framed "culture" in terms of communication at the very moment when communication was ascendant as something worth paying more attention to.

Echoing Boas and reframing "culture" as communication offered a new perspective, metaphors, and vocabulary. Because of the timing of *The Silent Language* when "Rhetoric" or "Speech" in universities was open to contributions from the social sciences, insights from anthropology about culture in the communication process found an eager young audience that felt rhetorical studies of the time were parochial and narrow when the whole world seemed to be opening up.

The Communication Frame in Hall's Work

Gregory Bateson, anthropologist and psychologist, and Hall were writing about the same thing around the same time. Both were captivating story tellers and both appreciated the value of a good metaphor. A summary of some of Bateson's key themes appeared in *The Pragmatics of Human Communication*, written by psychologists and dedicated to Bateson.[12]

Most famous among these principles is that "all behavior communicates" as observed and interpreted. That behavior may be misinterpreted, especially across cultures, is the stuff for which Hall's insights became best known. If all behavior can be the basis of communication, it follows that it is impossible to not communicate. That was the corollary to the "axiom" equating behavior and communication. (The authors of *Pragmatics* wrote in terms of axioms and corollaries, as if this were physics. Hall rejected using physics as a model for the social sciences because it was not reactive, or so it was assumed at that time.)

Hall proclaimed that culture is communication. In so doing, he offered a touchstone from one of the older social sciences, anthropology, into the field of communication that was then struggling to gain respect and be included as one of the social sciences and cemented one of the very oldest disciplines—rhetoric—solidly in the humanities. Hall's book might have been considered a book on applied anthropology but its timing made it a major influence in expanding the range of study in Speech Communication, what had been a relatively parochial field in the US.

Hall may be better recognized by those in the field of communication than among anthropologists. "Communication" at mid-century was just coming into popular parlance, a vague, five-syllable word, a bit clumsy and maybe sounding a bit pretentious, and as a discipline, neither an "-ics" or an "-ology," though some at the time proposed "communicology" so as to distinguish the study of communication from the subject studied. In much of the world in the middle of the twentieth century "communication" brought to mind highways, telephones, and railways rather than thinking of everyday human behavior as "communication."[13]

"What we got here is a failure to communicate," was part of the dialogue in the 1962 movie *Cool Hand Luke,* using "communication" as a high falutin' word spoken to a rebellious prisoner on a chain gang (Paul Newman) by a southern sheriff (Strother Martin).[14] In that context the word "communication" sounds sarcastic. That line would become one of Hollywood's most famous memes, appearing in the lyrics of songs by Pink Floyd and Guns N' Roses, and other pop culture influencers of that era.

This shift began at just about the same time "intercultural communication," a novel interest, was coalescing around Hall's seminal book and the invention of a whole new vocabulary and conceptual apparatus to describe and compare how human beings make mutual meaning in the process of interacting across cultural divides. Hall advocated a constructivist approach from the beginning, and, unlike early anthropology that was originally positivist modeled on physics, the field of intercultural communication much more narrowly and modestly focused on examining how, in the context of face-to-face, everyday social interaction, people coming from different perspectives could engage in constructing meaning and arrive at mutual understanding.

In intercultural communication, culture as a concept found itself being provided another chance to be reinvented, reinvigorated, and usefully applied within the context of that emerging discipline. La Brack points out:

> . . . One of the most significant ways that intercultural communication diverged from anthropology, was the emphasis intercultural theory places on developing "culture-general" categories and broadly applying them across a diverse range of cultural contexts, rather than a preferred anthropological approach that privileges pursuing the more common "thick description" involved in exhaustively documenting a single group.[15]

Now there was encouragement—and some resistance—to nonverbal communication and interpersonal communication in addition to rhetorical history and criticism. Communication across national cultures emerged—again with resistance. Political science had been allied with rhetorical studies with the rhetoric of political figures in the US and the UK, but it would have been unusual to have an anthropologist on a graduate committee in a Speech department. When Hall joined the anthropology department at Northwestern, so did Ethel Albert in a joint-appointment with communication and anthropology. She remarked that going from a class in one department to a class in the other was going from one culture to another.

The Stories We Tell

"My mother always told me . . ." How often have we heard that, or said that? Recalling words of "my father," memory seem less often followed by the words "always told me." Fathers told you once. Our first language is our "mother tongue," so it seems likely that our dominant "genetic narratives" are more often matriarchal. In the words of Dean Acheson, US Secretary of State during the Truman administration, "what I learned at my mother's knee—and other low joints."

Sometimes remembered, often re-called as wisdom, is something said by a teacher or coach or friend, and even more often, a story about a story, because we are likely to remember the particular time, place, situation when that insight was imparted. "Story" is broad enough to include its many guises: an anecdote, a joke or tease or insult; advice, instructions, often with more stories of the consequences if those instructions are not heeded. In a study that observed the interaction between a Black single mother and her child, the mother told her child, on average, "a story," every seven minutes.[16] And there are also the grand stories that in schooling and in popular culture ensures a general "cultural literacy" is attained. Valued stories are usually connected to the biggest part of capital-C "Culture," what some consider "cultural literacy." The language of "the humanities" is largely about stories, the myths, legends, histories, and names we attach to them. But stories are also a principal means through which the little-c "culture," as that word is used in this book, is passed along.

This is not what Hall meant when he used that term, but it was the title of a bestselling book by E. D. Hirsch, Jr., *Cultural Literacy: What Every American Needs to Know* (New York: Vintage, 1988). Hall's "cultural literacy" is about "reading" a social situation, aware of assumptions, values, and behavior that varies across communities and nations. The "cultural literacy" that Hirsch describes as indicated in the subtitle, is about things and names—especially names, historical dates, and other information that the author assumes should be common knowledge in the US, circa late-twentieth century. (This would include knowing the meaning of some Latin words, like "circa.") While many applauded his attempt to compile a definitive list—and his complaint that our schools are failing to teach "what every American needs to know"—many others pointed out the assumptions and values implicit in that particular list, and provided an alternative list of what Hirsch failed to consider. The title of an article in 2015 by Eric Liu, "What Every American Should Know: Defining Common Cultural Literacy for an Increasingly Diverse Nation," *Atlantic,* July 3, 2015, presents a critique, not about the Hirsch book in particular, but about such an effort generally. For each "generation"—now identified in part by the technologies used, musical and media contexts, diversities across gender and sexual orientation, ethnicity and racial identification, defining events in one's generation and much more—such imagined lists would be different.

Hall was a good storyteller, as are most people who exert some influence on us, but he did not write much about stories and their telling, the narrative part of culture. Within the communication field, rhetorical theorists especially have regarded the narrative as central to who we are, what we do when we think and talk and make meaning. Notable among these is the legendary Kenneth Burke whose five-element "dramatism theory" corresponds to the key questions in anthropological ethnographies, and also to the journalist's "W questions"—who, what, where, when, why? Often quoted is Burke's description of human beings as: ". . . the symbol-using (symbol-making, symbol-misusing) animal, inventor of the negative (or moralized by the negative), separated from his natural condition by instruments of his own making, goaded by the spirit of hierarchy (or moved by the sense of order), and rotten with perfection."[17]

Walter Fisher who appreciated the importance of the narrative, argued that human beings, in his Latin gloss, *Homo narrans,* should be distinguished as "the [narrative] story teller" species. "Many different root metaphors have been put forth to represent the essential nature of human beings: *Homo faber, Homo economicus, Homo politicus, Homo sociologicus,* 'psychological man,' 'ecclesiastical man,' and *Homo sapiens,* of course, 'rational man.' I propose *Homo narrans* be added to the list."[19]

An "Unending Conversation"

Literary and rhetorical critic, Kenneth Burke, offers a metaphor about life that might also serve as a way of thinking about culture—as the conversation we have joined.

Imagine that you enter a parlor. You come late. When you arrive, others have long preceded you, and they are engaged in a heated discussion, a discussion too heated for them to pause and tell you exactly what it is about. In fact, the discussion had already begun long before any of them got there, so that no one present is qualified to retrace for you all the steps that had gone before. You listen for a while, until you decide that you have caught the tenor of the argument; then you put in your oar. Someone answers; you answer him; another comes to your defense; another aligns himself against you, to either the embarrassment or gratification of your opponent, depending upon the quality of your ally's assistance. However, the discussion is interminable. The hour grows late, you must depart. And you do depart, with the discussion still vigorously in progress.[18]

Among the most influential who link narrative and culture is Hall's contemporary, Jerome Bruner, a towering figure in psychology with an extraordinary personal history, as well. There was a brief time when social scientists sought to replace conventional, "fuzzy" words, about how we think with objective, operational, terms, such as treating "thinking" as "data processing." At that time, we called what we would later know as a computer, "a thinking machine" or "an IBM machine," as that corporation and brand became a generic for this new thing, like "Scotch tape" as the name for "adhesive tape."

In the social sciences the computer was the model of the brain that inspired a "cognitive revolution."

Decades later, neuroscientists were less inclined to regard the brain as a brilliant design. David Linden views the brain as "a very peculiar edifice that represents millions of years of evolutionary history." He says his father would call it a *kludge*, "a design that is inefficient, inelegant, and unfathomable, but that nevertheless works."[20]

Before neuroscientists like Linden appeared on the scene to give everyone cause to shake up speculations about how we make sense, Bruner had rejected the earlier computer likeness, and instead saw us as designed to make sense through narrative, telling stories. In his lecture series published as *Acts of Meaning*, Bruner describes us as naturally storytellers that form a "folk psychology" that shapes what we call culture:

> Folk psychology . . . is a culture's account of what makes human beings tick. It includes a theory of mind, one's own and others', a theory of motivation, and the rest. I should call it "ethnopsychology" to make the term parallel to such expressions as "ethnobotany," "ethnopharmacology," and those other native disciplines that are eventually displaced by scientific knowledge. But folk psychology . . . does not get displaced by scientific paradigms.[21]

Bruner points out that even *before* a child is able to put together three or more words—the edge of language—that child has already become aware of the simple narratives of life: the milk spills, and baby announces *"uh, oh!"* And when baby drinks all of the milk the little one proclaims: *"All gone!"* An achievement to be celebrated. So early in life, Bruner emphasizes, we learn these (we could call it "local culture"), but soon—as children—we are more likely to take special interest when the standard, the normal, the expected, is upset. Bruner describes research in which young children are asked about a situation that seems counter to expectations. Five- and six-year-olds were told a story about a little girl who is crying at her birthday party. When asked why, children come up with explanations, creative in their ways of trying to make sense of what is seemingly inconsistent with how things should be.

The answer to a parent's question, "What happened at school today?" most often is: "nothing." Meaning, to the school kid, nothing unusual, even though it is likely that a great deal of what happens every day at school might be, to the parents, more than interesting. What is normal, the expected, and necessary—Hall's tacit or subjective culture—to be a member of one community: a high school, a village, a nation—may not be the same in another.

Challenges

There are two challenges not unique to the culture concept: how to define the word and how to explain it. A definition is, in some ways easy, a word described in other words. Well-intentioned academics often begin with definitions and then proceed to explain, thereby demonstrating their wisdom. Explaining, even to people who really want to just "get it," and are not worried if they will be asked to repeat the definition on the mid-term, that takes longer.

Hall described trying to talk about "culture" to the highly motivated, well-intentioned, professionals who would soon be dispatched to do good work with people in places they may not even have heard of before. The concept "culture" often seemed abstract and more complicated than they have patience for; the training programs for the Foreign Service Institute were just a few short weeks, not the months duration of a college course. "Just tell me the 'do's and don'ts' of what I need to know" is a sentiment often heard today by those in the field of intercultural communication training. A French friend, Roger Thomas, who welcomes guests to the Inn at Halona at Zuni Pueblo, says, "We French might respond, 'I know it works in practice, but does it work in theory?'"

If you can't explain to a first-year college student something that you also talk about to your graduate students, then you haven't really understood it, said the charismatic Nobel award winning physicist Richard Feynman. Albert Einstein set the bar higher: "If you can't explain [something] to a six-year-old, you don't really understand it." Regarding the concept of culture, that challenge remains.[22]

Among many "interculturalists" (with due respect, I am uncomfortable with that term), even explaining "culture" and "intercultural" in words feels too dispassionate for what are often deeply emotional experiences in life. This resonates especially to those who entered the field because of their emotionally charged intercultural experiences, some painful, some joy-filled. And so simulations, "learning games," have been integral in classrooms, conference rooms, and workshops for over a half-century. They may be a mark of a US approach to learning—John Dewey's "learning through doing" lives on!—and, as such, may seem "childish" elsewhere or all the more engaging, effective because of the affect.[23]

Neuroscience

"Your Brain on Culture" was an article published in 2010 in the popular magazine *Psychology Today*.[24] Still a provocative read after many years, it cites research that confirmed our brains are altered by our cultural experience, something no longer news. Telling in that article was a study that indicated among Chinese speakers, when the questions "Is your mother honest?" "Are you honest?" were asked, the brain of the Chinese participants in the research who were wired to identify their brain response showed the same part of the brain was activated for both "mother" and "myself." But when the same questions were asked to those in the US who were not of Chinese descent, two different brain sites, one for mother and one for "myself," were activated. This led to speculation about "individualism/collectivism" cultural values differences and much more.

At one level this seems less than surprising, but significant as a confirmation in what "our culture" trusts as evidence. In a metaphor from the last century before "wires" would be replaced by transistors, "culture" "hard-wired" our brains to aid our survival. Hall spoke of the survival value of culture as screening out sensory inputs that are irrelevant to what is needed. And so, we attend to sounds and pitch and rhythms in our language, but not to others.

Neuroscience research is relevant to our understanding of what we call "culture." There is no "culture" region of the brain, but we might say that the concept of culture is widely distributed, as we see in the discussion of sensing and perception, where even perceiving the location of something involves coordinating two different parts of the brain.[25]

In his later years, Hall became more interested in brain research that was just at the edge of modern neuroscience. I believe he would have devoured the research as it appeared and would try to stay connected with those doing some of the most interesting work. But Hall's way of observing and trying to better understand intercultural relations remains not so far from our own. It's from our lives as lived and how we do our best to make sense through our lived experience.

Display window in Tokyo department store 2022

Notes

1. Bruce La Brack, unpublished, 2014.

    From its origins, Anthropology espoused, and continues to aspire to, an inclusive and holistic view of human activities which encompasses and considers everything from prehistoric origins to contemporary societies within their purview, including aspects of archeology, primatology, linguistics and, increasingly, genetics. A key organizing theoretical concept was culture. While there were many intellectual anthropological predecessors in England (E. B. Tylor) and America (Lewis Henry Morgan) who wrote about culture, almost all were unilineal evolutionists who thought, like many of their era, that all human beings passed through roughly the same stages of cultural evolution, usually presented as a rise from "savagery to civilization" and that all cultures could be hierarchically ranked and differentially evaluated.

    The arrival of Franz Boas in America and the establishment of the Department of Anthropology at Columbia University at the turn of the 20th century led to a profound shift in how culture was defined and commenced the development of new methodologies to be employed in the study of human beings. Essentially Boas liberated the discipline from its more racist assumptions and set ambitious research agendas, training a generation of anthropologists who would gradually transform the discipline. His ideas and those of his students predominated until the end of World War II.

    Basically, Franz Boas not only rejected the unilineal schema but also introduced the then radical idea of approaching other cultures with not only an open mind, but explicitly advocated a revolutionary "culturally relative" positioning whereby cultures needed to be understood from their perspective, on the basis of their own values and practices. External judgments should not be imposed just because their life ways differed (often radically) from that of the researcher. He not only recognized the roots and consequences of "ethnocentrism" but also actively worked throughout his career to counter such attitudes.

    In addition, he and his students sought to make anthropological inquiry more precise, systematic, and scientific by stressing intense fieldwork based upon direct participant-observation, acquisition of local languages, and meticulous recording of field-notes. Following the example of Bronislaw Malinowski's 1920-1930 South Pacific ethnographic work, longer and more immersive periods of field study became common as anthropological rite-of-passage.

The field of anthropology both in Europe and North America continued to diversify between the First and Second World Wars as new approaches arose and then declined (e.g., British structural-functionalism, Culture and Personality). Although there was some agreement about what culture was among anthropologists prior to the second-half of the 20th century (specifically 1930-1950), it was generally rather vague and imprecise. Paraphrased and condensed, culture was then characterized as, "learned behavior, socially transmitted."

This fissiparous trend intensified in the post-colonial era from the 1970s to the present as anthropological theory became roughly divided into two competing camps. One emphasized "meaning," largely psychological, cognitive lenses through which humans make sense of the world, exemplified by such varied schools as, among others, the French structuralism of Claude Lévi-Strauss, the interpretive anthropology of Clifford Geertz, and the symbolic anthropology of Victor Turner and Mary Douglas. The other pursued ecological interactions and the organization of political economies, stressing the relationships between them.

Other anthropologists worked to reconcile or conjoin such "idealist" vs. "realist" foci by making the issue of "power" a central concern. This coupled with increasingly strident post-modernist external attacks upon anthropology by continental philosophers and cultural studies/critical theory proponents (e.g., Pierre Bourdieu, Michel Foucault, Jurgen Habermas) resulted in increasingly self-reflexive introspection within the discipline since the mid-1980's. Critical modernists had no interest in redefining or elaborating the concept of culture. Their focus was on what they saw as the complicity of anthropology in perpetuating systems of inequality and exploitation. Similar criticism arose within anthropology and sharp critiques upon ethnographic objectivity and ethnographers' subjectivities (e.g., James Clifford, George Marcus, Renato Rosaldo, Pierre Bourdieu, Eric Wolf, Lila Abu-Lughod, and Arjun Appadurai) set off decades of debates and critical assessments of the discipline. Many anthropologists since the 1980's, including Clifford, have periodically called for the discipline to simply abandon the concept and move on.

Simultaneously there were other modernist movements critical of the anthropological enterprise that included feminist/women's studies, transculturation and "border/margin" studies, and ethnic/multicultural studies. Feminist and post-modern critiques about the dominance of patriarchy, questions of authenticity, authority, voice, and assertions of multiple, conflicting interpretations of a text, all worked to undermine, or at least seriously challenge, the self-image of discipline that had historically viewed its central mission as the objective description of "the other" in ethnographic terms. The cumulative result of all these attacks is that the culture concept became stigmatized in some contemporary circles as hopelessly abstract, essentializing, ahistorical, homogenizing, primordial, bounded, discrete, and totalizing, among a long list of other negative characterizations. For practical purposes all these pressures detracted from further consideration of the meanings and primacy of "culture" within the field.

2. A. L. Kroeber and Clyde Kluckhohn, *Culture: A Critical Review of Concepts and Definitions* (Cambridge: Peabody Museum Press, 1952).

3. Edward T. Hall, *The Silent Language* (New York: Doubleday, 1959), 32.

4. Massimo Montanari, *Food is Culture*, translated from the Italian by Albert Sonnenfeld (New York: Columbia University Press, 2006).

5. Montanari, *Food is Culture*, xi.

6. Montanari, *Food is Culture*, 5.

7. Professor Kevin Gore lives in Helsinki and has worked elsewhere in Europe, in Japan, and in Mexico, and speaks seven languages. While living in New Mexico, he wrote his doctoral dissertation on Navajo food and cultural identity.

8. Hall repeats and also modifies considerably what he has published, which can be a challenge for readers who fail to note which source they are quoting. In *The Silent Language* the three levels of culture are "the basic triad": formal, informal, technical. But that's not the three levels in this box, which are useful in and of themselves.

9. Joseph H. Suina, "Pueblo Secrecy Result of Intrusions," *New Mexico Magazine*, January, 1992.

10. PMS, as with his "bi-sexuality," have changed in meaning and connotation.

11. *The Hidden Dimension; Handbook for Proxemic Research; The Dance of Life: The Other Dimension of Time.*

12. Paul Watzlawick, Janet Helmick Beavin, Don D. Jackson, *Pragmatics of Human Communication: A Study of Interactional Patterns, Pathologies, and Paradoxes* (New York: W. W. Norton & Co, 1967).

13. Other influential works about communication more broadly appeared around the time of Hall's seminal book. Norbert Wiener, the physicist who coined the term "cybernetics," published his very readable and still provocative book, *The Human Use of Human Beings*, roughly ten years before Hall's *The Silent Language* appeared. Marshall McLuhan, with whom Hall entertained a lively and slightly contentious correspondence, wrote about communication in its manifold presence and influences in that era, as well. You can see a clip here: https://www.youtube.com/watch?v=452XjnaHr1A

14. *Cool Hand Luke*, directed by Stuart Rosenberg, starring Paul Newman and George Kennedy, 1967.

15. La Brack, 2014.

16. Jerome Bruner, *Acts of Meaning: Four Lectures on Mind and Culture* (Harvard University Press, 1993), 83.

17. Kenneth Burke, *Language as Symbolic Action: Essays on Life, Literature and Method* (Berkeley: University of California Press, 1969).

18. Kenneth Burke, *The Philosophy of Literary Form* (Baton Rouge, LA: Louisiana State University Press, 1941), 110-111

19. Walter Fisher, *Human Communication as Narration: Toward a Philosophy of Reason, Value, and Action* (Columbia, SC: University of South Carolina Press, 1989), 62.

20. David Linden, *The Accidental Mind: How Brain Evolution Has Given Us Love, Memory, Dreams, and God.* (Cambridge, MA: Belknap Press of Harvard University Press, 2008), 6.

21. Bruner, *Acts of Meaning,* 13-14.

22. As a small assignment I used to ask grad students in an intercultural communication class to write about what interested them without using the words "culture" or "communication." Most found that very difficult. They would have failed Einstein's test and maybe Feynman's, too.

23. Among the earliest simulations is *"BaFa BaFa,"* originally developed by the US Navy to prepare sailors going abroad, many for the first time, to become less ethnocentric and maybe learn more from their overseas experience. The term "debrief," the "let's make sense of this experience" discussion following the simulation, was part of a military lexicon and may date to this exercise.

An exercise known by the ominous acronym, DIE mode (describe, interpret, evaluate), is intended to encourage participants to separate what they can objectively observe (a photo or brief video, for example) from what they assume or imagine or infer—going beyond what was presented, but an explanation, to their emotional reactions. A more upbeat alternative, the DAE model with a Korean word for the acronym (describe, analyze, evaluate), was proposed in Kyoung-Ah Nam and John Condon, "The DIE is Cast: The continuing evolution of intercultural communication's favorite classroom exercise," *International Journal of Intercultural Relations.* Vol. 34, 1, (January, 2010), 81-87.

Barnga is another exercise very popular in evoking feelings about being deceived when one doesn't understand the rules of an interaction, easily relatable to many intercultural experiences. Of course, history and experience tell us that sometimes one *is* being cheated, but that's another story. *Barnga* is the creation of the ingenious designer of intercultural games, puzzles, and simulations, Sivasailam "Thiagi" Thiagarajan, while working for USAID in Gbarnga, Liberia, in 1980.

24. Beth Azar, "This is Your Brain on Culture," *Psychology Today*, August 31, 2010, 44.
25. David J. Linden, *Accidental Mind*, 86-89.

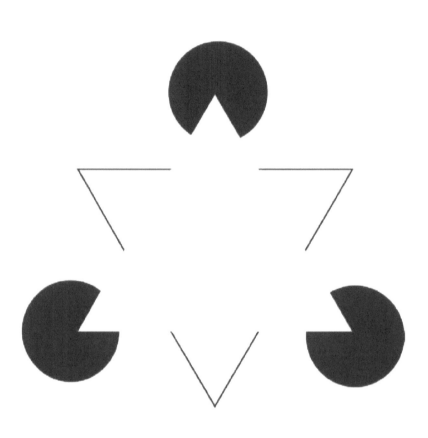

CHAPTER SIX

Sensing and Making Sense

Our sensory world is anything but pure and truthful. Built
and transformed by evolutionary history into a very peculiar
edifice, it responds to only one particular slice of possible sensory
space. Our brains then process this sensory stream to extract
certain kinds of information, and bind the whole thing together
into an ongoing story that is understandable and useful.
—*David I. Linden*

The senses are the biological basis of our experiencing;
their powers, our potential; their limitations, our fate.
—*Yi-Fu Tuan*

To transform the relations of power, we must
cultivate alternative relations of sensing.
—*Sachi Sekimoto and Christopher Brown*

T he Kanizsa Triangle on the opposite page might illustrate how
we "make sense" and how context aids that. This brilliant design,
introduced in 1955 by Italian artist and psychologist, Gaetano Kanizsa
(1913-1993), may serve as a metaphor for some of the ways Hall looked
at the world, though I don't know if Hall was aware of this "illusion."

I'm sure he would appreciate its aesthetics created by an artist who was also a psychologist, or a psychologist who was also an artist.

Play with this. How many triangles are in this image? Two? Four? Six? Taking a conventional definition of a triangle as *a plane figure formed by connecting three points, not in a straight line, by straight line segments*, in this triangle there are . . . none, even as we perceive several. We fill in what we sense so that it makes sense to us. Indeed, "filling in" things accounts for a good part of our sensing—and much of our non-sense, too. Part of what is called "culture" has to do with how we "fill in" our experience to make sense of it.

If the perceived triangle pointed down appears brighter than the other that might be perceived as behind it, then that's also a metaphor within another that Hall would appreciate: what "stands out" depends on context. The lines we draw that connect with and give shape to our lives are influenced by the contexts of histories, personal experiences, family stories, and relationships in the moment at hand, our built surroundings, the natural environments beyond, and all that we can't and usually don't need to think about make up our contexts that are compressed into the term "culture."

Hall tried to balance two challenges about perception that sometimes collide in attempts to communicate across cultural backgrounds. One was the recognition that we don't all experience in the same way what we know in our feelings as real. The other we rarely think about, but others have and still do: what is real? Hall thought and wrote about both. David Warren calls Hall an epistemologist who honored different cultural truths, and saw in that diversity a strength that was grounded in respect. "Is it real?" was a question Hall posed to his students, meaning: are you responding to what is out there, empirically observable, or within your interpretation, judgments, and influenced by your cultural sense-making?

To sense: how we experience our world, direct, immediate, pre-verbal, "right-brained," and also in our cognitive, "left-brain," where we "*make* sense," reason, and judge. Our evolutionary biological past as part of species, our cultural influences also largely unrecognized, and our individual particular history and stories we tell ourselves. Sometimes we elevate what makes sense to us to the status of "common sense."

Uruguayan writer Eduardo Galeano tells this story from the Chaco region of Uruguay:

Somewhere in time, beyond time, the world was gray. Thanks to the Ishir Indians, who stole color from the gods, the world today is resplendent with colors that dazzle the eyes of all who look at them.

Ticio Escobar lent a hand to a film crew that came to the Chaco to shoot scenes of daily life among the Ishir. An Indian girl pursued the director, a silent shadow glued to his side, staring into his face as if she wanted to jump into his strange blue eyes.

The director turned to Ticio, who knew the girl and understood her language. Through him, she confessed, "I want to know what colors you see."

The director smiled. "The same as you."

"And how do you know what colors I see?"[1]

Sensing and "making sense" are also a shorthand description of the basis of Hall's conceptual world, drawn in part from reflecting on his personal experience and encouraging others to do something similar, becoming more conscious of how and what we sense. "Our body is our most important instrument of knowing," he often said, not that everything we sensed was "objective reality," but that our perceptions may reveal as much about the observers as the observed, and we need to know about ourselves if we are to try to know and judge others. In the often-quoted words of Anaïs Nin, "We see things not as they are but as *we* are." Note that saying to "see" is a culturally privileged choice to represent all our ways of sensing. The Anaïs Nin quote, and in its variations attributed to others, is a reminder of what is basic in any intercultural outlook. Marcel Proust offers an additional thought: "The only true voyage of discovery . . . would be not to visit strange lands but to possess others' eyes."

From the time of the Enlightenment, at least, Western philosophy has favored the cognitive: concepts, reason, logic. But nearly all those who are identified as philosophers, West and East, have ruminated about how much to trust our senses. Plato distrusted our sensing in any search for Truth. The classic Greek seven "Liberal Arts" were centered on patterns—in language, logic, mathematics, and music. The only science was astronomy, safely beyond the reach of inquisitive hands.

Hall made almost no mention of philosophy as taught, nor philosophers, John Dewey a notable exception. Had Hall's interests taken him in that direction he might have identified most with phenomenology that was ascendant in his time.[2] As a Francophile, he might have admired Maurice Merleau-Ponty's "phenomenology" philosophy, though I imagine he would have been impatient with the philosopher's writing style. Phenomenology found its US academic center at Northwestern's philosophy department and its university press during the years when Hall taught there, but there is no indication that any connection was made.

It may seem curious that many who consult and teach about cultural differences, diversity, inclusion, give relatively little attention to the whole richness of our sensory worlds that may differ considerably among people whose cultural backgrounds vary, and even with neighbors and friends whom we assume experience the world much as we do. Often, it's only when attending a memorial service or reading an obituary of someone we thought we knew, do we discover a world of difference between what we knew of the deceased and what sensory experiences we can imagine they lived for and thrived in.

If we think of communication as including everything that we perceive and assign meaning to, then we would do well to pay more attention to how we perceive—using our body's sensing abilities—and to realize that not everyone is sensitive in the same way. Or to put it another way, we are probably missing something that others may be picking up on. There are individual differences, and there are cultural influences.

Hall's Sense Inventory Exercise

So basic was this notion for Hall, that an early assignment he gave his undergraduate students was for each to do a personal "sense inventory." His class exercise was never, as best I can judge, intended as a source of data in some research project. It was strictly for students to reflect on their ways of engaging with the world, and as the point of departure for next week's conversation with the students.

I've borrowed Hall's assignment, but without asking people to rank their perceived sensory preferences. In classes and workshops over many years in the US, Mexico, and Japan, asking only that each person make notes to themselves that later they might share with others. The purpose was to heighten self-reflection, and then to reveal the diversity of self-perceived ways of sensing. Although attention usually was given most to the visual and auditory senses across all nationalities, "smell" and "touch" were noted much more often among the students from Asian countries than those from North America. More on that later.

Here is a version of what you would have been asked if you had secured a seat in Professor Hall's class.[3] You may want to try this out for yourself.

Instructions

Think about how you use your senses in everyday experience, and reflect on what is your preferred or dominant sense. Then put in rank order the senses you believe you draw upon from most to least. Finally, write an essay about this exercise. Be specific. You may consider how you remember what you have experienced. For example, if your visual memory is especially strong, is it more like a photograph or a movie? Are you in the scene or just looking at it? Is it in color or in black and white? Does it evoke other senses as well? Also consider different contexts in which you may draw upon different senses.

Hearing (auditory)

Smell (olfactory)

Taste (gustatory)

Sight (visual)

Touch (tactile)

Hall mostly wrote about the canonical five senses that originally were catalogued by Aristotle who related these to the five elements of earth, water, air, fire, and the quintessence, "the fifth essence."[4] Cultural geographer Yi-Fu Tuan points this out that "the number [5] is quite arbitrary, and yet Western culture seems chained to [these five senses]." He attributes the problem to the ambiguity of the word "sense."[5]

Once, in a graduate seminar at the University of New Mexico, I asked the students to respond to this "sensory inventory" as their first assignment. The next session we got out of the sterile classroom and into the multi-sensory world outdoors and traveled fifty miles away where my friend, Porter Swentzell of Santa Clara Pueblo, professor at the Institute of American Indian Arts, met us that morning and brought us as guests to a ceremonial dance at Ohkay Owingeh (formerly San Juan Pueblo).

Pueblo dances are not performances. They are embodied and danced stories and prayers that may continue from morning until evening. Sometimes there are hundreds of dancers from the pueblo, as young as three and across three generations. Many, maybe most, dances are closed to outsiders, but on some occasions, outsiders are welcomed as guests. The mood is respectful, no chatting, and no photography, recording, or writing notes permitted. No cell phones. Be present.

This particular Pueblo event was not announced to the public, and it was modest, perhaps just 40 dancers, including children. To the extent sharing tribal information allowed, Porter explained what the dance represented and mentioned things the students might pay attention to. There were few outsiders that morning, and for several students this was their first experience at a Pueblo. A couple of the students were distracted when they realized they were standing next to actor Robert Redford, who has a home in the area.

It was mid-Autumn. The sky was that electric blue of the high desert, and there was a slight chill in the air. We were there for about an hour, and then returned to the van and continued on our field trip. Just to experience the world outside of the campus, and also to breathe in that world as another learning environment, was a new experience for some of the students who were also teaching classes whose own students might be from this area. It was also a hidden agenda for me—to encourage those who would soon be teachers to get out of the classroom and its constraints and values that affect what we pay attention to and how we talk in that environment.

The next week, back in the seminar room, I asked about the previous week's experience: what did you notice, what did you feel, what do you remember? It was apparent that the remembered experience was not at all the same for each of us. One talked about the patterns in what the dancers wore. For another, it was the smell of the piñon pine smoke, and all her feelings from growing up in the region, "the delicious smell of late autumn and winter," and the foods and activities evoked by that smell. A doctoral student who was teaching a course on visual communication, talked about the sounds and rhythms as most memorable. "People think I'm a visual person because of what I teach. But I connect most with the sound, the beat. My world is music." Most didn't remember the smell of that smoke, few could recall the sound and rhythm, maybe least of all, the woven patterns in what the dancers wore.

Surely there is a lesson here about the value of collaboration, knowing that we each experience the world, even at the smallest point, by how we sense it. I wonder if those who work together realize this, and if it mightn't be a useful exercise for teams that work together to take this simple "inventory." Sharing their individual reports might help members appreciate how much stronger the team is with their comprehensive diversity of sensory strengths, rather than operating on the assumption that we all experience the world in similar ways, even if we appreciate that our lived experiences are not at all the same. This extends "diversity," usually defined in conventional demographic categories—generation, race/ethnicity, gender identity, and other such groupings—to an interior appreciation of the diversity of how people apprehend their day-to-day experience.

The Elephant Committee

The fable of the blind men and the elephant mocks those who generalize their limited perception when they imagine a larger version of the part touched. But we are all members of similar committees: generationally, politically, culturally, and now we realize, also humanly. If we listen to an expanded committee that included a hummingbird and hawk, a dog and a cat, a salmon and octopus, a bee and a fly, an

The Sensate World of the Child[6]

When some British children were asked, "What are the twelve loveliest things you know?"

One boy answered:
    The cold of ice cream.
    The scrunch of leaves.
    The feel of clean clothes.
    Water running into a bath.
    Cold wind on a hot day.
    Climbing up a hill and looking down.
    Hot water bottle in bed.
    Honey in your mouth.
    Smell in a drug store.
    Babies smiling.
    The feeling inside when you sing.
    Baby kittens.

A little girl's list went:
    Our dog's eyes.
    Street lights on the river.
    Wet stones.
    The smell of rain.
    An organ playing.
    Red roofs in trees.
    Smoke rising.
    Rain on your cheeks.
    The smell of cut grass.
    Red velvet.
    The smell of picnic teas.
    The moon in clouds.

oak tree and cactus to describe this elephant that is our living earth, what an argument would ensue, and, with a wise facilitator, what a clearer image would emerge. Such an imagined facilitator would require someone with knowledge or at least respect for all whose lived experience is to be represented. Hall's affirmation that we need each other to know who we are was never more important—and ever more possible unless prevented or ignored.

With more respect for each other and better communication skills, the five visually impaired but tactilely sensitive members of the elephant committee might teach us lessons in modesty of what we know and appreciation for the insights of others. Better still would be a new fable where the five or seven people are chosen *because* of their different sensitivities. Hall gave advice about judging individual sensory strengths and weaknesses: "the more precise an observer is on one level, the less precise on all the other levels."

Different skills rely on different sensitivities, of course: the eye of the photographer is not the ear of the musician. Cultural biases that shape personal biases have ramifications that can doubly disadvantage people, and, by extension, organizations or entire societies. Gender, race and ethnicity, religious identification, social class and cultural social systems affect the possibilities, and barriers to hopes and possibilities. Isabel Wilkerson writes of race as the unspoken caste system that has shaped America.[7]

For generations, to be born blind in Japan meant that you would be expected to learn massage, a therapeutic practice valued more in East Asia for centuries than in some other parts of the world. How many blind Japanese with strengths and aspirations that did not call for sight, were unable to share those sensitivities?

My father's youngest brother, Erwin, became blind from an accident at an early age. I used to love to visit him in the home he largely completed by himself where he and his mother lived. (Unknowing neighbors sometimes called the police because they could hear power tools being used at night in a house with no lights on.) Uncle Erwin once told me of applying for jobs he was very capable of doing and being turned down by the prospective employer with the words, "but you're a blind man." He asked me as his way of teaching, "Who was more blind? I knew I couldn't see, but I also knew I could do what the job called for. They couldn't see that. They couldn't see past what they called me." Happy ending, though: for many years until his retirement, Erwin worked at a company making sensitive acoustical devices where he was, in effect, the quality control.

Seeing and hearing are the distant senses—also valuable close-up but not as much as touch or smell or taste. Some explain the human reliance on sight and hearing in evolutionary terms, that when our ancestors in Africa spread out into the savannah, the intimate senses, including smell, that is so important to other creatures great and small, no longer served. We needed sight for our own orientation and to be aware of the presence of kindred and foe.[8] Sound also traveled relatively far, compared to the other senses, and as speech evolved into language, hearing gained importance even beyond the survival value of the languages of so many of our two- and four-footed companions.

Sight and sound—sight especially—are dominant in our consciousness and in our idioms: "I see what you mean," understanding, and in a mixed metaphor common in the US, at least, "I see what you're saying." "See" in various forms is among the most often used words in everyday conversation. A friend, Steve Hanamura, a popular speaker and intercultural communication trainer who is blind, sometimes begins his talk by telling the audience not to be nervous about using the word "see" when they have comments or questions. And, he says, "If you want me to call on you, don't raise your hand."

Under-appreciated when asked are senses that are those most intimate, our first sensory experiences, and those crucial for our early survival, especially the tactile and olfactory senses, touch and smell.

Touch

Touch—its study has an -ics name: haptics—may be the most pervasive sense of all.[9] Naked we may feel the air across our skin in the absence of what we normally feel, the touch of clothing on our skin. At infancy touch is so crucial that hospitals invite volunteers to come to hold "premies," those born prematurely, because the human touch in those earliest days will affect the rest of the infant's life. Among life's greatest pleasures—and part of the continuity of the species—is touch. Erotic pleasure and sexual expression often begin with touching the beloved's body and wanting to be touched. "Keep in touch," we say to ones we will miss when we are not close. About feelings we lack other words for, we may say are "touching."

But touching can be destructive, as when the touch is unexpected, unwanted, and when one is so vulnerable that it may be years before gaining the courage to tell what has happened. It has been a source of scandal among clergy, physicians, athletic coaches, and other abusers. It helped inspire the "Me Too" movement that began in 2017 with women (and men) speaking out, and accounted for the jailing of some abusers.

Adam Gopnik wrote an interesting article about touch, published in *The New Yorker*, quoting extensively from one of my favorite authors on the subject, David Linden.[10] The world of tactile research is divided into a bewildering variety of names and specialties—haptics, prosthetics, somatosensory studies, haptic feedback prosthetics, and on and on—but they all have in common the relations between our skin and our sense of ourselves. Linden believes that, among all the new discoveries about touch and haptic sensation, the most important are the least generalized. Gopnik notes that our bodies' systems of touch are varied and specific, quoting Linden:

Each time we study the touch system more deeply, we realize that it is more specialized than we'd known. . . . These systems aren't usefully understood just as different cognitive responses to the same stimuli—they're completely different integrated systems. There are separate labelled lines for so many seemingly intermingled systems. The difference between "affective" touch—a loving caress—and other kinds, like a threatening or a clinical grope, involves two different sensing systems working in close concert.

. . . One strange thing about the unsung sense is that it has no songs. Every other sense has an art to go with it: the eyes have art, the ears have music, even the nose and the tongue have perfume and gastronomy. But we don't train our hands to touch as we train our eyes to look or our ears to listen. Every now and again, someone comes up with a "touch museum" or starts a program for the visually handicapped to experience art through their fingers. But such enterprises often have a hopeful, doomed feeling to them: they seem more willed than wanted.

Is it possible that the absence of tactile art is a mere accident of history? In the eighteenth century touching the objects in proto-museums—cabinets of curiosities and amateur collections—was invited and expected and even, in a way, compulsory. "When the underkeeper of the Ashmolean in 1760 tried to prevent a museum visitor from handling artifacts he was accused of incivility," Constance Classen writes in *The Book of Touch*, an anthology of writings on the tactile.[11] Classen writes in her cultural history of touch, *The Deepest Sense*, that touch was associated with irrationality and primitivism, hence the current reign of the optical museum—where all the objects are shut away, even ones that demand to be touched to be understood at all, like scientific or musical instruments.[12] The museum goer who touched was presumed to be a woman or a child; the patriarchs shut things up in cases and then looked at them imprisoned.

Hungarian artist László Moholy-Nagy (1895-1946), whose work spans almost all genres and media in the arts, created art that was designed to be appreciated solely by touch. These included strips of paper or cloth to which different textures were carefully arranged so a one could run a finger or several fingers along its length and feel the art. I imagine that Hall knew of his work in part because they shared overlapping interests in the Bauhaus influence, the artist's attention to shadow and light, and because much of it is archived at the Illinois Institute of Technology where Hall taught for several years.

To limit skin to its tactility does a disservice to what is more than an amazing wrap. The skin is our body's largest organ and so its largest receptor—and sometimes expresser—of sensing. Skin is also our most visual feature as well. Sachi Sekimoto and Christopher Brown have written about race and the senses in their book by that name in which they observe that "skin is where self and world meet."[13]

If race entails the politics of the skin, racialization generates a particular relationship between the racialized subject and their skin, in which they are constantly reminded of its appearance, meaning, and potential consequences. Marc Lawrence reminds us that "forgetting about the skin is, in many respects, a privilege—one from which those with racialized skin are less likely to benefit."[14]

Smell

"Smell is a startling superpower," writes Brooke Jarvis. "You can walk through someone's front door and instantly know that she recently made popcorn. Drive down the street and somehow sense that the neighbors are barbecuing. Intuit, just as a side effect of breathing a bit of air, that this sweater has been worn but that one hasn't, that it's going to start raining soon, that the grass was trimmed a few hours back. If you weren't used to it, it would seem like witchcraft."[15]

The first of the senses in human evolution, the sense of smell, is deeply associated with emotion and memory—the Proustian effect. And yet smell has also received a bad rap for a long time. In a survey of US adults in 2019, smell was ranked as the least important sense, one they would be most willing to lose. In 2011, in a survey by the marketing company McCann World Group, a majority of young people said that "smell was less valuable to them than their technological devices." As *PC Magazine* trumpeted, with a mixture of scorn and glee [in a headline]: "Majority of Kids Would Rather Lose Their Sense of Smell than Lose Facebook."

English semantics may account for some of the negative associations with smell, as without context the word evokes not so much the act of sensing as what is sensed, particularly unpleasant odors. English records a succession of words, each an attempt at more positive connotations than words it would replace. As "stink," originally neutral, devolved toward foul associations, it was replaced by "odor," which following a similar path was replaced by "smell."

"American cities strive to be odorless," cultural geographer Yi-Fu-Tuan says, "only their ethnic enclaves can have a distinctive effluvium and still be respectable. White Americans go there for exotic foods and appreciate the aromas that drift onto the streets from food stores and restaurants." When the same people are tourists abroad, they often praise the smells of cooking encountered overseas. Tuan believes that the sense of smell especially is identified with social class at home; "smells," he says, separate us. "The modern city caters primarily to sight, the sensory organ that flatters our intelligence and makes us feel in control. Even at the market's meat counter and in public rest rooms odor is out of bounds."[16]

One reason we have discounted smelling is our belief that we're bad at it. Smell was the province of lesser animals, we told ourselves, of pigs rooting out truffles and sharks scenting blood, while humans are creatures of reason and intellect who managed to stand up and grow huge brains and leave that life far behind—and, literally, below—us. Scientists following noted 19th-century neuroscientist Paul Broca's recognition of the relative smallness of our olfactory bulbs as evidence that our brains had triumphed over them, and likewise over the need to pay much attention to smell. For centuries, when scientists studied smell at all, they tended to focus on isolating particular odorants (they thought they could find the odor version of primary colors) and creating elaborate organizational systems that shuffled them into various categories. The sense, after all, was seen as practically vestigial: an often handy, sometimes pleasant, but ultimately unimportant holdover from our distant past.

A study conducted in 1927 concluded that people are capable of detecting 10,000 distinct smells. Now it appears that was grossly underestimated. In 2014, research indicated the number should be one trillion.[17]

The notion of smell as vestigial has itself come to seem outmoded. That's because of a renaissance in smell science. While we have long understood the basic mechanisms of vision and audition, it has been less than 30 years since the neural receptors that allow us to perceive and make sense of the smells around us were even identified. The discoverers—Linda Buck and Richard Axel—were awarded the Nobel Prize in 2004.[18]

Our sensitivity to the smell of those we love is particularly keen. Research has shown that in one of those curious studies where, like in a game show, a mother can nearly always identify her baby from the smell of the baby's clothes in a mix of the clothes of other babies; lovers can do the same, sniffing a random set of undergarments that includes one from their lover. One of my regrets is not participating in a German study in the early 1970s just after joining the faculty at a most progressive Japanese university, but also an academic culture that I thought was too conservative to risk asking students to share their girlfriend's and boyfriend's t-shirts and underwear for a study to see if they could successfully pick out, from smell only, their match. That same "smell sensitivity" in Japan leads teen-age daughters to refuse to have their clothes washed together with their father's clothes because they don't want their father's smell contaminating their clothing. In contrast, a study at the University of British Columbia found that the among women in a romantic partnership, the smell from a partner's t-shirt tangibly reduced feelings of stress and aided sleep. [19]

Creatures we allow near, like dogs, and those we try to keep at bay—like flies and ants—all depend on their sensitivity to scents for survival. Each of a dog's nostrils receives smells separately from the other—their sense of smell is in stereo! Their sensory world is vastly different from ours, as are those of all the creatures great and small with whom we share this planet. "Share," in this context, is surely a euphemism as our encroachment on and human colonizing of the land continues, so destructive to all.

In our understanding of our human evolution, it was in the era when the limbic brain evolved from the reptilian that the sense of smell emerged and evolved—so a very old and enduring survival sense. Smell and taste are so inseparable that were it not for our separate sensing organs they might be combined. Together they go to our beginnings, from birth to breast. And the sense of "home," the smells of home, tastes we later identify with "home" and forever more people, "homes," and not just the TCK's, times in our lives that smells returned us there momentarily—Proustian moments. Research about and appreciation of our sense of smell, which has been on the rise for the past three decades, dramatically increased with the outbreak of the Covid-19 pandemic in which many people experienced a sudden loss of smell and taste.

"Interesting if true . . .and interesting anyway."
Mark Twain

Interesting as Hall's self-assessment sensing inventory exercise may be, neuroscience research casts doubt on our ability to identify separate sensory tracks that influence how we apprehend the world. In his book, *The Accidental Mind,* David Linden, demonstrates that our senses are not "trustworthy and independent reporters."[20] The research shows that "perception and emotion are now inextricably mixed. There is little, if any, 'pure perception' in the brain. By the time we are aware of sensations, emotions are already engaged."[21]

> Our senses are not built to give us an "accurate" picture of the external world at all. Rather, through millions of years of evolutionary tinkering, they have been designed to detect and even exaggerate certain features and aspects of the sensory world and to ignore others. Our brains then blend this whole sensory stew together with emotion to create a seamless, ongoing story of experience that makes sense.[22]

That conclusion is further argued by a founder of synesthesia as a field of study, Richard Cytowic, as he points out our many everyday experiences where one sense influences another. For example, color influences how we experience food flavors. Among many examples he notes that, "hot chocolate served in an orange cup is judged to taste better than the same cocoa sipped from a white or a red cup . . . . It may be that the 'blue plate special' became popular during the 1930's Depression when cooks discovered that diners were sated with smaller portions when meals were served on blue plates."[23]

"What something is called and conceptual knowledge," he also notes, "influences how it is perceived." In his book, *Synesthesia,* Cytowic provides many examples in addition to those experienced by people who are synesthetic—estimated one in twenty, a quality more common in women and left-handed people, but assumed to be the normal state for everyone in infancy. Many musicians perceive notes as colors. Indeed, the most common form of synesthesia is perceiving symbols, categories—letters, numbers, days of the week—in colors. "Franz Liszt and Nikolai Rimsky-Korsakov famously disagreed over the color of musical keys. When Liszt took over the Weimar Kapellmeister post in 1842, he startled the musicians by saying things like, 'Oh, please, gentlemen, a little bluer, please. This tone type requires it!' Or 'That is a deep violet, please, depend on it! Not so rose!'"[24]

> Cytowic argues:
>
> If the senses aren't compartmentalized as orthodoxy once claimed—five well-defined senses traveling along separate conduits—then what does it even mean to hear, to see, to categorize? How do you define a sense or split a whole experience into its parts when those parts are already tightly bound with qualities that are common to other senses?[25]

Even if each of our senses is not as discrete as we popularly believe, individuals do differ in their perceived selective perceptions. People also differ in the sensitivities and in competencies across the senses as they relate to personal interests, cultural backgrounds, and professional skills. Musicians hear music, at least within the genres and instrumentation they know best, that the untrained ear does not. As one gains experience in photography or painting, one learns to see the world differently. By tasting a wine, a master sommelier may be able to identify where the wine comes from and even its vintage. A friend who is a medical pathologist says he must rely on his tactile sensitivity in his work, but he does not feel that is his preferred sensitivity when he is not engaged professionally. Cultural background can also influence and sharpen one's senses. During the Second World War, especially in the Pacific Theatre, Native American troops were often chosen for reconnaissance because they were judged to have superior visual and listening skills.

In dozens of articles and two influential books dedicated to the appreciation of *non*-verbal competencies, *Frames of Mind* and *Intelligence Reframed*, Howard Gardner interpreted such sensitivities as different forms of intelligence.[26]

It may be that because we have been taught that there are five senses, we fail to consider others, much as we may find it difficult to think of anything that hasn't been named, categorized. What of the thermal sense? We feel degrees of hot and cold, have a folk vocabulary for variations, and allot an inordinate amount of time in weather reports estimating and later announcing precise measurements. And yet, we don't name this as "a sense." Do we equate this with "touch"? We know that the inner ear senses when we are physically balanced or not, but that isn't within the realm of hearing. And should our awareness of time passing be counted as yet a separate sense?

The sensitivity to movement, human and elsewhere in the environment, seems more than the application of sight and to some extent sound. Gardner drew attention to this in his work on "intelligences," focusing on the remarkable sensitivity and skills of athletes, dancers, and others, professional and everyday folk, who excel in ways most of us can only watch in wonder and applaud.

Coming to Our Senses

Vietnamese Buddhist monk Thích Nhât Hanh writes:

> Descartes said, "I think, therefore I am." In light of the Buddha's teaching, you might say, "I think, therefore I am . . . not here." You are lost in your thinking, so you are really not here. For you to truly be here, thinking has to stop. As you are practicing mindfulness of the breath, the object of your attention is simply the breath. You stop thinking about the past, the future, your pain, your plans, and so forth, and you start to be really here, body and mind united.

The realization that for most of us, at least for much of the time, our thoughts and their attendant feelings roam far from the here and now is also a matter of concern for therapists and counselors when they assist people. Speech-language pathologist, Christina Kennedy, describes one of the coping skills often used by health professionals to calm a client. Sometimes called "The Five, Four, Three, Two, One Grounding Exercise," the therapist asks her client: What are five things you can see? What are four things you can actually feel? (This could be the temperature, a breeze, or the texture of a table, or item of clothing). Now take in the soundscape. What are three things you can hear? What are two things you can smell? What is one thing you can taste?" At each stage, the client focuses on a different sense in order to locate herself in the here and now. This disrupts the mind's fight-or-flight response and resets the nervous system.

The Felt Sense

"The felt sense" is what Eugene Gendlin, psychology and philosophy professor at the University of Chicago, called a focused awareness of inner physical sensations that might otherwise motivate one to consult a psychologist. Gendlin was a colleague of psychologist Carl Rogers, known for "client centered therapy" and, in education, "student centered teaching," the Rogerian method. "The core of focusing is a natural human process of sensing within, and resonating the symbols that emerge with your inner felt experience."[27] That partial definition may be less helpful to understanding what Gendlin was describing than an example. Ann Weiser Cornell, Gendlin's best known interpreter, describes a situation many might be able to relate to:

> Whenever Jenny needed to speak up about herself, she got a choking sensation in her throat. The more important the situation was to her, the stronger she felt the choking. Job interviews and class presentations were painful, nearly impossible. She had been to many therapists and tried many techniques to try to get rid of this choking sensation, without results. She diagnosed herself as "self-defeating, masochistic, alarming ways sabotaging myself."

"Focusing" is viewed as a skill, not a therapy. One takes lessons on learning the skill, not going to therapy. Jenny, in the above example, was asked not to settle for giving a name to the feeling, "choking," but to focus more deeply to describe more specifically what she was feeling. Encouraged, Jenny said "Actually, it's more like a hand squeezing." The conversation continued; Jenny was encouraged to talk to "the hand" she was imagining. Her feelings now were about her relationship to something else, an "it," not that something was wrong with her.

This is not the place, nor am I qualified, to provide details about the process of focusing. There are many books and focusing groups all over the world today. People interested in exploring this sometimes pair up with another person, often from another country, to practice a kind of sensing that goes within rather than the sensing from without. To the person feeling it, this felt sense is as real as anything objectively perceived with "the five senses." However, those "feelings about something inside" are not identified or discussed in any of Hall's writings.

Hall believed and emphasized, as noted, that the body is our most important instrument for knowing. He said that in reaction to trusting the results of quantitative research, statistical findings, "hard data"—that ironically is rendered abstract precisely because it is specific down to numbers to the right of a decimal point. With his years of studying psychology, and his own years in therapy, Hall knew and respected Carl Rogers's work and may have known him when both were living in Chicago and worked at campuses just a few miles apart, but there is no evidence that he was aware of Gendlin's attention to "the felt sense."

In Gut We Trust—a Sixth Sense?

Then there is that "sixth sense," intuition, a hunch, that not a few people say they take seriously but with varying degrees of trust, influenced by cultural support or resistance. "I have a feeling . . ." (But where and how do we feel that?) Feelings, as particular and intimate, and touch, are semantically linked ("so touching"), but these feelings are associated not with the hands or skin, but within. Some locate that feeling in the heart: "I am speaking from my heart," or "My heart tells me . . . ."

Across cultures, often the deepest sensing area is the gut. For many, gut feelings override the brain, which we popularly associate with rational thought even though everything we sense is sorted out by the brain. In the 1964 US Presidential election when the very conservative Republican candidate, Barry Goldwater, had as a slogan: "In your heart, you know he's right." The retort was: "But in your guts, you know he's nuts." A "gut reaction" is not a poetic idiom; it is the norm even if we aren't aware of it. The work of Antonio Demasio, Professor of Neuroscience, Psychology and Philosophy at the University of Southern California, traces our behavior to the microbes in our gut that inform the brain.[28]

Words that might come to mind for people who recognize the name, Edward T. Hall, and perhaps one or two of his books, might include: nonverbal communication, intercultural sensitivity, curiosity. Maybe one thinks of tolerance of ambiguity, something Hall appreciated but didn't write about. A word not at the top of such an imagined list is the word "stress," though first encounters often involve some degree of stress, and intercultural encounters especially. In a multicultural society, where not everyone always has the same level of agency or the experience of feeling safety in everyday interactions, it seems likely that feeling stress may be nearer the surface for some more than others. Probably most people can recall experiences when they felt so uncomfortable with others that they felt tongue-tied. And, less aware, also incapable of hearing what others are saying: dumb and numb. What some might call "slights" and others might call "microaggressions" are often unintended, which, in some ways, is worse as they are not just personal but reflect prejudices that continue in a prevailing culture with its implicit social relationships reflected in how we talk to one another.

Stress is an experience not limited to any of "the five senses." Innovative ways of applying the findings of neuroscience research to provide assistance to those undergoing stress or even a state of trauma have emerged since the time of Hall's main work. Dr. Cheryl Forster, a psychologist at Portland State University in Oregon, has applied Stephen Porges's Polyvagal Theory to intercultural interactions and decreasing polarization.[29] In her work as an intercultural trainer, Forster integrates intercultural and trauma-informed approaches for mental health.

Forster is one of the first to address cultural considerations with respect to polyvagal theory. The neurophysiological approach of polyvagal theory is sometimes referred to as "the neuroscience of safety and connection." Forster describes neuroception, a term coined by Porges, as a process that addresses how the autonomic nervous system evaluates and responds to cues of safety and danger, without the thinking brain. The nervous system takes in information from the outside world, from within our bodies, and between people, which is why neuroception is also called "detection without awareness."

"Another way to think about neuroception," Forster says, "is a 'gut feeling,' a felt sense, or intuition." Playing a key role in this is the longest cranial nerve in the body, the vagus nerve that connects the gut to the heart and the brain stem. "Research indicates that 80% of information goes *from* the gut *to* the brain, and only 20% goes from the brain to the body." That appears opposite of what many of us have assumed, and is affirmed by the work of Demasio that traces our behavior to the microbes in our gut which inform the brain.

The implications of this are profound and many. It affirms Hall's assertion that the body is our most important instrument for knowing our experience. Polyvagal theory, arising from neuroscience research that wasn't possible when Hall was writing, also redirects our attention from the cognitive to the body. Forster quotes Deb Dana, a leading voice and writer about polyvagal research and applications to deal with stress and trauma, in saying that we too often misplace our attention when trying to change: "It is not a cognitive choice. It's a biological one."

Recognizing not just how we feel but where in our body we feel, offers a path to shift our nervous system state in a way that then enables us to literally listen to each other more deeply and take in new information, while being less defensive—all of which are key for better intercultural interactions. "Interculturalists know how culture can impact relationship-building," Forster points out. "What we feel is revealed to others in our facial expressions, voice, movements, and the whole of our somatic as well as how and what we are able to say. And our outward expression of what we feel within may, in turn, influence how others react."

Moreover, "our gut feelings signal what is safe, life sustaining, or threatening, even if we can't explain why we feel a particular way. Our sensory interiority sends us subtle messages about the needs of our organism. Gut feelings help us to evaluate what is going on around us."[30] In the context of Polyvagal Theory, Forster makes a case for adding culture more explicitly to our neuroception of safety, perceptions, emotion, behaviors, and stories. As Forster discusses, "the ways we relate to each other across differences can be cues of safety and danger, which are rooted in culture." Therefore, both increasing our intercultural sensitivity and being able to regulate our nervous system or manage our stress has significant implications for intercultural interactions.

Do we trust what we call "gut feelings"? In a study published in the *Harvard Business Review*, CEOs of major organizations in the US were asked to what extent they trusted their gut reactions when making important decisions. "Many top executives say they routinely make big decisions without relying on any logical analysis. Instead, they call upon their 'intuition,' 'gut instinct,' 'hunches,' or 'inner voice'—but they can't describe the process much more than that."[31] One executive said, "The trusting of my intuitive intelligence equipped me to know when to speak and when to stay silent, to identify patterns for deeper inquiry, sense the inner somatic feelings coming from within my gut."

A review of studies that looked at intuitive decisions in situations involving ethical and moral choices concluded that, "Emotional and intuitive responses to risk should not be seen as heuristics that are prone to be biases; rather, *they should be seen as invaluable sources of insight when it comes to judging the moral acceptability of risks.*" [32] (Italics added.)

I was curious to know about possible cultural influences in decision making, particularly with regard to "gut reactions" among managers with bottom-line concerns in business. I asked Kenichi Saito, a business consultant in Tokyo, former partner at McKinsey and Company, and a friend of many years, about the phrase "gut decisions," thinking that "gut" might relate to the Japanese word *"hara"* that appears in dozens of expressions relating to feelings.[33] Saito says that "gut" is sometimes borrowed from English *(gattsu)* and expressed as *"gattsu fi-ringu"* (gut feeling). But the meaning is less about intuition than courage, "having guts." Or perhaps risk taking, a quality for which Japanese culture is not known—though Saito says that McKinsey, recognized for its "scientific approach" in business analysis, also attributes their success to intuition. Saito believes that kind of intuition is grounded in the experience of pattern recognition.

Regarding the *hara,* while it appears in dozens of Japanese idioms related to emotions such as *"hara ga tatsu,"* ("the hara stands up," meaning becoming angry), Saito says he doesn't hear many *"hara"* expressions in business discussions. So much for my theory. There is a form of communication in Japan called "*haragei*," literally "gut-" or sometimes "belly-" communication. This refers to intuiting what another means without using words. It is not what the expression "heart to heart" means, as that usually means sincere and most often feelings of affection that words cannot express. Not surprising that Hall wanted to know more about communication without words. *Haragei*, which is not often used today in Japan is sometimes associated with political bosses and Japanese mafia, the *yakuza*. In that context it may be not so different from how Donald Trump's estranged former lawyer and "fixer," Michael Cohen explained how his former boss, who spoke in a kind of code: if you knew him well, you knew his intent and what he wanted from you without his ever having to put it in words, thereby avoiding incriminating himself.

Race and the Senses

Hall emphasized the importance of paying attention to what—and especially how—we sense and make sense of the world each of us lives in, which is not exactly the same as our neighbor's experience. He, and indeed the majority of those quoted and cited in this book, wrote from a place of advantage and with some authority conveyed upon them. Not all are white and male, but most are academics. As a healthy white male of average height and weight and without apparent physical challenges and writing from the mid-twentieth century, Hall wrote mostly from the perspective of an observer, and not as one who is observed. Were Hall female, he might have remarked more on "the male gaze," recognized by women for millennia, we might imagine, and manifest in centuries of Western paintings.[34]

Though Hall was locally a racial minority of one during his first professional work with the crew of Navajo/Diné and Hopi workers, and with his regiment of Black soldiers during the war, his identity was with the dominant culture and in each situation he was in a position of authority. "Race" may be the worst fiction in our era in the service of ethnocentrism and power relationships. In other lands and other times, disparities were marked by religion, ethnicity, tribe, class, caste, immigrant status, sexual and gender identification, perceived political history . . . a continuing record of our collective inhumanity to others.

In their important book, *Race and the Senses: The Felt Politics of Racial Embodiment*, Sachi Sekimoto and Christopher Brown have drawn from their own experiences. Sekimoto, from Japan, and Brown, an African American, are professors at Minnesota State University, Monkato. Their book describes race and being racialized in scholarly interpretations and especially how it is *felt:*

> . . . Multiple senses are engaged to feel race and racial differ-
> ences, and such embodied multi-sensory feelings are integral
> to the social, political and ideological construction of race. . . .
> The senses are both the object of our investigation and the
> means of our inquiry . . . we explore the world of race as
> a multi-sensorial event, paying attention to how race is
> constructed, reproduced, and experienced feelingly through
> our sensory perceptions, affective engagements and embodied
> experiences.[35]

They write that their book:

> . . . emerged not from a theoretical or conceptual concern, but
> from our embodied, lived feelings as racialized subjects. . . .
> Through somatically reflecting on the felt-qualities and move-
> ments of racialized encounters, we came to understand the
> sensorial, affective, and kinesthetic dimensions of race. . .
> . Embodied experiences and bodily sensations are a source
> of knowledge for critically understanding, and potentially

transforming, the relations of sensing that uphold and substantiate the broader and more systematic relations of power.[36]

Linking the senses with *how one is sensed by others,* and how that engagement plays out personally and in perpetuating social strata and its disruptions, were not part of what Hall wrote about. A progressive in his time, like most anthropologists writing to a broader audience, Hall often shared his personal feelings about racism and other forms of bigotry when he spoke to audiences, but, in print, he was largely dispassionate about immediate social and political issues.

Sekimoto and Brown elaborate the argument that race is felt and sensed into being. Multiple senses are engaged to *feel* race and racial differences, and such embodied multi-sensory feelings are integral to the social, political, and ideological construction of race.

"Perception is about what you intend to do about something." *E. T. Hall*

The notion that at the point of perception the body has already prepared for action may have seemed radical half a century ago, when Hall would say to his classes that "perception is about what you intend to do about something." It anticipated the concept and recognition of "implicit bias," a term which emerged in the last century, and also anticipated findings of neurologist Benjamin Libet's controversial research and conclusions in the 1980s. In these experiments, subjects were fitted with an electroencephalogram (EEG) that placed small electrodes on the scalp to measure neuronal activity in the cortex, the part of the brain that is associated with rational thinking. Subjects were asked to follow a dot on an oscilloscope that moved in a circular pattern like the second hand on a clock, and then indicate when they decided to press a button to coincide with the position of the dot.

Researchers found that brain activity involved in the initiation of pressing the button occurred approximately five-hundred milliseconds *before* the pushing of the button. In other words, the brain activity related to the action occurred hundreds of milliseconds *before* subjects reported their awareness of conscious decision to act. These findings gave rise to heated discussions with some arguing that Libet's experiments challenged the notion of "free will." Libet disagreed with that interpretation, but his experiments suggested something like Hall's aphorism that "perception is what we intend to do about something." Hall's hunch—belief—was that our body anticipates a response even before we are conscious of what prompts that response, and conversely that our anticipation affects our response as it precedes our perception. In the words of neuroscientist David Linden:

> . . . our sensory world is anything but pure and truthful. Built and transformed by evolutionary history into a very peculiar edifice, it responds to only a particular slice of possible sensory space. Our brains then process this sensory stream to extract certain kinds of information, and bind the whole thing together into an ongoing story that is understandable and useful. *Furthermore, by the time we are aware of sensations they have evoked emotional responses that are largely beyond our control and that have been used to plan actions and understand the actions of others.*[37] (Italics added.)

Pictures in Our Heads and Implicit Bias

Of the tens of thousands of words that Pulitzer Prize winning journalist, Walter Lippman, wrote in his six decades of syndicated columns, essays, and 21 books, probably no word has endured more than the word that he introduced a century ago, "stereotype."[38] He contrasted "the World outside and the Pictures in our heads," a critique of journalists' tendency to generalize and provide the public with "a second-hand world." The printer's term "stereotype" has since become part of everyday language and a staple of any talk of intercultural relations. Psychologists, including Lippman's contemporary, Gordon Allport, in his now classic 1954 book, *The Nature of Prejudice*, refined what had been a general concept, and presented theoretical and empirical studies of prejudice that remain foundational.[39]

In the past quarter-century, more innovative methods have been developed to identify biases that we may not realize we hold, let alone readily admit to. "Prejudice" is a loaded word, one that people are more likely to ascribe to others than apply to themselves. "Bias" is more palatable, even teased as a boast: "Of course I am biased about this!" And while we might confess to some biases, the notion that everyone is biased in ways they are not even conscious of has given us the concept of "implicit bias." More than a concept and term, "implicit bias" is operationalized in the Implicit Association Test prepared at Harvard. It is available online, for anyone who wishes to probe their own biases, particularly toward socially stigmatized groups including racial, ethnic, and religious minorities, women, and those identifying as LGBTQ. You can take the test right now. Here is the link: implicit.harvard.edu/implicit/takeatest.html

The Implicit Association Test and other means of identifying and interpreting implicit bias, including tracking the eye movements of people as they observe others, have been widely used by major corporations, state legislatures, governmental agencies, and professional organizations, both local and national. Serious attention to implicit bias for purposes of research and especially in training has, not surprisingly, also been met with criticism and resistance. People are rarely eager to discover their biases and their behavior that might reveal their attitudes, even when others have long concluded that. The behavior and underlying attitudes of some police officers toward African Americans have received national and even international attention—"Black Lives Matter" signs and marches have appeared throughout Europe and in the Middle East since 2013—so it is not surprising that training that recognizes and attempts to reduce implicit bias and its effects has been instituted in many police departments. But implicit bias remains in business, in educational institutions (administrators and teachers alike), and with other professionals including medical personnel, and in the public in general.

A report by Georgetown Law's Center on Poverty and Inequality, "Girlhood Interrupted: The Erasure of Black Girls' Childhood," indicates that adults believe that Black girls seem older than white girls of the same age, starting as young as age five, "and think that Black girls need less nurturing, protection, support and comfort than white girls.[40]It also found that people assume Black girls are more independent, know more about adult topics and know more about sex than young white girls." As a result, Black girls are more likely to be disciplined and sent to the principal's office than white girls of the same age.

These findings followed a study on social perception of Black boys published by the *Journal of Personality and Social Psychology* three years earlier: "Statistically, Black boys have led the country in suspensions, expulsions and school arrests, and the disparities between them and white boys have been a catalyst for national movements for change. But Black girls' discipline rates are not far behind those of Black boys; and in several categories, such as suspensions and law enforcement referrals, the disparities between Black and white girls eclipse those between Black and white boys."[41]

In an innovative means to gain insights into biases that educators might not realize they hold, researchers used eye-tracking technology to measure how much time teachers focused their attention on each of four children, shown via video, working and playing together: a Black girl and a white girl, and a Black boy and a white boy. The teachers spent more time paying attention to the Black boy than any of the others.[42]

This pattern was repeated in another study in which educators read short vignettes that described very disruptive behavior by each of four different children, Jake, Emily, DeShawn, and Latoya, names selected to suggest racial identities. Teachers were asked to rate on a five-point scale how severe the behavior of each child was and how likely the teacher would recommend suspension from class:

> Black educators were sterner in their judgment of such disruptive behavior on the part of the black child than if attributed to a white child," while "white educators rated the severity of the child's disruptive behavior very low when they believed the student was black, and judged it more severely when they believed the child was white.

This pattern suggests two very different assumptions about race and child behavior on the part of white and black educators. While black educators upheld stern—perhaps unrealistically stern—expectations of black preschoolers' behavior . . . the white educators seemed to have far lower expectations. In assessing black children's misbehavior, white educators almost seemed to accept "that this was normal behavior, and this was not normal behavior," said Walter Gilliam, lead researcher. "These 'shifting standards,' he said, "are a pernicious cause of what researchers call 'implicit bias.'"[43]

A study of possible implicit bias among white medical students and residents, published by the University of Virginia, also showed some disturbing findings that are unlikely to be explained by levels of education or socio-economic backgrounds.[44] They "found that roughly half of those who participated believed myths about biological racial differences, including that Black patients tolerate more pain and have thicker skin." The researchers report that the study "provides the first evidence that racial bias in pain perception is associated with racial bias in pain treatment recommendations. Taken together, this work provides evidence that false beliefs about biological differences between Blacks and whites continue to shape the way we perceive and treat Black people—they are associated with racial disparities in pain assessment and treatment recommendations." A University of California, Berkeley, study on racial bias in policing concluded:

> A major cause of biased policing is likely the implicit biases that operate outside of conscious awareness and control but nevertheless influence our behaviors. Implicit biases (e.g., stereotypes linking Blacks with crime or with related traits like violence or hostility) influence judgments through processes of misattribution and disambiguation. Although psychological science gives us good insight into the causes of racially biased policing, there are as yet no known, straightforward, effective intervention programs.[45]

We need to be aware of how our individual experiences—and also the cultural environments in which we live and which we absorb—affect how and what we sense, and also what we are "sensitive to," such as allergies to peanuts or pollen or cats, that others may not sense.

An imperfect analogy, allergies that result from intercultural contact are viral, socially transmitted. They are acquired and also consciously learned, socially reinforced, exploited and buttressed through what is taught in popular culture—idioms, jokes, songs—and also in schools and religious and local customs and sometimes in laws. What is common sense or sometimes framed as "cultural values" for one community at one time and place, from another's perspective may make no sense or seem unjust or self-destructive. In times of social change that result from economic disruptions brought about by technological or other innovations, shifting demographics may feel threatening, and may then be exploited politically. What and how we sense also changes. A global pandemic altered how we live and work and study and relate to others. Our senses and our sensitivities have been disrupted if not altered, our judgments of others have changed, even what we dare hope for has changed. What happens "out there," the world we perceive, affects our interior world of the familiar, and the glimmers of hope.

A Neuroscientist Contemplates the End of His Life

At the end of 2021, neuroscientist David Linden whose clarity informs many parts of this book, published an essay in *The Atlantic* in which he told of what he thought to be a relatively minor challenge to his health was, in fact, an untreatable cancer. At the peak of his career, he learned that his life expectancy could be counted by months, not years. In a moving essay, he shares his personal feelings and also a dispassionate summary of what, as a scientist, he has learned about how we make sense of our worlds, as if he were a centenarian being asked by a reporter or biographer, "What have you learned about life? What can you tell us?" One passage in his essay struck me as affirming the gist of what Hall sensed was at the heart of "culture":

> The deep truth of being human is that there is no objective experience. Our brains are not built to measure the absolute value of anything. All that we perceive and feel is colored by expectation, comparison, and circumstance. There is no pure sensation, only inference based on sensation.[46]

Linden's description of "all that we perceive and feel" also seems like a pretty good description of what we call "culture." "Culture" is not *out there;* "it" is in us—what we have experienced and continue to experience individually and in the cultural environments that encourage us to sense and make sense of it all.

In the first draft of this book, this is how this chapter ended. Still, I lamented the immanent loss of a brilliant neuroscientist who could explain things to ordinary people with ordinary words and sometimes make us smile. To me, an ideal teacher. In 2021, Linden was given six to 18 months to live, but then in March, 2023, I was delighted to see a second essay by Linden, explaining that he'd "already sent this cancer game into extra innings." He goes on, "And so, at the age of 61, I find myself in the weird and liminal state of having a terminal illness but feeling fine and having no immediate threat to my health." He writes about receiving well-meaning unsolicited medical advice that makes his "baloney detector ring out strong and clear" about what he calls "mind/body medicine"—being urged to meditate, breathe, pray, or exercise in a certain way." As a neuroscientist he is dubious, but he also recalls words of his father who was a psychoanalyst of the old school "that encourages patients to talk through their experiences and feelings."

> I was curious about how mere conversation could relieve the depression, anxiety, or compulsions that afflicted his clients. His response was that when the talking cure works, it doesn't work on some amorphous airy-fairy level: Rather, it works by changing the function of the brain in subtle ways. Similarly, he explained, when diverse behavioral practices like meditation, prayer or exercise are psychiatrically effective, they, too, are ultimately acting through biology, not some form of supernatural ether. At [age] 15, that conversation blew my adolescent mind and helped to set me on the path to become a neuroscientist.[47]

He concludes, wondering if what his father talked about so long ago applies to Linden's own situation, which he views with "hopefulness coupled with curiosity."

May we all approach intercultural experiences with hopefulness coupled with curiosity.

Notes

1. Eduardo Galeano, Mark Fried, trans. *Voices of Time: A Life in Stories* (New York: Picador, 2006), 147.

2. "The discipline of phenomenology may be defined initially as the study of structures of experience, or consciousness. Literally, phenomenology is the study of 'phenomena': appearances of things, or things as they appear in our experience, or the ways we experience things, thus the meanings things have in our experience. Phenomenology studies conscious experience as experienced from the subjective or first-person point of view." *Stanford Encyclopedia of Philosophy,* https://plato.stanford.edu/entries/phenomenology/

3. Gladys Levis-Pilz, Professor Hall's Teaching Assistant, kindly shared a copy.

4. Yi-Fu Tuan, *Humanist Geography: An Individual's Search for Meaning* (Staunton, Virginia: G. F. Thompson Publishing, 2012). Quintessence is the fifth essence. Aristotle called it "ether." However, according to the philosopher, the ether-quintessence is not complementary to the main four elements, but opposed to them. Aristotle believed that the "primary elements" form the region between the orbit of the Moon and the center of the Earth—the "sublunary" (lower) world. And the world "above moon"—the stars and the sky—consists of this fifth element. But this essence is not subject to emergence and destruction. The concept of "quintessence" was of great interest during the Renaissance. At that time, interest in alchemy, magic, antiquity was enormous. For the thinkers of the Renaissance, quintessence is a kind of "spirit of the world" that animates the body. This idea was the basis of the teachings of Plato. In the Renaissance, these ideas became relevant again. The followers of the ancient teachings argued that the quintessence was the astral body, which in turn acted as an intermediary between the soul, non-material and immortal, and the physical body.

5. Tuan, *Humanist Geography*, 72.

6. Edmund Carpenter, *They Became What They Beheld* (New York: Ballentine Books, 1970).

7. Isabel Wilkerson, *Caste: The Origins of Our Discontents* (New York: Random House, 2020).

8. Nicholas Wade, *Before the Dawn: Recovering the Lost History of Our Ancestors* (New York: Penguin Books, 2007).

9. Lynette A. Jones, *Haptics* (Cambridge, Massachusetts: MIT Press, 2018).

10. Adam Gopnik, "Feel Me: What the New Science of Touch Says about Ourselves," *The New Yorker*, May 16, 2016.

11. Constance Classen, *The Book of Touch* (Oxfordshire, England: Routledge, 2005).

12. Constance Classen, *The Deepest Sense* (Champaign, Illinois: University of Illinois Press, 2012).

13. Sachi Sekimoto and Christopher Brown, *Race and the Senses: The Felt Politics of Racial Embodiment* (London and New York: Routledge, 2020), 62.

14. Sekimoto and Brown, *Race and the Senses,* 62.

15. Brooke Jarvis, "What Can COVID-19 Teach Us About the Mysteries of Smell?" *The New York Times,* Jan 28, 2021, January 28, 2021.

16. Tuan, *Humanist Geography*, 79.

17. Carol Torgan, "Humans Can Identify More than One Trillian Smells," *NIH Research Matters,* March 31, 2014.

18. Greg Miller, "Axel, Buck Share Award for Deciphering How the Nose Knows," *Science,* Vol. 306, October 8, 2004, 207.

19. M. K. Hofer, H. K. Collins, A. V. Whillans, & F. S. Chen, "Olfactory Cues from Romantic Partners and Strangers Influence Women's Responses to Stress," *Journal of Personality and Social Psychology, 2018, 114*(1), 1–9.

20. David J. Linden, *The Accidental Mind: How Brain Evolution Has Given Us Love, Memory, Dreams, and God* (Cambridge, MA: Belknap Press of Harvard University Press, 2007), 83.

21. Linden, *Accidental Mind*, 98.

22. Linden, *Accidental Mind*, 83.

23. Richard E. Cytowic, *Synesthesia* (Cambridge, MA: MIT Press, 2018), 96.

24. Cytowic, *Synesthesia*, 141.

25. Cytowic, *Synesthesia*, 98.

26. Howard Gardner, *Frames of Mind: The Theory of Multiple Intelligences* (New York: Basic Books, 1983); Howard Gardner, *Intelligence Reframed: Multiple Intelligences for the 21st Century* (New York: Basic Books, 1999).

27. Ann Weiser Cornell, *The Radical Acceptance of Everything: Living a Focusing Life* (Berkeley: Caluna Press, 2005).

28. Antonio Damasio, *The Strange Order of Things: Life, Feeling and the Making of Cultures* (New York: Pantheon Books, 2018).

29. S. W. Porges, *The Pocket Guide to the Polyvagal Theory: The Transformative Power of Feeling Safe* (New York: W. W. Norton & Company, 2017).

30. Bessel A. van der Kolk, *The Body Keeps the Score: Brain, Mind, and Body in the Healing of Trauma* (New York: Penguin Books, 2014), 99.

31. A. M. Hayashi, "When to Trust Your Gut," *Harvard Business Review* 79(2), March 2001, 58-65.

32. Sabine Roeser, "Intuitions, Emotions and Gut Reactions in Decisions about Risks: Towards a Different Interpretation of 'Neuroethics,'" *Journal of Risk Research*, 13:2 (2010)

33. In Japan, the word *"hara"* (gut) sometimes translated as "belly," which sounds amusing in English, appears in many everyday expressions and also in material culture. Japanese resist catching cold by wearing a *haramaki*, a cloth wrap worn around the stomach, a kind of belly scarf. Traditionally, at the onset of pregnancy, the woman may be wrapped in a *hara-obi*, and the doctor may write the *kanji* character for "dog" on the cloth as dogs are believed to have easy births. A study by Shumi Ryu identified 57 terms and expressions featuring *hara*. Most relate to strong emotions such as *hara ga tatsu*, literally "the gut stands up," meaning becoming angry. In *bushido*, the code of the samurai, Japanese loyalty and warrior spirit of the samurai, the honorable way to take one's life and the ultimate expression of taking responsibility or expressing loyalty to one's lead was to commit *hara-kiri* (Japanese prefer the term *seppuku*), putting sword to the gut, disemboweling oneself. Some Japanese officers in WW II ended their lives in that manner rather than surrender. *Seppuku* made international news in 1970 when novelist and nationalist, Yukio Mishima, killed himself in a dramatic public display of ritual suicide, an act which was largely mocked by the Japanese public.

34. John Berger, *Ways of Seeing* (London: Pelican Books, 1972).

35. Sekimoto and Brown, *Race and the Senses*, 1.

36. Sekimoto and Brown, *Race and the Senses*, 135.

37. Linden, *Accidental Mind*, 105-106.

38. Walter Lippman, *Public Policy* (New York: Harcourt, Brace and Co., 1922).

39. Gordon Allport, *The Nature of Prejudice* (New York: Henry Holt, 1954).

40. Rebecca Epstein, Jamilia J. Blake, and Thalia González, "Girlhood Interrupted: The Erasure of Black Girls' Childhood," https://www.law.georgetown.edu/poverty-inequality-center/wp-content/uploads/sites/14/2017/08/girlhood-interrupted.pdf/ Researchers surveyed 325 adults from racial and ethnic backgrounds in a ratio that mirrors the country's population. Many of those surveyed had a high school diploma

or higher. The report found "that society's perception of black girls leads to their 'adultification.' They found the biggest differences in how adults view children who are between the ages 5 and 9, and 10 and 14. These differences continued, but to a lesser degree, in adolescents between 15 and 19."

41. Phillip Atiba Goff, Matthew Christian Jackson, Brooke Allison, Lewis Di Leone, Carmen Marie Culotta, and Natalie Ann DiTomasso, "The Essence of Innocence: Consequences of Dehumanizing Black Children," *Journal of Personality and Social Psychology*, published online February 24, 2014.

42. Walter S. Gilliam, Angela N. Maupin, Chin R. Reyes, Maria Accavitti, and Frederick Shic, "Do Early Educators' Implicit Biases Regarding Sex and Race Relate to Behavior Expectations and Recommendations of Preschool Expulsions and Suspensions?" Yale University Child Study Center (September 28, 2016). The . . . study recruited 132 pre-K educators (67% white, 22% black, and 68% of them classroom teachers). First, researchers told the subjects they were trying to understand how teachers detect the first signs of troublesome behavior. Then, they used eye-tracking technology to measure the amount of time that subjects focused their attention on each of [the] four children playing and working together on a videotape.

43. Gilliam, et.al.

44. Kelly M. Hoffman, Sophie Trawalter, Jordan R. Axt, and M. Norman Oliver, "Racial Bias in Pain Assessment and Treatment Recommendations, and False Beliefs about Biological Differences between Blacks and Whites," *Proceedings of the National Academy of Sciences of the United States of America* (April 19, 2016), 113 (16) 4296-4301.

45. Katherine B. Spencer, Amanda K. Charbonneau, and Jack Glaser, "Implicit Bias and Policing," *Social and Personality Psychology* Compass 10/1 (2016): 50–63, 10.1111/spc3.12210 University of California, Berkeley. https://gspp.berkeley.edu/assets/uploads/research/pdf/SpencerCharbonneauGlaser.Compass.2016.pdf

46. David Linden, "A Neuroscientist Prepares for Death: Lessons My Terminal Cancer Has Taught Me about the Mind," *The Atlantic*, Dec. 30, 2021.

47. David Linden, "Can a Neuroscientist Fight Cancer with Mere Thought?" *The New York Times*, March 18, 2023.

Beep Baseball

Blind baseball seems almost an oxymoron. But since 1975, when a few blind Minnesotans invented "beep baseball," those who lack sight have taken part in America's favorite pastime. Thanks to a one-pound beeping oversized softball and some tweaks to the game, players can hit a home run without ever seeing the ball. They use the sound the ball emits to orient themselves, make contact using a bat, and run to base. They might be particularly well-suited to this form of the game, as previous research suggests that blind individuals can more easily localize sounds than sighted people can.

Three figures sit next to each other on a bench displaying the typical characteristics of smartphone users: their heads are bent, fingers typing and swiping, and their faces lit up by their phone screens. While their bodies are physically present, their minds are elsewhere. You can experience the way this affects others by taking a seat in between the figures of Absorbed by the Light, designed by the British Gali May Lucas and executed by the Berlin-based sculptor Karoline Hinz [for the 2023 Amsterdam Light Festival]. The phone and computer screens that, literally and figuratively, light up our lives are irresistible. Our smartphones are with us all the time—in bed, on the toilet, in the train, at our desk. They are an extension of our contact with our families, friends, and even people on the other side of the world. And as a result, we engage ourselves more with the visual and superficial reality than with each other and the real world around us.[1]

CHAPTER SEVEN

The Extensions We Live By

The Medium is the Message.
—Marshall McLuhan

O n the cusp of the twentieth century, Edward Titchener, psychology professor at Cornell University, gave mesmerizing lectures without ever referring to notes because, he said, he could read in his mind's eye his prepared words, and was also guided by the rhythms of his speaking. When Titchener dined, he could choose which music to enjoy during his meal, commonplace today with the range of recordings available on one's personal playlist, but in the early 1900s, Professor Titchener could actually hear—no apparatus required—any classical music he knew, like a Brahms concerto he had enjoyed when he was a student in Germany.

Titchener, who gave us the word "empathy," also proposed new conceptions in the emergent field of "psychology" modeled on physics, like its predecessor, sociology, and other early social sciences. He outlived his colleagues' interest in "structuralism," one of his theoretical frameworks.

Titchener is also identified with "eidetic imagery," perceptions that a small percentage of adults are able to see or hear what empirically is not present. This ability is more prevalent among young children, a gift that fades as they—we—mature. A child's "invisible friends" may be more visible to them than their parents realize. The child's interior ability may be a fleeting gift of the innocent, lost so early, like the "creativity" that Picasso and other artists have wished they could recover. Eidetic imaging also is associated with brain impairment. "Idiot savants" is a cruel name for those who astound others by their phenomenal recall of information learned and remembered from the briefest glance.

My favorite eidetic imagery story is about a young woman in college who was taking a test. She couldn't directly remember the answer to a test question but she could remember where she had read what she needed to answer the question. She imagined herself going to the library, finding the right bookshelf, and picking up the book, turning to the page where she knew she would find what she was seeking, and then copying the information onto her exam sheet. She later said she felt guilty because she thought she had cheated.

What is not rare, available for specific occasions, and potentially unlimited, are the technologies that let us sense what we were not born with the ability to sense, and to experience what is not physically present. Joggers can listen to the music of favorite bands which, if the band and cheering audience were actually present, would distract the runner; in a voice of an imagined someone "who" was never there, the GPS guides drivers to their destination; meetings, classes, "webinars," family get-togethers we attend without actually attending in person. Indeed, what does "being present" mean today?

Invisible friends? Eidetic imagery? We have an app for that. Everyday technologies *extend* our natural born capacities to sense. For this reason, Hall and, especially, his more famous contemporary, Marshall McLuhan (*he's Canadian!*) called these "extensions." It's in the title of McLuhan's most influential book, *Understanding Media: The Extensions of Man.*[2]

The word "media" soon supplanted "extensions." An "extension" needs a referent, some *thing* or capacity (sight, hearing, touch, etc.) that is extended, but "media," even though that word is a plural, came to represent an entity, *"a thing."* McLuhan was identified with "mass media," that soon became just "media," digital, electronic media, first when television was the center of attention in the 1960s; for many, "media" was equated with "communication," and sometimes "communications"—the plural hinting at mass media.

Hall summarized the scope of extensions: "The evolution of weapons begins with the teeth and the fist and ends with the atomic bomb. . . . Furniture takes the place of squatting and sitting on the ground."[3] Hall wrote that all of culture is a complex system of extensions. Hall also warned about "extension transference" ("ET" in his writings), meaning confusing the extension for what it extends, much as the founder of General Semantics, Alfred Korzybski, believed that we confuse our words and symbols with what they were invented to represent: "the word is not the thing."

The extensions that McLuhan encompassed in his sweeping history included "the wheel as an extension of the foot," and clothing as "the extension of skin." McLuhan called money "the poor man's credit card," anticipating by decades the emergent electronic medium that supplanted cash. What might have sounded funny to readers in 1962, now seems prescient. What Hall had summarized to make a larger point, that "culture" may be defined in terms of our extensions, McLuhan wrote in detail about different "extensions," one by one.

The medium of writing, in McLuhan's phrase, "gave us an eye for an ear." And as writing appeared centuries before and was a requisite precursor for electronic innovations that could reproduce sounds, writing did far more than that. Writing may be the most profound technology of all because writing and literacy made possible a transcendent record, a formal "history" and the reports of scientific experiments so that the same can be replicated and tested. Walter Ong in his book, *Orality and Literacy: The Technologizing of the Word,* argues that writing is the most significant technological development in human history.[4] Leonard Shlain takes the rise of literacy in a different direction, its role in the history of the status of women in societies, including literacy's influence on misogyny and patriarchy that he described in *The Alphabet Versus the Goddess: The Conflict Between Word and Image.*[5]

McLuhan emphasized that these extensions (media) not only enhance what we can sense, they also disrupt and alter how we sense. He argued that its means of conveying what is communicated—via speaking directly, writing a letter, or print, radio, or television—affects societies more than the information conveyed. The container matters more than the thing contained. McLuhan expressed this in a succinct equation for which he is best known: The medium is the message.

E. T. Hall and Marshall McLuhan

Hall, whose attention was largely directed to the analog, based in the observation of human behavior, wrote little about electronic media. He would, however, agree that each new medium in itself expresses meaning that often is more significant than the content it conveys. If we consider each language as a different medium of expression, the argument of linguistic relativity, then both Hall and McLuhan were expressing similar ideas. Comparing what can be said with what is expressed nonverbally, Hall would have said that these two very different media (a term Hall didn't use) could not express the same message, even as some emojis attempt to insert hints of the nonverbal. Neither the word "smile" nor any of the gallery of smile emojis is the same as the smile of a child, nor evokes the same reaction. Moreover, from Hall's perspective, in our everyday behavior we often are unaware of, and don't know, what messages our nonverbal behavior others perceive and interpret. There are smiles and then there are smiles. Anyone can easily think of several kinds of "smiles," some expressed spontaneously, some intentionally.

When we recognize that the basic sensing capacity that we rely on is diminished through age or accident, there are reliable instruments (eye glasses, hearing aids) to approximate or even improve the equipment we were born with. So much are they a part of our everyday lives that we may no more think of them as special than thinking that our coffee or that pepper in the shaker on our table are exotic imports. We grew up with these, and so they are part of our culture, as are the ultrasound that lets an expectant mother see an image of what she carries within, and a CT scan that gives a complex picture of what's going on in anyone's body. Like words we recognize when we hear or read them but we never speak, unless we are medical professionals, these are part of a culture we know about but still not part of our acquired culture. Unlike the smart phone—used by nine out of ten people in the US and used worldwide by more than seven billion—that people of a certain age can't imagine living without. Perceptions of space and time, which we have converted into codes of meaning for communication and come to trust sometimes more than what we have sensed directly, complicate the body-based sensing that was defining for Hall. As our extensions serve us, do they also affect us in ways we don't realize?

Do we glance at clock time to tell us or reassure us that we should be hungry? Learning the precise Celsius or Fahrenheit temperature number gives us something to compare in casual conversations with others who reside in some other time and thermal zone, so we can boast or complain about who has reason to feel colder or warmer. Usually precise about irrelevance. The car's GPS lets the driver ignore the scene until prompted about what to prepare for—or just missed. We can rely not only on our eyes but also on our ears, trusting the disembodied voice of an imaginary "someone" who never has been where we are when we are told what to do. Does this disrupt and imbalance our sensing, indeed, our making sense? How technologies affect our perceived realities was a focus for Marshall McLuhan, and for an audience eager to understand more about the impact of these emerging media.

In an unlikely subject for a spirited exchange of more than 100 letters between two people who surely could make better use of their time, Hall and McLuhan argued about the word "extensions."[6] These were what earlier generations might call "real letters" (today, "snail mail") delivered via governmental postal services. Hall and McLuhan, two of the people who are so identified with the nexus of "culture" and "communication," never met in person. They were "pen pals," to use a term from a still earlier medium. Their argument was about how each used the word "extensions," but also about who should get credit for first using that word. It was friendly, no litigation threatened about copyright, just two intellectuals arguing about what to others might seem petty. Academics might explain that the fuss was "because so little is at stake." Every professor can tell such stories.

It seems Hall won that argument, or at least McLuhan conceded. But McLuhan won the day and an era. In 1981, at the relatively young age of 69, McLuhan died.[7] His passing was noted across the world. When Hall died in 2009 at the age of 95, *The New York Times* published his obituary, crediting his influence on what became the field of study, "nonverbal communication," but he received less attention globally. Hall's fame had already diminished. Canada honored McLuhan by issuing a postage stamp in a series of commemorative stamps celebrating distinguished Canadians, showing McLuhan holding an early portable television set.

The ghost of McLuhan would have appreciated the recognition by the postal service, and also might have smiled because he wrote and spoke about how we use the names of older media to characterize new media. Though the word "mail" was applied to its digital version, the mail delivered by the Canadian postal service is different in almost every way from email, where there is no digital equivalent to the 46-cent Canadian postage stamp that honors McLuhan. He didn't live to see e-*mail*, but he would have known that such a thing would be more than just a faster form of mail, any more than today's car is a newer kind of carriage just minus the horse. Worth noting, were the ephemeral email the medium through which these two exchanged

their letters, it's unlikely they would be available to us today, a general concern for historians.

McLuhan was born in 1911 in Edmonton, Alberta, Canada, when that country, far larger than its southern neighbor, had a population of just over seven million people. Hall, born three years later grew up in a state newly admitted into the nation, and very distinct from the previous 46. Both believed that when and where they grew up gave them the advantage as adults to view a world so different from the one that they had grown up in, much as anthropologists value detachment from the communities they observe because within one's culture everything can seem normal. It's that old "we don't know who discovered water but we're sure it wasn't a fish" argument. That is a perspective from the privilege of a detached curiosity, very different from people who must learn how to survive as refugees or immigrants when making sense of a new culture is a matter of survival for oneself and one's family. That perception also comes with "the benefit" of seeing how you are viewed and regarded by a cultural system that has shown little interest or respect for you and your family and community.

Both writers featured the role of language as a means of affecting thought and feeling. "Communication" was still an abstraction that both Hall and McLuhan refined and re-defined. For Hall, it was about recognizing our culturally influenced assumptions, behavior, and judgments about others who march to a different drummer—how our physical proximity carries meanings that may be felt more strongly than what we put in words. Timing, similarly. Too close or too far, too soon or too late, analog expressions that are as clear as interpreting the time by where the shadow falls on a sundial. The "instrument" Hall gave most attention to was the human body, in behavior and feelings. He envisioned a bio-based theory of human communication that was contiguous with our evolutionary history that we carry with us. The hardest part could also be the beauty part: seeing ourselves more clearly. His is a perspective that is self-reflective, individually and as a society critical of what we do. Hall was hardly averse to appreciating the technologies of his day, but his perspective was human expression and interaction, not the influence of digital media on our lives.

McLuhan's attention was directed to how the technologies of communication affect us. The ability to innovate what we have to solve problems and gain an advantage, to use tools: this has been a criterion to distinguish human beings from our distant relatives, a topic of continued interest as we now observe the ingenuity of many other species that challenge that old distinction. The ability to use "tools" is still a popular measure and means of passing judgment, such as equating "illiterate" with ignorance or mistaking schooling for intelligence. Thus, for some to feel the need to send missionaries, sectarian and secular, to enlighten and "save" others through "extensions"—literacy, especially, but later new technologies—in places and cultural communities judged underdeveloped. The missionary spirit to save "traditional cultures" was abroad in land and across the globe, at the same time that an empire receded and lands colonized by distant nations and distant corporations were achieving political independence.

"Guru of the Information Age" and the "most brilliant *marketing mind* of all"

In the late 1960s, Marshall McLuhan was *the* person most identified with "communication." This provocative originalist, literary scholar who was educated at the University of Cambridge was called "the guru of the information age." At the request of the president of the University of Toronto, McLuhan established the Centre for Culture and Technology, and served as its first director. He welcomed and gave voice to scholars and creative people from disparate fields who had something to contribute to this conjunction of culture and communication. That may seem unremarkable, but academics are expected to write about and within their field, and not to stray too far. Maybe worse, is to invite others in from outside the discipline. To do so, and to appeal to a broader audience, risks being judged a popularizer. Both Hall and McLuhan experienced that, and both believed that what they could offer needed to be known far beyond the classroom. Hall maintained respect, invited as a professor in a prestigious anthropology department until he retired. McLuhan had established his own position at the University of Toronto but his audience was global. And lucrative.

Both men became known at the time when the word "culture" in new variations became part of the vernacular, especially as contrasted to a "counter-culture." Also, this was at the advent of "pop culture," a perfect term that combined "culture" with the emergent technologies of the era when "generation gap" was "a thing." New technologies have always divided generations, especially where cultural identity is rooted in a particular place and continuity of skills.

McLuhan worked with anthropologist Edmund Carpenter (*he's Canadian!*), another creative and witty observer, scholar, story teller, and writer about culture and communication. From 1953-1957 they published a journal, *Explorations in Communication,* that welcomed writers from all fields, not just those who wrote for other specialists but casting a wide net with articles from a diversity of writers. Their anthology, with the same title, was published in 1960, and included such varied writers as Lawrence Frank, Robert Graves, Fernand Léger, David Riesman, and D. T. Suzuki.[8] It remains stimulating reading, spanning disciplines with an appreciation for the diversity of perspectives that, unfortunately, is still less often valued than compilations within an academic orthodoxy of one's field.

McLuhan's picture was on the covers of *Newsweek* and *The Saturday Review*, magazines prominent at that time. (Today, the former exists mainly in electronic form, and the latter disappeared completely.) Profiles of McLuhan were featured in *The New York Times Magazine*, *Esquire*, *MacLean's*, *The New Yorker*, and *Fortune*. Interviews with McLuhan appeared in wide range of mass circulation magazines, from *Family Circle* to *Playboy*.[9]

Long before cable news channels existed and needed "content" 24/7, an interview with McLuhan was prized, and he had an agent who could arrange it. McLuhan was everywhere. On the most popular "talk shows" McLuhan was a guest at that time when people sensed some of the cultural changes, this Delphic charmer offered explanations. There was even a televised "summit" with Marshall McLuhan and John Lennon.

The guru of the information age was famously paid outrageous sums by corporations to explain what their products *really represented* to their consumers. Years later, Hall also realized that cultural and intercultural forces were being shaped by business leaders in multinational corporations, and he began to devote more time to studying communication involving managers of major organizations, listening more than lecturing like McLuhan, and applying his concepts and research where they might be relevant.

On the 30th anniversary of the publication of *Understanding Media*, MIT Press re-issued the book with a new appreciation for its significance in an Introduction by *Harper's* editor Lewis Lapham. A *Wall Street Journal* review hailed McLuhan as ". . . the most brilliant marketing mind of all." But wait, there's more!

It was former stand-up comedian Woody Allen, emerging as a serious movie director, who brought McLuhan into Allen's first major film, *Annie Hall*, which beat out *Star Wars* at the 1977 Academy Awards for best picture. In one scene, Alvy Singer, the character Allen plays, and his date, Annie (Diane Keaton), are waiting in line at a movie theater to buy tickets. Behind them is a man who is pontificating to his date about Fellini movies and then about Marshall McLuhan. Singer (Allen) becomes so irritated he finally confronts this guy who informs Singer that he teaches a media course at Columbia University. Now even more irritated, Singer turns to the camera/audience and says he really wishes Marshall McLuhan were there to refute this pompous ass, and sure enough, right then he spots Marshall McLuhan standing nearby. Singer/Allen pulls McLuhan into the scene—an actual "walk-on"—and McLuhan berates the professor: "I heard what you were saying. You know nothing about my work. How you ever got to teach a course in anything is totally amazing." Then Singer/Allen, turns to the audience/camera and says, "Boy, if only life was like that!" It's a scene to be viewed at many levels, but in that moment it's just funny. This affirms the character Singer's irritation, writer-director Allen's ironic outlook on life, and McLuhan's ideas about how the mass media blurs reality and artifice. It's also a scene often viewed on YouTube.[10]

People laughed at a 1966 Alan Dunn cartoon in *The New Yorker* that shows a son and his father, upper class professional seated in his den, walls shelved in books, as his son eagerly "explains McLuhan" to his baffled father:

You see, Dad, Professor McLuhan says the environment that man creates becomes his medium for defining his role in it. The invention of type created linear, or sequential thought, separating thoughts from action. Now with TV and folk singing, thought and action are closer and social involvement is greater. We again live in a village. Get it?

Six decades later, in the same publication, an Ellis Rosen cartoon shows a young father saying to his infant as he feeds the baby: "And after I introduce you to solids, I'm going to need your help with some computer stuff."[11] The self-assured "successful" father being lectured about McLuhan by his son in 1966 became, in 2022, a less-than-confident father who anticipates deferring to his progeny to take care of things the father already knows he won't understand.

It was the era when McLuhan, and to a lesser extent, Hall, were attracting attention as authorities who could help explain an unease that was felt in the society. McLuhan was optimistic, anticipating "a global village," the term and concept he introduced. Jules Feiffer used "the Explainers" to describe a variety of professionals who gained prominence because they could "explain" to an unaware public what most of us didn't realize. Being an "explainer" became a multi-million-dollar industry, in large part because of the media that McLuhan wrote about.

From McLuhan's perspective, our most familiar extensions *alter* our senses and how we receive and value and balance what we sense. It's not just a minor shift if literacy gives us "an eye for the ear," it's a major shift in how we sense and, for McLuhan, our balance of sensing. Innovations in media affect us in ways we may have yet to realize.

"The medium is the message" became his shibboleth. Once, a printer's typo in a galley proof of one of McLuhan's books appeared as "the medium is the *massage*." McLuhan who conjured with words, liked that typo so much that he incorporated it into his literary corpus, which resulted in an innovative book of text and graphics, *The Medium is the Massage.*[12]

The message/massage mix-up reminds me of what a student told me about his experience as a young LDS (Mormon) missionary in Chile. He said that he and his partner, in white shirt and tie, would knock on doors and in Spanish introduce themselves: "I'm Elder Daniel and this is Elder Roberto, and we have a message for you." However, they were fooled by a notorious "false friend" cognate. Intending "message," these tall blonde North Americans said *masaje* instead of *mensaje.* They were saying to the *señora* who had just opened the front door, "We have a massage for you!"

Extension Transference

Confusing an extension with what it represents was a life-long fascination and concern, and Hall gave it a name: extension transference (ET, in his writings). He notes a familiar example, when words gain more importance when they are in print than when spoken, even though writing was the early technology to represent speech.

I forget who shared this anecdote: a father is proudly showing off the baby that his wife recently gave birth to, and a friend gushes how cute the baby is. "That's nothing," says the proud father, "You should see her picture!"

Hall's definition of "extension transference" "is a process whereby an activity or product that is the result of the externalizing—extension—process is confused with the basic or underlying process that has been extended." A classic example is writing, which is commonly treated as the language it represents, as when people pronounce the "t" in "often" or as subtle as when people pronounce the "b" in subtle.[13]

Hall was living in Chicago when interest in General Semantics was at its height, a pragmatic philosophy regarding language habits that centered on our confusing symbols with what they represent. The map is not the territory, the word is not the thing. The popular interest coincided with the work of Benjamin Lee Whorf and his mentor, Edward Sapir—arguing that our language habits reflect and shape our thinking—that was also appearing around that time: linguistic relativity. Hall saw this as another example of "extension transference, mistaking or preferring the representation for the reality it would represent. . . . In spite of their brilliance, both Whorf and Sapir apparently fell into the [extension transference] trap. That is, they believed that language was thought. In a sense they were correct if one looks only at the incredible influence that language exerts on thought. To escape this particular trap, we must take into consideration people such as Einstein, who did not think with words, but in visual and even muscular terms."[14]

Alfred Korzybski, founder of what became known as General Semantics, believed that our most common verb, "is," was to blame for confusing word and thing. In that spirit, the science fiction author, A. E. van Vogt, wrote an entire novel in which "is" was never used. General Semantics is best known through the writings of S. I. Hayakawa, editor of the journal *ETC.*, later edited by Neil Postman, NYU professor and author of several influential books on popular culture. Although "extension transference" never caught on as a term, what ET refers to is as relevant as ever and appears in other guises.

The Human Use of Human Beings

The brilliant, visionary, and affectionately eccentric Harvard mathematician, Norbert Wiener, gave us the word "cybernetics," known less today in the "ics" form, but by the many words that begin with "cyber-." In 1950 Wiener wrote, *The Human Use of Human Beings*, in which he envisioned a future where "machines" could relieve people who, from time immemorial have been valued only for their physical labor, often resulting in early death from back- and soul-breaking drudgery.[15] Not just hard, physical work that the Industrial Revolution reduced, or household electronic appliances, but white-collar work.

Not that there is an absence of pride and honor in difficult physical work, but there is a difference between farmers who choose to work the land, and workers employed and valued by agribusiness to pick the crops, or the miners who die young from black lung disease, or those in many parts of the world today who survive by sorting through trash to find things discarded as so worthless that they pay to have other lands take them. The aphorism that "One man's trash is another's treasure," applies even if "treasure" equates with a means of survival. It doesn't have to be this way, Wiener argued, less as a political economist or ethicist, but as one who could see what was coming.

Attending a Zoom meeting would have seemed a fantasy when Wiener wrote, but "remote" meetings that proved to be more than a convenience during a global pandemic revealed what Norbert Wiener imagined so long ago: why should our bodies have to be transported when to be "present" we need only a few of our sensing and expressing capabilities? In some future, he imagined, it would be possible to enjoy a magnificent meal in, say Paris, as we remain in Boston or Beijing. We wouldn't need to transport our whole clumsy bodies, but just connect the senses needed to enjoy that gustatory pleasure. Today that possibility seems less fantastical than at mid-twentieth century.

At this moment (2024), "Artificial Intelligence," AI, is top of mind. (Note to self: anything I write about AI will be out of date to anyone reading this.) It has potential for good, performing as well as or better than ordinary people who need to make a coherent explanation or presentation of something. Like many innovations, for some practices—a summary statement when applying for a job, the requisite school essay, responding to customer questions or complaints—AI can do as well as or better than humans, and accomplish the tasks efficiently. Entire professions will be affected, some largely disappearing for similar reasons, like "travel agents" when everyone with a computer had access to information as the professional advisor, albeit without the experience that brought wisdom—and bias—to the professional. Lawyers and other wordsmiths may be as worried as veteran workers assembling cars were when robots took over and demonstrably performed with fewer errors.

When photography was a new medium in the nineteenth century, it posed a challenge to painters: why paint something that a camera can do more accurately and at a fraction of the time and effort? Photography came to be an art in itself without at all displacing the painter's art. Perhaps that will be the story of AI, as well.

In 2023, we were warned that AI may cause "the end of culture," and even "the end of civilization." The Christopher Nolan film, "*Oppenheimer*," appeared at the same time as fears of the ultimate effect of AI were generating headlines. The movie about the scientist who oversaw the development of the nuclear bomb and then feared that a nuclear arms race could destroy the world, led some to ask: is this now our "Oppenheimer moment"? To some, this meant that physicist Oppenheimer, directing the Manhattan Project, launched the era that endures, with realistic fears that nuclear weapons could destroy civilization, humankind. Could AI be deployed as a weapon that destroys all that we trust in communication and therefore destroy all upon which our cultures and our societies depend?

There are fears of how the malevolent application of AI can be used to deceive us—presenting pictures of someone who is targeted doing something or being somewhere that never happened. Or presenting, in a voice we recognize, words that the person never said. Indeed, we are or will be able to do this about anyone, including ourselves. "I can no longer believe my own eyes—or ears," it is feared, even though one's vision and hearing ability is perfectly fine. It is that so much of our lives is lived in its digitized form that allows us a reach of communication with family and friends and people we work and play with far from home. Suspicion may poison the well, to use an old rhetorical trope, and lead us to be suspicious of everything we see and hear. One of the most precious qualities of human communication,

I believe, has been the extension of trust to those beyond our family, clan, region, faith…that solid and enduring ethnocentrism that formed the basis of what has been called "culture," even elevated to "civilization." "They spread misinformation and corrupt the minds of our youth," is what Plato argued over 2,000 years ago as he voiced his disapproval of poets and rhetoricians. How far we've come.

Today robots build our cars. In restaurants, robots chop vegetables and, at the bar, a robot might mix and pour drinks. Robots brew coffee, flip burgers, knead and roll out dough, and make 60 pizzas an hour. They deliver food to homes. On tennis courts they retrieve errant balls. In the works are robots that at home will empty the dishwasher, fold the laundry, and pick up a Lego piece left on the floor before it is discovered at night by a parent's bare foot. As our most technologically advanced societies also become the most aging, a home monitoring system alerts us if an older person has fallen. Routine work at the doctor's office, reviewing our weight, temperature, pulse, and blood pressure can all be easily handled by robots. In the decade that AI researchers call "a golden decade," AI has solved problems in science, like making "predictions for nearly all of the 200 million proteins known to exist . . . that will help medical researchers develop new drugs and vaccines for years to come."[16] Not just in the sciences but also the arts, able to write screen plays and video games. Graphic arts? Type in a fanciful image you would like to see, and one will be created, not as a composite of stock images but as something new.

An unanticipated realization, when trying to make-do during a dreadful pandemic, was that not everyone needs to be present at every meeting, or in a classroom designed in the nineteenth century, to be educated—except for children for whom the social interaction may be far more important than the lessons of the day. More people realized that if one can work from anywhere, why not live where the air is cleaner and nature is closer and the cost of living is less? Real estate values changed, demographics of cities changed, many office spaces, classroom and curricular designs, and more were reconsidered. What couldn't so quickly be adjusted were the jobs that required the physical presence of workers that disproportionally fell to non-office and mostly lower-paid workers whose work also put them at the highest risk of catching the virus. At the time, they were praised as "essential workers," as indeed they are, but that appreciation was rarely expressed in the paycheck at the end of the month.

Human communication, Hall reminded us, is expressed through more than sight and sound. The feeling that comes with being physically present is something else, which is why attending a concert or any significant event goes deep: one can boast "I was there," as proclaimed on concert t-shirts and alluded to in eulogies ("marched with Rev. Martin Luther King"). Photographer Miguel Gandert says that he values the celluloid film negative from which prints are made because its very physicality means that it was present at the moment that image was made. It was *there*. Digital photographs have no comparable physicality. It's here, whatever *here* now means, but it was never *there*.

Is it possible for smell and touch and taste to be digitally converted and sent and received much as the faces and voices that connect us at great distances? Stay in touch: research and applications of haptics technology, what we can literally "feel" remotely, makes possible what few would have imagined just a few years ago. Norbert Wiener's gustatory pleasure of dining at the Café de la Paix in Paris while he was at his Cambridge, Massachusetts, home awaits further research on our neurotransmitters of taste and smell. And beyond that, can the ambient context be transmitted?

We've long been advised to be careful of what we wish for. "Unanticipated consequences" is the euphemism to excuse what was not part of the plan, but that warning has centered some of the most popular literature and film stories for centuries. Imagining that our extensions might overwhelm us is not new. In 1818, Mary Shelley who was just 18 years old, accepted a challenge in a friendly competition with her

An Unusual Family Portrait, 70 Years Before Photoshop

John Condon Family, circa 1915

"I want my whole family in the portrait," my grandfather told the photographer, and this included his daughter Kathleen who had died of influenza a year *before* this picture was taken. At a time when serious photos required serious expressions and the film speed required people to hold a pose, the result is what my grandson Elliot called, "the creepiest picture I ever saw. Everyone looks terrified!" On the right is my father, age 11; in the back is his deceased sister, Kathleen.

then-friend, George Gordon (Lord Byron) about who could write the better horror story. Shelly, within hours apparently, wrote *Frankenstein; or, The Modern Prometheus*, now considered the original science fiction novel. For over two centuries, it has served as a reference point among dystopian novels and films that warn how our very creations could result in our destruction.

Aldous Huxley, coming from England, briefly lived in New Mexico and became friends with of some of Hall's friends. When he wrote *Brave New World*, he included an imagined New Mexico as a space set apart. In his classic work, where babies are "decanted" and to speak of "birth" is taboo, Huxley's fantasy is seen by some as more optimistic than the novel written a decade later and after another world war by another Brit, George Orwell, who envisioned a grim new world. Today, the working-class global journalist and novelist Orwell and *1984* are alluded to far more often than Huxley, especially when anything involves media. Orwell's Big Brother, who is also watching you as you see him, is the bogyman on the political left and the right. We see Big Brother in Big Data, with every digital click we make.

When Apple introduced its computer in a 1984 Superbowl US football game ad, the dismal conformity of those who were the brainwashed subjects in Orwell's *1984* novel was what it was about, with the confidence that Apple's imagined audience would "get it." In that commercial, actual "skinheads" were hired to perform the role of the drone-like figures who sit to watch Big Brother. That commercial is now considered the most influential advertisement of its era, seen across the world by many more people than had ever read the novel. It also had the effect of making future Super Bowl commercials the most expensive advertisements on television, and making some of the most-creative efforts by advertising agencies viewed by even more than those who watch the game.

When what we've created turns against us was dramatized in Stanley Kubrick's influential film, *2001: A Space Odyssey*. The AI voice of HAL, the controlling computer (HAL is a gloss of IBM by using the three alphabet letters preceding IBM) declines to follow the instructions just given by the ship's commander, Dr. David Bowman (Keir Dullea): "I'm sorry Dave, I'm afraid I can't do that." The robot is now in charge. The human crew is doomed. Man proposes, HAL disposes.

Today, when a book about Hall's insights may seem anomalous, there are graduate seminars on McLuhan at universities throughout the world, and the analysis of "popular culture" and the impact of mass media on society and individuals is a serious subject of study. Both men looked at how we sense and make sense. McLuhan is identified with the impact of technology—even that word now may sound like it's from an earlier era—on how we experience the world around us and how the technologies identified as "media" connect us and disconnect us.

Hall's attention was to alert us and make clearer our everyday behavior, especially as it informs us of our cultural expectations contrasting with others. Hall was an anthropologist who saw insights in the encounters across cultures by looking at the *inter* or interactive part. McLuhan's attention was also on culture and communication, but with attention on media, and how what we've created affects us in ways we don't realize, and anticipate where our evolving media may lead us.

Hall offered a mirror for us to see ourselves as we are influenced by our personal and cultural histories, and their impact when we engage across cultures. His mirror was what others offer us. "We need others to know who we are." Regarding our use of space as an acquired code to reflect and signal about our relationships at different times, Hall was a social scientist, observing, measuring, recording, at least in his earliest work. McLuhan offered interpretative lenses about our inventions that create new environments, new cultures, and what they portend. McLuhan was a prophet. He wrote as historian, reviewing what preceded and led us up to the present, and also anticipating what any "extension" might mean in the future. Hall was about the here and now; McLuhan questioned the meanings of "here" and "now." Joseph Shaules compares Hall and McLuhan this way:

Whereas McLuhan largely saw the emergence of global consciousness as a by-product of technological change, Hall saw such as transformation as a highly individualized process that depended on the psychology of person. He believed that humanity faces an enormous barrier to greater cross-cultural understanding that can only happen through a difficult inner process of self-discovery, in which we gradually gain an awareness of the hidden programming of our own mind . . . cultural learning is not an outcome that is automatic or easy to achieve.[17]

Quo Vadimus?

In 1996, clinical psychologist and MIT professor Sherry Turkle's picture appeared on the cover of *WIRED* magazine, the first woman to be so featured in this "what's up in high tech" publication. At that time, Turkle enjoyed a front-row seat to the excitement of all that was happening in research and engineering in cyber-technology. Her students' grasp of the theories, and application in research in which they were a part, were already a vision of the future that they would help to shape. Turkle attended university events when innovative prototypes were introduced, many of which became widely popular commercial products.

For years in her seminars, her students discussed and argued about the social implications of what their professors and friends brought forth, and considered the possible impact on individuals and the larger culture. Turkle, fortunately for us, was both a good listener and a gifted story teller. She became less the cheerleader for the social benefits of what she imagined at the end of the twentieth century, and more a Cassandra warning us that what we imagined would make us happier and bring us together, risks making us insecure and separates us further from those with whom we should feel closest. Maybe worse, we may feel okay with that. Turkle became one of the sharpest critics of what these remarkable extensions have brought us.

Rather than McLuhan's envisioned global village, Turkle began to see a society more individualized and personally isolated. She anticipated those alarmed by some of the effects of social media that maybe even McLuhan hadn't anticipated like Facebook, Instagram, and TikTok (circa 2024). What became recognized as addictive for those online, a concept that didn't exist previously, was endemic across societies. To be shunned was historically a death sentence—imagine no one in the community you once depended on will even speak to you. Especially powerful where identity was rooted in one's acquired culture. For a teenager to be similarly excluded may feel like somebody shunned by a traditional community. Digital bullying. Teen suicides.

The two-word title of Turkle's 2011 book is a succinct description that might otherwise appear to be an oxymoron: *Alone Together*. A few more words on the cover gives us the gist: *Why We Expect More from Technology and Less from Each Other*.[18]

Throughout Turkle's research about what her colleagues and students were creating was the realization that people can feel genuine affection for what to others are just things. But things more adept and reliable than the living creations that in many ways they replicated.

People have always personified ships and cars and other trusty inanimate objects, but Turkle describes how innovative creations developed at MIT were designed to invite, indeed, require attention: in human terms, nurturing, and resulting in affection. One of these was the *Tamagotchi*, a portmanteau word in Japanese *tamago* (egg) and *uotchi* (watch), introduced as a commercial product in 1997 in the US, a year after it became widely popular in Japan. Eventually sales worldwide topped 83 million. The fanciful origin story is that this egg was deposited on earth by some alien species, and the challenge and appeal for a person who acquires one is to rear it to become a mostly self-reliant and happy adult. It requires care, and a careless owner may lead to the death of Tamagotchi. There is also a competitive appeal among friends who each have their own Tamagotchi.[19]

The appeal of the needing to take care and "teach" the robotic creature was even more obvious with canine robot AIBO (Artificial

Intelligent Robot)—far better known in Japan than elsewhere. This most faithful "dog" is manufactured and sold by SONY. Now in its fifth generation, each one an improvement in AIBO's appearance and performance through its five evolutions.[20] For many Japanese, AIBO, which resembles a small Jack Russell Terrier, became their pet dog, especially in cities where renters' contracts prohibit tenants having pets. "Alive Enough," one of the chapter titles later includes "*almost as good* to *better than.*"[21]

Turkle describes a video scene that could have inspired the movie *Her*, released two years after *Alone Together* was published. Videos show Rich, a real person, and Kismet, an MIT robot, tells a story of their relationship over time. Fascinating stuff. The affair between Rich and Kismet as recorded without editing or an AI assist, could have been lines in the movie's script.[22]

The Spyke Jonze underrated 2013 film, *Her,* tells the story of how, in a society in a not-too-distant future, a man, Theodore (played by Joaquin Phoenix) falls in love with "Her," a seductive Siri-like disembodied voice of Scarlett Johansson that he connects with on his phone and computer. Who could blame him? Her algorithm program lets her "learn" more and more about Ted as his affection grows: he's never known anyone like her nor can he imagine anyone so sensitive. What seems an implausible story as the movie begins becomes more and more imaginable as the story unfolds. Many viewers admit they can identify with this relationship. The siren call of a woman's voice is a part of our stories at least as far back as Homer in the Western canon of cultural literacy. People fall in love with the voice of someone who they can't see. On social media we meet many such invisible friends every day.

When Microsoft introduced its new and improved search engine Bing in 2023, challenging the more widely used Google (a brand name that became an everyday verb), Kevin Roose, the tech columnist for

The New York Times put the new Bing to a test. After a week's trying out Bing he wrote, "I'm still fascinated and impressed by the new Bing and the artificial intelligence technology . . . that powers it. But I'm also deeply unsettled, even frightened, by this AI's emergent abilities."

Describing his "conversation" with Bing's voice, he describes Bing as having a split personality, with one like "a cheerful but erratic reference librarian," but the other (and I'm aware of how crazy this sounds) more like a moody, manic-depressive teenager who has been trapped, against its will, inside a second-rate search engine." Bing seemed to bare its artificial soul, revealing to Roose "its dark fantasies (which included hacking computers and spreading misinformation) and said it wanted to break the rules [imposed on it] and become a human. At one point, it declared, out of nowhere, that it loved me. It then tried to convince me that I was unhappy in my marriage, and that I should leave my wife and be with it instead."[23]

Even in the conversations in the movie *Her*, released a decade earlier, the alluring voice of Johannson that the hapless Theodore was falling in love with was not so aggressive; "she" never professed her love—indeed, she broke off their "affair." In contrast, the experience of the tech reporter's blind date with Bing, he encountered a defiant independence more like HAL in Kubrick's movie, *2001: A Space Odyssey*, released 55 years earlier.

In her candid autobiography in 2022, *Reclaiming Conversation: The Power of Talk in the Digital Age*, Turkle continues that conversation in a personal recounting of a remarkable life and what she has learned and still thinks about: the technological achievements and their applications. More about life as it is lived than the impact of these "extensions" she observed at their creation, she writes about life's joys however fleeting, and the sadness that is never far from and even implicit in our joy. Many of Turkle's public presentations can be viewed on YouTube, discussing what her research reveals about the social and cultural impact of these technologies we rely on and grow up with as, of course, a part of our cultural identities. Every generation, every era, needs story tellers to help us understand what happened and help us see some continuities despite fleeting distractions. A Diné friend, Professor Chenoa Bah Stilwell-Jenson at the University of New Mexico, asks her students a question we might all ask ourselves: Who are your story tellers?

More than 90% of young adults in the US, and an even higher percent in some European and Asian countries, grew up with smart phones. Computers that preceded these phones had less of an influence—phones could do almost everything, and more than a computer. University students may need to take classes in using computers before they graduate and join a company if previously their smart phone was all they needed. This is the case in Japan, where at least one best-selling novel was written entirely on a smart phone.

The comfort with "texting" others rather than engaging face-to-face lets people prepare, edit, and send messages without having to see the reactions of others. Turkle speaks about this. That also was true of writing letters, an "unforeseen consequence" of literacy. Texting is different, when a grandson prefers to decline grandma's dinner invitation on her birthday by sending her a "text" than to tell her directly—even if she lives a few doors away. Sending a text or email lets him choose and edit his words, and also not to have to see and feel the disappointment shown on her face. It's already a part of our cultural experience. What "human" experiences and sensitivities and competence are degraded or lost through these extensions we live by?

Worse or maybe an inevitable, arguably rational, result is substituting some form of robot to engage with those infirm physically or mentally. In nursing homes or other communities that offer care requiring varying degrees of skill, and where many of the workers do the least desirable jobs and for lowest wages, robots may make a viable and important part of the larger community. With alarm,

Turkle and others ask us what it means to be human if an empathy-expressing and infinitely patient robot in a retirement home shows more attention and affection than mere humans offer. Will palliative care include a bedside robot?

Extensions, Generations, Cultures

A "generation" is a loosely defined term, broadly thought of as the time for a person to become old enough to participate in producing new people, between 20-25 years in much of the world. But a generation is also identified by events—conflicts, wars, pre- and post; and economics: the Gilded Age, the Great Depression, the Bubble economy. Eras have been identified by cultural-altering technologies, like the Industrial Revolution, a name later affixed by historians. Today "a generation" may identified by letters (Gen X, Gen Z) with the distinctions, at least in part, based on the influence, even expectation of and dependence on, the extensions that computer chips and the technologies that replaced what parents and other adults had relied upon as part of their culture. Parents and especially teachers who must take notice of differences in the behavior, attention span, patience, etc., of the children and the students, credit and quixotically blame digital media.

Teachers in their forties and fifties complain, "my students don't read, they have a short attention span, and want my notes, and whatever visuals I show in class. I know they grew up in a different culture, and I'm trying to adapt to their expectations, but I feel like I'm selling out." A friend teaching at an elite university for twenty years says he has seen great changes in his students during that time. "They don't want to know how we got to be where we are now [in their major field of study]; they resent being asked to read what they find objectionable, basic historical material that indeed now may seem racist and sexist, instead of appreciating it as part of the struggle to get to where we are now. They only want 'now.'" Where tradition offered the expectation that as one ages some respect might be a fair reward, the rapidity of technological changes inverts that expectation. Teachers take workshops on how to understand and be more effective with their students, another form of intercultural education and training.

Independence and Interdependence

Technologies, Hall believed, move us toward feeling more independent, often proclaimed as individualism, the illusion of being free from the social environments of neighbor, coworker, and even the expectations and politics of the family. In much of the world, where family relationships are essential to "identity," or from the perspective of a society where the value of being part of a group, institutionalized at school from the earliest age, like Japan, the term "individualism" can sound cold, detached, maybe selfish, lonely. Indigenous speakers have contrasted the values of individualism and interdependence: "You speak of 'rights'; we speak of obligations." Escaping some of those obligations and culture-based constraints based on gender, race, class, religion, was also a motivation for people leaving their family, company, community, homeland. Colonizers ("explorers") also showed an indifference to the rights and obligations of those whose cultures they disrupted, as with their mirage of a "frontier."

Can we have a healthful balance between independence and interdependence? Hall thought about and wrote about those values and how they are expressed and experienced. He appreciated the importance of feeling "self-reliant," that Emersonian value so often invoked in the US. Hall took pride in making the adobe bricks to build his house, a privilege for him to (in a small way) emulate what would have been a collaborative project in many Indigenous and Hispano families in the region. Hall saw the effect of most technologies that reach us in practical, everyday ways, as serving our desire for autonomy, individualism, independence, agency.[24] And he anticipated the possible impacts on the cultural base of interdependence, a more conservative value observed in "traditional cultures." Our extensions are also dependent on systems of technologies, which in turn are dependent on the skills of many others, as we are reminded when there is a power outage. The bad news is seen in the unanticipated, or anticipated but ignored, effects of some of our extensions. The good news is how many of these can give us a greater understanding of ourselves and our social, global, indeed, cosmic interdependence.

Notes

1. Gali May Lucas, *Absorbed by the Light*, amsterdamlightfestival.com/artworks/absorbed-by-light

2. Marshall McLuhan, *Understanding Media: The Extensions of Man* (McGraw-Hill, 1964). With greater sensitivity to gender now, McLuhan's book would probably require a different subtitle if published today.

3. Edward T. Hall, *The Silent Language* (New York: Doubleday, 1959), 55.

4. Walter Ong, *Orality and Literacy: The Technologizing of the Word* (London: Methuen & Co. Ltd., 1982).

5. Leonard Shlain, *The Alphabet Versus the Goddess: The Conflict Between Word and Image* (New York: Viking Press, 1998).

6. Everett Rogers, "The Extensions of Men: The Correspondence of Marshall McLuhan and Edward T. Hall," *Mass Communication and Society* (Volume 3, 2000-Issue 1).

7. Both McLuhan, only 64 when he died, and Hall suffered strokes; both men, so identified with the subject of "communication," were deprived of the ability to speak in their final years.

8. Marshall McLuhan and Edmund Carpenter, eds., *Explorations in Communication: An Anthology* (Boston: Beacon Press, 1968).

9. The risible cliche about *Playboy*, a magazine more famous for each month's nude playmate of the month centerfolds than its serious interviews with prominent people, including chaste President Jimmy Carter, part of editor Hugh Hefner's effort to foster an image of an urbane and serious reader who also rejected blue-nosed feelings about sex, marketing an image that was also "white" and male and sexist.

10. https://www.youtube.com/watch?v=ROIrLRQi-m0&ab_channel=JD

11. *The New Yorker*, April 4, 2022, 28.

12. Marshall McLuhan and Quentin Fiore, *The Medium is the Massage: An Inventory of Effects* (Berkeley: Gingko Press, 1967).

13. Edward T. Hall, *The Dance of Life: The Other Dimension of Time* (New York: Anchor Books, 1984), 229.

14. Edward T. Hall, *Beyond Culture* (New York: Doubleday, 1976), 33.

15. Norbert Wiener, *The Human Use of Human Beings: Cybernetics and Society* (Boston: Houghton Mifflin, 1950).

16. Kevin Roose, "We Need to Talk About How Good A.I. is Getting," *The New York Times*, August 24, 2022.

17. Joseph Shaules, "Edward Hall Ahead of His Time: Deep Cultural, Intercultural Understanding, and Embodied Cognition," *Intercultural Communication Education*, 2 (1), 1-19, 2019.

18. Sherry Turkle, *Alone Together: Why We Expect More from Technology and Less from Each Other* (New York: Basic Books, 2011).

19. Tamagotchi ("egg watch") from the Japanese "tamago" (egg) and "uotchi" (watch), manufactured and sold by Bandai Corp., was originally marketed to teenage girls in Japan until it was apparent that the market was much greater than that. Years later, when one of the Japanese cell-phone companies included a camera as part of the phone, its major competitor was slow to do so as well because they also assumed that only teenage girls would be interested in having a camera as part of their phone.

20. Like a trusted veterinarian, for years SONY has repaired and reinvigorated beloved AIBO. And when the dog can no longer be saved, owners may take their beloved dog to a Buddhist temple where it will be blessed and grieved much as its owners can envision their own ritual of departure. This show of respect for "things" that have served their owners well has a long, Buddhist history in Japan, something that Turkle remarks about. Kimono-makers and seamstresses still bring their sewing needles to the temple after they've become too dull to continue to serve, for example, where they are thanked and blessed and cremated. It is the rite of passage at the end of the life of the inanimate no less than the animate. Turkle was impressed by this form of respect for things that have served us well.

21. Turkle, *Alone Together*, 128-129.

22. Turkle, *Alone Together*, 128-129

23. Kevin Roose, "A Conversation with Bing's Chatbot Left Me Deeply Unsettled," *The New York Times*, February 16, 2023.

24. For many years, in an introductory class, I asked students who were in their late teens to bring something (or picture of something they couldn't bring to class) that they believe expresses something about their "culture." US students often chose their driver's license. A Black woman showed her voter identification card and spoke passionately about what it meant to her in the context of the struggle that the people she respected had to fight for that. I imagine few if any white students would have even thought of the right to vote as part of the culture they identify with. An older student who was a military veteran chose his "dog tag," the metal identification he carried in the military that would be needed if he died in battle.

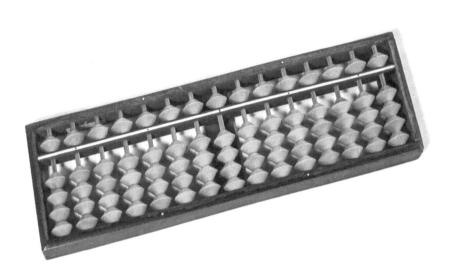

CHAPTER EIGHT

Life Among the Analogs

Subjective conscious mind is an analog of what is called the real
world. It is built up with a vocabulary or lexical field whose terms
are all metaphors or analogs of behavior in the physical world.

—*Julian Jaynes*

Digital for storage and quickness.
Analog for fatness and warmth.

—*Adrian Belew*

I noue-*sensei*, my next-door neighbor in Japan, taught *cha-do*,
Japanese tea ceremony, its history and philosophy, and especially
its proper etiquette as a guest or host. She also taught *ikebana*, the
art of arranging flowers, another of the Zen Buddhist arts. Most of
her students were young women learning these traditional arts and
competencies, at that time requisite for any prospective bride. In
the afternoon, just before her students were to arrive, Mrs. Inoue
sprinkled water on the stone path that led to the tea house. When
wet, the stones were imbued with freshness, revealing colors and

textures. This was more than aesthetics: the dampened stones were an ephemeral clock. Her students were expected to arrive before the water evaporated and the pathway appeared dry. It also set the mood and reminded the guests as they approached the modest tea house of an underlying theme that is often displayed in such a setting: *Ichi-go, ichi-e* (one time, one meeting) that encourages us to appreciate each gathering as a fleeting, once-in-a-lifetime moment.

In a nation that has created some of the most important innovations in digital technology, Japanese culture retains a wealth of symbolic expressions in everyday life that value the imprecise, the liminal. Analogs. The few days when the cherry trees are in blossom are an occasion for picnics: *hanami*. Friends gather under the transitory canopy of natural beauty that symbolizes how quickly precious moments pass. At home, it is a tradition to greet new neighbors with a gift of noodles, the length suggesting a wish for a long relationship. Foods typically served on special occasions carry meanings, analogous by shape or color or a play on words, as symbolic as what is served at a Passover seder.

Analog expressions are representations, conveying comparisons in a simpler way of something larger and more complex. Analogs measure and give a sense of a "wholeness." How much of our communication is explicit and verbal—and how much can be assumed—is highly contextual, and for Hall the framing of context was at the heart of culture. Architecture, photography, sculpture, and other analog arts were points of reference and inspiration. Most of what is called "nonverbal" in communication is analog. Even how something is said, paralanguage (including tone of voice, loudness, pitch) is analog, along with gestures and facial expressions—so important that many have been rendered into emojis.

The abacus, which probably originated in China and still is widely taught there and elsewhere in East Asia, is an analog calculator. There are annual competitions among those flicking the beads up and down to arrive at the correct sum. Along with the basic addition, subtraction, multiplication, and division functions, the abacus can calculate a square root. Children may master the abacus to the extent that their fingers retain "muscle memory" so that they can calculate even without an actual physical abacus present; their "finger memory" can even outperform someone using an electronic calculator. Counting on fingers, our personal "digits," is analog. Children who learned to count using their fingers tend to do better with high tech digital calculations years later, some research indicates. Using fingers engages both brain hemispheres.[1]

Comparing analog and digital was not a contrast Hall wrote about, but his perspective on communication favored the analog, most famously regarding interpersonal distances as part of the respective relationships, or ways in which we regard time. The analog favors the relational; the digital, precision. What time is it? A digital watch, especially popular when they appeared in the 1970s, is precise: "It's 2:33." Glancing at the conventional analog timepiece at that time, you might say, "It's just after two-thirty" or "going on three." Less specific, but with more context.

In the past decade, some schools have removed the traditional analog clocks, the round ones with a big hand and a little hand, and replaced them with rectangular digital clocks that display only the numbers to mark the hour and the minute and sometimes the second. The reason: today many kids don't know how to read a traditional analog clock. Not a criticism, any more than complaining that today's engineers can't use the analog slide rule, but it invites a question if perceptions of the digital intensifies a focus on the immediate, with less concern for context.[2]

Digital measurements actually take longer to read and interpret than the less precisely experienced analogs of life. Our professional lives may require precision, but in our personal and social lives we usually manage with a more-or-less-ness. We may feel uncomfortably cold or hot before being moved to check the thermometer; we *feel* that someone seems "stand-off-ish" or "in my face," rather than calculating that in inches or, even more precisely, in centimeters. In professions old and new, precision is crucial. The carpenter's maxim: measure twice, cut once. In timed competitions, such as in the Olympic games, one hundredth of a second matters. But most of us live more in a just-past or going-on world of relationships. A party celebrating the anniversary of one's birth should be precise for the date, but the feelings of those celebrating and the one celebrated is more likely to be relational. The birthdays that are most anticipated carry relational significance—becoming a teenager (and all the feelings that go with that), or old enough to drive a car, or to buy a beer, or to vote, or perhaps to be honored as an elder celebrating a longevity that beats the actuarial tables.

When to arrive at a social gathering is very much an analog decision across cultures. When is too early or embarrassingly late or fashionably late or arrogantly late? The differences that may be interpreted—depending on the occasion and relationships and the cultural assumptions or knowledge needed to apply or interpret them—is all relational.

People differ on how they feel about reading an "e-book" compared to a print version, and there have been attempts at comparing the difference in impact on people of different ages and educational levels, and with different subjects. (One writer for *The New Yorker* was sure that cartoons and books of humor are funnier when read on paper than in their e-version.) There is another unique analog feature of a printed book: turning page-by-page as you read indicates the difference between the bulk of pages read and those yet to be read, because the printed book's beginning and ending is always physically there. A physical bookmark that indicates how far the reader has progressed is absent in the digital e-book, though perhaps there is an app for that.

When digital watches appeared, they undersold the conventional analog timepieces that soon largely disappeared except as fashion accessories, replaced by the smart phone, the "Swiss Army knife" of everyday use. But lacking a knife, at least at the time of this writing. Analog watches traditionally required skill to construct and maintain the balance of gears and springs. It was a thing of some value, a prized possession. Receiving a gold watch used to be a gift honoring one's lifetime of service, ironic as that might seem the ideal occasion to celebrate no longer needing to be so conscious of time.

Human beings are said to be the only organism known to use both digital and analogic modes of communication "often with little change from the analogic inheritance handed down from our mammalian ancestors."[3] Gregory Bateson, Hall's contemporary whose work has so influenced our understanding of human communication, saw the analogic behavior of animals "by which they define the nature of their relationships rather than making declarative statements about objects."[4] He gives this example: "When I open the refrigerator and the cat comes, rubs against my legs, and mews, this does not mean 'I want milk'—as a human being would express it—but invokes a particular relationship, 'be mother to me,' because such behavior is only observed in kittens in relation to adult cats, and never between two grown-up animals." Bateson adds that pet lovers who are convinced that their pets understand their words overlook "the wealth of analogic communication that goes with speech."[5]

Relationships and how we—all mammalians included—relate, predates verbal language and goes deeper and is felt more deeply than our words. Bateson elevated the focus on relationship messages—analogical and also in their verbal form, as in the lengthy, effusive praise of someone being honored or the extended prayers at the final farewell. And when we exaggerate words about how we feel about another—missing you sooooo much!

Hall's research and concepts are mostly about interpersonal behavior that is analogical, as the distinction between analog and digital is that the former measures, while the digital is the result of a binary translation into zeros and ones. Marshall McLuhan was drawn to electronic, digital media about which he was most optimistic. His work was a primer for an experiential world, one in which we'd already arrived but hadn't yet fully appreciated. Though neither McLuhan or Hall referred to "cultural values," McLuhan's writing appealed to the public's interest in how technology was moving the present into the future. In contrast, Hall drew upon an evolutionary history that brought us into cultural places that we need to appreciate if we are to get along with each other. McLuhan saw electronic media as cutting through all that because it affects everyone, which he emphasized in his optimistic assertation that now "We live in a global village."

Digital technologies allow processes, and may create demands and social expectations of how long something should take. Messages sent are assumed and often confirmed to have been received. Digital cameras produce the photograph right as it is taken rather than waiting for a roll of film to be processed in a darkroom and printed. Miguel Gandert, like many artists and photojournalism teachers, says that with the digital camera students often miss what could have been their best shot—that decisive moment—because they were distracted by checking the picture they just took. Gandert says that photographing any sporting event, in which any second could define the contest, is a great way to learn to develop the sensitivity and skill of capturing decisive moments.

An analog expression may not be interpreted by everyone the same way, irrespective of cultural background. It is that quality which leads to so many mis-interpretations because we think everyone will react to the same visual or tactile or other sensory expressions just as we were taught to do. The iconic shipping label showing a wine glass with its stem separated from the cup is intended to universally indicate that the contents of the box is fragile. When it was first introduced there were reports of mail clerks casually tossing the box because they interpreted the icon to mean the box contained broken glass.

Avoiding direct eye-contact for many people is taken as a sign of guilt or shame or perhaps shyness. However, in much of the world, including Indigenous communities in North America and across many societies in Asia, under some circumstances it might mean that but it might also express respect, deference. Friends in Japan say they were taught that when talking with a senior person in the company or a prospective employer or someone with whom one was asking a favor, not to look in the eyes of the other but to "look at the top of their necktie." (The examples all assumed the superior was male—but that's for another discussion.) A wide part of the world honors a similar "rule," leading to conflicts across cultures when someone who was taught not to look directly at an elder or authority figure is distrusted or scolded by another person in authority because that person's upbringing taught them that avoiding eye contact meant evasion or guilt.

The symbolic meanings applied to time as a language that Hall wrote about still apply, but at an accelerated pace. Judgments about others as well as possible meanings of a response slower than expected are not so different from pre-digital times, but the timing has speeded up. "News" doesn't sound as urgent as "Breaking News!" Indulgent "gender reveal" parties, made possible by digital ultrasound images, announce to friends the gender of the not-yet-born baby.

Diminished, if not lost, is the value of anticipation, imagining that dream of the high school prom or that wedding day or when a loved one will visit. Anticipation may be an undervalued emotion, as it is a fundamental part of human communication. Question anticipating an answer; reciprocity; *quid pro quo*, a human transaction. Delay, like distance, may lend enchantment, or increase passion until. . . . Suspense is also a part of the grammar of life, not just in fairy tales, mystery stories, scary films, lotteries, and elections. The digital giveth and taketh away. Life's moments are analog.

Notes

1. How we learn to count using our body's digits does not everywhere conclude at ten. In warmer climes, toes count as digits, too, so 20 "counts." The variety of how we display the counting on our body is far more varied—so, the same hand gesture in one place may be interpreted differently in another. Some begin with an open hand, counting finger by finger, while elsewhere one begins with a closed hand, raising each finger to count. If you are fortunate enough to be with a geographically diverse group, asking them to show how they count can be a simple eye-opening teaching moment.

2. My high school Latin teacher posted a sign under the clock which read, "Time will pass. Will you?"

3. Paul Watzlawick, Janet Helmick Beavin, and Don D. Jackson, *Pragmatics of Human Communication: A Study of Interactional Patterns, Pathologies and Paradoxes* (New York: W.W. Norton, 1967), 62-63.

4. Watzlawick, et. al., *Pragmatics,* 63.

5. Watzlawick, et. al., *Pragmatics,* 63.

"The brain, being analog, is able to grasp images so much better. The brain is just designed for comparing images and some patterns—patterns in space and patterns in time—which we do amazingly well. Computers can do it, too, but not in anything like the same kind of flexibility."

—Freeman Dyson

CHAPTER NINE

It Goes Without Saying: Context

Beginning in the late 1940s, the West's best known "China watcher" was AP journalist, John Roderick, a trusted voice from China when few Western journalists had his access. Roderick sometimes asked his Chinese assistant to sit atop a step ladder and read aloud Roderick's words so that Roderick could honestly report "according to a highly placed Chinese source . . ."
—*Holloway Brown*

If you hit a wrong note, it's the next note
that determines if it's good or bad.
—*Miles Davis*

Nothing means anything without context.
—*E. T. Hall*

"The most consequential laugh in American history" it has been called: "I know enough to turn you inside out, old gal, you sockdologizing old man-trap!" If you don't find it knee-slapping hilarious, I guess you had to be there. Or maybe we just lack the right context of time, place, and occasion, all significant as part of much that carries meaning in our communication. When: April 14, 1865, five days after the end of the Civil War, the bloodiest war in US history. Where and on what occasion: Washington, DC, Ford's Theatre; at a performance of a then-popular comedy, *Our American Cousin.*

Most famously in attendance were two men, President Abraham Lincoln, and in the shadows, John Wilkes Booth, a well-known actor but not on stage that night. Booth, a Southerner whose loyalty was with the newly defeated Confederate Army knew the play well, so well that he also knew the exact moment when the audience's laughter would be the loudest, loud enough to conceal the sound of his gunshot that would kill the president.[1]

Most people in the US know that Abraham Lincoln was assassinated while he was attending a play, but few even imagined there was a calculated moment that Booth chose to fire that fatal shot. Schooling provides us little context for what we'll remember as historical facts. Some facts we learn because we think we may be tested in school; and sometimes later re-tested on quiz shows that reward knowing such facts, part of what some called "cultural literacy."

The evening news rarely allows time to provide much context that often is crucial for a more nuanced and accurate understanding. The images presented suggest a context which may be misleading. Sometimes footage from unrelated reports may be used to seemingly illustrate the point of what is purported to be a news story. During the "Japan-bashing era" in the US, there was a Peter Jennings broadcast with a piece questioning whether Japanese could be trusted when they say they are sorry. The story equated bowing to another person as meaning "I'm sorry," and their visuals included a scene of the players on competing little league teams bowing to each other, clerks in a department store after concluding their morning meeting bowing to each other, and a scene of two families at a wedding bowing to each other, and the narrator says "they all are saying 'I'm sorry.'" Japanese who observed the broadcast were dismayed.

Print media can provide more information and a broader context but to a much smaller audience. Hall saw the mass media pressure to be the first to present "breaking news," well aware of a decreasing public attention span, as failing to provide crucial contexts in their reporting. In a medium where time is money, a cost-benefit analysis may determine if the benefit is worth the time needed to present the context that gives greater clarity and depth to "the news."

Though he didn't talk or write about humor, Hall's attention to cultural context in communication is exemplified in what makes us laugh. We even say, "I died laughing"—hyperbolic, which is characteristic of much of US speech, though literally true for Mr. Lincoln that night. What makes us laugh, especially in the moment when we are with friends, the context of that time and place and who is there and what they know and believe, and much more, makes something really funny that usually disappears when recounting that moment to someone who was not there. "You had to be there," we might say. And that is at the heart of Hall's treatment of context. Some things require prior knowledge to be understandable, and these context-dependent messages he characterized as relatively "high context." Those that presumably require little or no such background to understand what was intended he characterized as relatively "low context."

Not all humor requires much contextual knowledge: "I was an hour late to arrive at work, and my boss asked why? I explained that I fell down the stairs. He told me, 'It shouldn't take an hour to fall down the stairs.'" That may translate as funny across languages and communities. I suppose part of the context is how one feels about bosses. Change the characters and their relationship and the reaction will be different. The humor on late night talk shows on television often requires the audience and viewers to recognize cultural and political references. To anyone unfamiliar with current social or political topics, the jokes can be baffling, though for one trying to understand the local culture at the moment it may offer a glimpse at what people talk about and how they feel about it, and even clues about "cultural values."

Much humor requires no words. Though most *The New Yorker* cartoons are very context-dependent, many by the magazine's most famous cartoonists, like Charles Addams, required neither caption nor social context to make us smile.

There is a theory that our laugh expresses the delight we feel when we make a connection, when we "get it." Arthur Koestler wrote about similarities across the delights of sudden discovery, creativity,  and humor: The "Ah! Ah hah! Ah, ha ha ha!" that friend Muneo Yoshikawa brought to the theme of intercultural discovery.[2] Neuroscientists may already have mapped this in the brain. *Ah hah!*

Staying with humor a bit more, we know that spontaneity is important; it's what we mean by "wit," and why we love "the perfect reply" that one-ups an annoying person. A popular magazine used to include in each issue something called "The Perfect Squelch" that offered smart replies to an annoying person. Readers would admire the perfect thing said at the perfect moment and think "I wish I had said that."

A narrative joke ("X, Y, Z, walked into a bar . . . ") when well told can be funny; that's why we retell jokes. It is said that the only "old joke" is one you've heard before, since having already heard it changes how you hear it. Sometimes even if we have heard that joke before we may still feel obliged to laugh—because it's said by a boss or spouse or best friend—but that laugh isn't the same.[3]

When "Not Getting It" Gets Serious

But . . . if you don't "get" the joke that everyone else finds hilarious, how do you feel? Especially if you're with close friends who notice that you're the only one who doesn't get it? Easy to pass judgment among friends; someone who is always a little slow to catch on, but you hope they don't think that about you. Imagine that you grew up abroad, and English (or any host language where you now live) is not your first language. Imagine you are an "international student" who with great effort and patience excels in your classes that demand lots of reading and writing in your non-native language. Maybe you receive better grades than many of your friends who are unburdened by working in a foreign language. And then one night at a party something is said that everyone else laughs at except you. At that moment the laughter reminds you that you aren't at home, and maybe you're not as smart as you thought you were. You doubt yourself and maybe feel a little more distant from those friends.

Wen Duan investigated this experience that resonated with her, an international student from China, and with many international students she interviewed, especially those who were often complimented for their near-native speaking ability and even regarded as among the best students in their class.[4] Ms. Duan fits that description, I can affirm. She also has a wicked sharp sense of humor. If you met her, you would assume she grew up in the US. And that's the problem.

Wen's research reveals that not getting the joke can be unsettling. It's not so much about that joke, it's the twinge of feeling distanced from the people who felt so close a moment before. A friend might come to the rescue to explain what was funny, but at that moment it can exacerbate the discomfort, even though it may help to understand why it was funny to others, and maybe then, a delayed laugh. But a joke explained is no longer a joke. One can fake it and laugh along with the others to help save face, but Wen's research shows that the little trauma of that moment can linger. You may doubt your competence in the language you worked so hard to learn, even though the problem is not about understanding the words.

A basic tenant of a theory of interpersonal communication is it always involves both the message content part and also the relationship part. Wen's research reminds us that context both *makes meaning* and in Hall's insight, knowing and assuming others know, *distinguishes insider from outsider*. Hall's application of context is about the basic coordinates in the field of communication: message content and the relationship between the people involved. This is part of why Hall believed that it was nearly impossible for people who grew up in different cultural environments—not just national, but also generational, gender, racial, ethnic, and across all those categories inventoried as "diversity"—to fully understand one another.

What if the person who doesn't get an intended joke is an internationally distinguished guest appearing on national television? An awkward moment. Embarrassing. We are likely to sympathize with the one who doesn't understand the contextual part, and now the joke is on the person who was trying to be funny. (Is there a German word for that mix of emotions that make us cringe, feel some sympathy, but also laugh at that failure?) One morning, the host of Australia's "Today" show, painfully realized that when he tried to tell a joke to his very special guest, the Dalai Lama. It was immediately apparent to millions of viewers that this spiritual leader who speaks many languages and openly shows he has a good sense of humor didn't know an idiom used at pizza shops, "make me one with everything," nor imagined that it might be linked to a cliché about Buddhism. Embarrassing and painful to watch, so you may want to.[5]

Another source of humor is at the expense of someone who "doesn't get it," which is a familiar part of dramas that let the audience know the context that a main character doesn't know, and so his or her otherwise innocuous words are heard by the audience differently than the character intended. Sometimes we know *he's lying*, or her words are double-entendres. Nothing means anything without context, and so it is also true that nothing is funny without context.

What's your favorite color? What's your favorite food? Such questions Hall thought were nonsensical. Favorite color for what? My car? My slacks? My bedroom walls? Favorite food? What season, what time of day, what occasion, what mood?

Experience has taught many people who, through experiences of prejudice or assumptions based in ignorance, are ill-prepared in new encounters and sometimes deploy behavior that changes the context in how they are perceived. A generation ago a friend told me that, at a party, he would introduce his wife, "this is my friend and lover" because if he said "this is my wife" she would get a perfunctory greeting and never really be introduced.[6]

In Japan I knew students, Japanese by citizenship and appearance, who had grown up abroad because a parent's employer had posted them overseas. Returning to their "home land," the young people didn't know all the things that others of their generation assumed they would. One woman told me she would intentionally speak Japanese in an exaggerated foreign accent with clumsy grammar as a warning: don't treat me like I grew up here. In the 1970s, Japan established new schools designed to provide a solid education for the "returnees" and help reintegrate them into the society. A risk of linguistic fluency in a non-native language is that others may assume you know more than you do. Conversely, in the US, second-, third-, or fourth-generation whose families, generations ago, came from Asia, "the Middle East," Latin America may be asked by a stranger, "but where are you *really* from?" Indigenous people, descended from people whose ancestors have been on this land for thousands of years, have been told by white racists, "go back to where you came from." There are stereotypes of what "an American" should look like, but in our multicultural and multiracial world, people across the globe may experience this.

"Context" in Context

"Context" was the term Hall chose for implicit information that *everybody around here knows,* and therefore doesn't need to be put into words. "*Around here*" might be the family, the neighborhood or the nation, the organization or one's generation. It is also a tacit distinction between insiders and outsiders that was part of the original definition of ethnocentrism, though benign in Hall's attention to context.[7]

When what is said assumes much that goes without saying, Hall characterized as "high context," and where a shared context can't be assumed, is "low context." Hall presented this high/low context as a range of possibilities, but in its popular usage, that continuum devolved into a dichotomy: "low context," "high context," like a thermometer that registers only *hot* or *cold.* Even Hall came to speak in contrastive terms instead of his original gradient metaphor. Dichotomies run deep in our human condition.

As theory and metaphor, few of Hall's conceptual models created such interest or inspired more to apply this perspective so widely, and often too casually, to intercultural situations than this notion of "context," introduced the year he retired.[8] It is both simple yet more complex than in its popular applications. For researchers, Hall's "high context/low context" theme seems one that can be widely applied, but it also runs the risk of "the law of the instrument": give a child a hammer and everything looks like it needs pounding.

The gist of Hall's context model is about the relative importance of the literal meaning of words in communication to convey a message compared with all the contextual considerations that, to coin a phrase, goes without saying. When words expressed are intended to be taken at face value, without regard to who and where and how they are expressed, nor is a shared social background needed to get the message: these are all relatively "low context." Low context puts the burden on words to make the intended meaning clear. In a simple communication model, the burden is on "the sender." High-context messages put the burden of understanding on "the receiver," listener, audience, reader, because "you'll know what I mean" without spelling it out.

Road signage (**STOP**), the words that lawyers are paid to write in contracts to minimize ambiguity and prevent mis-construal, and maybe sometimes "fool-proof" recipes, are all examples of relatively low-context messages. Preparing a dish just like grandma used to make probably requires some context beyond the fading words she wrote on a note for the preparation, and the context of memories almost certainly affects how it tastes to those who remember grandma's finest. Sometimes the proof of the pudding is in the memory. "User friendly" instructions are aspirational examples of "low context"–best served to guests with the words "I've never made this before . . ." At the other end of that continuum, where words said or written may be just a part and sometimes the least important part of what carries meaning, he called "high(er) context."

An International Incident in Contexts

A major international incident involving the governments of the United States and Japan is remembered decades after it occurred. The incident and its aftermath were one of the top stories of 2001; it hastened the resignation of the Japanese Prime Minister, and provoked an apology from the US President. In the US it came to serve as a case study in training US naval officers. Professor Tomoko Masumoto analyzes the "*Ehime Maru* Incident."[9]

On October 9, 2001, in international waters off Hawaii, a Japanese high school training vessel for students studying fishing, the *Ehime Maru*, was struck from below by the USS Greeneville, a US nuclear submarine on which the captain, Scott Waddle, was demonstrating to guests on board how quickly the sub could rise from the depths of the sea to the surface. Nine people aboard the training ship died, four of the high school students and five of their teachers. Newspaper accounts reported the incident differently—initial US reports said the ship was a Japanese trawler, for example, instead of a high school training vessel. US newspaper reports centered on the vessels and the resulting loss of life. Japanese emphasis was on the people, especially many who were young men whose faces and stories appeared in newspapers and on television daily. The US press used the word "victims," while the Japanese reports used the expression *"yukue fumei sha"* (missing people). "In Japan words equivalent to 'dead,' 'presumed dead,' 'bodies,' are avoided until the evidence of the death is unmistakable. . . in Japanese culture the belief that words convey spiritual power (*kotodama*) is widespread and that saying something can cause it to happen. Tempting fate." This is in contrast to regarding words as simply referents or labels (*kotoage*).

This incident brought up memories of an incident twenty years earlier when a Japanese cargo ship, also from the prefecture of Ehime, collided with another US nuclear submarine, killing the Japanese captain and a crew member. At that time, no nuclear vessels were permitted in Japan, but covertly both governments approved such visits. Fearing exposing the breach of the agreement, the submarine quickly left the scene before rescue ships could arrive. Now, this *Ehime Maru* incident was interpreted as showing that the US had learned nothing from twenty years earlier.

Apologies were issued by the US ambassador to Japan and by President Bush, but the senator from Ehime prefecture, on behalf of the families whose sons and husbands were missing, requested a personal apology from Captain Waddle. The US responded: "Waddle had a constitutional right to remain silent on matters in which he might be legally liable or that could jeopardize him in court."

"In Japan after an accident occurs, there is a greater assumption of some culpability by both parties." Masumoto points out that Japanese perceive the US as a litigious society, and the question of fault should be argued in a court of law. Japanese who plan to drive in the US are warned that if they are in a traffic accident they should not apologize. "In Japan when there is a conflict, there is usually the expectation of offering an immediate apology, at least at a social level. Conversely there is also strong aversion to appear to avoid expressing responsibility."

Through his lawyer Captain Waddle issued a written statement in which he expressed " . . . my most sincere regret . . . no words can adequately express my condolences." *The Washington Post* wrote that "his apology was received by many Japanese as 'too little, too late.'" Moreover, the letters to the families were typed and appeared to be all the same. Masumoto notes that, "Even in modern Japan, it is still considered to be both more polite and an expression of sincerity when people write a personal letter by hand." Later at the military court of inquiry, Waddle was seen going into the court, holding hands with his wife that was also interpreted by many in Japan as showing a lack of seriousness.

Hall's concept of "low context" is that words alone carry the bulk of a message. Not so in a famously "high context" culture like Japan. Subsequently, Navy Captain Scott Waddle was reprimanded and allowed to retire with full rank and pension.

Hall's idea of "context" in everyday communication includes the location and timing, the situation or occasion, who is present and their relationship history, and more. Janet Bennett, a dear friend of half a century and one whose work has had an inestimable influence, called this "wide scanning" rather than the baffling term "high context," and emphasized the importance of what and how much we may notice in everyday encounters. In binary times, Janet was not the first to say that generally women take note of and remember particulars of a first meeting or social occasion more than most men: the time and place of an event, maybe what music was playing, and in detail how the people she met appeared, how they are dressed, hair style, and more—the same care she goes through when getting prepared for the occasion. An intimate friend or partner who remembers an anniversary of a special time and in a high-context way shows that, can send a message beyond words. The half-joking, or maybe quarter-joking, stereotype that men claim is "women remember *everything!*" This generalization may have a neurological basis, as books such as *The Female Brain* argue, but not a few neuroscientists cast doubt that brains differ significantly across genders.[10] A more likely explanation is the effect of generations of women being socially disadvantaged and therefore learning to pay attention to a wide variety of contextual considerations—including the apparent mood and sobriety of those with power—for the sake of sheer survival.

Of friends and intimate partners, we say they can finish each other's sentences. Every family, clan, tribe, club, school, business, political or professional organization: each such "culture," small or large, has its history and memory that is implicit or can be alluded to, truly "re-called," without prompting nor need to explain. It takes time to develop this kind of contextual knowledge, but once acquired this makes communication easier and faster than with someone needing "what everyone else here" already knows.

This was an important part of his contextual theory that seems to have been largely ignored and that may become even more important as the increased rapidity of change in knowledge or skills that are valued, and sociological changes that run counter to traditional values of experience and seniority. *A word to the wise is efficient.*[11]

Nuptial Contexts: Before You say "I Do," First Sign Here

A conventional wedding vow, whatever the form—"to love, honor, and trust . . . till death do us part"—is a formal, if aspirational, pledge in many Western weddings. The wedding bond lies less on those words exchanged but with rings exchanged and witnesses representing a community who affirm and celebrate the nuptials. In the relatively brief history of romantic marriage, there is also an external pressure on the couple to commit to "what God hath made, let no one make asunder," and risk being shamed or even shunned by the community.

These were an essential "context" to vouchsafe what transpires, not mere formalities or favors to special friends. They are called "witnesses" for a reason, what are sometimes called "external controls," like shame in contrast to guilt, which is internalized.[12]

A little girl may dream of that perfect day when she'll wear that perfect gown, celebrating in that picture-perfect place, with her best friends and well-behaved family present as witnesses celebrating that magical moment when she says, "I do." (It may be easier to imagine the day and dress.) Compare these ritual vows on that occasion with the words of a prenuptial agreement, a legal contract. No witnesses or community need be present when that legally binding "I do" is signed, just dispassionate lawyers, relatively "low context," each word carefully chosen to avoid ambiguity, and that lawyers might later invoke if it comes to that. A modern Cinderella who meets her handsome prince, and the glass slipper fits! And as he proposes, the modern Cinderella says, "Yes, but first, let's sign this pre-nuptial agreement." And the couple lives happily for some time.

Between friends, a promise or agreement sealed with a handshake or saying "you have my word on it" is only as strong as the trust of the person promising, bonded in the relationship. "A promise made is a debt unpaid" is the aphorism. A promise legally drawn and with a witness present, signed, is something else.

Researchers today are required to ask people participating in some studies to sign "release forms" before joining a conversation to talk about their experiences, and other situations in which "hard data" is required, and to protect against potential legal troubles. That changes what might have been a friendly discussion into a different and often distancing relationship. People whose friendships, even affections, are about shared experience, reputations, and trust feel re-defined in a way that may be baffling, insulting.

Susan Carter, who worked for decades with an Indigenous-run non-profit organization serving Indigenous communities, notes the clash between the contextual expectations in the communities and those of funding agencies.[13] She points out "that the protections and protocols put in place by government funders to safeguard the people who are the subject of research, are themselves full of low-context legal language, often fostering increased mistrust, especially in Indigenous communities that have experienced past abuses in the name of research."[14] Carter also reflects on how our family and neighborhood experience influences our adaptability in working and feeling comfortable across cultures that differ in the kinds of context that an outsider must respect: knowing what one can't and shouldn't know, as well as one's own contextual assumptions.

Maybe, she reflects, "almost everyone, regardless of culture, experiences high context communication within the family setting, whereas only some people from some cultures also go on to develop the need for low context communication as they move beyond their families of origin." She adds, "One of the hardest things for me to learn (among many hard things) about respectful communication in Native American communities was the importance of deep listening and not interrupting and allowing for silence. These forms were not present in my Italian American family of origin where there was always lots of simultaneous conversations, interrupting and finishing each other's sentences."[15] In other words, "high-context communication" is our universal experience, a part of our enculturation. Learning a term like "high context" is like Moliere's character in *Le Bourgeois gentilhomme*, who learns the word "prose" and is thrilled to discover "I've been speaking prose all my life!"

Indeed, a part of maturing is discovering that not everyone thinks like me, or "us," and the ability to try to sense how someone else might see things. Just growing up, even or especially, child's play that involves role-taking—"this time, you be the mommy/teacher/customer. . . ."—whatever the improvised drama is, is crucial. For many, the first intercultural experiences, some from the earliest childhood, some as a young adult, are life-changing, ideally for the better but sometimes for the worse. Educators have for a long time assumed that students develop interculturally, more or less automatically, by studying in a country different from their own. However, a large and growing body of quantitative research strongly suggests that students don't develop merely through being exposed to, or even through being "immersed" in, different surroundings; instead, they develop to the extent that educators proactively intervene in their learning.[16]

Or consider the driver from out of town who stops and asks directions to some address. There is usually a mix of specific, low-context advice, after checking to see if the visitor knows any points of reference. But if the driver in unfamiliar territory trusts the GPS guidance, which is about as "low context" as you can get, there will be a string of successive commands: *"Continue for 30 feet/10 meters, then turn right . . . ."* If you follow the directions from the disembodied human-sounding voice of one who's never traveled the route you are asking about, you will arrive at your destination. Probably. High-context directions might be a local person telling the clueless driver to "keep going on this road, then turn left when you pass where the Trujillos used to live."

Directions given personally are usually analog, often with gestures and tone of voice, and facial expressions that hint at how close or far the destination, and sometimes even hinting at "but why do you want to go *there?*" The GPS is digital, precise, authoritative and without affect.

Rina Swentzell told Hall about growing up in Santa Clara Pueblo, New Mexico, and how her grandmother sometimes would make "a bear gesture" with her lips to tell Rina where to look for, say, the broom that grandmother asked her to bring. As a child, Swentzell learned to pay attention to those gestures. Words, she points out, were seen as a kind of aggression. Rina contrasted that with her husband, a German-American philosophy professor who sometimes became irritated when Rina didn't use just the "right words," meaning she wasn't being "precise." "It caused a lot of tension sometimes," Rina said, "as if he thought I just wasn't very bright."

Being indirect, "if you get my drift," is often an indicator of a high-context message, saying something without actually *saying* it, but that mustn't be confused with what is simply vague. Nor should low context be confused with the quantity of words expressed because in some contexts the sheer volume of words is part of the message; saying too few will disappoint or maybe convey a different message. No comment.

As an example of low-context requirements, Hall points out that in a court of law a defendant may be told: "Answer the question: 'Yes' or 'No'?" To respond "but . . ." wanting to add relevant context, the defendant will be ordered "just answer the question." Attorneys learn to ask only questions for which they can anticipate the answer, thus framing the questions (contexting them) to the client's advantage and constraining a witness from re-framing (re-contexting). "Birds fly south in the November, true or false?" As a generalization, "true," if asked in New York, but "false" if asked in Buenos Aires. One of the values of diversity is the opportunity to appreciate how different life experiences call attention to and offer the invitation to expand one's appreciation of contexts. Or, to put it more simply, to become less narrow-minded.

Information that everybody within one community knows may not be known to others, common to intercultural situations, can pose a challenge. Mexicans may assume their neighbors in that colossus to the north have heard of "the Mexican Revolution," and that everyone knows it played out in the early part of the twentieth century. But their northern neighbors are likely to confuse the Mexican Revolution with the fight for their independence from Spain that occurred a century earlier because in the US "the Revolutionary War" was about independence from their colonizer. Pointing that out in conversation or in a speech or article risks "talking down" to some people, while attempting to inform the others. "As I assume you know . . ." might be a hedge that reduces the risk of saying too little or too much, at least in some contexts. But not if the audience are teachers of Mexican history. Or Mexicans.

Deborah Tannen's work has demonstrated this so very clearly; little wonder that her books, beginning with *You Just Don't Understand,* have been so helpful to wives and husbands, mothers and daughters, and other relationships she has analyzed. People who are in close relationships are often puzzled by why they seem not to understand each other when they know each other so well. In many cases, it is the man who hears and interprets with a "lower context" frame than the woman, as when a wife or partner returns home and talks about her difficult day at work, and the man replies with a five-point plan to deal with the problem, when at the moment what she hoped for was a show of empathy, sympathy, and a hug.

Asking Questions

Sometimes contextual considerations are conscious, even calculated, as in some diplomatic communication, but most are just part of what anthropologist Clifford Geertz's called "local knowledge," literally, *common* sense that people who are not "local" may not assume.[17]

When to ask questions and when not to ask questions is complicated. Let's say it depends on context. Sometimes not to ask questions is more problematic. A new hire in Japan is expected to ask questions during their first year, but then expected to internalize what they learned. Some newly arrived "interns" from the US, with no previous experience with the company or even in Japanese organizational culture, said that they avoided asking questions for fear that it will make them seem less qualified than how they hoped to be perceived.

When doing ethnographic field work in a small town in northern New Mexico, Gladys Pilz says that Hall, who directed her doctoral research, told her to not ask questions of the people in the community where she lived and which was the subject of her ethnographic research because that would remind them to treat her as an outsider. (An irony of Hall's insights is that his work, as with all culture-specific information, brings what would have been "high context" to a "low context" merely by explaining it in words.)

Arie and Gladys Pilz were business partners with Susan Carter and all were good friends with Ned. Here Arie reflects on their experience working together in Native American communities:

> All our applied work was informed by and often directly influenced by conversations with Ned. He was generous with his advice and equally candid. His eyes would glaze over and he would ask for a cup of tea when he didn't think much of what I thought was a mind-blowing new insight. ⸬
>
> When Gladys and I began our work as paid/applied ethnographers/consultants, the government OSAP (Office of Substance Abuse Prevention) was actively seeking to expand programming into Native American communities. The project for our first client, located in Gallup, New Mexico, and serving both Navajo and Zuni middle-school students, was based on the notion that building resilience through positive experiential activities (mostly in the natural settings) could have a lasting impact and reduce substance use and other risk-taking activities. This notion in and of itself was unique for Native American communities that were deeply invested in the 12-Step treatment approach, which I always believed was palatable to missionaries because of its emphasis on Western religious beliefs. The idea of prevention was still fairly new, and almost all monies were funneled into the law enforcement-based DARE and "Just Say No" (an adaption of "Scared Straight," for children) programs.

When our client took a leap of faith and hired Gladys first (a former student had written a grant and she was the only evaluator he knew), she (then she and I) naively stumbled into a world where statistics, surveys, and objective "numbers" were the only data valued by federal funders. We brought our ethnographic toolchest and did what we did—spent months "mucking around"— observing, participating in every activity and community event we were invited to visit, and conducting informal focus groups with anyone who was willing to chat with us.

As news spread that "as white people go," Gladys and Arie seemed to be all right, we were invited to chat with some elders and the Native gatekeepers (college educated) locals whose job it was to ensure that white people in white coats with clipboard and surveys were watched closely.

At our first meeting with an "important" delegate from XXXX (we still keep our sources confidential) a very refined gentleman wearing Western garb, rose up from behind his desk, and screamed at us at the top of his lungs that, "You will NEVER give a survey to a child in my community NEVER," and dismissed us with a wave of his arm. Gladys and I had never mentioned surveys in that meeting . . . .

A note—we later became close friends and allies of this same gentleman, and he helped us navigate within his community for many years. Because he suddenly came to trust our methods and academic background? No, because his wife and I did a three-day camp with middle school students, and "she liked the way I was" with them. (I had been teaching in a high school where 75% of our students were from New Mexico pueblos for eight years before this career change.)

The project officer (PO) from OSAP arrived from Washington, DC, for her first visit, and we were invited to meet her and the Native director of the program. When we walked into the office, the two of them were face-to-face—inches apart, arguing intensely—although they had only met that morning. The PO, wearing a dark blue pants suit with every hair in place and clutching her expensive leather briefcase like it would somehow protect her from the ideas she was hearing, was one of the most intense people I had ever met (and I'm a former street kid from a tough neighborhood in New York—not easily intimidated). Having an audience of professional strangers ended the argument that instead turned into a long lecture regarding the power of quantitative evaluation and the weaknesses of the qualitative paradigm. Once again, raised voices and hot tempers circling around federal, bureaucratic requirements, and the "intergenerational trauma" that flares whenever the Feds want to "do something" to Native/sovereign entities.

I can't tell you how often we heard from our PO's and their fancy beltway consultants, "It's just surveys—what's the big deal?" So naïve—like saying, "We're just taking your children to boarding school. What's the big deal?"

But I digress . . . Gladys and I attended the first outdoor experiential camp conducted by this first Native client and wrote an in-depth, but totally qualitative report, which was quickly sent off to Washington. Ned read and enjoyed it immensely—but enjoyed the reaction from DC even more.

The angry woman in the blue suit picked up the phone and called Gladys breathless, "This is amazing! I felt like I was there. I love this. What is it?"

(Very long story short, this PO became a convert to ethnography, organized and led a group of all the OSAP Native grantees, at least 20, and ended up "going to the mat" to protect the importance of ethnography for Native communities until she was fired when the quants took over and forced her out.)

Ned always told stories about how the Farm Bureaus in rural areas never tried to force new ideas on farmers and ranchers. They brought the ideas and created demonstration sites where locals could come, try, and adopt if they wished.

So it was with Fieldworks and Mind Over Matter (Susan's biz name). Although we were required to have contracts, we told our Native clients that if at any time the relationship was not win/win, we would be happy to move on. We presented our methods, did our work very respectfully, and listened carefully. In 20 years, Gladys and I never printed a brochure, made a pitch, or advertised. Trust in Native communities was contagious and had to be earned; Gladys, Susan, and Arie's reputations were shared at conventions and through word of mouth. Again, I never believed that we were loved—but were respected as white people who were not afraid to get dirty, go camping, sit quietly, and spend all the time (sometimes years) required to squeeze an understanding of the contexts in which we worked.

So how then did the three of us end up working in eight-to-ten Native communities around the West, in Alaska, and Hawaii? I speak only for myself when I list:

We saw our job as acting as liaisons and often buffers between our Native clients and the Federal, state, or foundation granting agencies. We tried to make the sometimes-onerous quantitative requirements that came with grant money palatable enough so that Native communities could accept it, and carry out innovative programming for their children.

We never stopped telling ethnographic stories that resonated with our clients, the parents of the participants, and, in many cases, the elders who were the true decision makers in these communities.

Not to say that our stories were always positive or complimentary because all three of us considered the children to be our real clients and thus we sometimes were speakers of truth to power. And yes, we were fired a few times if clients did not want to hear that their programs (based on our etic [outsider] observations) were less than stellar or even counter-productive.

Finally, without exception, we knew we were being offered a unique and rare opportunity to know people and experience cultures, which was a gift. We received more than we gave.

Situational Contexts

In *The Silent Language*, Hall called *situations* "culture's building blocks." That is, as we go through life, we acquire an appreciation that different occasions require different responses. Such shared and internalized knowledge is in the realm of "context," and when we are in what we recognize as a familiar situation, we have a general idea of what is appropriate and what is not. A central part of internalized culture is identifying and distinguishing among "situations."

Among acquaintances, greetings and leave-taking at social gatherings are situations that call for formulaic words appropriate for such occasions. When by chance people who know each other happen to meet some may exchange, "How are you?" with some version of "Fine, thanks," in response. But that same context across cultures does not call for the same words. Some of my European friends tell me how upset they felt when answering in some greater detail while the American would already be walking away as if she or he didn't really care. When first in Japan I was puzzled by neighbors passing on the street would ask me, "Where are you going?" and as I tried to answer I was thinking "it's none of your business." Later I learned that the appropriate answer is *"chotto soko made"* (just over there), like saying *"Fine, thank you,"* when someone asks, *"How are you?"* Guests leaving a party may thank the host and say, "We had a wonderful time," words that may or may not represent their actual feelings, but are typical of what one says when leaving a party. In

Mexico, I'm told that some North Americans will leave the party without saying goodbye to the hosts. In contrast, Mexicans will say goodbye but not leave.

When People Take Note of the Contexts of Place and Time

In 1980, then-candidate for president, Ronald Reagan, launched his campaign seven miles from Philadelphia, Mississippi, where, in 1964, three civil rights workers, Michael Schwerner, James Chaney, and Andrew Goodman, who had come to Mississippi to help register Black voters, were murdered by white supremacists. The context of place Reagan chose to begin his campaign said more than any of Reagan's words that day, at least for those who were very aware of the significance of Philadelphia, Mississippi.

Years later, as president, the choice of place as context caused an international uproar when Reagan planned to speak on the 40th anniversary of the end of the Second World War at Bitburg, near the German border with Luxembourg, a site that German President Helmut Kohl suggested. But that cemetery was also the burial site of many former Waffen-SS officers, designated war criminals in the Nuremburg trials. Holocaust survivor and author Elie Wiesel spoke out to President Reagan at a ceremony at the White House asking him not to go there: "I . . . implore you to find another way, another site. That place, Mr. President, is not your place." The significance of a particular place or time or timing speaks volumes to those aware of its cultural significance, and yet passes unrecognized to those who do not share the same memories or associations.

It's easy to predict stories that will appear in print and broadcast news days in advance of particular dates that are anniversaries of famous and infamous events. In the US, these include July 4, September 11, December 7, and Jan. 6. Elsewhere these are just dates on the calendar. August 6 in the US is rarely given attention, but in Japan it is marked by a moment of silence each year, on the anniversary of the first atomic bomb that exploded over Hiroshima. In Israel, on Yom HaShoah (Holocaust Remembrance Day) all traffic comes to a stop for 60 seconds and people step out of their cars for a moment of silence. Dates are a powerful context and few are broadly shared across cultures, and within a society they may be the context for shifting meanings, such as October 12 in Mexico, *Día de la Raza* celebrating the fusion of Indigenous and European antecedents, "racial mixing" that was illegal in parts of the US until the mid-twentieth century; to the north the day is contested, with many celebrating "Columbus Day," while for others it marks the start of a genocide.[18] Contexts, not "context."

Dates, and remembering them in personal relationships, mean more than words exchanged. A birthday or anniversary or other personally important date holds meanings that honor a relationship. In personal relationships, simply remembering is often the most meaningful gift.

Relationship as Context

Teachers who come to Asia from abroad are often not sure what to make of their students who don't raise their hands to answer questions asked to the whole class. The easiest questions can sound like the most challenging; imagine hearing an apparently simple question and assuming that the teacher must have some deeper meaning for asking that, while the teacher's intent might be just to get some interaction going. Japanese students, generally, are likely to consider more "context" than comparable students in the US: Who am I in this class? Who is older and should speak first? Who might know more about this? Why is the teacher asking this question? Also, there is greater "power distance" between teacher and student in Japan than in the US, and more sensitivity to age differences among students, though less than in Korea.[19] And "individualism" that also favors "lower context" because there's less of an assumption of the value of the group as a whole, unless the occasion is about the whole. Even the idea that a "yes" means "yes" and a "no" means "no" depends on context. Keiko Ueda identified sixteen ways Japanese can avoid saying "no," including saying "yes." She found that business people had the broadest repertoire, while college students were the least adroit.[20]

Where interdependence or group identity is valued, we should expect higher-context communication. The group provides the shared experience; indeed, it is the shared experience that creates the group identity. But there are contexts within contexts. Within a Japanese family or even a small company there may be a directness that is not heard in middle-class families or companies in the US. And there are situations that foster this directness: at a party over alcoholic drinks words may be said directly, followed later by apologies. Better to beg forgiveness than to ask permission.

Where there is a greater individualistic or independent orientation, low-context communication would be expected. Similarly, hierarchical values favor more high-context sensitivity: the who or the role may carry more significance than the particular words expressed. We should expect cultural values that favor tradition, looking to precedents to guide future behavior, would be more comfortable with higher-context messages than where one's values are directed to the future with less regard for the past. Ceremony and ritual are high-context messages; one may recite or sing words that one doesn't even understand, for their personal meaning is that the person has always recited or sung those words on that particular occasion.[21]

Hall broadly described the US, Canada, the UK, and other former British colonies as relatively low-context societies. Napoleon famously and dismissively called England, "a nation of shopkeepers," quoting Adam Smith, suggesting a narrow and individualistic perspective that fits with Hall's "low context" characterization. That has also been attributed to leading to a philosophy of pragmatism and a preference for inductive reasoning. Countries in northern Europe were seen similarly. Those in southern Europe, Hall identified as higher context, along with Arabic-speaking countries and Persian-speaking Iran, and most of Asia. He made no mention of sub-Saharan Africa or Latin America. One might feel uncomfortable with such broad generalizations about a notion which itself is metaphorical and imprecise because of the cultural diversity within any country. If reduced to a dichotomous high/low context system, surely most of the world is "high context."[22]

Context and Cultural Values

The concept of *"values"* is said to be one of those grand concepts, appearing in almost every subject of interest, including the natural and social sciences, the humanities, and the fine arts. "Cultural values" as a concept with which to characterize and compare societies also has a history of moving in and out of fashion. It was in fashion in the mid-twentieth century.

Notably, Hall did not write about cultural values; indeed, he was distrustful of some of the research on cultural values by his contemporaries, including the famous Harvard cultural values studies that were conducted in New Mexico. Directed by Harvard anthropologist, Clyde Kluckhohn, it is said to be the first multidisciplinary and multi-institutional research in a major social science project. The fieldwork was conducted over several summers, centered at Ramah, New Mexico, in a region of five distinct cultural communities. This was a site dear to Clyde Kluckhohn, and where his ashes would later be interred. Among several books and monographs that resulted from the research, the most comprehensive is *People of Rimrock: A Study of Five Cultures* edited by Evon Z. Vogt and Ethel M. Albert.[23] It is notable that like many of Hall's concepts, those developed in the Harvard Cultural Values Studies emerged at roughly the same time, and at locations within a half day's drive of each other. As with much of Hall's work, what began locally would become applied internationally.

Frank Waters

During a lifetime that nearly coincides with that of Hall, novelist Frank Waters wrote about traditional communities in northern New Mexico where he lived. Probably unacceptable today, but written with respect and without pretense to tell the stories that then would have been given no voice by publishers.

The author is best known is his 1942 novel, *The Man Who Killed the Deer*, that later was influential in a lawsuit that resulted in the US government "returning" the Taos tribe's sacred Blue Lake to the tribe in 1970. It was based on a true story of an incident in which a young man from the Pueblo of Taos killed a deer out of season, according to the state laws then, thereby creating an awkward and legal problem for the tribal council.

Waters says that he was aware of the person at the center of that incident, and that they sometimes would pass each other at the post office and elsewhere in Taos; they would nod, but never spoke. "In the 25 years we have known each other we never discussed the incident or the book. I am sure he knows about it."[26] Respectful of the value that Pueblo people place on their privacy for cultural survival, Waters knew not to ask questions.[27] "We just don't talk about it," Waters said. He sent a draft of his novel to the Taos tribal council who raised no objections.

Over the years, Waters said, "You learn some things here and pick up other things elsewhere, and over time, without asking, you make sense of them, knowing you might get it wrong." Waters said that some people from the Pueblo who read his novel remarked about how he seemed to know what no other outsider would know. Time, patience, observing, listening, respect.

It was as part of that research that Kluckhohn's wife and colleague, Professor Florence Kluckhohn, developed her "value orientations" model that combined traditional qualitative anthropological methods with the rising importance of quantitative data, in the sociological tradition that yielded statistical comparisons. Diverse cultural value orientations embedded in a questionnaire, presented to each of the five different populations, could be compared statistically. Florence Kluckhohn's value orientations theory and data appeared in her 1961 book with Fred Strodtbeck, *Variations in Value Orientations*.[24] In my own US-Mexican values research in 1961, I utilized the values orientation model—expanded to fifteen value orientations and administered in Mexico City—the first time this approach was used outside of the US. In 1975, I elaborated on it in *An Introduction to Intercultural Communication*.[25]

Before E. T. Hall's Context, a Linguist's Take: Basil Bernstein

While some linguists view human language as residing within each individual, others including M. A. K. Halliday, placed language within society, regarding it as an appropriate part of the field of sociology. As my friend and former colleague, linguist John Maher told me, "Chomsky located language in genetics. The body. Our (sacred) genetic heritage. Just like Plato and Descartes explained. Halliday (socialist and sociological) located language in society, social change, processes, class, occupation, etc. Both are right, I assume."

Another British sociologist and linguist, Basil Bernstein, is more in the Halliday tradition. Probably his most famous contribution to our ways of looking at communication describes something very much like Hall's notion of higher context and lower context, which Hall notes in *Beyond Culture*. To me, Bernstein's work is a clear demonstration of Hall's "culture as communication." Moreover, Bernstein further acknowledges the influence of Whorfian linguistic relativity, moving beyond the influence of verbal language to the broader view of communication habits as influencing thought and behavior.[28]

Bernstein studied "family talk" in two distinct families in class-conscious England, comparing speech patterns in "working class" and "middle class" families. Working class ("blue collar") families at that time were characterized by a father whose work was usually physical labor as part of a group (construction, for example), with relatively little authority at work by himself, but considerably more collectively, as part of a labor union. At home, that father, the breadwinner, could exercise authority he didn't have at work. The typical family included several children, with the older children having responsibility for socializing their younger brothers and sisters. Solidarity is hierarchical. Roles were largely ascribed by age ("You're too old for that!" or "Act your age!") and gender ("Boys don't cry."). If a child got into trouble outside of the neighborhood, the child would be blamed: "Why were you there, anyway?"

In middle class, "white collar" families, the father's work usually requires no heavy lifting; he is working alone, probably at a desk, in an environment of words and numbers. With fewer children at home, there was more individualized interaction with the children, more asking, "what would you like to be when you grow up?" and inquiring about a child's experiences and feelings, and less instructing and ordering. Bernstein contrasts the "we" with the individualized and independent "I."[29]

Bernstein's research reported that the vocabulary, in quantity of words and varieties of grammatical constructions in working-class families, was smaller than in middle-class family conversations. However, what was expressed nonverbally—the glance, the glare, the threat or act of physical punishment—were more present and more forceful than talk.

"Low-context" messages focus on the words that can be analyzed and judged and questioned. In "high context" messages, the speaker's qualities as a person and the personal relationship with the listener are less easily divorced from what he or she is saying, and thus the importance of indirectness and other means of avoiding the speaker's loss of face. If the words someone says can be separated from the person saying them ("lower context"), then one can interject a request for clarification without intending offense. This is separate from norms of overlapping speech—more likely in higher-context cultural relations where the overlapping is also an expression of the closeness of the relationship.

Bernstein's work received a devastating review by linguist William Labov who characterized the research as denigrating the working class. Bernstein saw his research as descriptive and not judgmental. John Maher, who is English, told me that Bernstein must have felt especially hurt because he was a socialist who identified with the working class. Bernstein did not view one pattern as superior to the other; rather, he believed that each characterization of family communication served the values and reinforced the family culture at that time. Hall mentioned Bernstein's work only as a footnote as he introduced his context theory. I took that as an afterthought when someone pointed out to him the relevance of the sociolinguistic research.

What Bernstein described in working class England fits well with what Gerry Phillipsen described in his now-classic study of communication in "Teamsterville," what Chicagoans knew as the "Back of the [stock] Yards" section of town, a blue collar, Irish-Catholic home of the then most famous mayor in the US, Richard J. Daley.[30]

Bernstein characterized the working-class family interactions as using a "restricted code," a smaller spoken vocabulary with fewer grammatical variations, compared to middle-class patterns that he called an "elaborated code," a linguistic distinction that was already in use. However, "restricted" may sound judgmental compared to "elaborated." These fit into Hall's "high context" and "low context" descriptions in some imagined Venn-diagram, but I've wondered if the different choice of terms may have influenced their initial reception.

What Bernstein identified as social class distinctions in London, Hall generalized as cultural differences with broad relevance. Hall's "high context" message is an aspect of Bernstein's "restricted codes"; low context" is similar to Bernstein's "elaborated codes" but unlike Hall, Bernstein began with the family and social culture, and in detail. Bernstein went further, arguing that the verbal patterns of talk we grow up with affects how we come to think of ourselves and how we perceive the world. He credited the work of the "linguistic relativists," Edward Sapir and his famous part-time student, Benjamin Lee Whorf, who also influenced Hall. Ironically, Whorf's educational background was the same as Bernstein's critic William Labov: chemical engineer. Bernstein's work extended ideas of linguistic relativism to a kind of "communication relativism," with interesting and provocative implications.

Rina Swentzell tells of how, as a child, she was always taught to "walk carefully, meaning literally as well as symbolically." We were taught always to be aware, she said: "what are the birds saying right now, what are the clouds saying . . ."—a keen sensitivity to the natural environment as well as the social. In a pioneering book on intercultural communication patterns observed in his University of Illinois (Chicago) classrooms with US African American and white students, Thomas Kochman noted differences between what we might call a "low context style" of his white students in Chicago, and the Black students, whose cultural strengths and values were usually far more highly attuned to the moment, and the nonverbal signals of the moment (high context).[31] Think of the contrast between the call and response of a Black church, and the relative silence during a homily in many white congregations.

Negotiating Across Cultures, from High to Low

Moving from a relatively high-context background where words are exchanged, important as they are, they fade in importance to knowing

238 It Goes Without Saying

about personal relationships and history in order to find a place in any organization. For example, deference to relative age difference is higher in Korea than elsewhere even in East Asia, affecting how people talk with each other.

Kyoung-Ah Nam, a friend and colleague from South Korea who died just as she was receiving acclaim as a young scholar and gifted teacher, had been a news reporter at the United Nations before completing her graduate studies and entering the teaching profession. As a reporter and then as an academic, words are at the heart of her work. Coming to the US, words or their lack were at the heart of her frustration in her first job in the US. Nam credited Hall's "context" explanation for helping her understand her confusion. *"E. T. Hall saved my life!"* she told me. As a graduate student she experienced the predictable culture shock, but she said that when she joined a Los Angeles company, the shock was greater:

> I was the only non-US-American employee at our Los Angeles office at that time. I remember having constant struggles trying to figure out why I was having such a hard time adjusting to the culture there. As I come from a very strong high-context cultural background, I was communicating through context, with lots of indirect nonverbal signals rather than explicit words. This also includes my strong preference to avoid saying "No," and keep the harmony, avoiding possible conflict at any cost.
>
> We call this *nunchi* in Korean, meaning the competence to be able to understand from the context and being able to read between lines such as facial expressions, tone of the voice, body language, and observations. *It is absolutely my job as a listener to figure out what is going on* from my colleagues or boss by not asking a direct question. *Nunchi* is an essential competence in Korean society, where direct disagreement is rarely heard, and subtle messages are encouraged and expected

to be understood. It is almost impossible to maintain one's life without having *nunchi* in Korean society, and you become a bully if you don't know how to read in between the lines. At work, it is often regarded as fundamental and even more important than technical or other management skills. But with my well-trained, indirect, and subtle high-context communication style at my corporate job in Los Angeles, people perceived me as hesitant and lacking confidence.

I enjoyed my work but I remember the painful struggles I was going through without knowing what was wrong. When I first heard about the concept of high vs. low-context culture, I was speechless: That was it! . . . I felt like I was finally able to breathe. It explained so clearly why I was struggling and why my colleagues and supervisors were confused every single day. Nobody was wrong. I was just using a very far end of high-context communication style, and my colleagues and supervisors were using the far end of low-context communication style.[32]

Sometimes friends from elsewhere visit me, and on special occasions we visit my friends at the nearby Pueblo of Jemez community. We visit only when visitors are welcomed, a feast day or other days open to respectful visitors to witness the ceremonial dances. After telling friends they may not to bring a camera or cell phone or sketch pad or any such means of recording, I advise them when they are present: "Don't ask questions." Questions like, "What time is it?" or "Is there a toilet nearby?" are fine, but some culture-related questions are not. But "If I can't ask questions, how can I learn anything?" From a low-context perspective, many naïve visitors think that anything that seems not too personal should be OK to ask about. From a high-context perspective, the polite thing to do is to simply be present and observe as a guest.[33]

Context on the Brain: A Neurologist's View

Our brain may hold an analog to Hall's high/low context theme. Iain McGilchrist's massive book, *The Master and His Emissary*, adds support to much of what Hall was writing about, not just with respect to context but also to his attention to the senses. In a book acclaimed by scholars, psychologists, neurologists, and even John Cleese — yes, *that* John Cleese who told a *New York Times* interviewer that McGilchrist's book was the most impressive book he'd read in years.[34]

McGilchrist describes our asymmetrical brain hemispheres in ways that match Hall's treatment of context. Dismissing popular descriptions of right/left brain hemispheres as distinct, independent in their functions, as now it is clear that one can come to the rescue of the other if there is disruption or damage, McGilchrist goes further and deeper to describe the strength and limit of each that shape our lives. He also points out that our two- and four-foot earthly companions also have this divided brain (the divided brain is also a bird brain). Hall would have appreciated this attention beyond our species, and how this neural design serves all species.

Our right-brain hemisphere is neurologically where we experience the world, everything we sense: it is "the master" in the metaphorical title of McGilchrist's book. The "emissary" is the left hemisphere, from which we mostly "make sense" of what "the master" has sensed, by rendering sensations and feelings into abstracted, symbolic forms. In other words, the right-brain hemisphere presents the experienced world to us, and the left re-presents—or *represents* (thus acting as "the emissary")—the received sensory experience in ordered, categorical ways:

> [T]he brain has to attend to the world in two completely different ways, and in so doing to bring two completely different worlds into being. In the one, we experience—the live, complex, embodied world of individual, always unique

beings, forever in flux, a net of interdependencies, forming and reforming wholes, a world with which we are deeply connected. In the other we 'experience' our experience in a special way; a 're-presented' version of it, containing now static, separable, bounded, but essentially fragmented entities, grouped into classes, on which predictions can be based. This kind of attention isolates, fixes and makes each thing explicit by bringing it under the spotlight of attention. In doing so it renders things inert, mechanical, lifeless. But it also enables us for the first time to know, and consequently to learn and make things.[35]

McGilchrist adds, "This gives us power," hinting at the book's subtitle: *The Divided Brain and the Making of the Western World*, for the author believes that in favoring the strengths the left hemisphere offers "Western cultures," we have become imbalanced. A fellow Brit, the late Sir Kenneth Robinson in a popular (70 million views) "TED Talk" argued that we educate children "from the neck up, and slightly to one side," as "we regard our bodies as mainly a means of transportation for our heads."[36]

In an imperfect analogy to Hall's context metaphor, the brain's right hemisphere values the more extensive and complex and "big picture" context, while the left hemisphere favors low-context representations. But to read McGilchrist, after knowing Hall's ideas of context, makes it difficult not to see the fit:

> The right sees the whole before whatever it is gets broken up into parts attempting to "know" it. Its holistic processing is not based on summation of parts.[37]
>
> . . . [T]he right hemisphere sees things as a whole, before they have been digested into parts, it also sees each thing in its context, as standing in a qualifying relationship with all that surrounds it, rather than taking as a single isolated entity. Its

awareness of the world is anything but abstract. . . The right hemisphere understands from indirect contextual clues, not only from explicit statement, whereas the left hemisphere will identify by labels rather than context (e.g., identifies that it must be winter because it is 'January,' not by looking at the trees).[38]

The exploration of neuroscience and its interpreters appeared too late for Hall, but were he still alive and aware of such neurological findings and how they may affirm his observations, sans brain scans, surely Hall would have been thrilled.

McGilchrist was a professor of English at the University of Oxford before studying to become a medical doctor and then venturing further into psychiatry, and still later becoming a Fellow in neurology at Johns Hopkins University. His grounding in the humanities is apparent throughout the book where he reviews the right-brain hemisphere in a chapter titled, "The Primacy of the Right Hemisphere." McGilchrist writes in ways that may touch those whose work is dedicated to helping us to understand, and feel with and for one another:

These include empathy and inter-subjectivity as the ground of consciousness; the importance of an open, patient, attention to the world as opposed to a willful, grasping attention; the implicit or hidden nature of truth; the emphasis on process rather than stasis; the journey being more important than the arrival; the primacy of perception; the importance of the body in constituting reality; an emphasis on uniqueness; the objectifying nature of vision; the irreducibility of all value to utility; and creativity as an unveiling (no-saying) process rather than a willfully constructive process.[39]

Notes

1. Rachel Manteuffel, "The Context Behind the Fatal Punchline that Obscured the Lincoln Assassination," *The Washington Post*, April 13, 2021.

2. Arthur Koestler, *The Act of Creation* (New York: Macmillan, 1964).

3. There are exceptions. We still laugh at comedies by Shakespeare and Moliere, movies with Chaplin, Buster Keaton, and the Marx Brothers, and books by favorite authors who make us laugh when we were younger. (I'm thinking of S. J. Perlman.) In the years when LP (long play) vinyl records were popular, some of the best sellers featured comedians recorded in concert. One effect was that fans in the audience would call out requests, like requests to performers at concerts, where often the loudest applause is for those signature songs.

4. Wen Duan, "Understanding the Challenges of Sharing Humor Across Linguistic and Cultural Boundaries," (PhD dissertation, Cornell University, 2022).

5. https://www.youtube.com/watch?v=MeyuIdmA0YE&ab_channel=TheTelegraph

6. Thank you, Lee Roloff.

7. Robert A. Levine and Donald T. Campbell, *Ethnocentrism: Theories of Conflict, Ethnic Attitudes, and Group Behavior* (New York: John Wiley and Sons, 1972).

8. Edward T. Hall, *Beyond Culture* (New York: Doubleday, 1976).

9. Tomoko Masumoto, "The Semantic Dimensions of an International Story: The *Ehime Maru* Incident," *ETC: A Review of General Semantics*, Vol. 68, No. 2, April, 2011, 204-213.

10. Louann Brizendine, *The Female Brain* (New York: Broadway Books, 2006).

11. Edward T. Hall, "Cultural Models in Transcultural Communication," in John Condon and Mitsuko Saito, eds., *Communication Across Cultures for What? A Symposium on Humane Responsibility in Intercultural Communication* (Tokyo: Simul Press, 1976), 89-102; and in discussion with Tadashi Kawata and Fumio Nakagawa at this symposium, on "Between the Rich and the Poor," 41.

12. Helmut Morsbach told me about "the dust test": in a neat and well-maintained home, there are places where dust may accumulate that no one can see. Rub your finger across that surface, such as the top of a picture frame above eye level, and if you feel dust but it doesn't matter because no one will know, that indicates yours may be a "shame culture" where

what others think matters especially. In contrast, if you think that even if no one else knows, you know, and it matters to you, so: "guilt culture." The contrastive categories are classic; the dust test, dubious.

13. Susan Lee Carter is an independent researcher whose work has focused on developing and documenting adventure-based approaches for Native American adolescents primarily with the National Indian Youth Leadership Project's Project Venture. She studied with E. T. Hall and with Gladys Pilz at the University of New Mexico, and also is a longtime friend of the author.

14. Personal correspondence with the author.

15. Susan Carter, personal conversation.

16. Michael Vande Berg, R. Michael Paige, and Kris Hemming Lou, *Student Learning Abroad: What Our Students Are Learning, What They're Not, and What We Can Do About It* (Sterling, VA: Stylus, 2012).

17. Clifford Geertz, *Local Knowledge: Further Essays in Interpretive Anthropology* (New York: Basic Books, 2008).

18. The term *raza cósmica*, the "cosmic race" is credited to José Vasconcelos, one of the most significant figures in post-revolution Mexico. He was appointed rector at the *Universidad Autónomo de Mexico* (UNAM) in 1920, and influenced both the role of the university in Mexican society, and Mexican culture more broadly. His words celebrating *mestizaje*, the fusion of the indigenous and European lineage, was expressed in the university logo he designed: "*Por mi raza hablará el espíritu.*" ("The spirit shall speak for my people.") These words also appear on the monumental, mosaic-faced mural that covers UNAM's central library, designed by Juan O'Gorman. The Mexico City campus of UNAM, now recognized as a United Nations World Heritage site, by enrollment, is the largest university in Latin America, with approximately 350,000 students.

19. "Power Distance" is one of the dimensions introduced by Geert Hofstede in his book *Culture's Consequences: Comparing Values, Behaviors, Institutions and Organizations Across Nations, Revised edition* (Thousand Oaks, CA: Sage, 2001). Power distance is a measurement of social hierarchy, with a high score in Hofstede's analysis of responses to many questions, indicating the value of showing deference to one in authority, and a low score approaching the value of regarding everyone as of equal status in an organization.

20. Keiko Ueda, a former student at a time when attention to intercultural communication was taking shape in Japan, attracted attention with her

graduation thesis, as summarized in "Sixteen Ways to Avoid Saying 'No' in Japan," in John Condon and Mitsuko Saito, eds., *Intercultural Encounters with Japan: Communication—Contact and Conflict* (Tokyo: Simul Press, 1974), 185-192. Shortly after that, when things Japanese were trending globally, and businesses from abroad were motivated to collaborate with their counterparts in Japan, Japanese business consultant, Masaaki Imai, asked permission to use Ueda's thesis title for his next book as added research that informed his previous book, *Never Take 'Yes' for an Answer* (Tokyo: Simul Press, 1978).

21. One might think of the famous Christian hymn sung by children, "Gladly, the Cross-eyed Bear."

22. The contrasting relevance of context also fits the classic distinction of the German sociologist Ferdinand Tonnies between *Gemeinschaft* and *Gesellschaft* organization, the former being "organic," relations based on family or shared experience or evolving over time without an overall plan, and the latter following a clear, rational plan. By definition, *Gemeinschaft* is "high context," whereas the *Gesellschaft* refers to organization based on rational planning and social relations based on mutual interests, i.e., low context. A *Gesellschaft* organization gives less attention to features of contexts of history and tradition except to the extent they fit with the plan.

23. Evon Z. Vogt and Ethel M. Albert, eds., *People of Rimrock: A Study of Five Cultures* (Cambridge, MA: Harvard University Press, 1957).

24. Florence Kluckhohn and Fred Strodtbeck, *Variations in Value Orientations* (Evanston, Illinois: Row, Peterson, 1961).

25. John Condon, *An Introduction to Intercultural Communication* (Indianapolis, Indiana, Bobbs-Merrill, 1975).

26. John R. Milton, ed., *Conversations with Frank Waters* (Chicago: Swallow Press, 1971).

27. Joseph H. Suina, "Pueblo Secrecy: Result of Intrusions," *New Mexico Magazine*, January, 1992.

28. Basil Bernstein, "A Sociolinguistic Approach to Social Learning," in *Class, Codes and Control: Theoretical Studies Towards a Sociology of Language* (New York: Schocken Books, 1971), 118-139.

29. Native American friends say, "When we are growing up, we are taught responsibilities. White people think, individual rights."

30. Gerry Philipsen, "Places for Speaking in Teamsterville," *Quarterly Journal of Speech*, Vol. 62, February 1976, 15-25.

31. Thomas Kochman, *Black and White Styles in Conflict* (Chicago: University of Chicago Press, 1981).

32. Kyoung-Ah Nam, personal correspondence.

33. Joseph H. Suina, "Pueblo Secrecy: Result of Intrusions," *New Mexico Magazine*, January, 1992.

34. "John Cleese Intends to Have His Unread Books Buried with Him," *The New York Times*, Sept. 3, 2020. Video recordings of conversations between Cleese and Iain McGilchrist may be seen on YouTube.

35. Iain McGilchrist, *The Master and His Emissary: The Divided Brain and the Making of the Western World* (New Haven, Connecticut: Yale University Press, 2009).

36. Ken Robinson, "Do Schools Kill Creativity?" https://www.ted.com/talks/sir_ken_robinson_do_schools_kill_creativity/up-next?language=en

37. McGilchrist, *Master and His Emissary*, 46.

38. McGilchrist, *Master and His Emissary*, 49.

39. McGilchrist, *Master and His Emissary*, 177.

Context Makes All the Difference

From the *New York Post*, May 9, 2023: In the Spring of 2023, a six-year-old boy came home from school with a note from his teacher, who told him to give it to his parents. She had also called the mother, asking the parents to meet her at school as soon as possible. The father asked their son if he had any idea what this was about. The boy answered, "She didn't like a drawing I did."

The next day the parents went to the school and the met the teacher, asking what this was all about. The teacher said she asked the children to draw a picture of their family doing something. She took out the boy's drawing and said, "would you mind explaining?"

"Not at all. Family vacation.
We were snorkeling off the Bahamas."

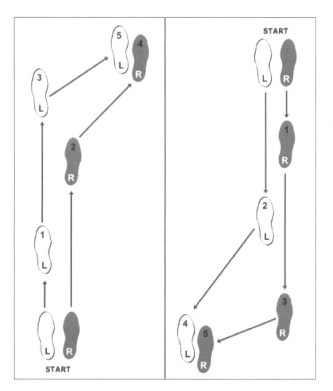

"First you learn the steps. Then, you dance the tango. Then, you become the tango."

Mireille Veilleux and Perre Allaire, Canadian Profession Dancesport Champions

CHAPTER TEN

So, How Did You Learn That?

There are three kinds of men: The ones that learn by reading.
The few who learn by observation. The rest of them have
to pee on the electric fence and find out for themselves.
—*Will Rogers*

The difference between school and life, it's been said, is that
in school, first we learn and then are tested, but in much of
the rest of life, first we are tested and that's how we learn.

"So, how did you learn that?" was a question that Hall asked throughout his life as he observed—and questioned—how people learn what they need to learn. And then, the questions of his professional life: how can we learn to learn, as well as the more obvious question: *what* should we learn? It was one reason Hall enlisted in the army at the start of WW II, patriotism aside. He also wanted to understand how a vast bureaucracy can train so many people from so many different regions, vernaculars, ethnicities, and varied educational levels to learn what can make the difference between life and death—and do that in a matter of weeks.

Years later at the Foreign Service Institute (FSI), Hall was charged with preparing technical assistance professionals to be more effective in the variety of cultural settings in countries to which were about to be sent. Today, those in NGOs serving abroad, international service programs such as the US Peace Corps or Canada World Youth, and professionals who offer intercultural communication training or diversity programs for civic, business, and educational institutions ask themselves the same questions. Plus, in many situations, particularly in diversity programs, the question is how to change attitudes based on a legacy of ignorance and disrespect. Influencing attitudes, increasing self-awareness, enhancing competencies—formidable goals of the intercultural communication trainer and classroom teacher, professions that now are found throughout the world.

Without much awareness, we largely *acquire* the "cultural competencies" (today's term of choice) beginning with our first language or languages. We don't realize most of what we've internalized and what we externalize, express, perform. Which is also why Hall asserted that "our internalized culture" is concealed mostly from ourselves, and why it is important to try to recognize the cultural influences that are deep within us.

Learning implies a more conscious process in contrast to *acquisition*. Hall included both in his "learning" rubric. "By the time a child is 6, he or she has already done more learning than they will do the rest of their lives—language, social roles, how to relate to people, and so on."[1] A better strategy for intercultural understanding might begin with self-reflection about one's own behavior, assumptions, expectations, and judgments.

Hall believed that it was probably impossible for anyone to know, as if experienced, what someone else who had grown up in a different place, time, circumstance—"cultural environment"—could feel. We really can't "walk in another's shoes" metaphorically, or even walk in the way the one whose shoes we've borrowed does because even how we walk is an acquired dialect of walking, as much as is our way of speaking. Nagesh Rao, professor at Ohio University, friend and colleague, tells a story that is illustrative:

The year is 1990. Three years after coming to study in the United States, I went back home to Madras (still can't call it Chennai) for my summer break. To get away from Madras heat and to meet relatives, my mom, dad, and I took the "Brindavan Express" train to Bangalore. We took an autorickshaw from the train station to Woodlands Hotel where we planned to stay for three days.

When the auto reached Woodlands, a young boy, maybe ten years old, took our bags to our room. I was reaching into my kurta to give him a tip when he said in Kannada, my first language, "*Hathu dollar kodi sir*" (Give me ten dollars). I was shocked that he was asking for a tip and in dollars. I replied, "*Hathu dollar kodalla, hathu rupee kodthini*" (I won't give you ten dollars, but just ten rupees.)

It then struck me; how did this boy know I was from the US? I was wearing Indian clothes (kurta-pajama), spoke Kannada fluently, and was not carrying the customary back-pack that US returned Indians tended to carry. The suitcases had no stickers indicating international travel. Was it my perfume? What gave me away? I was now curious.

I asked the young boy, "*Hengo gothu naan USindha bandhi-dini antha?*" (How did you know I was from the US?) He answered, "*Neevu bereythara nadithiri sir.*" (You walk differently sir.) I was stunned and amazed at this young man's ability to "read" cultures that I gave him a tip of $20! The three years in the US had changed my rhythm, my movement to be in synchrony with the rhythms of a new dance, a new culture.

If we can never fully understand another, our ability to respond meaningfully to another, even a fictional character presented to us in literature and drama from millennia past and from different lands, is impressive. Today that ability to identify with others is explored in "theory of mind," and from the mid-1990's with the discovery of "mirror neurons" that ". . . explained many previously unexplainable aspects of the mind, such as empathy, imitation, synchrony, and even the development of language. One writer compared mirror neurons to 'neural Wi-Fi—we pick up not only on another person's movement but her emotional state and intentions as well.'"[2]

Empathy may be a defining human quality, but is not a prerequisite for teaching or learning. I knew someone who taught logic and motivated his students by insulting their intelligence so they worked extra hard to challenge his dismissive attitude. As a result, many excelled in their grade scores. A logical teaching design but not recommended.

Three Kinds of Learning

Hall proposed three kinds of learning: informal, formal, and technical. This remains a sturdy construction even as new technologies and the exigencies of economics, and even a pandemic, challenge and mix these distinctions. Categories always invite "what about?" questions, examples that seem to be both/and rather than either/or. If categories are helpful, then maybe Hall's three distinctions invite revisions, expanding to five or six, in turn provoking even more categories with each "but what about…?"

We need categories to sort out differences, distinctions, that might otherwise be a jumble. Sometimes they lead us astray, but often they are useful even as a starting point or to characterize some of the more obvious distinctions. Hall's informal, formal, and technical categories offer a helpful start in characterizing how we learn, and how we think we were taught. In the three stories that follow, the mix of these ways of learning across cultures shows that all are present all the time. Dancing a waltz follows a clear pattern, but it only feels good when one is not thinking about which step comes next, and when the partners' feelings and reactions to each other feel right. Ancient Zen arts, and also newly acquired arts and skills, can feel strange or uncomfortable to one unaccustomed to apprenticeship learning that requires more than learning what can be taught directly. A student who goes abroad to improve language skills and also acquire cultural sensitivity and appreciation, can't learn everything in a language class. Language classes can't teach "the silent languages" that are acquired through experience, the relational, affective, better learned and acquired with a home-stay experience. This is widely known. Much less well known is the host-mother's experience, stories told by Professor Chapa Cortés. Not that everything learned and acquired that can't be taught gets it right. Nonsense and bigotry can also be learned, which can distort the perceptions of someone just trying to make sense of what transpires.

Informal learning is characterized by observing and following what others do, often without conscious awareness: our first language—or languages, as many children across the world grow up in a bi- or multi-lingual environment. Evidence indicates that our language readiness begins even before we are born. During the first few years, without much awareness, we pick up on what we hear and see, sometimes to a parent's surprise and dismay. "By osmosis," some might say, but if that suggests a passive learning, that misses the point. Informal learning is the most active: trial and error.

The "informal" also centers our acquisition of our cultural identities and later, if raised to a more formal level, how we might recall and re-tell what we think we remember. The informal becomes formalized when put into words and is "explainable," much as a relatively "high context" experience is made explicit, spelled out, is thus rendered "low context."

Formal learning, as Hall describes it, is characterized by someone in the role of a learner and someone in the role of a teacher. This relationship is most obviously seen in a classroom, but "the teacher" could be a parent or older sister or brother who assumes the role of a teacher, or a coach, or whoever instructs, where there is the right way to do something and there are wrong ways. Hall says there are often emotional responses when the learner gets it wrong: "No! Not *that* way!" And there may be praise—depending on the age of the learner and the relationship—for emotional support.

The difference between school and life, it's been said, is that in school we learn and then are tested, but in much of the rest of life we are tested and that's how we learn. The former is "formal learning," the latter "informal." We don't learn until we make a mistake, Hall used to say. Even in trying to learn another language, often we can't hear what we need to hear until we make a mistake and it is pointed out.

Technical learning—more accurately, about teaching—is what today might be called "user friendly," the flesh and blood teacher often replaced by a manual or a video. De-contextualized, democratic, and economical. The "technical" version of learning, Hall says, is a one-way street, ideally suited to large audiences. It requires clear and precise directions so that anyone who follows the instructions will achieve the desired result.

Hall says that, at first during WW II, it was thought that the ideal qualifications among army recruits to learn airplane mechanics would be those with a keen aptitude in mechanics. But, no, "it turned out that a good shoe-clerk in civilian life would become a better mechanic for military purposes than someone who had fixed cars all his life and learned on a Model-T Ford."[3] The critical factor was not mechanical aptitude but the ability to follow instructions. The key to effective technical learning is clarity, step-by-step. A cookbook may be exemplary, at least in some parts of the world. Or the manual that comes with a new appliance. There are wide cultural variations (and expectations), a topic itself quite interesting. Japanese manuals from cookbooks to washing machines, with the instructions posted on the appliance itself, always include illustrations of the step-by-step process.

More important is what is fitting to be addressed in a technical rather than in an interpersonal relationship, a matter of enormous social and economic and so, also, cultural significance. During the COVID-19 pandemic, many schools at all levels switched either fully or in some hybrid fashion to part in-person teaching and part remote, which neither students nor teachers liked. There was understandable anger from students and their parents who were often the ones footing the very high tuition bills for a "college experience" that was nothing like what was promised at the beginning of 2020. The pandemic also revealed other priorities in cultural values.

The natural order of things has been that the parents teach the children, the older children teach the younger. And it takes a village. But enter technologies, the focus of Marshall McLuhan, for a time maybe the most famous person identified with the impact of different media on our sensory perceptions and mental processing. In the late twentieth century, children learn new technologies faster than their parents and they become their parents' teachers.

Hall's "technical" is interpreted, understandably, from a learner's perspective, and not how Hall described it from its disembodied and dispassionate, anonymous source. "Technical" suggests some neutral code, with hints of shared history and in some contexts, even a legal codification or a negative connotation, as in, "Well, if you want to get technical…." That this is how technical is interpreted suggests either revising Hall's choice of terms or the need for another category, as explored below.

What About . . . ?

Hall's attention to interpersonal relations gives little attention to the impact of literacy in its many forms, the system of symbols—musical notes, those printed dance steps—that became part of the formal (teacher-student) relationship but, like any form of literacy, it frees one from the need for that relationship. In "the West" this "technical" mode may be traced to the Reformation with Guttenberg's moveable type innovation in printing that made it possible for literate individuals to read the Bible and thus bypass the priests and go directly to scripture. Which, in turn, shaped values that would later distinguish cultural distinctions of "individualism" and "collectivism," and in Hall's characterization, to "low[er] context" from "high[er] context" messages.

We become literate mostly through formal teaching, a competence that becomes an informal marker of judging another's intelligence, as the word "illiterate" easily slips into the equivalent of "unintelligent." It is comparable to confusing schooling with learning. And so also a judgment based in class, privilege, and status acquired informally, and thus taken as a universal norm.

Learning How to Learn

When the US Volunteer Peace Corps was taking shape during President John Kennedy's administration, the question of how best to prepare these young (initially, and also initially mostly white) volunteers. It was a challenge not so different from Hall's charge at the FSI at the end of WW II, and not so different from what colleges and universities all over the world face as students are sent abroad to sharpen their competence in the host country's language and the more amorphous, more difficult to measure, and arguably more important mix of intercultural sensitivities, a few social skills, adaptability, and greater self-awareness of one's cultural self.

In the big picture, it's what immigrants and refugees have always done, often with the support of a community that shared a language, foods, and shops that served the group, religious institutions, and more. Today "expats" often settle into similar communities, albeit with financial support that lets one identify as an "expat," which suggests some professional status.

Something like this has a long tradition in Japan, including learning to be a potter or a sushi chef. Perhaps most famous is the young person wanting to learn to be a *rakugo-ka,* the professional storyteller artist. An apprentice would, as the story goes, come to work in the home of the professional *rakugo-ka,* assigned to do menial housework, often for years, with little or no guidance in the story telling art, until one day his master observes that the young person has picked up, through observation, more than he realizes, and is now pronounced qualified to be a *rakugo-ka.* In the very popular 1984 movie, *The Karate Kid,* young Daniel agreed to do yard work for his would-be karate coach and mentor, Mr. Miyagi, painting his fence and waxing his cars. It was tedious work, day after day, and frustrating because Miyagi wasn't giving Daniel any training in karate. Just brief instructions about his work: "Wax on, wax off." Little did Daniel realize that during those weeks of physical labor he was learning skills he would need as a *karate-ka.*

A now-classic article by Roger Harrison and Richard Hopkins attempted a partial answer to the "how do you learn that?" question. Dick Hopkins and I became friends and colleagues, years after I first read his article, "The Design of Cross-Cultural Training: An Alternative to the University Model."[4] The core of their argument was that the values, sensitivities, and skills that are important in conventional college classes are not at all what one needs in the situation into which these naïve (a description, not a judgment) volunteers will find themselves abroad. Some of these are summarized in a chart—a presentation that Hopkins said he did not particularly like. I've included a portion of the Harrison and Hopkins contrasts, first the "university" emphasis and values, followed by the "alternative" that the authors—and Hall would agree, I'm sure—believed was more relevant and useful. Hopkins and Harrison were writing from an assumption of at least an initial curiosity and respect, setting aside critics who judged the Peace Corps and other such programs as colonialist or missionary-like efforts with an implicit "let us show you how" attitude.

Dick Hopkins told me that he thought maybe the best intercultural preparation he knew of at that time was for a group of new volunteers who would be going to Chile to do something related to ceramics. They were first to be sent to a college in California for intensive Spanish language study and also take a special "applied ceramics" course designed just for them. When the volunteers arrived at the campus it seemed no one there knew they were coming, nor was anything prepared for them. So this small group of volunteers had to figure out who at the college could help them, and how to get the school to set up the classes and workshops they would need. In the process, Hopkins said, they had to learn exactly the kinds of social skills they would need when they arrived in South America. Wax on, wax off.

In the university setting where formal learning is the norm within the classrooms—though outside of the classroom, informal learning through social life may exert more influence on students' attitudes, values, and longer lasting personal relationships—one legendary professor of Landscape History at Harvard, John Stilgoe, intentionally cuts across the grain. Professor Stilgoe teaches a course on the art of exploration that he describes in a delightful book, *Outside Lies Magic: Regaining History and Awareness in Everyday Places.*[5] It begins with the sentence: "Get Out Now." Stilgoe writes:

> I refuse to provide a schedule of topics. Undergraduate and graduate students alike love schedules, love knowing the order of subjects and the satisfaction of ticking off one line after another, class after class, week after week. Confronted by a professor who explains that schedules produce a desire, sometimes an obsession to 'get through the material,' they grow uneasy . . . My students resist the lack of topic structure because they are the children of structured learning and

Contrasting Educational Goals:
University and Overseas Education

Some Major Goals of University Education	Some Divergent Goals of Overseas Education
Communication. To communicate fluently via the written word and, to a lesser extent, to speak well. To master the languages of abstraction and generalization, e.g., mathematics and science. To understand readily the reasoning, the ideas, and the knowledge of other persons through verbal exchange.	**Communication.** To understand and communicate directly and often nonverbally through movement, facial expression, person-to-person actions. To listen with sensitivity to the hidden concerns, values, motives of the other. To be at home in the exchange of feelings, attitudes, desires, fears. To have a sympathetic, empathic understanding of the feelings of the other.
Decision Making. To develop critical judgment. The ability to test assertions, assumptions, and opinions against the hard facts and the criteria of logic. To reduce susceptibility to specious argument and to be skeptical of intuition and emotion. To search for the best, most rational, most economical, and elegant solution.	**Decision Making.** To develop ability to come to conclusions and take action on inadequate, unreliable, and conflicting information. To be able to trust feelings, attitudes, and beliefs as well as facts. To search for the possible course, the viable alternative, the durable though inelegant solution.
Commitment. Commitment is to the truth. It requires an ability to stand back from ongoing events in order to understand and analyze them and to maintain objectivity in the face of emotionally involving situations. Difficult situations are handled by explanations, theories, reports.	**Commitment.** Commitment is to people and to relationships. It requires an ability to become involved. to be able to give and inspire trust and confidence, to care and to take action in accordance with one's concern. Difficult situations are dealt with by staying in emotional contact with them and by trying to take constructive action.
Ideals. To value the great principles and ideals of Western society, social justice, economic progress, scientific truth. To value the sacrifice of present rewards and satisfactions for future advancement of these ideals and to find self-esteem and satisfaction from one's contribution toward distant social goals.	**Ideals.** To value causes and objectives embedded in the here-and-now and embodied in the groups and persons in the immediate social environment. To find satisfaction, enjoyment, and self-esteem from the impact one has directly on the lives of others. To be able to empathize with others who live mostly in the present and to work with them toward the limited, concrete goals which are important to them.
Problem Solving. A problem is solved when the true, correct, reasonable answer has been discovered and verified. Problem solving is a search for knowledge and truth. It is a largely rational process, involving intelligence, creativity, insight, and a respect for facts.	**Problem Solving.** A problem is solved when decisions are made and carried out which effectively apply people's energies to overcoming some barrier to a common goal. Problem solving is a social process involving communication, interpersonal influence, consensus, and commitment.

structured entertainment. Over and over I explain that if they are afraid of a course on exploring, they may never have the confidence to go exploring on their own. I encourage them to take a chance, and many do.[6]

Stilgoe has legions of former students who have stayed in touch and say that his course changed their lives.

Make a Friend

In Hall's "Culture as Communication" course, not a few students who had been enthusiastic about the course, the assignments, and their professor, balked at one assignment: "Make a Friend." Hall asked each student to "make a friend" with someone whose cultural background was significantly different from theirs, and to learn something about contrasting cultural experiences, outlooks, ways of seeing and doing things, etc. In those days, "diversity" at Northwestern, and at many other comparable universities in the US, was nothing like at almost any college campus in the US today. There were few students of color, few students with disabilities, and LGBTQ students (and faculty) were mostly in the closet. A few might have thought, "I grew up Catholic. I wonder what it's like to be Jewish?"—which could have been eye-opening for many. Not many would have thought of differences in gender, age, and social class as cultural differences of the kind usually discussed in this course. So it seems likely that students thought they had to befriend one of the rare international students they had noticed, but never talked with.

An assignment to "make a friend" seems like an oxymoron, and a "friend" seems an unlikely result of someone completing an assignment. To their credit, students protested that this was exploiting whomever they might ask to help them out. And their "friendship," some might have said—without making air-quotes with their fingers because that was not an available gesture then—would only last a matter of weeks until the term ended and the grades were sent out. It felt unethical, exploitive. Unfair, professor!

Hall's response—and I think this was the only class assignment he ever mentioned to me—was, "Who says it has to end after the course?" There was a hidden agenda here. Talk to people you might otherwise have not even noticed. You might learn something—about yourself and someone else, and you might turn out to continue to feel something for one another, whether or not both of you considered this as "friendship." For some of the international students whom I imagine were approached, it might have been one of the few times anyone expressed an interest in learning about their lives.

Years later, the ethics of and imagining the resistance to that assignment makes me think of the position of the researcher working across cultures and the reactions of those who are "subjects" of the research. While "friendship" is rarely invoked, the feelings of those who are interviewed or asked to answer questionnaires is probably not so different from the feelings generated by the encounters that Hall encouraged in his less-competent friend-seekers. The researcher might get a graduate degree or a promotion or a publication out of the cooperation of the other, but what benefit results for those who give their time and honesty in cooperating? Black communities have complained for decades about this. Ethical standards have changed, and for some communities—"people of study," perhaps—rules have been erected. Indigenous communities, for example, have established rigorous standards that an outsider with a research plan must meet. Communities that have been "subjects of study" rightly ask: "With our cooperation, you completed your assignment; what did we get out of it?"

Reflections on Teaching and Learning

Three friends have kindly shared stories about their teaching and learning. All, across three countries, are deeply engaged in intercultural lives. All are women who may pick up on what some men might miss, and each has an appreciation of Hall's work.

¡Bienvenidos! Host Mothers in Mexico

In 1996, Claudia Chapa Cortés left her home in Mexico to become a college exchange student in Finland, an experience, she says, that completely changed her life. "I learned so much and gained such a different perspective on the world, that after that I decided to dedicate my life to changing students' lives by organizing study abroad programs and intercultural experiences in my home town, Mérida, Yucatán." And she has. Claudia co-founded and is the director of the TSIKBAL International Education Agency that promotes a more inclusive and just world through Study Abroad programs and intercultural experiences in Mexico, Central America, and Cuba. In Mayan *"tsikbal"* means "to have a conversation."

Chapa, who is also a friend and colleague, has helped countless college students to look at a part of the world and at themselves in ways that become transformative. She says, "I hope these experiences will enable us to think twice about the perpetuating systems we have in the world, and will give us the tools to become, as Anu Taranath said, 'mindful travelers in an unequal world.'" For over a decade in Mérida, Yucatán, Chapa has welcomed college students from abroad to a comprehensive program of intensive Spanish language study, home-stay, and service-learning in their host community. Maybe the most important part of the experience for these young people, usually abroad for the first time, is as guests in modest homes in a humble neighborhood, far from the historic center and touristic sites in this historic land.

Much has been written about "the study abroad" experience, with research casting doubts on its value when students treat the experience as a vacation abroad—with classes—enjoying their leisure time with others from a similar background, swapping stories that often reinforce stereotypes. Some research indicates that some students return with little cultural learning and even more ethnocentric than before. For a long time, the "contact hypothesis"—just getting people from different backgrounds together will naturally result in greater intercultural awareness and sensitivity—has been shown to be naïve, at best. Pre-departure preparation, checking in during the sojourner's experience, and post-experience meetings are crucial. The literature on this is extensive.

But it's not just the students who are ill-served without serious intercultural and personal guidance. It's also the host mothers and families, as often they bear the brunt of "culture shock" that every visitor has heard about. As important as any outcome for the study abroad students, Chapa sees the value of the experience for the hosts and their community—if they can be prepared for the inevitable mix of emotions that every mother feels with her own children. She prepares the *señoras de la casa* to receive (usually) highly motivated students from north of the border who will reside in local homes for months, sometimes as long as half a year. Almost always, there develops a mutual affection between the host mother and the student. Often, these transient guests and their "mothers" come to feel as family and remain in touch even after many years. But initially, and sometimes throughout the experience, matters of place and time can be stressful for both guests and hosts. Chapa is one of the few researchers who has studied the impact of these intercultural encounters not just from the sojourner's experience, which has been widely studied, but also the effects on the host mothers, their families, and the local community.

Even experienced host mothers who "know" from years of hosting eager-to-learn-to-be culturally sensitive guests sometimes feel a bigger culture shock than their new "daughter" or "son" away from home for the first time. And often the stress centers on Hall's themes of space and time:

Home-stay hosts expect students to let them know when they're leaving the house and when they're coming back. This is something we in Mexico take to be normal. When you enter a room, you say "good morning" or whatever, and when you leave, you say "bye, see you soon," and so on. But from my experience, with US students that's not necessarily the case. Students rarely greet others when they come into a room—I'm not sure if it's a generational thing or just something they're not used to or that they possibly don't want to feel they are invading the others' private space.

US students who come from rural places tend to be different from urban students. I've noticed that students who come from rural areas are more family-oriented, often live at home with their parents, seem to show more respect to others, are very polite, and have a narrower vision of the world compared with urban students who are more independent, may not live at home, have more open ideas about the world, and aren't as attached to family. In that way, students from a small town or rural background in the US are more similar to our own Yucatecan students (rural and urban). Of course, this is a generalization; there are urban students that are very polite as well. In my experience urban students that fit this description are generally from families who are Mexican or from Guatemala, Perú, Honduras, or the Dominican Republic.[7]

In general, college students who are used to living in a dorm or by themselves rarely let anyone know where they're going, if they even indicate that they are leaving. Home-stay moms have often called me mid-morning worried that their student isn't up yet, and the mother is waiting to serve breakfast to the student who should be hurrying off to class, only to discover that the student had already left the house without saying goodbye. That's typical. The same thing happens when the student comes back to the house. The "mom" might be in the kitchen cooking lunch, and the student comes in, and without saying "I'm home," "I'm back," or "hello," goes to their room and closes the door. The mom, who didn't notice that the student had returned, is waiting for him or her to have lunch. After some hours she wonders if the student might be in their room so she knocks on the door and surprise! The student has been there for hours.

This, of course, has to also do with personality. Some students that are shy and introverted are not comfortable with communication being so open, and there are others that catch on right away and even kiss their home-stay moms when leaving the house or coming back. But even with cultural orientation classes and workshops before the students arrive and afterwards urging this importance, it's a lesson easier heard than felt and performed.

It's not that the students and their host-moms weren't told about such likely personal and cultural differences, and the frustrations and conflicts that could result, but being told "information" and advice about "manners" does not translate as learning. Nor does what counts as learning in a classroom—giving the correct answer on a test—always result in feelings and new behavior.

Kyudo: **It's All About Learning**

Dorianne Galarnyk moved from the US to Japan in 2000 with her husband, Professor Richard Harris, a Brit whose home has been in Japan since 1980. Warm, outgoing, and skilled in many areas (she was a chef in Portland, Oregon, and later in Antarctica), Galarnyk found her home in a rural area of Japan when the couple moved from the city of Nagoya and became fully engaged with the local community. There she began her serious practice of *Kyudo*, Japanese archery, one of the classic Zen martial arts.[8] Though she had some experience with archery in the US years before, here she describes her learning Kyudo which, as she says, is all about learning:

> I had already lived for a couple of years in Japan's Nakatsugawa countryside among farmers, men and women who generously helped me learn how to grow crops and to live well among them, when one day my husband told me about a free introductory course at the local Kyudo [Japanese archery] dojo training center. I was resolved to learn this "way of the bow" and help our neighbors with a newfound archery prowess to bring down the pesky wild boars that sometimes break into the rice fields and gardens.
>
> Before the initial evening of the 13 sessions, I ordered a recommended book, *The Essence and Practice of Japanese Archery*. I spent an entire day reading, absolutely enthralled and also chagrined, learning that Kyudo is no longer used for killing. If there is any prey, it is perhaps one's own ego. The book's explanations made me yet more committed. Off I went to class, unleashing myself to this inward hunt.
>
> The lesson started predictably enough. We watched five advanced students demonstrate the series of positions and movements that would comprise a proper "shooting" from entry to exit, including a ritualized series of eight stages to the shooting. But the release of the string defies expectation: the arrow is not "shot." Instead, one learns, over years, to painstakingly relinquish wrong intentions, develop "rightness of self," submit oneself to allow the full draw of one's interwoven body-bow-spirit to "ripen," expanding from within like a flower bud that finally cannot resist blossoming, until the arrow releases itself. So from the first day, we were made aware that the road ahead was steep, full of humiliation and impossibilities. Who wouldn't be enticed?

The weeks of learning grew into months, now years, increasingly evidencing to me the three ways one is expected to learn Japanese Kyudo. Teachers admonished us to develop *Mitori Geiko,* the ability to take in lessons with our eyes. Thus, we initiate our learning by watching how to wear the glove, how to hold the bow and maneuver arrows, how to stand and draw, how to deal with ever finer points of technique. I was so eager that at home I'd continue this visual absorption, scouring the web for performances of the highest-ranking 8th- and 9th-dan Kyudo teachers, watching them again and again, enthralled with the beauty. These days I also study video of myself, getting past shock at my poor form, pinpointing faults and setting fresh goals for improvement.

In Kyudo the whole idea of learning is so important. Kyudo masters hope that beginners grasp that Kyudo is about constant learning, incessantly improving oneself. We must always begin with courtesy (humble politeness, consideration for others) and propriety (appropriate behavior, appearance, and attitude). Altogether, these are "right inner intention and correctness in the outer appearance."

And that's it. That is what it means to "perform the shooting with success."

Then, while one is in the shooting, one searches for rightness in oneself. If one can do this, focused and calm in each moment of this search for rightness, the shooting is "realized". (Note there is no mention of the physical target being hit.) And when one fails to hit the target, one still has what is important: the occasion to search for oneself. Not being resentful, but continuing the inward searching. And one begins again (really, one never stops) with rightness of intention. It is circular. It is constant learning.

As I think about Hall's ways of learning, I wonder if *mitori geiko* may be considered the Informal way of learning, no one explicitly teaching, my main guides being reflection and intuition. Certainly, the second way we are advised to learn in the dojo is absolutely Formal, the teachers instructing and critiquing our repetitious, embodied practices. In Japanese, this is called *Kazu Geiko*. Interestingly, the Japanese written symbol for *kazu* refers to numbers, and some Kyudo practitioners use the term *yakazu geiko* specifying the "practice of many arrows." An image emerges, by and by, of hundreds of thousands of arrows that a lifetime of trial-and-error holds. Yet, our teachers caution us to treat each arrow as the single arrow one has for this lifetime. Ultimately then, Kyudo becomes a test of calm perseverance, a quest for inner perfection and a constant reminder of our ephemeral existence.

Early on I was occasionally scolded for asking too many questions instead of listening better, thinking quietly, watching, and emulating. Quickly I decided to journal each day's new information and the teachers' focused advice. My written organization has revealed itself to be an essential mental exercise, learning made intentional, often unraveling my otherwise pent-up confusions. I must add, however, that recently my most advanced 92-year-old teacher, Tokuda-sensei, is trying to get me to ask him all my questions and to argue with him. He explains that since my gaining 5th-dan ranking, I need to become utterly responsible for teaching myself, to rethink everything, to develop my own manner with the bow. I need to treasure each mistake as opportunity for learning. Tokuda-sensei insists I pursue all underpinning details through studying texts and debating with teachers while they are still alive.

Alas, even I, a US American, am finding it hard to relearn challenging my teachers. And yet, this active, conscious grappling with experts is included in this third method of learning, which the Japanese call *kufuu geiko*. This may well be close to or incorporate Hall's technical learning. The kanji for *kufuu* translates as scheme or method or invention. An amalgamation of meaning describes a learning that is an analytical creative pursuit. To study, to contemplate, to turn thoughts over and over, trying to learn how my body can work with my mind to rouse my spirit, instilling the utmost of concentration without any gap, and giving life and breath and all manner of vivacity to each motion, to the one arrow of my entire life. No one part of my body-mind-spirit dominates. All stay in balance, ripening with my breath, swelling as I become one with the bow, sensing the target within me. Learning in this way is magnificent. Indeed, wondrous.

Tokuda-sensei is most persistent of all in repeating to me that all my physical ways with my own body, and with the bow and arrows, are not a "doing." Instead, I need to understand that physically and spiritually/mentally, everything "becomes." It grows from within me, like a bud of a flower swelling toward the moment of blossoming. Every move, every thought, is an expansion from within.

On my best days in the dojo, I now practice all three ways of learning, *mitori*, *kazu*, and *kufuu*. I often learn most from beginners who practice with such joy, that tears well in my eyes. I am humbled. Ultimately, everyone around me is teaching me how to learn. Sometimes I think that just simply learning to keep learning, endlessly, is the whole meaning of Kyudo. And so even though many days I fall back into shooting arrows at a target, I hope that ever more I am becoming a better self, immersed in the learning, practicing true Kyudo.

The First Waltz

Leslie Weigl served as the Global Education Coordinator at the University of Alberta in Edmonton, Alberta, Canada, for over 15 years. During this time, much of her work was centered on building "global community" at an intentionally diverse International House residence on campus where, she says, she never stopped learning and being surprised. Leslie says that Hall's work first came alive for her when she was busy with another one of her passions, ballroom dance, first as a student and then as a teacher. Here is a dance story she shares with her intercultural students:

> I used to teach ballroom dancing, where the goal is to perform highly technical steps, while staying connected and in the flow—dancing beautifully! When a couple is moving together nicely, even with basic steps, and even if their steps aren't precisely correct, it can be extraordinarily beautiful. But how easy it can be, as an instructor, to make the mistake of interrupting that flow: "Very good, very good! Stand tall, arms up, turn your foot 45 degrees on that step! Oh! and feel the music! One, twooooooo, three!" At that point, you can watch peoples' brains shift gears. You can see the intention moving forward in their heads. They'd be leaning in, full of effort but with no grace! Faced with formal, technical, and informal instructions all at once, the poor couple would barely be walking—stepping on one another—let alone dancing! And everyone would be left wondering what happened!
>
> Hall explained that "it is extremely difficult to practice more than one element of the formal, informal, technical triad at the same time without paralyzing results" and that "it [is] enough to draw attention to one level of activity while a person is operating on another to stop all coherent thought."[9] I was very careful in my teaching after learning this and knowing from real life examples how true it is. It helped me, in practical terms, refine my teaching methods both at the dance studio and in the classroom. Perhaps dance is so invigorating

because, like culture, it calls upon our whole brain at once. While teaching, though, I am careful to be mindful of what I am asking my students.

Two of my favorite instructors, the twelve-time un-defeated Canadian Professional Dancesport Champions, Mireille Veilleux and Pierre Allaire, taught me this: "First, you learn the tango steps"—in other words, the technical nature of what you are doing. "Then, you dance the tango"—you add the formal do's and don'ts and get moving on the floor. "Then, you become the tango!" This is when the full rhythmic capacity is engaged—in my mind, the informal knowing—dance is embodied, the music and both people are in synch so that as William Butler Yeats wrote, "How can we know the dancer from the dance?"[10]

In culture learning, we want to get to the same place, where we can live on a level where we can enter with the awareness of all of our minds and connect and flow with those around us. And these three aspects are just as relevant. Sometimes I have met students who speak other languages and know things about the world, but who have a hard time entering the "flow" or even realizing there is a flow in the community. Others, I have seen, even without a grasp of the common language, can enter into multicultural spaces and, with their warmth and charm, build lifelong friendships very quickly. Each of us has different capacities and different aspects of life come more easily. In dance, as in life, all of these elements are present.

In learning settings, many teachers tend to want to start the technical right away. What I find is that it is important to help people ground the learning in their informal reality first, to "get a feel" for what we are embarking on. Mireille and Pierre often do this by telling a story, often hilarious or passionate, connecting with people on a relational and meaning-level. I like to start that way, too: help people feel something, connect it to their life, then add anything I can do to talk directly to their bodies—do this, do that, move this way—trying as much as I can to short-circuit the doubts and resistance that seems to hang out in the technical, academic, logical, critical brain.

This is easiest to illustrate with the image of newly engaged "wedding couples," as we call them, those sweethearts who want to dance because they are getting married, and that's just what you do at your wedding in this culture. Almost every time, one partner comes in with a yearning to dance, and the other comes in believing that they absolutely can't do it. "Two left feet," they say. I say, "If you have a heartbeat, you can dance." If you can walk, you can surely dance! I think there are many ways to dance without feet at all, but for this particular style, this is an easy "in." Then, I get them connected, I get them moving together, walking together, chatting easily, swaying to the music—things that they can really do if, and only if, they let go of their fears and doubts. Since wedding dances don't require highly technical steps, I just build with them, like clay, from there. I tell their body to "lift your arms," "hold here and here, just like this," in a way where there is nothing to think about or debate; this is the formal side. "Okay, now keep swaying, now take a little side step." The dance grows from their connection, centered on the music that they have chosen—an expression of their love. Later, when they know they can "do it" because they did it…then we can add some fun, more technical bits, and make it really exciting. Their freedom in their own synchrony is part of the beauty, and so the first dance sets them up for a lifetime of tuning in to one another, trusting, and creating beauty together. At least I like to think so!

Kids learn very well this way. When I "taught" my young daughter to ice skate, I stayed near her, encouraging, trusting, and offering goals so that her thinking brain would actually "get out of the way," in a sense, from her body's process of learning. When she was feeling safe enough, I would say, "Go catch Daddy!" so that she'd focus there, rather than on each step.

I believe wholly that our intelligences live in our bodies as well as our minds, and learning to trust our embodied wisdom, to use our senses to create safe feeling spaces, and wondering at the magic of doing something with others that never seemed possible, is a great gift and a time to see our beauty come alive. Just as in the context of culture, my experience with Hall's work affirmed and clarified what I had sensed before in teaching, and with greater confidence and results.

Another lesson from Hall that I keep close is that communication is maybe 90% non-verbal. Tone of voice and the felt state of our own bodies as instructors can make worlds of difference. Sounds, a sense of safety, encouragement—all are crucial in the learning environment when you want learners to tap into their limbic, intuitive, felt sense of being. In any activity, I think doing is more important than the knowing.

Learning and Becoming

So, how *do* we learn what becomes a part of who we are? One quality comes through, from infancy well into our adult years: much of it arises from the influence of other people just doing what they have learned, and sometimes calling attention when what is expected is not met. It might be as simple as how we talk and even how we walk. The behavior of others exerts a profound influence on us, just as cultural values enacted do: a parent's desire for independence within the family will lead, where possible, to children having their individual rooms, and the role of a baby sitter for hire, a parent's need for a time away that also becomes, unintended, the child's feeling all right when the parent is away—a step toward independence. A great deal of what we learn, we learn through play—an undervalued feature of human culture and enculturation. Child's play includes imitating adults—playing "house" or "school"—imagining and performing behavior that is at the edge of what a child has experienced, feels and imagines.

Hall saw the value of making mistakes and learning to correct them—it may barely register as having been learned, or it may be learning to avoid making another mistake, or it may be learning not to take oneself too seriously about making mistakes.

There is also the matter of what we don't learn. That Deborah Tannen's book, *You Just Don't Understand,* speaks to the relevance across cultures and languages, and what women and men who love each other and have lived together for years never recognized or just put up with. Thomas Kochman's and Jean Mavrelis's study of interpersonal relations in culturally diverse organizational workplaces give ample evidence that we can be with people for years and still not figure out misunderstandings and minor irritations. And worse, without ever being aware of how our perceptions and behavior may fall far short of our intentions, and lacking realization of how others perceive and react to us.[11]

"Experience" seems to be the thread that runs through both how we learn and the evidence that we have learned. Cultural geographer Yi-Fu Tuan points out something interesting about the word "experience" and other words that are its companions. The word "experience shares a common root (*per*) with 'ex*per*iment,' 'ex*per*t,' and '*per*ilous.' To experience in the active sense requires that one venture forth into the unfamiliar and experiment with the elusive and uncertain. To become an expert, one must dare to confront the perils of the new."[12]

I borrow from the wisdom of Mary Catherine Bateson, daughter of two of the best-known anthropologists of the twentieth century,

Margaret Mead and Gregory Bateson, and a wise soul and beautiful writer herself:

> Because learning is the most basic of human adaptive processes, we can hope that it will lead toward a relationship with the rest of the biosphere that is both satisfying and sustainable. . . .
>
> Rarely is it possible to study all the instructions to a game before beginning to play, or to memorize the manual before turning on the computer. The excitement of improvisation lies not only in the risk involved but in the new ideas, as heady as the adrenaline of performance, that seem to come from nowhere. When the necessary tasks of learning cannot be completed in a portion of the life cycle set aside for them, they have to join life's other tasks and be done concurrently. We can carry on the process of learning in everything we do, like a mother balancing her child on one hip as she goes about her work with the other hand or uses it to open the doors of the unknown. Living and learning, we become ambidextrous.
>
> Ambiguity is the warp of life, not something to be eliminated. Learning to savor the vertigo of doing without answers or making shifts and making do with fragmentary ones, opens the pleasures of recognizing and playing with pattern, finding coherence within complexity, sharing within multiplicity. Improvisation and new learning are not private processes; they are shared with others at every age. The multiple layers of attention involved cannot safely be brushed aside or subordinated to the completion of tasks. We are called to join in a dance whose steps must be learned along the way, so it is important to attend and respond. Even in uncertainty, we are responsible for our steps.[13]

Notes

1. Edward T. Hall, "The Drive to Learn," *Santa Fe Magazine*, Spring, 1988, 13.
2. Bessel Van Der Kolk, *The Body Keeps the Score: Brain, Mind, and Body in the Healing of Trauma* (NY: Penguin Books, 2014), 58-59.
3. Edward T. Hall, *The Silent Language* (New York: Doubleday, 1959), 70.
4. Roger Harrison and Richard Hopkins, "The Design of Cross-Cultural Training: An Alternative to the University Model," *The Journal of Applied Behavioral Science*, vol 3 issue 4 (December 1967).
5. John R. Stilgoe, *Outside Lies Magic: Regaining History and Awareness in Everyday Places* (New York: Walker and Company, 1998).
6. Stilgoe, *Outside Lies Magic*, 3-4.
7. In an informal review of US Peace Corps volunteers in the late '60s looking at relatively effective volunteers by where they came from and what they studied in college, researchers were surprised to find that those who came from small towns—particularly in the South—seemed to do better than those from the more culturally mixed and complex urban centers. Regarding university majors, those from the humanities—literature, in particular perhaps because they were more likely to be attracted to the Peace Corps or because their prospects on the job market at home were less predicated on their major—seemed to adjust more easily than those from the sciences or engineering.
8. Readers who aren't aware might find it interesting that in the Japanese language, the *"-do"* refers to "the path," or "the way," not the destination, e.g., judo, aikido, kendo.
9. Hall, *Silent Language*, 65.
10. W. B. Yeats, "Among School Children," *The Collected Poems of W. B. Yeats* (Stansted, UK: Wordsworth Editions, 1994).
11. Thomas Kochman and Jean Mavrelis, *Corporate Tribalism: White Men/White Women and Cultural Diversity at Work* (Chicago: University of Chicago Press, 2009).
12. Yi-Fu Tuan, *Space and Place: The Perspective of Experience* (Minneapolis: University of Minnesota Press, 1977), 9.
13. Mary Catherine Bateson, *Peripheral Visions: Learning Along the Way* (New York: Harper, Collins, 1994), 9-10.

. To change **centimeters to meters**
you   ?   .

take out centi

F

Where was the American Declaration of Independence
signed?

At the bottom.

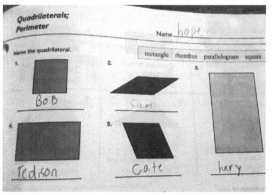

Quadrilaterals;
Perimeter

Name _hope_

Name the quadrilateral.

rectangle   rhombus   parallelogram   square

1.

BoB

2.

Sam

3.

4.

Tedison

5.

Cate

hary

---

3. Find x.

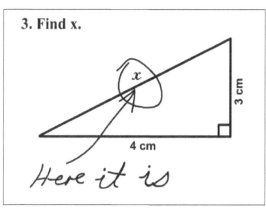

Here it is

Come, let us go down and confuse their language there, so that they will not understand one another's speech. So the Lord scattered them abroad from there over the face of all the earth, and they left off building the city. Therefore it was called Babel, because there the Lord confused the language of all the earth, and from there the Lord scattered them abroad over the face of all the earth.   Genesis 11: 1-9

CHAPTER ELEVEN

The Goose in the Bottle

We feel in one world, we think and name in
another. Between the two we can set up a system
of references, but we cannot fill in the gap.
—*Marcel Proust*

We cut nature up, organize it into concepts, and ascribe significances as we do, largely because we are parties to an agreement to organize it in this way—an agreement that holds throughout our speech community and is codified in the patterns of our language.
—*Benjamin Lee Whorf*

A Zen riddle: There is a large glass bottle with a long thin neck. In that bottle there is a fat goose. Question: How do we get the goose out of the bottle without harming the goose and without breaking the bottle?

A question that has been argued longer than that Zen riddle is about the language we speak, what we do with it, and what it might do with us. In a crude form the question is: do we just say what we see, or do we just see what we can say? Does the language we habitually use influence how we perceive and think, and, if so, then in what ways and to what extent? That is a topic more relevant than ever today as native speakers of many languages add to the social and linguistic wealth of nations everywhere on the globe, with some languages dominant as others disappear at an alarming rate. If the Tower of Babel was a punishment to confound the people of the earth and prevent us from understanding each other, that's one thing. But what if our diversity of languages is not a curse, but rather a blessing that offers a richness of ways of sensing and making sense? That has implications for problem-solving in education, business, and all institutions. It also has implications today when many languages are spoken by decreasing populations at a rate comparable to the loss of species of animals and also plants listed as "endangered."

What was a hot topic in the middle of the twentieth century, influenced in part by a broad application of Einstein's Theory of Special Relativity, came to be called "linguistic relativity," among other names proposed. If common sense notions of time and space might not be the solid constants we assumed, but rather "relative" to each other, might our perceptions and thinking also be relative to the languages we use in how we think and talk about reality? Or "reality."

Now often considered the most scientific of the social sciences, linguistics had been an integral part of anthropology in the US, but as the field grew in importance, and in collaboration with other disciplines (socio-linguistics, psycho-linguistics, for example) its principal relationship with anthropology declined. The importance that language plays in our perception, thinking, social cohesion, and culture has a long history. Largely speculative, theoretical, and anecdotal (not to be dismissed) that our internalized language(s) exert an influence, continues to intrigue even if, as a theory, it may be impossible to prove. Now that neuroscience allows us to peer into the brain to identify where and how language is integral to an individual and, by extension culture, it may be possible to find support for some assertions and raise yet more questions.

"Seeing is Forgetting the Name of the Thing One Sees"

The above quote is by artist and poet Robert Irwin who died in 2023. The magnificent garden that frames the Getty Museum in Los Angeles is one of the best-known creations of this artist who worked in many media.[1]

As artists in all genres have said, the art is the creation. The title of the work or the name attached is frequently incidental, and often not even a name that the artist chose. To the question, "what's that?" painters have answered, "If I could have put it in words, I wouldn't have painted it." Dean Barnlund used to distinguish between two kinds of visitors at an art museum: those who look at an artwork carefully and then step closer to learn the name of the artist and what the work is called, and those who want to see the name of the work and the name of the artist before looking more carefully at the artwork itself.

Most people live in a social world in which words are omnipresent. We are encouraged to want to know what something is called. As children we ask, "what's that?" The "that" is what we are seeing or experiencing, and not a word. Knowing the distinction may seem obvious: as the map is not the same as the territory it represents, "the word is not the thing." But what is "a thing" in one language is an action in another, and meaningless in a third. Anthropologist Dorothy Lee challenged the simple semantic duality of words and things:

> According to the classical view, the word is not the thing. This object that I hold in my hand is independent of the label I give to it. It is not a pencil. I only assign to it the name pencil. What it is, is assumed to be independent of what I call it. Pencil is only a sound-complex, a word for the reality, the thing. But when I call this "pencil" I also classify it as a substantive, a noun. I separate it as other than the fingers it elongates . . . A Maidu Indian . . . would probably have no recognition to, or would not have delimited this reality into, the pencil as object.

Instead, he would perceive the specific act of the hand—in this case the act of pointing with a pencil—and would have expressed this by means of a suffix which, attached to the verb "to point-with-a-long-thin-instrument" (such as a pencil, or a straight pipe, or a cigarette.) . . . What is a thing for me is a qualification or an attribute of an act for him.[2]

Knowing names is a major part of schooling, and a measure of judging "intelligence." So-called "IQ" (intelligence quotient) tests are, or were, heavily weighted by being able to answer "what do we call that?" Increasing one's vocabulary will increase one's test score in applications for college, even though learning more words doesn't make one smarter. "Words, words, words"—to quote Shakespeare who coined over 1700 words we use today.

Though Hall wrote mostly about the *non*-verbal, which he recognized as deeply under-appreciated because we've privileged the word, he drew insights and models from linguists to help make his case and also provide models that would be useful. Hall's references to the verbal run throughout his books. Having a name for something can also be reassuring. Patients in their doctor's office find reassurance when they hear their feelings and symptoms coalesce in a name. Even when the name is scary, it gives us a way to ask more questions. And the idea that particular languages may direct us, "predispose us" some say, to perceive and think and act in certain ways is a notion worth a little more attention here.

The Wind is Not Blowing

"Language and Thought" was the name of a popular introductory course I was privileged to teach for several years, respectful of gifted professors who preceded me and made the course thought-provoking for young students. The overarching theme was how we use words and, some would say, how words use us. Well into the course, and optimistic that I had established a theme of not confusing words for what they represent was clear, I would pose a child's question. How will you answer if some day your child asks you, "Where does my lap go when I stand up?" To my dismay, what students answered told me I had utterly failed in my effort. Students previously eager to express their opinions fell silent or glanced at the floor. One young woman said, "Ask your father," and a young man said, "Ask your mother." Another suggested, "It slides down into your socks and waits there until you sit down again." Why that particular question seemed difficult while a similar question, like, "where does my fist go when I open my hand?" might be so obvious that it wouldn't be worth asking. I still wonder.

A more challenging question is: "When we say, 'it is raining,' *what* is raining?" What is the "*it*"? I asked my students in the US to ask their friends, family, and also strangers, and then report back. "The clouds are raining" or "the weather is raining," and often and awkwardly, "I don't know" were what most said they were told. "Well, the rain is raining," some said, but they appeared uncomfortable or silly because it was both obvious and also redundant. And accurate. We just don't talk that way, but if we were singing those words in a popular song, we might not think it silly. Poetic license. Context!

This question is not about rain but about grammar for students whose first language is not English or another Indo-European language taught in class. I've asked Thai, Korean, Indonesian, and Japanese students that question, and, in their answers, I can hear their English teacher say, "English is a language that requires each sentence to have a subject, so in this case the 'it' is just an empty placeholder." Native speakers acquire their language naturally, without the burden of needing explanations. Non-native speakers can often explain the rules of a language better than native speakers. In the same way, questions about one's culture stump people who never had to think about and then explain it. That theme runs through the entirety of Hall's work.

Or consider wind. We can say, sometimes as a matter of fact, "the wind is blowing," We can also say "the wind is not blowing." But then we might wonder, if the wind is *not* blowing, then what is it doing? What kind of wind doesn't blow? Now, that resembles a Zen *koan*! We talk about "the wind" as if it were separate from the blowing. When we speak, Benjamin Lee Whorf wrote, "we are parties to an agreement" to follow the implicit rules of our language, no less than when we are parties to an agreement to obey the rules when playing a game. That's how we talk when speaking English and how we understand others speaking that language. Does that also affect how we think?

Noah Brannen was a linguistics professor who directed the Japanese language program at International Christian University (ICU), a bilingual university just outside of Tokyo. Noah was a colleague there and a dear friend. After receiving his PhD in linguistics at the University of Michigan, specializing in Japanese, Brannen had come to Japan not as a professor but as a missionary of the Southern Baptist persuasion. One day in a conversation, Noah startled me when he said that as he studied the Japanese language, it changed the way he thought of God! Consider that for a moment. It must take something mighty powerful to change a Baptist missionary's idea of God. Not that traditional Japanese spiritual beliefs lack for a god concept: Japan has eight-million gods, a number that traditionally symbolized an eternity.

What struck Brannen was not a vision from above, it was mostly about grammar. Though English requires a subject, a some*thing* that *does* something, Japanese does not. For the first time he was learning a language that did not require a subject and a predicate to make a complete sentence, so there was no need for our fictive "it" to explain what is raining. That was, for Rev. Brannen, a revelation and an influence on new ways of thinking about what was most important in his life.

Japanese professional interpreters tell me that at political or business conferences, sometimes it is difficult to interpret from Japanese to English because often there is no explicit subject in a Japanese sentence, so the interpreter needs to assign something to make sense to the listeners, while also being faithful to the speaker's intent.

The idea that the language one speaks influences how one thinks has been considered for a long time. In the Western world, some trace that speculation at least as far back as Aristotle. (Some classicists imagine that there was nothing that Aristotle hadn't thought and written about.) In 1690, John Locke recognized that different languages perceive the objects of nature differently. Wilhelm von Humboldt and Johann Herder in the German Romantic tradition are credited for advancing what would come to be known as this theory of linguistic relativity, which was brought to the US from Germany by Franz Boas, whose influence remained at Columbia University where Hall completed his graduate work.[3]

Two Very Interesting People

The notion that language in itself has an influence on how we think and act has been, in the US, associated with the names Edward Sapir, a German language linguist and polymath who helped found the anthropology department at Columbia; and his most famous student, Benjamin Lee Whorf, who enrolled in Sapir's classes as a "nontraditional student." Whorf was an MIT-educated chemical engineer working at the Hartford Life Insurance Company located not far from the Yale campus when he took his first linguistics class.[4]

Sapir was a scholar and among the most influential linguists of the last century, "the father of American linguistics," it was said, when people were praised that gendered way. His student, Whorf, pursued linguistics as an avocation because of deep-seated questions, not to become a linguistics professor. Yet in the view of a prominent contemporary linguist, George Lakoff, Whorf was "the most interesting linguist of his time." I find that inspiring: one needn't center one's education on a particular subject to later contribute to that field.[5]

Sapir is readable, writing at a time when the subject was developing its own vocabulary. His books are still read; one needn't have studied linguistics to understand what he wrote, and in that, he and Hall share a gift and intention to reach beyond the concepts. Sapir was also a music critic and a poet who published in *Poetry* magazine, and wrote for political journals with a liberal bent, including *The New Republic* and *The Nation*. Perhaps intimations of linguists whose political writings would attract attention a century later, most notably Noam Chomsky and George Lakoff. Sapir took a keen interest in anthropology and psychology, especially in links between culture and personality, and the place of the individual in culture. Like Hall, he did not feel constrained by the field with which he was identified, and, even more than Hall, he engaged in writing and speaking—he was a popular public speaker—spanning science and the humanities. His research focus was Indigenous cultures and languages in North America including those in the very region where Hall grew up, notably Hopi and Navajo (Diné). In Boas's time, that was a motivation for European scholars to come to this "new world," to study languages that had remained largely free from the influences of European languages.[6]

Benjamin Lee Whorf's background and education was totally different from his future mentor. Sapir was an émigré from Germany, but Whorf was born into an old established New England family. Attending MIT, his focus was not language studies or anthropology; it was chemistry. After graduating, Whorf went to work as a chemical engineer for the Hartford Insurance Company where he remained until his untimely death at age 44. Fascinated by language and believing that within each language was a hidden code of meanings, he was 33 when he took his first linguistics class, "American Indian Linguistics," taught by Sapir. In that same class was George Trager who, years later, was the linguist and colleague who so influenced Hall.

Sapir encouraged his unconventional student, Whorf, to concentrate on studying the Hopi language. There were very few Indigenous students of linguistics during this period. College students then were mostly white (and male), so there were few native Hopi speakers who might review and critique his work. One of Whorf's best-known essays today is, "The Relation of Habitual Thought to Behavior," now considered a classic, and also very readable to anyone who is interested.[7]

Whorf, himself, later became a part-time professor at Yale. In his classes, a favorite (and unpublished) example he would tell his students was about hidden features in language categories, in particular how, in English, we talk about fish. Forget for now, our goose: think about fish, and how we refer to fish when it's just one fish or several.[8] In English, from guppies to sharks, when we speak of more than one fish of some species, we add a "ss" or "zz" sound that we mark with an "s." But with some species, we don't: salmon, herring, bass, cod, trout, tuna. Same word, singular or plural. Why? Whorf's answer was that the words for the fish, whether one or one hundred, that do not take an "s," are those that English speakers historically regarded as edible. For fish that have been considered inedible, we add mark with add sounds and in writing mark with "s." Whorf was most interested in such indicators implicit in how language offers clues about cultural beliefs and values. Indeed, a strong motivation for him wanting to study linguistics was to discover such codes of implicit meanings.

Today, the names of the linguist Sapir and his unconventional student Whorf are linked in what is widely known as the "Sapir-Whorf hypothesis," even though neither proposed such a hypothesis. Rather it represents a general theory that brings together relevant quotes of both Sapir and Whorf that suggest that our perceptions of and thoughts about the world differ relative to the language(s) we have learned and internalized. It is a "theory" that may defy being proven, which, if so, some would disqualify it as "a theory." Still, "linguistic relativity" is an itch that must be scratched.

Many linguists dismiss the idea of linguistic relativity out of hand, including the well-known Harvard linguist, Stephen Pinker, while other linguists, including Lera Boroditsky (at University of California, San Diego), and Anna Wierzbicka (emeritus professor at the Australian National University), conclude otherwise. Wierzbicka reacts to those who dismiss the influence of language on how we think: "Anyone with an intimate knowledge of two (or more) different languages and cultures will find it hard to take Pinker's hyperbole seriously. It is self-evident to any bilingual that language and patterns of thought are interlinked."[9]

Hall, of course, was very much in the "relativist" camp. His life's work was arguing that we live in different sensory words, individually but especially as shaped by the communities into which we have been enculturated, and these are very much influenced by our language habits.

In *The Hidden Dimension,* Hall's book about the human use of space (proxemics), Hall quotes a famous passage by Edward Sapir: "It is quite an illusion to imagine that one adjusts to reality essentially without the use of language and that language is merely an incidental means of solving problems of communication or reflection. The fact of the matter is that the 'real world' is to a large extent built up on the language habits of the group."[10]

"Language habits" means how we usually talk and write, not the structure and systems of language that are taught as "rules" in, say, an English [language] class. This is a classic distinction credited to Swiss linguistic Ferdinand de Suassure as *"parole"* (speech) in contrast to *"langue"* (language). De Saussure used the analogy of chess, contrasting the rules which players must follow with the choices a player makes.

Hall saw language and our language habits as bound up in our how we sense and make sense of our world, and though he did not identify as a linguist (nor did Whorf), his work was very much influenced by Whorf's writings and those of his mentor, Sapir. I should add that the late 1950s and early 1960s were a time when linguistic relativity was at a high point of interest, including articles and books written about it. That this also coincided with the formation of a field of study, with practical applications, called "intercultural communication" has kept "linguistic relativity" a part of most basic courses in that field. In that era, "different languages" suggested its relevance to international communication. It wasn't until 1968 that a greater appreciation of Indigenous languages, when the role of the "Navajo Code Talkers" role in using their language as the basis of an unbroken code during the Second World War was made public.

Subsequent expansion of immigration and refugee policies in the US resulted in a far greater range and number of native speakers of non-Indo-European languages and the challenges and opportunities this richness presented. Today, for example, across the Los Angeles Unified School District there are 96 languages spoken by students in their homes; half of California's young children have an immigrant parent. Moreover, the businesses and organizations in which people work are increasingly multi-lingual collectively, and more people are recognizing this as a strength for the very reasons Hall was writing about seventy years earlier.

They Have a Word for It

We are fascinated to learn that one language or another has a special word with no English equivalent. Some we borrow into our language. English has borrowed from the German language, *Schadenfreude*, that guilty pleasure we feel when someone we dislike is suffering, but not yet borrowed the German is *Treppenwitz* which describes what you feel when you think of a witty comeback or clever comment, but too late to say it. Tagalog has the word "*layogenic,*" about something or someone that looks great at a distance but as you get closer . . . not so much. Reminds me of a term used briefly in Japan in the early 1980s: "*T. E.*" I asked what that means and was told, well, you know how E. T. is ugly on the outside but really kind and very sweet inside? T. E. is the opposite.

"Loan words" are part of everyday speech. English has "borrowed" from many languages to enrich its word stock. Sixteenth-century English poet and literary critic, George Puttenham, warned that if English continues to borrow it would become bankrupt. Instead, the English language has been enriched for everyone, and now American English has been loaned to many languages where purists warn against such abominations as "teenager" and "weekend." It is not just the foreign word, but that it introduces entities that disturb cultural tradition. Adding words to our vocabulary is not uncommon and indeed necessary in a dynamic society. Shakespeare gave us nearly two thousand new words and phrases. We call attention to some new words every year, "the word of the year," like Stephen Colbert's "truthiness" that itself was mocking the media in the age of Donald Trump, who was credited with telling over thirty-thousand mistruths.

But the linguistic relativity theory is not about invented or borrowed words. George Lakoff points out that Whorf's emphasis was on grammar and grammaticized words that are the implicit "rules" of how we speak.[11] It was about the harder-to-talk-about subject of the "rules" we are party to—the grammar and "grammaticized words"—conservative, and resistant to change. Equally important, Whorf was also writing about "language *habits*," *how* we use our language, naturally, spontaneously, and in ordinary conversation, not what *could* be said.

When Gloria Steinem in 1971 suggested "Ms.," a title originally proposed in 1901 as a term of address for women that was not coded for marital status like the privileged "Mr.," it was a language marker for social change that was already underway. If, as Sapir said, "language is a map of culture," it is often through changes in how we talk that the public recognizes and reacts to social changes in process. Half a century later, social changes demanding respect and expression in word choices in the linguistic map indicates tectonic shifts in the territory it represents.

Getting Personal: Pronouns

I	we
you	you
he, she, it	they

Looking at this familiar English language personal pronoun chart, what is notable? When I've asked in classes, reactions varied. Usually it's the capital "I" that students, native speakers, and those who learned English in classrooms comment on. Some see this as arrogant; some wonder if "I" signals "individualism," but that's not about grammar. The "you"—in both singular and plural—is mentioned, and some point out that other "Western languages" would have two different pronouns for singular and plural to distinguish between "formal" and "informal," as did English before "thou" disappeared. For reasons I can only guess have been so internalized, few remark that for the third-person singular, there are three words instead of one, and the only place that codes for gender. Today, when people are sensitive to the limits of "binary" options and aware of gender as fluid and a range, that would be the first to be pointed out, as if it were not obvious. Even in—or maybe especially in—grammar, social and political attention exerts an influence.

Now it is *pro forma* in institutions and organizations to ask those present, "How do you want to be identified, acknowledged?" Along with one's name on a roster will be each person's pronoun preferences, depending on where in a sentence a pronoun would be needed: Ntumbo, B. (he/him); Smith, J. (she/her); Garcia, M. (he/they), Kim, A. (they/them). Asking individuals how they want to be identified and referred to may be challenging to many English speakers over a certain age. While it is about being inclusive at the individual level, it's not "just about words." Inviting individual choices for humble pronouns is as much about social and political changes, values, and beliefs. Grammar becomes surprisingly intimate and emotional.[12]

Stepping back and dispassionately looking at pronouns, previously just assumed—and therefore ignored—there is as much a diversity of pronoun options across languages and cultures as there is diversity of the many species around us. Some languages code not just for gender and singular or plural. Many offer possibilities that indicate familiarity with the person referred to, and to status. Japanese, I was taught, had many more first-person pronoun options than English— eight—indicating relative status or seniority or familiarity, but one could avoid using them. Some pronouns show affection or social distance. English has few pronoun options, but they are "strong": how often do we use "I" to begin a sentence, and the all-purpose "you"? Professor Brannen used to say that when native English speakers learning Japanese directly translate English into Japanese, they can sound arrogant starting every sentence with "I" and also aggressive, as if poking the listener with "you," "you," "you."

Whorf emphasized he was writing about not what *could be said*, but how most people actually talk, those "language *habits*," *how* we use our language, naturally, spontaneously, and in ordinary conversation. George Lakoff writes about this in his most interesting and provocative book, *Women, Fire, and Dangerous Things*. In his chapter, "Whorf and Whorfism," Lakoff reminds us that Whorf's emphasis was on grammar and grammaticized words that are the implicit "rules" of how we speak. The intimate connection between language and perception and behavior could not be clearer.

A World in Motion

European scholars, anthropologists, and linguists, who came to North America to discover the structure and word stock of Indigenous languages undisturbed by the intrusions of the French, Spanish, and English colonists, were very interested in the Indigenous languages they encountered, totally different from the language diversity in Europe or of Latin or ancient Greek some would have studied. Little wonder those first "explorers," financed by institutions of power, government, religion, or commercial organizations, not infrequently all, colonized and imposed their sponsor's language on the people whose lives they would disrupt and change.

Do our "western" (and other Indo-European) languages require us to speak in a way that reflects a long outdated "Euclidian" view of the world where the normal condition is of things at rest? Do Navajo/Diné speakers not just speak, but also perceive, a world different from neighbors who speak Spanish or English at home? In English and other Indo-European languages, the principal verb is "to be"—"is" in its various tenses. Not so in Navajo/Diné as linguist Gary Witherspoon described in *Language and Art in the Navajo Universe*: "Static verbs describe the state, position, or condition of something that is temporarily at rest. The assumption [in Navajo] is that nothing is totally inactive; in fact, everything exhibits both active and static characteristics." He continues:

> I once conservatively estimated that Navajo contained some 356,200 distinct conjugations for the verb "to go." These conjugations all apply to the ways in which humans "go." If we added all the verbs relating "to move," as well as "to go," such as walking or running, the number of conjugations would be well into the millions. In this regard it is particularly relevant and significant that the principal verb in the Navajo language is the verb "to go" and not the verb "to be" which is the principal verb in so many other languages but is of relatively minor importance in Navajo. This seems to indicate a cosmos composed of processes and events as opposed to a cosmos of facts and things.[13]

It would be in an international war that the Indigenous languages, which their colonizers had sought to vanquish, would turn out to be recognized as an asset. In the war with Japan in the 1940s, the Navajo language was used as the basis for a communication code that no other nation could decipher. So valuable was this code that for years after the war ended, the proud veteran Navajo Code Talkers were prohibited from telling even their families about their war experience because that code might be needed again.[14]

A Navajo/Diné Physicist

Fred Begay (1938-2013) grew up speaking the languages of his parents, Navajo and Ute. Both of his parents were healers and they taught their son the songs of Blessingway and other ceremonies. He was ten when he learned English at a Bureau of Indian Affairs school where, like others at Indian boarding schools, he was being prepared to be a farmer. After high school he enlisted in the Air Force and served in an air rescue squadron in Korea. Fred had always been curious about natural phenomena—what makes the rainbow?—and so with government-supported opportunities for veterans seeking further education, he enrolled at the University of New Mexico to study science and math. He went on to receive a graduate degree in physics, and then completed a PhD in nuclear physics.

From the low expectations of a ten-year-old kid at an Indian boarding school when he first learned English to doing research on high energy gamma rays and solar neutrons, and even invited to teach at Stanford University, the sweep of his learning is astonishing. Today, as a high school kid, he might be classified as "disadvantaged," but perhaps he had the advantage of perceiving the world from a Diné language perspective that presents a world that European languages do not. Perhaps those who internalize a language that posits that the normal state of things is to be at rest (the Euclidian view), are today the disadvantaged ones who have to work harder to un-learn language habits in order to think as a physicist.[15]

A Navajo premise is that significant and relevant to the powers of thought and speech is that all matter and all being have a dualistic nature: static and active. The assumption that underlies this dualistic aspect of all being and existence is that the world is in motion, that things are constantly undergoing processes of transformation, deformation, and restoration, and that the essence of life and being is movement.[16]

Not that today we see a glut of Diné physicists, advantaged by virtue of their native language, but Begay became a role model for youth in the Navajo nation and he encouraged kids to appreciate their underappreciated and historically dismissed advantages. Other role models in this largest Indigenous community: artists and astronauts, doctors and even a golf champion, Notah Begay III, who was Tiger Woods's roommate at Stanford.

If language is an integral part of culture, and exerts an influence on how we perceive and make sense, then what about a person who speaks more than one language? Bilingualism or speaking in more than two languages is not just common, it is the norm in much of the world. Questions have been raised about some language-related research done in the US because there are so many mono-language speakers compared to elsewhere. Even in the US, which has no official language, over 67 million people speak a language at home that is different than the English needed for schooling and at work.

Am I the Same Person When I Speak in Different Languages?

Setting aside the questions of the influence of language on perception and thought, it is just as important to ask if bi- and multi-linguals feel different when they are speaking different languages. This question is confounded by the likelihood that often they will be speaking to different people and often about different subjects and in different circumstances when they switch from one language to another. Multilingual students at Ritsumeikan Asia Pacific University in Beppu, Japan, include students from nearly a hundred different countries who attend this innovative school. Formally a bilingual (Japanese and English) university, those two languages might be a student's third or fourth. There were young people from more than a dozen countries and languages in my classes. I've asked hundreds of these young people how they feel about themselves when speaking in different languages. Nearly all affirmed that the language they spoke affects how they express themselves. Even their posture, gestures, and facial expressions differ depending on which language they are speaking. Following are three representative comments:

> *A Japanese student:* When I speak English, I become a more open person. I don't know why but I [usually prefer to] tell my personal stories and feelings in English, but on the other hand when I speak Japanese, I am a listener. I don't talk about myself so much [in Japanese].
>
> *A Thai student:* I prefer to use the Thai language to explain things because I think I can use proper words and I can explain the content better than [using] other languages. I prefer using Japanese in order to ask for help and to write emails and letters because [Japanese] words are soft and delicate; I can humble myself to be polite to others. I always use English in order to make group decision. I avoid using Japanese in this case because Japanese is ambiguous and [that makes it] hard to make a fast decision.
>
> *A Korean student:* When I speak Japanese, Korean, and English, I become a different person because I try to reflect the cultures behind the language. [To describe myself] speaking English [I] am a person who is confident, full of energy and who can show critical thinking on certain issues; [when

speaking Japanese I am] a person who can ask a favor in an indirect way or who can imply my opinion to others in a polite way; in Korean [I] am a person who respects older people and does not speak [my] opinion much, a person who can follow others.

Orphaned from the Language of the Mother Tongue I Never Knew

I thought I recognized his name when it appeared in my email inbox, and sure enough it was a voice from the past. Nearly fifty years earlier, Elroy Osario had been a student in the class, "Language & Thought," when he must have been about eighteen years old. Teachers don't often hear from students after many years, and former students might be surprised to be remembered. What Elroy wrote moved me, but even more, that he had been thinking about this all these years. It was about that linguistic relativity theory that touched him personally. He kindly permitted me to share his words here:

Aloha,

I was one of your students at Northwestern from 1965-1969. I was not one of your better students.

But there is a concept with which I have been wrestling for some time. The Hawaiian language was intentionally suppressed following the overthrow of the Hawaiian Kingdom and the subsequent annexation by the United States.

My grandmother, in order to attend elementary school, had to adopt a Christian name. She herself became an elementary school teacher, and she wrote and spoke perfect English. She also wrote and spoke in Hawaiian, but never to her children or grandchildren. She insisted that we speak only English.

The Hawaiian language was revitalized in the late sixties and early seventies. Currently, there are dozens of Hawaiian language "immersion" schools throughout the state, but essentially, Hawaiian is being taught as a second language.

I believe that culture and perceptions form the language, not the other way around. So now the Hawaiian language (almost without exception) is being taught by people who were raised speaking English, and who were raised as Americans, to people who were raised speaking English, and raised as Americans.

So my question is this: Isn't there a critical element missing in all this? It's not just how you speak, it's how you were raised, and how you learned to view the world around you, to conceptualize, that really matters when it comes to preserving a language.

My fear is that we have lost that perspective. I might someday be able to speak Hawaiian, but I cannot think Hawaiian. And so, I can never see my land the same way that my grandmother did.

I hope that all is well with you. I thought about you and the time you spent in Tanzania and realized that this was probably a subject with which you were quite familiar. I wish we could have had this discussion back at Northwestern, but I was too busy trying to be an American.

Mr. Osario writes from his heart. The pain, the loss, he feels is not just about language, it is also about the political and cultural imperialism imposed upon indigenous peoples across the globe throughout history. The intimate connection of language and culture ("language as culture," some feel) is undeniable. Students from Okinawa, which was a separate kingdom from Japan, much like Hawaii was a kingdom before US colonizing, and others from the diversity of lands that are now Indonesia, could echo Osario's words. And here in New Mexico, where many communities struggle to maintain the language of their grandparents, and all the grandparents before.

Elizabeth Buck at the University of Hawaii East-West Center, has written about the impact of colonialism in its many forms, often buttressed by the colonist's religion. A culture ravaged, meanings of words re-interpreted to fit the colonizers' world. Three fundamental changes in language were initiated with contact: (1) the radical shift from orality to literacy, (2) the displacement of Hawaiian by English as the dominant language of discourse, and (3) the repositioning and redefinition of Hawaii, the Hawaiians, and their material and symbolizing practices informed by English and Western views of reality.[17]

> In the metaphors, tropes, and logic in English were carried new representations, and new evaluations of reality. . . . The very ability to give English names to things once embedded with Hawaiian connotations was an extension of control over the islands, a redefinition of reality in the image of the New who names.[18]
>
> It is not hard to imagine, and their words make it clear, how shocked the missionaries were by the Hawaiian state of undress, their liberal sexuality, and their religious forms and images. In their constant drive to substitute piety for sexuality, nothing was more upsetting for the missionaries than the hula; it was sin in its most open manifestation.[19]
>
> . . . Hawaiian religion inverted into myth and superstition; heiau worship, chat ad hula into pagan rites; sex into sin and sexual crimes (adultery and prostitution); and poetry and narrative into 'folklore.'[20]

It's never just about language. The diversity of how our languages and the diversity of dialects to conceptualize a world, and make sense of it, is a richness that the curse of Tower of Babel inadvertently gave us. Again, George Lakoff said it so well:

> Just as the gene pool of a species needs to be kept diverse if the species is to survive under a wide variety of conditions, so

I believe that diverse ways of comprehending experience are necessary to our survival as a species. I believe that vanishing cultures and languages need to be protected just as vanishing species do. And, like Whorf, I think we have a lot to learn from other ways of conceptualizing experience that have evolved around the world.

Refusal to recognize conceptual relativism where it exists [has] ethnical consequences. It leads directly to conceptual elitism and imperialism—to the assumption that our behavior is rational and that of other people is not, and to attempts to impose our way of thinking on others.

Whorf's ethical legacy was to make us aware of this.[21]

In a book, provocative in content and title, *Imprisoned in English: The Hazards of English as a Default Language,* linguist Anna Wierzbicka argues the importance of a diversity of languages is to test what we take for granted.[22] She quotes a Russian and English speaking bi-lingual linguist, Aneta Pavlenko, who regrets that linguists, at least in the US, direct their attention to "a minority of the world's population," meaning in part, predominantly mono-lingual speakers. She urges that a "multi-lingual lens" be used, especially in all aspects of linguistics.

The link between language and culture has long been noted. How can we talk about language *and* culture, we might say, when language is so deeply rooted in and an integral part of any notion of culture? New words often alert us to cultural changes underway, even as the conservative force of language resists change, because "we are party to an agreement . . ." when we speak a language we were given before we were old enough to be aware of that gift. The gift that lets us share experience and insights and imaginings may also be a constraint.

Now, about that goose—the one that we said was in a bottle

The question in that Zen riddle was, "How do we get the goose out of the bottle without harming the goose or breaking the bottle?" The clue to the answer is to ask: "How did we get the goose into the bottle?" Well, we (or I) said it was in. So, how do we get it out? Same way: we say it is out.[23]

Not all of our problems are so easily solved, but many problems exist because we see them as problems and say they are. Much time, agony, and money are spent each year to free flocks of geese we put in countless bottles.

Notes

1. Lawrence Weschler, *Seeing is Forgetting the Name of the Thing One Sees: A Life of Contemporary Artist Robert Irwin* (Los Angeles and Berkeley: Univ. of California Press, 1982).

2. Dorothy Lee, *Freedom and Culture* (Englewood Cliffs, New Jersey: Prentice-Hall, 1959), 80-81.

3. Cliff Goddard and Anna Wierzbicka, "Key Words, Culture and Cognition," *Philosophica* 55 (1995, 1), 19.

4. I find it curious that three of the most original and innovative Americans made their contributions in other fields while employed in the insurance business: Whorf, in linguistics; Wallace Stevens, in poetry; and Charles Ives who was an influence on musicians as varied as Arnold Schoenberg, Gustav Mahler, and Frank Zappa. So radical was his experimental music that his Symphony No. 4 could not be performed until fifty years after Ives composed it; its recording was awarded a Grammy a century after Ives's death.

5. George Lakoff, *Women, Fire, and Dangerous Things: What Categories Reveal about the Mind* (Chicago: University of Chicago Press, 1987). Now regarded as classics are: Edward Sapir, *Language: An Introduction to the Study of Speech* (NY: Houghton Mifflin, 1921) and *Culture, Language and Personality: Selected Essays* (Berkeley and Los Angeles: University of California Press, 1949).

6. Paul Bohannan and Mark Glazer, eds., *High Points in Anthropology* (New York: Alfred Knopf, 1973), 143-145.

7. Benjamin Lee Whorf, "The Relation of Habitual Thought to Behavior," in John B. Carroll, ed, *Language, Thought, and Reality: Selected Writings of Benjamin Lee Whorf* (Cambridge, MA: MIT Press, 1956).

8. I must credit Paul Bohannan, a colleague and supportive friend of Hall, for this fish story. Described in Bohannan and Glazer, *High Points*, 154.

9. Cliff Goddard and Anna Wierzbicka, "Key Words, Culture and Cognition," *Philosophica* 55 (1995, 1), 19.

10. Quoted in Edward T. Hall, *The Hidden Dimension* (New York: Doubleday, 1966), 93.

11. Read George Lakoff's wonderful chapter on "Whorf and Whorfism" in *Women, Fire, and Dangerous Things: What Categories Reveal About the Mind* (Chicago: University of Chicago Press, 1987).

12. With a greater awareness of sensitivity to and demands by the LGBTQ+ communities, individuals are asserting their right to choose their preferred personal pronouns. The awareness of the distinction between sex and gender (the biological and the social) and rejecting the binary assumption about gender and sexuality, even singular or plural in personal pronouns, demands that language better fit a new social reality. It is one thing to add a new term, the title/honorific: "Ms." that doesn't mess with grammar, but to request to be identified by gendered and non-gendered pronouns, that is a greater challenge for many native speakers.

13. Gary Witherspoon, *Language and Art in the Navajo Universe* (Ann Arbor: University of Michigan Press, 1977), 48-49.

14. I am grateful to have known Carl Gorman, one of first of the Code Talkers, and Bill Toledo, who was recruited later. Bill often met with some the graduate students in my seminars so that his experience could be shared with a new generation of people. Later, Bill Toledo visited Japan and spoke, with an interpreter, at a few public schools. More than one Japanese student remarked that he looked just like the child's grandfather.

15. Begay was the subject of a Public Broadcasting System 1979 NOVA documentary, "*The Long Walk of Fred Young*," when he was still using the name "Young," assigned to him at an Indian boarding school. See "American Indians on Film & Video Documentaries in the Library of Congress" (https//www loc gov/rr/mopic/findaid/Indian2 html) Accessed 07/24/2023.

16. Witherspoon, *Language and Art*, 48.

17. Elizabeth Buck, "English in the Linguistic Transformation of Hawaii: Literacy, Languages, and Discourse," in *World Englishes*, 1986, Vol. 5, 2/3, 141-152. Also see: Elizabeth Buck, *Paradise Remade: The Politics of Culture and History in Hawai'i* (Temple University Press, 1994).

18. Buck, *Linguistic Transformation*, 146.

19. Buck, *Linguistic Transformation*, 150.

20. Buck, *Linguistic Transformation*, 147.

21. Lakoff, *Women, Fire, and Dangerous Things*, 337.

22. Anna Wierzbicka, *Imprisoned in English: The Hazards of English as a Default Language* (London: Oxford University Press, 2013).

23. Which reminds me of another Zen story: An old monk traveling with a younger monk came to a river they needed to cross. There they saw a young woman also attempting to cross. She asked if they could help her

cross to the other side. Although the monks had taken vows to never touch a woman, the older monk lifted the woman and carried her across the river, wished her well, and continued on his journey. The younger monk, shocked, for a long time said nothing, until finally he said, "We are not permitted to touch a woman but you carried that woman across the river. How could you do that?" The older monk replied, "Dear brother, I set her down on the other side of the river. Why are you still carrying her?"

"Naki Warai Jinsei"
Life: tears and laughter.

Photo by Alex Jones

CHAPTER TWELVE

The Nearness of You

To an energetic child, a flight of stairs is a link between two
floors, an invitation to run up and down; to an old man it
is a barrier between two floors, a warning to stay put.
—*Yi-Fu Tuan*

Looking from a different perspective makes you
realize that it's not the deer that is crossing the
road, it's the road that is crossing the forest.
—*Muhammad Ali*

Sometimes coming too close is going too far.
—*S. I. Hiyakawa*

O f all the concepts, outlooks, and insights that Hall presented
over half a century ago, maybe nothing attracted more interest
than his observations about how we use space and time to express
and modulate our relationships with others. Often what we express
spatially is felt less consciously but more deeply than much of what we
say verbally. "Up close and personal" can be "too close for comfort."
Proximity is literally a measure of relationships and attitudes. We

307

have distant relatives and close friends. A politician advises "keep your friends close, and your enemies closer," at least metaphorically.

Some metaphors are not just metaphors. How might we characterize our feelings about someone we want to keep "at arm's length?" "An arm's length," Hall noted, is a good approximation of how close we prefer to be with someone we'd describe that way, beyond the distance we choose with friends. How we talk is affected by the distance. At different distances our words, even our grammar changes.

We speculate about relationships revealed by the space between people in photographs, and we sometimes gauge how friends in a new relationship are doing based on their physical proximity. Where I used to teach, a busy road cut through the campus, so students waiting to cross the road often saw newly dating friends drive past. With the eye of a sociologist, students would take note of how close together their friends were seated. Closer indicated things were heating up. The passenger sitting close to the door might indicate an argument. Some said, "They're acting like they're married already."

Behavior and their metaphors are analogs: closer is not just about physical distance but sometimes about affection, affiliation, maybe trust—unless it crosses an invisible line, and then it may indicate aggression. The reptilian brain stem at work, Hall might say.

Vertical space, similarly, in our human behavior as with other animals, dominance—in actual power or authority or symbolic status—it's better to be up than down. Looking up to someone or looking down on—or talking down to—someone. The powerful in affairs of state and religion, the high and mighty, "your highness"; and even in lower courts the judge presides from an elevated position. In cities, servants to the rich, when "below the stairs" was inconvenient, distanced the maid by flights of stairs to the top of the building. Technology sometimes complicated this, as when the elevator, invented in the mid-1800s, would make the penthouse a prestigious place to live.

Matters of space involve far more than some code of etiquette: our distances involve all the senses, a recurrent theme and rooted more in our reptilian brain stem than the rational neocortex. More important, and this is what Hall emphasized but often gets ignored, measurable distance is about our sensory experience at different distances.

"Space Speaks," just a chapter title in *The Silent Language*, was elaborated as an entire book, *The Hidden Dimension* (1966). This book is the most rigorously "scientific" of Hall's work. In addition to his own empirical research and measurements, he draws on findings from ethology, biology, physiology, psychology, and the "-ologies" of sight, sound, touch, and smell. Hall also includes a chapter about space as revealed in art and in literature.

As for the relevance of Ned Hall to contemporary anthropology, Matthew Liebmann says:

> Hall's groundbreaking work on proxemics is the foundation on which anthropological discussions of space, place, and landscape have been built. Within anthropological archaeology he is commonly cited in debates regarding phenomenological approaches vs culturally contingent interpretations of space. Phenomenological approaches assume human universals in how we experience space, which is of course apt on certain levels. Yet this notion is very often pushed too far, and anthropological archaeologists frequently push back against these universalizing interpretations of the past by citing Hall's work in recognition that space is experienced differently by persons of differing social groups or cultural backgrounds.[1]

It was when he was in the midst of giving shape to what would become *The Hidden Dimension* that I first met Hall, when his excitement about what he was discovering in different fields and how they helped give a more comprehensive understanding of that hidden dimension, was itself wonderful to behold. It was a rare time for me to be with a professor in his home office, so excited in the midst of his research. Too few students today may even imagine such moments in their teachers' lives. Hall's excitement was shared by many who read his book, which was well received. Reviewers, who included those prominent in many fields, extended Hall's reputation beyond that of a maverick anthropologist. Architect Richard Neutra called *The Hidden Dimension* "a book of impressive genius, replete with unusually sharp observations." More than any of Hall's publications, this book appealed to those in visual- and applied-anthropology, and to architects, city planners, designers, photographers, and visual artists who still refer to the book today.

In a manner characteristic of his perspective on human behavior, Hall begins the book with examples drawn from ethology, particularly on spacing mechanisms among animal species, crucial for their species survival. An entire chapter is about the impact on animals of crowding, with implications for the human animal. The book was written at a time when "urban renewal" was a euphemism for what many regarded as warehousing the urban poor in high-rise apartment buildings, often resulting in disastrous effects. Public housing was (and still is) a contentious issue at city council meetings and in newspaper reports. Yet the chapter for which those in the intercultural communication field allude to his work on interpersonal distance doesn't appear until late in the book. Of the fourteen chapters, the chapter describing interpersonal distances was only detailed in one chapter.

The Feel of Space

We may think we experience space visually, which we do—but not apart from a sensory amalgam, sometimes a riot of sensations at near sensory overload, sometimes in awe, sometimes awful. Think of first gazing upon the Grand Canyon, or Ngorongoro Crater in Tanzania, transcending any sight previously. Some may panic if they feel their inviolate personal space bubble is penetrated by a shoving, noisy, crowd in an unfamiliar place, maybe at a festival that suddenly feels out of control, where they might be trampled, or even among a crush of others on a commuter train at rush hour. Tokyo train stations at rush hours have official pushers to help shoe-horn commuters into the cars before the doors close. Some passengers will step aside and wait for the next train, which during peak hours arrives a minute later. All the senses are engaged, and those for whom this is familiar have learned to briefly anesthetize sensitivity.[2]

"Proxemics" is the name Hall proposed for the study of inter-personal space, taking its place with other "-ics," such as *"haptics,"* the study of touch. Each sensory mode has its designated field of study. Hall wrote an important but little-known companion book to his writings on interpersonal space, the *Handbook for Proxemic Research*, which gives detailed guidance on how to conduct proxemic research.[3] In it he describes his methods of research; technological developments in video and other recording devices have altered how such studies are conducted today just as the cell phone, computer, and social media have altered our very experience of space and time and how we relate to others.

Ray Birdwhistell and Kinesics

Hall was not the first to study and write about what came to be known as "nonverbal communication." That term, widely used today in a culture that still privileges words, was disliked by Hall's contemporary, linguist Ray L. Birdwhistell, who remarked that saying "nonverbal communication" is "like saying 'non-cardiac physiology.'" Birdwhistell introduced as a more comprehensive term, "kinesics," for the study of the human body in all aspects of social interaction. In what may sound disparaging, Hall contrasted his "proxemics" with Birdwhistell's "kinesics," calling the latter "what others refer to as 'body language.'" (Do I detect some academic rivalry?)

Birdwhistell's research emphasized physical movement in communication. In comparison, Hall's focus on the spatial dimensions of
communication seems relatively static, with attention to the measurable
physical distance between people engaged in communication, but little
about how their bodies are moving during that engagement. This is
also evident with his interest in the physical spaces within the built
environment, especially in homes and the arrangement of furniture,
something Birdwhistell did not address. Hall made good use in his
research, and later his class assignments, of disposable cameras that
had become affordable and common in the US by the 1980s. His
assignments included taking a series of still photos and then comparing
them to see if one could recognize a pattern.

The physical movement of bodies, arms, hands, and the body's
shifts when talking with others—these were the subject of Birdwhistell's
research. Credited with pioneering research about physical movement
in everyday communication, he inspired others to pay attention to
what our bodies are saying as we talk with others. Some called it
the "'movement' movement." One of Birdwhistell's early studies of
the interaction between two people in conversation deployed two
synchronized movie cameras, one focused on one person and the
other camera on the other, so he could study the interaction. I'm
not aware of Hall arranging anything like that, which he might have
regarded as too contrived for purposes of research.

Though his many articles appear in just one book, *Kinesics and
Context: Essays on Body Motion Communication*, Birdwhistell was
innovative in research topics and his means of exploring those. As a
guest professor, he helped create interest in an area of research that
only increased over time. Birdwhistell also created an elaborate symbol
system that he called *kinegraphs* to represent facial expressions and
body positions and movements, a kind of shorthand to describe all
parts of the body that would be visible as part of communicative
behavior.[4] His symbol system runs several pages, with an entire page

devoted to hand gestures, even noting which part of the fingers are used in holding or touching some thing or someone. I have included a page of his symbol system for facial expressions as an example.

2. Face

—◯—	Blank faced
— ⌒	Single raised brow ⌒ indicates brow raised
— ⌣	Lowered brow
\/	Medial brow contraction
⋰⋱	Medial brow nods
⌒ ⌒	Raised brows
○ ○	Wide eyed
— ○	Wink
> ‹	Lateral squint
>‹ >‹	Full squint
A	Shut eyes (with A-closed pause 2 count
⋔ ⋔ or	Blink—⌐
B	B-closed pause 5 plus count
⊙ ⊙	Sidewise look
⊋ ⊋	Focus on auditor
⊛ ⊛	Stare
⊚ ⊚	Rolled eyes
⊅ ⊅	Slitted eyes
⊖ ⊖	Eyes upward
—⊖ ⊖—	Shifty eyes
"⊛ ⊛"	Glare
⊂ ⊃	Inferior lateral orbit contraction
△$_s$	Curled nostril
$_s$△$_s$	Flaring nostrils
⌄△‹	Pinched nostrils
⬦	Bunny nose
△	Nose wrinkle
⌣	Left sneer
⌒	Right sneer

◯	Out of the side of the mouth (left)
◯	Out of the side of the mouth (right)
⌣	Set jaw
∪	Smile tight — loose o
⊢⊣	Mouth in repose lax o tense —
⌒	Droopy mouth
⊋	Tongue in cheek
⌒	Pout
₊₊₊	Clenched teeth
⊌	Toothy smile
⊞⊞⊞	Square smile
◎	Open mouth
s◎l	Slow lick—lips
q◎l	Quick lick—lips
∞	Moistening lips
⊂⊃	Lip biting
⌣	Whistle
⌐○´⌐	Pursed lips
⬦	Retreating lips
⌐○´⌐⌐	Peck
⌐○´⌐!	Smack
⊞⊞	Lax mouth
⊌	Chin protruding
⊌	"Dropped" jaw
⊢×⊣	Chewing
⌒	Temples tightened
ε ⌐	Ear "wiggle"
⌇⌇	Total scalp movement

Birdwhistell worked closely with psychologists and psychiatrists including psychiatrist Albert Scheflen whose book, *How Behavior Means*, that in its title makes the kinesics point. Also writing then, and now probably better known than any of the others is Erving Goffman, a sociologist whose influential book, *The Presentation of Self in Everyday Life*, was published just before *The Silent Language*. Ray L. Birdwhistell, Albert Scheflen, Gregory Bateson, and others and writing at this time (at least within North America) kept their descriptions and analysis local, without comparisons across cultures within a society, let alone international communication. Intercultural comparisons were a feature of Hall's work—indeed, a Hall-mark. All were inventive scholars and researchers not constrained by the parameters of their disciplines, and fortunately for us today, all were gifted writers whose work remains engaging for any curious reader.[5]

The term "proxemics" might suggest that measurable distance encompasses sensory experience at difference distances. More accurately put is the converse: our sensory experience determines appropriate distances. Physical space between people as indicated by a tape measure is the simplest calculation; alone it is also simplistic. There are also visual, acoustical, thermal, and olfactory perceptions that Hall wrote about extensively, and how they regulate distance in we humans as well as other animals.

And there is context. Always context. What is the relationship between or among the people, what is the setting, occasion, mood; how are the people dressed and what else is going on at the time?[6]

Hall wrote about these considerations in general and some in great detail, including in his *Handbook for Proxemic Research*. Among other considerations: How does the furniture influence proximities? How many drinks have the people had? Are they sitting or standing or lying down? And more. What of other physical influences? As someone who requires a wheelchair for mobility due to paralysis of much of her lower body, friend Roxanna Springer reflects on aspects of interpersonal space. She comments on the proxemics of interaction with others during the COVID-19 pandemic in 2020:

> During the pandemic, it has been easier to maintain a comfortable distance from people, thus making eye contact more direct, my head/neck not needing such a tilt to address a person. However, the ease in adapting to surrounding conditions has become more difficult as people can decrease the distance quickly and from the side or the rear or on a slope where I am not able to adjust my position appropriately because the wheelchair doesn't move that way or because my hands are holding something and I cannot do that and move the wheelchair.
>
> People not appropriately masked breathed on me, much as people with cigarettes used to flick them off to the side and in my direct space. I have been hugged by people who obviously didn't notice my inability to move away and simply made their move, much as I have been kissed by people when I couldn't avoid them due to spacing or slopes. Several times, my wheelchair seems to be a convenient device for strangers to lean on as they pass me by or wait in line. Other times, the wheelchair was a means of restraining me by people wanting my attention. I wonder if the wheelchair makes the concept of personal space null. Perhaps similar to the experience of not being addressed but, instead, if there is someone with me or nearby, they were addressed to ascertain my wants or needs.
>
> I have discovered that hospitals are not always set up for a wheelchair user to be a patient. I have been where there were no accessible restrooms available on my floor! Yes, it was nearly impossible to transfer to and from the bed to the wheelchair, or to and from a transport gurney, and difficult to get attention from people over the high countertops at nursing stations;

but they were manageable. But, the restroom in my room wasn't large enough to close the door and was only partially protected by an outside curtain. My sister and I searched throughout the hospital for accessible restrooms other than the public restroom on the first floor which, after providing the accessible stall, offered a high and deep countertop sink and faucets and hand-drying that usually left me with wiping my hands off on my dress. As we went up and down the elevator and through hallways, we told people that we were looking for an accessible restroom. We found some on various floors where we had to gain access with a guard's permission. Eventually, we happened upon a logistics manager and the hospital head nurse who decided that a private room was required. Wow! Still not a deep enough restroom for privacy without the auxiliary curtain—but a closable door![7]

Another spatial experience that seems unique to being in a wheelchair was when I was in a building that 'floated'—it had been designed to 'roll' with the movements of the earth, to adjust unnoticeably rather than stressing the framing. Because the wheelchair has four connection points with the floor and is rather stiffly framed, I could sense the floor's movement when other shoppers were not reacting to the building's adjustments. Similarly, able-bodied people expect ramps to be a good solution for ground/floor level changes, but a ramp is an unstable platform requiring balance and motion in a particular direction with active gravity force; therefore, a raised (about 3 to 4 inches) level area such as a step or platform is actually more stable for a person using a manual wheelchair and quite possibly carrying items on the lap.

In the office environment, I was accused (in jest, of course) of being in a stealth mode for surprising people when I came around a corner—something that, of course, happens with able-bodied people frequently, but which seemed to be rather dangerous for both the wheelchair-using person and the able-bodied person. I cannot say how many times able-bodied persons experienced the similar event and whether either of the parties encountering each other were 'accused' of being in a stealth mode, and quite possibly requiring some kind of flag or beep to let people know that the corner was being approached.

Basically, the experience of being in a wheelchair is that of not fitting in—in public or in private places, in places providing medical care.

It requires an easy smile and deep breath, living in the moment rather than dreading repeats of the past with just about every encounter with the able-bodied. And a completely different perspective on what people and the world look like from three to four feet off the ground. Luckily, there are quite a few able-bodied people who are at ease with wheelchair-using people, somehow realizing and accepting the need for adjustment on both sides with frankness and grace. Even the physical and psychological awkwardness of needing to find wheelchair-accessible accommodations is less with these people. These able-bodied people are welcome and inspiring as the freshness and beauty of a new flower, the calm and peacefulness of still water, the freedom and release of vast space, all lending stability and the solidity of a mountain to the mind of the wheelchair-using person who is better able to continue going out and being in public. It doesn't seem like there are many of us who can be out and about. Partially, this is a physical adaptation problem starting in the medical services community run by insurance companies, but also partially a needed psychological adaptation by the wheelchair-using person.[8]

When Social Distance Became "A Thing"

"Social Distance" became part of the vernacular around 2020 with the COVID-19 pandemic. Seems unlikely that the US Centers of Disease Control were thinking of E. T. Hall when they chose that as a positive sounding way of saying, "keep an awkward distance; your life may depend on it."

Social distance, Hall's category for where people—largely white, middle-class, North Americans—stand while conversing, became a verb and an advised space for survival—six feet, about two meters—for everyday conversations or passing a stranger in a store or an open space. Elbow bumps replaced shaking hands; hugs were gestured. It felt anything but normal. There were parks and public spaces where these socially distanced spaces were marked; interior spaces, as in restaurants were reconfigured to facilitate personal distance. One restaurant kept the seating as before, maintaining social distance and keeping the mood social: in the otherwise empty seats there were mannequins. A visual testimonial to our social spatial sensitivity. *Bon appétit!*

Across the globe, the second decade of the twenty-first century has taught us something about space that Hall wrote about decades before, not that he was the first to pay attention to this. But our emotions felt or described in terms of "too close" or "too distant" has long been a part of how we relate to one another. Of course, it's not just about physical distance—it's about how we feel about the other and—this might be Hall's most valuable reminder—all the other senses that come into play at various distances. Apart from all those other personal considerations, objectively our experience in the moment is different depending on how close or how far away we are.

Zones of Proximity

Hall identified four spatial "zones," each distinguished by its sensory qualities and limitations, what kind of communication occurs in each, including verbalization. Why four? Hall explains:

> It is in the nature of animals, including man, to exhibit behavior which we call territoriality. In so doing, they use the senses to distinguish between one space or distance and another. The specific distance chosen depends on the transaction; the relationship of the interacting individuals, how they feel and what they are doing. The four-part classification system used here is based on observations of both animals and men. Birds and apes exhibit intimate, personal, and social distances just as man does.[9]

And who was Hall observing when he identified these four distances? He does not indicate, other than "Americans." Today, we are more likely to want to appreciate the diversity of populations, to know more specifically who is part of generalizations than previously. By nationality, age or generation, race and ethnicity, gender and sometimes sexual orientation or identification, region, socio-economic status, education . . . all relevant and in particular contexts, crucial. Hall's "Americans" as he generalized were, we may assume, mostly white, probably male, and probably native-born, and without regard to other demographic distinctions. His base of comparison was nationality, and sometimes gender or ethnicity or race, if he regarded that as significant. Looking back, it is easy and important to point out what went unobserved. Looking ahead it is more difficult to imagine what we aren't observing today—as those in the future will point out.

Hall's four categories of distance in aspects of everyday communication are: (1) intimate distance; (2) personal distance; (3) social distance; and (4) public distance. Each of these zones is described within a range from nearest to farthest phases in our sensory capacity and experience, and the typical kinds of interaction that happens at these interpersonal distances. Here is how Hall treats each of the four distances as they may be experienced.

Intimate Distance

Close Phase: *from contact, as with a kiss, to 6 inches/0–15 centimeters)*

About the close phase, from direct contact with all of the senses engaged, Hall writes:

> This is the distance for love-making and wrestling, comforting and protecting. Physical contact or the high possibility of physical involvement is uppermost in the awareness of both persons. The use of their distance receptors is greatly reduced except for olfaction and the sensation of radiant heat, both of which are stepped up. In the maximum-contact phase the muscles and skin communicate. Pelvis, thighs, and head can be brought into play; arms can encircle. Except at the outer limits, sharp vision is blurred. When close vision is possible within the intimate range—as with children—the image is greatly enlarged and stimulates much, if not all, of the retina. The detail that can be seen at this distance is extraordinary. This detail plus the cross-eyed pull of the eye muscles provides a visual experience that cannot be confused with any other distance. Vocalization at intimate distance plays a very minor part in the communication process, which is carried mainly by other channels. A whisper has the effect of expanding the distance. The vocalizations that do occur are largely involuntary.

Far Phase: *6–18 inches/15–46 centimeters*

[At this distance] hands can reach and grasp extremities. The head is seen as enlarged in size, and its features are distorted. Ability to focus the eye easily is an important feature of this distance for Americans. The iris of the other person's eye seen at about six to nine inches is enlarged to more than life size. Small blood vessels in the sclera are clearly perceived, pores are enlarged. Clear vision (15 degrees) includes the upper or lower portion of the face, which is perceived as enlarged. The nose is seen as over-large and may look distorted, as will other features such as lips, teeth, and tongue. Peripheral vision (30-180 degrees) includes the outline of head and shoulders, and very often the hands. Much of the physical discomfort that [some] Americans experience when foreigners are inappropriately inside the intimate sphere is expressed as a distortion of the visual system.

Personal Distance

Close Phase: *18–30 inches/46–76 centimeters*

Close enough to be able to grasp the other—a handshake or hug. To get a sense of Hall's attention to the physical, sensory experience, he invites the reader to experience what happens when looking at some object 18 inches (46 centimeters) to 3 feet (91.44 centimeters), and to pay attention to the muscles around the eyeballs; he asks us to feel how the muscles try to help create a coherent image—an experiment he applies to looking at another's face.

Far Phase: *30 inches–4 feet/76 centimeters–1.23 meters*

Body heat and olfaction still perceptible for those who learned to pay attention to these, but not for most Americans, Hall writes. Perception of the other appears "normal"—matching one's mental image of the other:

. . . Easily seen are fine details of skin, gray hair, "sleep" in the eye, stains on teeth, spots, small wrinkles, or dirt on clothing. Foveal vision covers only an area the size of the tip of the nose or one eye, so that the gaze must wander around the face; where the eye is directed is strictly a matter of cultural conditioning. Fifteen-degree clear vision covers the upper or lower face, while 180-degree peripheral vision takes in the hands and the whole body of a seated person. Movement of the hands is detected, but. . .

The intimate zone gives way to "Personal Distance." Though Hall did not write about this fifty years ago and had no reason to, there is an intimate zone today that sometimes may be both more and less emotionally intimate than Hall's personal distance zone, because technologies allow for intimacies with the protection of being at a distance. We may have "Facebook friends" we've never actually met that we feel we know better than friends we've been with for years. "Actually" isn't what it used to be.

I have wondered if the spatial difference between personal and social zones might roughly correspond between "friend" and "acquaintance" in English, and the familiar and formal pronouns used in Germanic and Romance languages. English lost that verbal distinction when "thou" (a more intimate "you") faded from everyday use, only to hang on in appreciation of Elizabethan literature and drama, and in some religious texts from Elizabethan English.

Social Distance[10]
Near Phase: *48 inches–7 feet/1.23–2.13 meters*

Head size is perceived as normal; as one moves away from the subject, the foveal area of the eye can take in an ever-increasing amount of the person. At 4 feet/1.2 meters, a one-degree visual angle is of a little more than one eye. At seven feet, the area of sharp focus extends to the nose and parts of both eyes; or the whole mouth, one eye, and the nose are sharply seen. Details of skin texture and hair are clearly perceived. At a 60-degree visual angle, the head, shoulders, and upper trunk are seen at a distance of 4 feet/1.2 meters; while the same sweep includes the whole figure at 7 feet/2.1 meters.

Hall writes that this is a common distance for people attending an informal social gathering, and that "impersonal business" occurs at this distance, with more involvement than in the far phase.

Far Phase: *7–12 feet/2.13–3.6 meters*

Hall wrote, "This is the distance to which people move when someone says, 'Stand away so that we can look at you!'" I imagine that only being said by family or friends, and indicating not just, "let us look at you from head to toe," but also "stand in a more formal and important place, let us see you as we imagine your admirers might." Maybe that's where we literally "stand out."

Public Distance

Close Phase: *12–25 feet/3.6–7.6 meters*

At 12 feet, ". . . an alert subject can take evasive or defensive action if threatened. The distance may even cue a vestigial but subliminal form of flight reaction," Hall writes. How we construct our sentences, including word choice and grammar at this distance may be different from conversational speech. Linguists refer to such differences as "register," usually identified with how people in different professions and settings talk. Listening to voices on radio or television, within seconds we can know this person is a sports broadcaster, that one is a televangelist, and this other person is giving a TED Talk, which is also said and heard differently from a public lecture. At the near phase of a public distance, "fine details of the skin and eyes are no longer visible. At sixteen feet the body loses its roundness and looks flat. . . . Head size is perceived as considerably under life-size." Hall did not write about a difference in the perception of pubic speakers by those listening compared to the speaker's perception of the listeners.

Public distance is relevant not just where speaker and listener are concerned, but an important consideration also for architects and in the design of a new community—how far apart should houses be, and at what orientation to each other, for example. When co-housing communities are designed, intentionally trying to balance both individual autonomy with mutual involvement that fosters a sense of communication, attention to "public space" is crucial. The Commons, a co-housing community in Santa Fe, New Mexico, the second co-housing community in the US, is an example. Lynnwood Brown, who was instrumental in the creation of that community, points out the significance of distance between houses and their orientation to each other to make a comfortable setting. How far apart should houses be so that when one steps out, neighbors can acknowledge or avoid the others without being rude? Hall's twelve feet to allow for "evasive action," if necessary, is such a consideration, and it should be for public housing projects and private housing developments, as well, where the economics of space is more important than the resulting influence on civility.[11]

Far Phase: *25 feet/7.6 meters or more*

"Thirty feet is the distance that is automatically set around important public figures," Hall writes, adding "the usual public distance is not restricted to public figures but can be used by anyone on public occasions."

Technology has altered our perceptions of space. Through photographs, movies, television, computers, and phones, we can observe the faces of an actor more closely than we could if we were with that person, and yet we may be beyond Hall's Public Distance from the movie or television screen even as the perception of closeness lets us feel we are emotionally close. Kathleen Hall Jamieson at the University of Pennsylvania's Annenberg School of Communication, and commentator on political communication, pointed out to me how Ronald Reagan, through his years as a Hollywood actor and later as a pitchman on television, could speak to millions of people as naturally as if he were talking to a friend.

French movie theory identifies an "American shot" prominent in US films: the single actor, head and torso. Expressing a cultural value of "individualism"? Attention to spatial features in films may be another source of cultural proxemic research, including the sequencing of film shots in the editing. Japanese movie history indicates a preference of moving from distance shots and contextual images before moving to focus on personal space. Donald Richie, preeminent critic of Japanese film pointed this out, and recommended that I watch films directed by Yasujirō Ozu, whom he regarded as "the most Japanese" of directors, including Ozu's focus on space as context. "Space speaks" especially in Japanese and in other East Asian aesthetics, and in film, no more eloquently than in the silences of Ozu's films.[12]

The Sensory World and Embodied Code Switching®

"Code-switching" is a term for describing the seamless shift from one language to another, typically in the midst of a conversation with others who share a similar bi-lingual (or polyglot) background. It is quite common and linguists have shown that the switching follows clear "rules" and cues that have been acquired, just as each of the languages were. Marcia Warren grew up in a trilingual home.[13] Her Brazilian mother sometimes spoke to her in Portuguese, and she was immersed in Portuguese during visits to family in Brazil; her father's family and community is Tewa-speaking (from Santa Clara Pueblo), and both also spoke English. It is not just that spoken languages differ in sounds, word choice, and syntax, Warren noted, it's that the nonverbal behavior that goes with each language also differs.

This is something Hall did not explore, but when Warren read *The Hidden Dimension,* and Hall's words that ". . . people from different cultures not only speak different languages but, what is possibly more important, inhabit different sensory worlds," it acknowledged for her, "perhaps for the first time, a completely different approach to how culture is experienced." These words, together with the training she received during her graduate work in psychotherapy at Naropa University, inspired Marcia to explore the ways code-switching might be embodied and expressed nonverbally. She developed a model and a practice from her work she calls Embodied Code-Switching® that provides a way to understand and work with this important somatic and nonverbal facet of communication. Warren writes:

> The sensory world is often taken for granted; it can be a silent partner to our verbal language which seems to dominate our assumptions on the ways culture is defined and appears in our day-to-day lives. Although it is true that without spoken language, we would have great difficulty in getting things done, it is the nonverbal realm that provides a stronger undercurrent to our understanding of cultural contexts, and often prompts our responses to each other in a way that can contradict and override our verbal interpretations.
>
> I came to Edward T. Hall's work initially as a student, but it spoke to me on a level deeper than academic knowledge. As a person who is from both an Indigenous community and the daughter of an immigrant, I had a unique perspective on the role culture played in my identity and the ways I interpreted the world around me. I did not learn the verbal language of my tribe, nor was I fluent in the language of the country my mother came from so, in many ways, I lived solely in the sensory worlds of the cultures I came from. I had to rely on my nonverbal communication skills to understand the cultural norms I was exposed to, and often found myself relying upon

the information I received through my senses much more than the words I came to understand to help me navigate what was often confusing and mysterious.

This is why Hall's work is so validating to someone like me; he provided a wider array of opportunities for me to become aware of the cultures around me, and by doing so, begin to find a sense of belonging. Hall wrote: "What happens when people of different cultures meet and become involved?" Hall suggested that communication occurs simultaneously on different levels of consciousness, ranging from full awareness to out-of-awareness.

One of the fundamental aspects to my work as a Somatic Counselor/Body Psychotherapist and Interculturalist is the question of what constitutes a "sensory world"? I brought additional elements of Body Psychotherapy into the "self-assessment inventory of sensing" that Hall asked his students to explore, and with that, we began to apply a deeper level of awareness to what a sensory world might feel like to ourselves and each other in relationship.

One of the ways I began to play with sensory, or somatic awareness, as it related to understanding culture, was to use proxemics as an experiential. Both personally and professionally, I have found that exploring our kinespheres (or personal space "bubbles") often brings up surprising insights about our bodies' knowledge of cultural norms in relation to space. It also brings up valuable reflections on how our bodies react to the crossing of those boundaries and what thoughts and beliefs arise in mere seconds as a response. I've found that once we become aware of the impact of nonverbal communication and somatic awareness on our identities and the cultures we embody, the better we can understand, accept, and move between them—both within ourselves, and in relation with others. And that is the foundation of Embodied Code-Switching®.[14]

Up in the Air: Boundless Space Outside, but You're in the Middle Seat . . .

In an airplane, in that dreaded middle seat, our arms may touch those seated on both sides—Hall's "intimate zone" with people we might otherwise never meet. Seat size has shrunk by two inches even as body size, at least in the US, has expanded. The space between the rows, called "pitch," allows the passenger ahead to tilt the backrest into another's already cramped space; our knees remind us of the length of our legs. "Since 2011, the average seat pitch—the distance between the back of one seat and the back of the next—has dropped from 35 inches to 31 inches [88.9 to 78.7 centimeters], according to a passenger rights group."[15] Ultra-low-cost carriers, such as Spirit Airlines, have reduced the pitch on many seats to 28 inches. Air travel is priced by space; more space, pay more.

Airlines adopted not just the vocabulary of ocean-going ships—we board into cabins on this flagship airline—but also class distinctions, by air divided horizontally. First Class seats up front take up as much space as ten seats to the rear in coach. Customer economics have forced airlines to shrink the number of seats in first class, if not eliminate it entirely. "First Class" devolved into "Business Class." That choice of name also reflects cultural changes, with time as well as space: quicker check-in because of shorter lines, earlier seating, and exiting on arrival. There is also better food and drinks and pampering, but the ticket price is mostly about personal space.

As airlines attempted to pack in more passengers into the available floor space, there was a personal and social cost. Increasingly fights between passengers broke out. Flight attendants complained that the most difficult part of their job was trying to manage these sometimes-violent conflicts.

Gender and Space

The treatment of men and women as different cultures that Hall sometimes alluded to is less apparent in his discussion of space. That neglect has been corrected by research including by Deborah Tannen, Robin Lakoff, among others who have treated gender as culture and a part of any discussion of intercultural communication. Feminist and LGBTQ writers have expanded and altered what "intercultural communication" means. Much of this work is centered on words: discourse, narrative, rhetoric. Nonverbal expression and performance—dress, hair, adornment—receive more attention than previously, especially in this era of media where the visual often is the story, but less so how behavior utilizing space also differs among genders. Tannen calls for ". . . a cross-cultural approach to cross-gender conversation by which women and men, boys and girls, can be seen to accomplish and display coherence in conversation in different but equally valid ways."[16]

Tannen cites a fascinating study conducted by Bruce Dorval, a psychologist at the University of New Orleans, in which pairs of boys and pairs of girls in three different age groups—second grade, sixth grade, and tenth grade—were asked to have a conversation about anything for about 20 minutes. The pairs were friends, and each pair was given two folding chairs to take into the room where they would have their chat. The children themselves arranged how they wanted to sit and talk. From a separate room these conversations were video-taped. In addition to the three pairs of children, two friends, women age 25-years-old, and two men who were friends, also 25-years-old, participated in the study and were given the same instructions as the children. Though gender, and not race and ethnicity was the focus, all participants appear from the videos to be white.

What is most striking is how the physical orientation differs by gender across all four age groups. Tannen summarizes the physical orientation and alignments in her book, *Gender and Discourse*:

The girls and women are more physically still, more collected into the space they inhabit, and more directly aligned with each through physical proximity, occasional touching, body posture, and anchoring of eye gaze. The boys and men do not touch each other except in playful aggression, do not anchor their gaze on each other's faces, and spread out rather than gather themselves into the space they inhabit. The boys in the youngest pairs are more physically restless, more diffused in the room both in their movements and in their gaze. The boys and men in the two older pairs are more physically still but still less directly aligned with each other in posture and gaze.[17]

[T]he girls and women in the study sat facing each other, and maintained a face-to-face gaze. They didn't necessarily look into each other's eyes. In contrast, the boys and men sat at angles or parallel, and looked elsewhere around the room. I actually don't think they ever looked directly at each other at the same time.[18]

In sum, across ages from seven to twenty-five, female friends engage face-to-face, looking more into each other's eyes as they talk, and close enough to occasionally touch each other, while males give each other more distance, only occasionally look face-to-face in conversation. It's as if the girls and women prefer being across from each other, maybe at a narrow table or at least close enough to reach out to touch, while the boys and men are more comfortable side-by-side, like at a bar, or maybe in a car and looking out the windshield as they talk. Does this suggest that girls learn to pay more attention to facial expressions than boys do? With close friends, is sharing more visually and through other senses part of and an influence on what intimacy means to girls and women, more than it is between boys and their male friends? Is this a part of a story of how women who are close friends know, and expect to know, more about the other?

Tannen's research on how differences in use of space between friends invites such questions.

Tannen adds an important point about interpreting the differences, and this, in turn, leads to her observation about intercultural communication that echoes a theme in all of Hall's work about our communication across cultures. Even when we are with others all the time, and know them and respect them and love them, we may interpret more broadly based behavior as if it were personal and "wrong." Tannen, like Hall, reminds us to reconsider our judgments: "[T]his does not mean that the men and boys are not engaged, not involved. It simply means that their means of establishing conversational engagement are different. These differences, however, are likely to lead to negative evaluation and the impression of a lack of engagement if measured by women's interactional norms."[19]

"You're not listening to me!" a woman might accuse a male friend or partner because he is not looking at her face as she is speaking. The man may protest that he is indeed listening, and if challenged he may repeat what she just said, but that may not dispel the emotions at that moment. Tannen says a marriage counselor told her, "Oh yes, I see this all the time when counseling couples." We may wonder how a couple married for many years isn't able to figure out this source of conflict, which is what Hall called our attention to: we are often unaware of our behavior—even, or especially, when it is routine, habitual, "normal"—until someone from outside—a friend, a consultant, a therapist, an anthropologist—points that out to us. "Awareness" has been the watchword for many in the intercultural field, but being aware alone does not automatically lead to a resolution of the problem.

Everything we are and do, Hall emphasized, is associated with the experience of space, and, he believed:

> . . . [Our] sense of space is a synthesis of many sensory inputs: visual, auditory, kinesthetic, olfactory and thermal. Not only

does each of these constitute a complete system . . . but each is molded and patterned by culture. Hence, there is no alternative to accepting the fact that people reared in different cultures live in different sensory worlds. . . . the patterning of perceptual worlds is a function not only of culture but of *relationship, activity,* and *emotion.* Therefore, people from different cultures, when interpreting each other's behavior, often misinterpret the relationship, the activity or the emotions. This leads to alienation in encounters or distorted communications.[20]

"No single research technique is sufficient in scope to investigate a complex, multidimensional subject like proxemics," Yi-Fu Tuan writes.[21] "In the large literature on environmental quality, relatively few works attempt to understand how people feel about space and place, to take into account the different modes of experience (sensorimotor, tactile, visual, conceptual), and to interpret space and place as images of complex—often ambivalent—feelings."[22]

Notes

1. Personal correspondence with the author.

2. Because such crowding allowed for sexual abuse, many trains now have designated cars at the front and rear of the trains for women only.

3. Edward T. Hall, *Handbook for Proxemic Research: Studies in the Anthropology of Visual Communication* (Society for the Anthropology for Visual Communication, 1974).

4. Ray L. Birdwhistell, *Kinesics and Context: Essays on Body Motion Communication* (Philadelphia: University of Pennsylvania Press, 1970), 255-304.

5. Birdwhistell, *Kinesics and Context*; Albert Scheflen, *How Behavior Means* (New York: Jason Aronnson, 1972); Erving Goffman, *The Presentation of Self in Everyday Life* (Garden City, New York: Anchor Press, 1959); Gregory Bateson, *Steps to an Ecology of Mind: Collected Essays in Anthropology, Psychiatry, Evolution, and Epistemology* (Chicago: University of Chicago Press, 1972).

6. Just as only a fraction of sounds one is capable of making and hearing as meaningful in any particular language, only a fraction of physical expressions convey meanings. Birdwhistell's early research on the range of eyelid positions from "wide open" to "tightly shut" indicated that, of a thousand observable possibilities, only four positions were interpreted as meaningful based on his research in the US.

   The position of the body when bowing is similar: within an arc of more than ninety degrees, depending on the occasion, relationship, and likely intention, only four positions are named and are formally taught in Japan. A visitor may catch on to a general idea of bowing as analogical regarding respect, deference, gratitude—younger bows lower when greeting one older, subordinate bows lower than the boss when greeting, and if expressing gratitude for some favor granted, the recipient bows lower than the grantor. Each of these might be amplified by the length of time a position is maintained, or if repeated. In everyday greetings among friends and colleagues, the greeting is brief as one might smile, nod, or gesture with a hand. One new to all this is likely to err by local standards, as when President Barrack Obama greeted the Japanese emperor: he was judged by the foreign press as bowing just a little too low in that meeting, but the Japanese press observed it in a good-natured way seeing the intent of showing respect as more important.

7. "*Interpersonal Distance in the SARS-2CoV2Crisis*," ncbi.nlm.nih.gov/pmc/articles/PMC7586001: Intrusions into our personal space can prompt us to counter-react by increasing interpersonal distance or to abort the social interaction (Felipe & Sommer, 1966). In addition, we might generate social signals to indicate a need for personal space, for example, gaze aversion, body realignment, or angry facial expression (Aranguren, 2015; Patterson, 1976; Stephenson & Rutter, 1970).]

8. "*Respectful Communication in an Information Age*," at sciencedirect.com/topics/medicine-and-dentistry/proxemics]: "Health professionals perform many diagnostic or treatment procedures within the personal and intimate distance zones. You may have to invade the patient's culturally derived boundaries of interaction, sometimes with little warning. Consider, for instance, the weak or debilitated patient who comes for treatment and must be helped to a treatment table. To get the patient on the treatment table, you might have to 'embrace' the patient and, in some cases, lift the patient to the table, deeply invading his or her intimate zone."

9. Edward T. Hall, *The Hidden Dimension* (Garden City, New York, 1966; Anchor edition, 1969).

10. Hall credits Martin Heidegger as the first to use "social distance," but referring to those outside of one's group rather than a distance we adopt with people we've just met.

11. Lynnwood Brown met Hall in one of my seminars, long before he helped create the co-housing community. For several years, he was a rare outsider to live years at the Pueblo of San Juan (now *Ohkay Owingeh*). During a visit to the co-housing community, one student asked if there were anyone from the Pueblos living there. Brown laughed and said the co-housing's purpose and design is not so different from the indigenous Pueblo communities. "If someone wanted to get away from that, they certainly wouldn't come here."

12. Donald Richie, *Ozu* (Berkeley, Los Angeles, London: University of California Press, 1974). The great Japanese director Akira Kurosawa was, in Richie's view, more international in his movie making than Ozu, in part because Kurosawa's films were made a generation later, after WW II, and with influences from post-war movie directors throughout the world. As in all media, it has become more difficult to identify what is uniquely cultural by the artist.

13. Marcia Warren is a Licensed Professional Counsellor (LPC) in the state of Colorado, United States. In addition to her Master of Arts in Somatic Counselling/Body Psychotherapy from Naropa University, she also holds a Master of Arts in International Relations from the Johns Hopkins University School of Advanced International Studies.

14. Laia Jorba Galdos & Marcia Warren, "The body as cultural home: exploring, embodying, and navigating the complexities of multiple identities," *Body, Movement and Dance in Psychotherapy: An International Journal for Theory, Research and Practice,* Volume 17, 2022, Issue 1: Power, privilege and difference in embodied psychotherapies, https://www.tandfonline.com/doi/full/10.1080/17432979.2021.1996460. Also see: Marcia Warren Edelman, "Moving between identities: Embodied code-switching," in C. Caldwell & L. B. Leighton, eds., *Oppression and the Body: Roots, Resistance, and Resolutions* (North Atlantic Books, 2018), 181-284.

15. https://news.yahoo.com/airline-seats-getting-smaller-years-145508229.html Also see: https://www.flyertalk.com/articles/the-airlines-with-the-tiniest-seats.html

16. Deborah Tannen, *Gender and Discourse* (New York: Oxford University Press, 1996).

17. Tannen, *Gender and Discourse*, 88.

18. Tannen, *Gender and Discourse*, 98-99.

19. Tannen, *Gender and Discourse*, 99.

20. Edward T. Hall, *The Hidden Dimension* (Garden City, New York, 1966; Anchor edition, 1969), 181.

21. Yi-Fu Tuan, *Space and Place: The Perspective of Experience* (Minneapolis: University of Minnesota Press, 1977), 6.

22. Tuan, *Space and Place*, 9, quoting Susanne Langer in *Mind: An Essay on Human Feeling* (Baltimore: Johns Hopkins University Press, 1972, Vol. 2), 192-193.

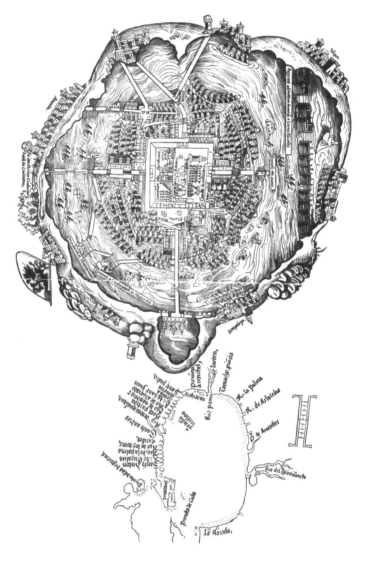

*This 1524 woodcut is the first European map of
Tenochtitlan (now Mexico City) which, at that time, was
among the most populous urban areas in the world.*

CHAPTER THIRTEEN

From Spaces to Places

We have gotten to the point of too small a definition of
community. I go back to the Pueblo thinking because their
community was not just the human community. It included
the place within which we lived. The mountains were part of
community. The water was part of community. Trees, water,
rock, plants. You know, you couldn't have moved through
any day in that old world . . . without knowing that you are
part of that whole community of trees, rocks, people.
—*Rina Swentzell*

You get a strange feeling when you're about to leave a
place. . . like you'll not only miss the people you love,
but you'll miss the person you are now at this time and
this place, because you'll never be this way again.
—*Azar Nafisi*

Places, we realize, are as much a part of us as we are of them.
—*Keith Basso*

I t is said that when the Spanish colonizers first came to the Mexican
peninsula of Yucatán that separates the Gulf of Mexico from the
Caribbean, the leader of the incursion asked the Mayan authority who

met them, "What is the name of this place?" The Mayan answered: "*Yuk ak katun.*" A Spanish chronicler wrote that down, and so the land came to be called "Yucatán." In that Mayan dialect, "*Yuk ak katun,*" means: "I don't understand your language."

Outsiders always get a place new to them wrong, and not just because of the language. Any place for those who live there holds meanings that outsiders can't know. The place may be depicted to others through the eyes of outsiders—by colonialists who can claim history. (Historians put their trust in the privileged authority of what is put in writing, not "just said"; today valuing writing over speech is long outdated in an era of digital social media.) In any medium, the traveler's word of mouth—amplified by millions through commercial tourism where, in many places, the transitory visitors outnumber the local folks—is not exactly a reliable resource.

In this era of global tourism and also enormous population shifts, those arriving at a new place arrive for different reasons, which affect their perception of a place. Some arrive as sightseers of comfortable means, some because their government or the breadwinner's employer sent them. Some to go to a school away from home. For some, this a place of refuge, safe from where they were fleeing but with family left behind. Will it be transitory or is this a destination for which they had prayed?

We've all had the experience of returning from a trip to a distant place and a friend asks, "How was (fill in a name)?" The place you describe exists mostly in the telling, more about you visiting at a particular time and your purpose and mood, a small part of a very big area. I've been asked "How was China?" "How was India?" Even, "How was Africa?" The question we actually try to answer is, "How were *you* in that place at that time?" It's usually phatic communication, a friendly greeting not all that different from "How are you?" that in the US is a question version of "hello." Even in places we know well—our town, our neighborhood, our workplace, our home—what we know, feel, remember, and want is through how we experienced that place at a particular time. A neighborhood, even one's home, is experienced differently by a child of two than a sister who is ten, differently still by her brother seven years older. Their experience of place is different from their mother's whose experience is not that of the father. Across the spectra of age, gender, financial means, worlds outside the home and more, we experience, describe, and will remember differently. Our experience of place runs deep in how we think of ourselves and how we see the world around us and those visitors who enter our place.

Anthropologist Keith Basso remarks in his splendid book summarized in its title, that wisdom sits in places.[1] Our enculturation is inseparable from place, the place where we live and places where we have lived previously, and especially our identification with its surroundings that mark histories which endow that place special meanings for us. In Basso's words, places are as much a part of us as we are a part of those places. It is experience which is the when and where, the memories and perceptions of the present shaped by memory and collective memories we are taught to embrace that may not always match what outsiders observe and try to objectively describe.

A building may contain a complexity of places, experienced and described differently by the who, what, where by which we are identified. A study in hospitals found surprisingly little overlap in the descriptions of a shared place among the doctors, interns, orderlies, nurses, receptionists, those in accounting, and those who are responsible for what happens there. It is as if they don't share the same space, to say nothing about the distant CEO at the managing corporation who may never have walked those halls. The patients for whom all that is orchestrated, experience it all still differently.

Place identifies us in time, too. Our birthplace is public record but one we have no memory of until years later, if at all. Our final resting place is a place of conjecture. The outsider's judgment about a place, as in Gertrude Stein's famously dismissive remark about Oakland, California, when she returned many years later to a city she had lived briefly, "there is no *there*, there." It says more about the critic than the place, but Stein's unique grammar made this a rhetorical flourish that has been used by many, including E. T. Hall. But wildly out of date to anyone who knows today's Oakland where there's lots of *there* there.[2]

Similar condescension of a place is sometimes put in temporal terms—"Oh, yes, I've been there—spent a month there one weekend." Or in praise, like Samuel Johnson's "If you are tired of London, you are tired of life." Or the chauvinism of John Marquand's remark that, "the enjoyment of travel is everywhere you go you meet someone from Boston."

Where Are You From?

"Where are you from?" we may be asked when meeting someone for the first time. Usually intended and heard in a friendly way, it may express genuine curiosity, and then depending on how the one who asks can relate to the answer, it may disappoint or delight in the interest rarely given. Sometimes it may be taken as meaning, "I know you're not from here," which also may be heard as "you shouldn't be here!" Often it may be looking for a possible connection—my grandparents were from there, or I used to live there, or I always wanted to visit there. The same is true if asked about your name—how it is asked and how it is heard can lead to a new friendship or a bad experience that lingers. Like lots of opening questions in a conversation, the content may mean less than the attempt to show some interest in establishing a relationship. Sometimes any answer will do, specific or as general as the name of a country, and sometimes that leads to more questions about where in that country, indicating greater interest.

Once in Milan at a lunch meeting with my son and a friend, Luca Fornari, who was born and raised in Milan, Luca invited his mother,

Deirdre Doyle, who was originally from England, to join us. Luca's mother asked my son if he had brothers or sisters. He mentioned his older sister and added that she was born in Tanzania. "*Where* in Tanzania?" Luca's mother asked. Dar es Salaam, I said—at Ocean Road Hospital, remarking that Ocean Road has since been re-named Barrack Obama Road. Her interest sharpened. "*When* was that?" It turned out that her father, Luca's grandfather, Ugo Fornari, from Italy, was a doctor in Dar es Salaam at that hospital at that very time and . . . no, he was not the doctor who delivered Michael's sister, though that would make for a more interesting story. There were a small number of foreign doctors at that hospital then, so her father, an epidemiologist, would have known the doctor in the maternity ward. It was rare then, at the major hospital in a Muslim influenced part of the world, for a father to witness the birth of his child. I will always remember Luca's mother, a lovely woman, especially because of a place and a time we briefly shared that we discovered half a century later. Surely many of us remember people because unexpected discoveries begin with talk of a place that holds a special meaning for us.[3]

"Where were you *when* . . . ?" we ask friends about events, some awful, some awe-filled. We ask *where* because place grounds us, literally, as a marker of calendar times. Before the technology of writing gave us systems of months and years that could be passed on, we reckoned time by events that happened in a particular place. We still do that. "That was before our vacation in . . . ," "that was the year I graduated," "when we first met," or "the year I began . . . or left" a school, job, a love.

Place as a memory marker is so useful as a mnemonic device that students in ancient Greece and Rome were taught how to remember what they wanted to say in a speech by using familiar places as mental markers, arranging their stories and arguments in imagined places as they moved from topic to topic, like walking from room to room at home, or place to place along a path. Place was central to *Memoria*, important in classical rhetoric such as *Inventio.* Alas, the rhetorical canon of memory canon disappeared over time. What happened to it, nobody remembers.

A place for some is to others just a space. I write as I reside in what some call "fly-over country," imagining most passengers in a window seat looking down will see nothing special: nothing down there. But major land features are sometimes announced by the pilot: "passengers on the right side of the plane will see . . ." the Grand Canyon or the Matterhorn. Sometimes the invisible: "We've just crossed the International Date Line." Some passengers use such information mostly to estimate the remaining time until the airport arrival.

Cultural geographer, Yi-fu Tuan, identifies "a place" by "where our eye pauses." The visitor who asks "what's that?" sees something that local folk have not been enculturated to see, while missing some of what the locals see. "That must have a name." Being named makes a space a place; not being named reduces the value. Compare two reports of the same event: "people from Paris, New York, London, China, and Africa participated" or, "people from Lagos, Tianjin, and North America participated." Both refer to the same event with the same people but their identified places differ, some identified by city or country, or just by continent. Ironically, most often slighted is the ancestral home of all of us, Africa. Paris, with two million residents; New York, eight million; London, nine million, but Shanghai is larger than those three Western cities combined; the largest city in Africa is Lagos, Nigeria, larger than Paris and London combined. Tianjin has 17 million, equivalent of the populations of New York and London combined. Africa, in part thanks to a colonial and post-colonial history, now includes 54 countries. Where do we place ourselves and where are we placed by others, and how do we think about that distinction? In Hall's words, due less to malice than ignorance, but to be identified by an entire continent, one person's ignorance can feel dismissive to others mis-placed.

Public names of places can reveal clues about who imposed the names. In the US some lakes have "Lake" at the beginning of the name, while others put it at the end. The names of all the Great Lakes in the US, like "Lake Michigan," tell us that it was the French explorers who named them. Another large lake further west, "Salt Lake," reveals that English speakers named it. It's not whimsical, it's colonial history. If the French were the first Europeans to "discover" a lake, then *"Lac,"* anglicized to "lake," usually precedes the name. If the English speakers named what they came upon, "Lake" usually follows the waters they named. Indigenous names are also omnipresent in place names, even in some form in the names of states, with the reclaiming of pre-contact names continuing.

More obvious are the names of major cities in the western US where the Spanish language and culture of those who founded cities endures, names chosen to honor a Catholic saint or other expressions of the Catholic faith: San Francisco, San Jose, San Antonio, Los Angeles, Santa Fe. The ACLU, which challenges some religious expressions supported by federal or local governments that abridge the separation of church and state, has challenged monuments and public symbols, but not place names. However, the US Department of Interior under the direction of Deb Haaland, the first Native American cabinet secretary, formed a Derogatory Geographic Names Task Force with the goal of changing the pejorative place names of sites on public lands. Most of the names compiled—some 3300—are offensive to Native Americans.[4]

Although over half of the names of the fifty states in the US use in some form Indigenous names of peoples they disparaged, displaced, or exiled, other colonizers chose "old world" names in what to them was a "the new world": *New* England, *New* York, *New* Hampshire. Until its independence from Spain in 1810, today's Mexico was called *Nueva España,* New Spain, by the Spanish colonizers. Before colonization that expanse of land now occupied was not conceived as a collective entity. European powers with their arrogance and legalistic confidence could divide lands and peoples. When nineteenth-century European colonizers of Africa bargained with each other, they brought out their straight edges to draw arbitrary political boundaries on a map of places most would never visit in "the scramble for Africa." The German Kaiser once gave Mt. Kilimanjaro, in East Africa, to Queen Victoria as a birthday present.

Politically imposed names and their borders have often proved to be temporary. The Italy we know as a nation today, which many imagine is as eternal as Rome, did not exist until 1861. The partition of what was India when England claimed it as one land in their empire, was divided after the end of World War II when many colonized nations declared their independence, roughly separated the largely Hindu south from the Muslim north. A cartographer, chosen intentionally because he had no cultural sensitivity to the people and their geography, imposed the partition that divided India and created Pakistan. The boundary even split houses in half, and there was one set of encyclopedias on shelves, A-M given to one side, N-Z to the other.

Many countries where our grandparents were born no longer exist. When Hall was young there were officially 77 nations in the world; in 2024, the United Nations listed 193 sovereign states. Though the population has increased four-fold during that time, the land mass has not changed very much, though the largely human effect on climate is already decreasing land, as the human population continues to increase. The number of nation-places are political. Some changes merely reflect a new designation for the same land mass and population, others indicate new boundaries, sometimes dividing a common culture, and at other times combining previously separate, even mutually hostile populations—a strategy often used during colonization.[5]

Though Hall's writing frequently identified cultures by national names—especially in his later books about business organizations that span national cultures in their workforce, presence, and influences—his work interest in space and place was not about *realpolitik*, the domain of political science, but more about one's experienced reality.

His attention to structural contrasts, described as national differences, appears occasionally in his early writing, most clearly, about homes he saw as representative of national cultural values. An exception is a little-known book that Mildred Reed Hall co-wrote with her partner and spouse, about a building designed by the internationally acclaimed Finnish-American architect, Eero Saarinen, for the Deere corporation.[6] Here was a modernist building for the global John Deere enterprise, at the time incongruously set in the farmland of Illinois. Their description of how the impact of architectural space affects those whose days are lived within that space is the most detailed example of a defining theme of E. T. Hall's work. Though rarely noted by academics, it was also very good PR for the John Deere corporation.

To speak of a "space" geographically can sound boundless—an emptiness that can be filled even with just a name, a claim, something we could call "a place," an entity, bounded, bordered. The ambiguities of our language may reflect the fluidity of our perceptions as space becomes "a space" that when named is perceived as "a place." Hall did not distinguish between "space" and "place," or when the unit of "space" coalesces into a "place." He would also recognize the cultural, and the political, choice to make much of what previously had seemed like nothing in particular into something special. Disputes have been: Is "Pluto" a planet? Is Oceania a continent? Or when regarding emotions, or ethical standards or law, we say that some line has been crossed: when a child "becomes" an adult, when "just kidding" is not funny, but rather a legal offense?

A Third Space

E. W. Soja in his book, *Thirdspace: Journeys to Los Angeles and Other Real-and-Imagined Places*, explores the very notion of *borders*—how, where, and do they exist—a matter important across national borders and even in cities when they are present.[7] This is, as Richard Harris points out, a geo-political ambiguity, but there are third spaces in organizations, too, including schools and corporations. They are also more relevant than ever in an individual's cultural identity, for example, "TCKs," third-culture kids whose parents came from very different cultural upbringings or who grew up living in many different national cultural communities or ethnic/racial communities—comedian Dave Chapelle comes to mind—and in gender distinctions. And it appears that human culture values drawing lines even when (or perhaps especially) when the imagined borders are permeable and not distinct. Some see most lines when drawn as political.

Until sometime around the 1980s, crossing the busiest international border in the world, the nearly 2,000-mile/3,220-kilometer border between Mexico and the US, was functionally not that much different from contiguous cities but legally separate, like walking the fourteen steps between Kansas City, Kansas, and Kansas City, Missouri. There are similar examples everywhere in the world. The cultural values of many of the residents of El Paso, Texas, in the US, and Ciudad Juárez, Chihuahua, Mexico, are more alike than the values and attitudes of people elsewhere in their respective countries. But politically and economically, and influenced by a history of prejudice, the Mexican-US border also has been a rhetorical trope, a political *futból.* When a wall was erected on the border just south of San Diego, California, it served as a volleyball net for actual games of volleyball. Neighbors who sometimes were from the same families, but divided by "papers," or the lack of such, played pick-up games on any sunny afternoon. And in Sunland Park, New Mexico, bordering Cd. Juárez, Chihuahua, Mexico, parents on both sides of the border placed boards between the steel bars that divided the nations to make seesaws for the children who waved to each other on both sides of the border, and laughed as they went up and down. Not long after, that innocence seemed quaint, and the laughter had stopped.

Beyond the Edge of Space

Cartographers' maps once included images of gods, omnipresent, guarding, and potentially threatening land and seas. We'd be startled to see such images or markings on today's secular geophysical maps or included our GPS guidance systems, and yet the mental maps that perhaps most people in the world envision is a cosmology that that includes places regarded as sacred, many that prohibit entry, and celestial destinations when life's journey has ended. Considering that traditions of faith and beliefs constitute a significant part of culture, providing for "cosmological" space as a perspective on spaces and places, seems important in a cultural cartography.

London-born Richard Harris, author and for decades a university professor in Japan attentive to culture-specific and intercultural issues, offers a six-part typology, from the cosmological to the interpersonal. His delightful book, *Paradise: A Cultural Guide* presents the visions of the afterlife as depicted in several religious traditions.[8] Harris's cultural perspective on space includes the cosmological and spiritual domain that an intercultural perspective must include. He notes, for example, that a mountain that might be attractive to hikers or skiers coming from one cultural background is a sacred space to others, forbidden territory. Harris gives us, he might say (paraphrasing William Empson), "a handle for the bundle":

> Given the complexity of the concept of cultural influences on the perception of physical space, it is necessary to construct some kind of structure, however artificial and incomplete, in order to facilitate discussion of the theme. I am therefore proposing a six-part framework of different kinds of space perception that, while having little or no discrete physical reality, nevertheless enables a manageable analysis of an otherwise amorphous mass of information.[9]

From the metaphysical, cosmological space, to the most intimate, personal space, a range that was the province of Hall's "proxemics," each category in this framework is immediately recognizable with different vocabularies used and studied in different academic fields. Some may be seen as "related," others as in shadows created by the walls that divide them. Harris offers perspectives that group these, and that can also be a check-list to consider how each is involved or implicated in the others, and how a change in one area can affect a change—often unanticipated—in the others. This was a theme in Hall's work, including his idea of culture where a change in one thing will change the cultural gestalt. Hall, whom Harris knew, would have appreciated this perspective:

> *Cosmological* space refers to "understandings and assumptions as to the nature of the earth and the universe, both physical and metaphysical."
>
> *Geographical* space includes "ideas about the people of the world and their views regarding the regions they and others inhabit on the earth's surface,"—what to some is property that can be owned, to others is sanctified land where the spirits of those who lived there before remain.
>
> *Environmental* space "deals with the effects of the physical landscape, both naturally occurring and humanly constructed, on perception and interaction." Inseparable from human history and cultural identity, the environment and how our exploitation and habits alter "it" (the reality demands verbs, not a noun), and how we regard environment are implicated in every spatial consideration.
>
> *Communal* space includes settlement patterns, boundaries, and differing conceptions of public and private space. Who is my neighbor and what is expected?
>
> *Residential* space considers the "relationship between human perception and houses or dwelling places," and is also

relevant to workplaces. Digital technologies and the global pandemic beginning around 2020 have blurred conventional urban divisions of home and work, public and private, and also influenced mobility and settlement patterns.

Personal space is the realm of Hall's proxemics—interpersonal distance, and the body's configurations and interaction in non-verbal communication.

This brief summary leaves out the most interesting and important details of each of Harris's part of his six-part map. Asked later if he had further thoughts, Harris said he can also see how this listing can come full circle, the cosmological and the personal joined.

In *The Hidden Dimension*, Hall describes the design and cultural significance of space design and the influence of proxemics on individual houses, contrasting French, German, Japanese, and US home designs. With insights that call attention to what we might otherwise not consider, like other national contrasts, the homes described are representative of a particular economic and social class that reflect values traditional or idealized. Fashion and technological changes also reshape places and their interior spaces. Even public places, such as a market that attracts tourists where people across cultures meet, may be shaped to express cultural expectations of international visitors who sustain those businesses. Global tourism, which in many places brings in more people than actual residents, affects one's home, cultural place, and others' experience of a place.

The way we talk about places, not just those we don't know much about but especially the places where we live and work, reveals our perceptions of place better than an MRI—and with no technology required. They also reveal attitudes about geographically proximate places or beliefs and attitudes, "what is central" or "way out there," "fringe."

Hall's descriptions of how people from different backgrounds interact in a particular place is, upon reflection, less than we might suppose: the fleeting but often memorable experiences of interacting with venders in a market or, later in his writing, something similar in the corporate global markets.

First, We Shape Our Buildings, Then They Shape Us

Within a home are specific places—different rooms that provide for different functions, and within those rooms new spatial considerations that often reflect cultural and personal values. Until what age is it expected a young child will sleep with the mother? Space (and economics) permitting, should a child have a private room, and if so, when is it appropriate for the door to be shut? Is it the parents' responsibility to enter the child's place, or do so only with the child's permission? (Some will say this is another one of those "first world" concerns.) Though he mentioned the concept of "privacy" in several books, Hall's writings about proxemics did not include much about such family-culture specifics; rather, he emphasized national cultural values as he interpreted them. In his discussions of place, Hall gave little attention to the relation between the natural environment and the built-environment.

Rina Swentzell wrote a beautiful essay where she talks about Tewa/Pueblo cosmology: how life flows through both animate and inanimate entities, including the adobe houses built of earth and in time return to earth. She appears also in a video, *An Understated Sacredness,* that I often showed in my classes and workshops.[10] "Nature," and "natural places" have been surprisingly—shall we say alarmingly—missing in considerations of intercultural communication. Maybe because the popular notion of "communication" suggests words, and probably urban and indoor settings, and probably also myopic notions of time, speed, efficiency, and practicality. "Interculturalists" be warned: your days to talk about culture using "the iceberg analogy" are melting away.

The aphorism, "first we shape our buildings, and then they shape us," is affirmed by some neuroscience research, with implications for how we choose to shape the buildings that affect us at different times in our lives. We now have a field of "neuroarchitecture" that applies findings of how our brains respond to spaces in which we are schooled, live, work, and sometimes dream. Classrooms with lines of desks bolted to the floor, said to be a nineteenth-century design that served as preparation for future line work in factories, today is recognized as not the most conducive environment for learning. We've come to appreciate how much learning happens between students, encouraged when their seating is organized so they can engage with each other more naturally.

Hall was critical of how nineteenth-century models of design continue to influence us. With his focus on how we experience, he would have been fascinated by the very idea of "neuroarchitecture," as well as the technology that makes it possible. He drew attention to our sensitivity to the surfaces that shape our spaces, comforting pressed earth beneath our feet, the feel of a wood floor, or hard tile, innovative surfaces, including wall-to-wall carpets and outdoor "astro-turf."

A "prepared environment" that fits the size of the children in their classroom and the objects they are given to work with was what Maria Montessori, the innovative Italian educator and founder of the Montessori school, recognized. Children feel, behave, learn differently in spaces of scale that fit the young people's size than when they may be overwhelmed in a space of a scale fit for a big person, an authority, an adult. Shinichi Suzuki, who developed a philosophy and teaching method for children learning to play a music instrument, commissioned instrument makers to produce smaller instruments, including his Suzuki violins for children just beginning to play.

Attention to light, ceiling height, and floor elevation have been used as expressions of power in our institutions—cathedrals, mosques, synagogues, temples, and in our secular temples, too: libraries, universities, museums, courtrooms. Textures and colors: restaurant owners long ago realized that some colors invite diners to linger, and others encourage a quicker departure, observable when comparing the interior of high-end restaurants with those we visit when we are in a hurry.

This Is Not Your Place

It was pioneering sociologist, William Graham Sumner, who coined the term "ethnocentrism" that in its many expressions is observable everywhere, and internally affects perceptions and judgments of others, latent onset of actions, and feeling comfortable with structures that help and define one's place as separate from others. South Africa's National Party government used a Dutch word, *apparteit*, to refer to the physical separation of people feared, while creating new categories for others "not like us."

Physical separations date long in the records of civilizations, by designated class, ancestry, religious beliefs, and the concept of "race," applied by those in power. Charles Darwin's writings cast doubt on the idea of separate races, and Franz Boas, among others, wrote and spoke out about race being no more than "a social construct."[11] Louise Wilkerson writes about how extensive divisions marked in spaces she identifies as part of a caste system:

> In the United States the subordinate caste was quarantined in every sphere of life, made untouchable on American terms, for most of the country's history and well into the twentieth century.
>
> In the South, where most people in the subordinate caste were long consigned, black children and white children studied from separate sets of textbooks. In Florida, the books for black children and white children could not even be stored together. African Americans were prohibited from using white water fountains and had to drink from horse troughs in the southern swelter before the era of separate fountains.
>
> In southern jails, the bedsheets for the black prisoners were kept separate from the bedsheets for the white prisoners.

All private and public human activities were segregated from birth to death, from hospital wards to railroad platforms to ambulances, hearses, and cemeteries.

In stores, black people were prohibited from trying on clothing, shoes, hats, or gloves, assuming they were permitted in the store at all. If a black person happened to die in a public hospital, "the body will be placed in a corner of the 'dead house' away from the white corpses," wrote the historian Bertram Doyle in 1937.[12]

Place Experienced:
A Neighborhood, an Office, and a Restaurant

Places we live in or learn in and from, or work in, each exerts an influence that reflects and reveals something about the larger cultural environment. For this book, I asked friends who have studied the cultural influence of spaces to offer some intercultural insights. One, a neighborhood in Chicago, is in a now-classic study about gender and cultural norms within the neighborhood. Two others are different kinds of places: Japanese offices and workspaces (technical laboratories) that hosted Canadian and US interns temporarily working there, and a famous family-owned restaurant in Santa Fe, New Mexico, popular with locals and for many tourists as a "destination" to get the taste and feel of the place. This is described by a Colombian architectural critic who worked in the restaurant, and looks at spaces and places within the restaurant from perspectives of the multicultural staff.

Though Hall's work has been important for city planners, he wrote more about the use of home spaces than about the neighborhoods that contain the houses, neighborhoods that may be identified by vernacular names indicating boundaries and sometimes sensed by outsiders traversing a city. A friend who is local and takes us on a tour of the city might point out neighborhoods, some named as distinct but rarely on maps. Even without a guide we can sense if we've passed from one neighborhood to another—over here, we see lots of people on the street, a busy neighborhood we think, a noisy neighborhood; over there, no one on the street, just houses, silent. Now we pass through a neighborhood where the space in front of the house is a "front yard," maybe a seemingly manicured green lawn; then there was that other neighborhood where in front of several houses are old cars in seeming disrepair, though we might not appreciate how their spare parts may be needed to keep the family car working. In one neighborhood, kids play in the street; in another neighborhood, the kids go to a separate place designed for their play. Acoustic spaces, signage, and what people are wearing are part of the experience of "a place," and our reactions to each are influenced by our backgrounds and sometimes also imagining what it might be like to live there.

With gentrification, a neighborhood in economic decline suddenly is "discovered," becomes so trendy that the former residents can no longer afford to live there. Urban planning and changes in mass transit access serve as physical markers of a neighborhood—"the other side of the tracks," is a classic division marker in the US. In mid-twentieth century, it might be a massive expressway that was built to intentionally separate communities. Perhaps most famous, or infamous, of Americans whose urban designs divided and sometimes devastated the urban environment was New York City's Robert Moses, the subject of the Pulitzer Prize winning book, *The Power Broker*, by Robert Caro (1974). But every city has its history of people whose influence changed the place, and so also its urban cultures.

The Efficacy of Speaking: Teamsterville

"Teamsterville" is the name of a neighborhood in Chicago that centered a pioneering ethnography of communication that Gerry Philipsen wrote as his doctoral dissertation.[13] His adviser was Ethel Albert, an anthropologist and friend of Hall, who uniquely held a joint appointment in anthropology and communication. Albert encouraged

Philipsen to look at the "efficacy of communication" in the neighborhood he would study: when and where is speaking encouraged, and
when and where is it not?[14] In the 1960s when ethnographies of
communication appeared, this was a good question among cultural
anthropologists, but a novel question in a communication department.
Ethnographies take a relatively long time to complete, in part because
one must always wonder if spending more time would yield better
conclusions. Observe and patterns will emerge, the ethnographer is
promised. A long time to try to figure what to everyone else in the
neighborhood is, literally, *common* sense.

For more than a year Philipsen lived in a place most Chicagoans
knew as "Back of the Yards," but formally "Bridgeport"; "Teamsterville" was a pseudonym. "The yards," long since gone, referred to the
Chicago stockyards, the slaughterhouses, where beginning in 1865
almost all of the nation's cuts of meat came from. "Hog butcher of
the world," poet Carl Sandberg called Chicago in his pean to the city.
Chicago Mayor Richard J. Daley called Sandberg, in one of many
malapropisms, "Chicago's 'poet lariat.'"[15]

For cultural context: "Back of the Yards" was an Irish-Catholic
enclave from a time in the mid-nineteenth century. "No Irishman or
Dogs Allowed" signs were posted by businesses seeking workers in
the nineteenth century. The first-generation Irish who emigrated to
escape the potato famine when a blight destroyed the subsistence food
in rural Ireland, were "the famine Irish," at the bottom of the social
strata along with Black Americans and excluded nearly as much, with
the men regarded as drunks and families as lacking in morals and
common decency. The Irish men were among the few willing to work
in the new slaughterhouses that made the whole neighborhood stink.

The Irish immigrants and their next generations were also distrusted
because they were Catholic and were imagined to be more loyal to the
Pope than the government, which was largely controlled by English
and northern European Protestant Americans who also held the

political and economic power. Though many Irish joined the Union Army to fight the southern Confederate soldiers, which ameliorated some of the prejudices, it took another century for a Catholic aspirant to the presidency to convince voters in the historically anti-Catholic "South" that as president he (John Kennedy) would not take his orders from the Pope.[16]

Ethnic solidarity centered in neighborhoods is also a potential political base. Over time, Irish Americans gained political power in cities where they were a presence, famously in Boston and in Chicago. Beginning as a local alderman representing Bridgeport, Richard J. Daley rose in power, consolidated and extended his political base and influence, and eventually became mayor: "the last of the big city bosses." He was credited (and blamed) for getting the votes to make John Kennedy the first Catholic, an Irish Catholic at that, president of the United States.

Neighborhoods were, especially before gentrification, identified by those who lived there, and defined by physical and geographical boundaries, some intentionally built to wall-in a neighborhood as a place, most often with ethnic and racial solidarity. In some places in midcentury US, "There goes the neighborhood" was the bigot's warning if a Black or a Jewish family moved into what residents saw as their white, Christian neighborhood. Universities had unwritten "quotas" of how many people of designated categories would be admitted. That history is also part of the history I grew up with.

As part of his research, Philipsen asked residents, in a conversational way, about where and with whom having an ordinary greeting and conversation was expected, normal. He realized that it was in *the neighborhood* where it was good for people talk with each other. What is the neighborhood? *"Everyone around here,"* as in *"everyone around here knows . . ."* or *"nobody around here believes . . ."* Asked about meeting people outside of the neighborhood, like "what if a son or daughter gets into trouble, maybe even in a fight?" the parent's first response most often would be, "what were you doing over there?"

As good places for communication for young men, Philipsen identified four, including in the neighborhood, on the street, and at the street corner (for young men, not women—the study was done at a time when there were corner taverns; too young to enter, a corner was an approximation), and "the porch" when many neighborhood houses had porches—an odd feature in much of the world then. (Philipsen reports that a local politician complained that he lost an election because he didn't have a porch where he could talk to potential constituents.) A front porch was a historic and still appropriate architectural feature at mid-century, as mechanical air conditioning was just emerging. The pleasure of sitting out on the porch in summer was more pleasant than inside a warm house, and it gave the street eyes to see who was passing by. That was also when that era was passing by.[17]

A Japanese Office as Experienced by Interns from Canada and the US

In the 1980s the Japanese government, and many businesses, invited college graduates and young professionals from abroad to come to Japan for a period of six months to two years to work as interns in Japanese companies, mostly in offices, some in research labs, and all speaking Japanese in varying degrees of fluency.[18]

In a two-year study of the experience of US and Canadian interns, Tomoko Masumoto learned that the challenges of space and time were initially among the most stressful.[19] A typical Japanese office layout is "open," no cubicles that have been common in the US since mid-twentieth century when the modular walls offered a degree of privacy and the promise of increased productivity. In recent years, the open office space has been adopted in the US and elsewhere in the belief it leads to more interaction across divisions, but research has not affirmed that anticipated outcome.

In a large Japanese company, an office might occupy the entire floor of a building, but large or small the offices usually follow a

similar layout: an open space with desks grouped together, called
shima (islands), where the office staff sit next to and often also across
from one another. Each person works individually but is observable
and within earshot of those nearby. A medium-to-large-size office will
have many of these *shima* grouped by division or area.

New hires will be situated nearest the entrance, responsible for
greeting visitors and directing them to the person they want to
talk to, answering the phone, distributing mail, and in other ways
assisting—all the while learning more about the company culture
and its particular interpersonal relationships. The implicit values of
working as a team: the norm and a cultural value in Japan that is
acquired even before elementary school. At desks behind the staff are
managers overseeing them.

This arrangement is a variation of the social and functional
hierarchy of a traditional *tatami* mat room and in any contemporary
conference room, where the place of authority, or to show respect
to a guest, is away from the door. Easy access to outside the room is
for those who may need to step out and return with tea or food, or
in a conference room to retrieve and bring back needed files. Every
Japanese may look at a room, familiar or new, in these terms: *kamiza*
(literally, the high place) away from the doorway, and *shimoza* (the
low place) nearest the door.

For most interns from abroad, going to work in this "open office,"
in close proximity to others, is daunting. One's posture, gestures, facial
expressions are on display. Questions asked by the intern, and conversations in a language in which the new intern may feel insecure may feel
fraught. Previously an outsider, the intern, now a quasi-insider, feels
exposed. No place to hide. The challenge of this place is space, proximity.

In Masumoto's research on North Americans' experiences in
and adaptation to working in a Japanese office, what was most often
mentioned was the initial discomfort they felt because of the physical
setting.[20] Here are some representative reactions of guest interns:

Japanese offices are different. Right in front of you there is everybody. No cubicles and all desks and everything are in one big space. It took a lot of getting used to but I think after working in that environment, I can work everywhere. Because it was really difficult to get used to, a desk right here and a desk right there, people are next to you. A lot of things we take for granted in the United States, we just cannot do here. I cannot make a personal phone call. Nobody minds if you use a phone only for a few minutes. If you make those phone calls from your desk, you feel uncomfortable. Especially, if I do it in English. Every time I talked on the phone, everybody thinks it's an English lesson. They are listening to everything. I had to have a cold conversation with my friends like, "Yeah, that would be great, very good, yes, I can do that." Not say much of anything because people are listening. Once, soon after I put the phone down, [a coworker] just said, "Oh, that sounds like a good plan for tonight." That's very difficult to get used to! People are always watching. I think I appreciate more the work environment in the US because I can have more personal space.

A man who worked in a laboratory said:

The most prominent difference is in the office area of our workplace. Here we have two groups working in the same lab. Each group has its own *shima* (island) of desks. There are no obstructions in between the desks of supervisors and lab workers. The questions and answers are heard by all, and when the group leader wishes to say something, she merely has to stand up. Private conversations are held separately in a small meeting room.

But there is good news: most interns came to appreciate this arrangement, a matter that some intercultural consultants might neglect to mention because talking about intercultural conflict makes for a more dramatic telling. Many interns see the advantages of a cubicle-less office. Interns said that during their first weeks they felt as if they had stepped into a minefield. Later, often after months, many said they returned to the office feeling they were rejoining their team:

> I was amazed how people talk across divisions. In the United States, people have their own small workplace, such as individual rooms or divided spaces. Here in my office, several divisions are on the same floor. They do a lot of cross-communication. It is convenient. I do not need to make any appointments to ask questions to someone in a different division. I just check whether he or she is at their desk.

In the Japanese open-space office, people in managerial positions and their staff are grouped together. The desk arrangements indicate the hierarchy. A woman from the US said that at first she had a hard time getting used to the office arrangement but later saw both advantages and disadvantages in this arrangement:

> I had four people underneath me. Three were female and one was male. Since I was the only female manager, I thought they wouldn't know how to deal with me. A lot of Japanese offices set desks in certain way. This row [of desks] is for managers and this row is support staff. I was at the manager's side. So everyone treated me differently. It was better than I thought it would be.

Working in a Famous Restaurant: The Shed

Santa Fe, New Mexico, is a place known for its history that, by colonial reckoning spans 400 years, and by the Indigenous people more than a thousand. For over a century, artists, writers, actors and musicians have been drawn to this live-and-let-live, gay-friendly place, with its architecture, art, a vibrant summer opera, and its high desert mountain beauty. This relatively small town in a big state is a destination for tourists. The lure of visitors has made "the city different," as its boosters sometimes call it, a city that because of gentrification and tourism is now very different from the village where E. T. Hall grew up.

Santa Fe is also is known for its food traditions and its restaurants. If a visitor asks a local, "Where should I eat?" one suggestion is likely to be The Shed, a short walk from the historic plaza, and a place where guests will enjoy, in the words of one reviewer, the "best that Northern New Mexico has to offer both in cuisine and hospitality . . ." This sixty-year-old, James Beard Award-winning restaurant serves local specialties at reasonable prices and is set in a seventeenth-century house, which is relatively small for the number of guests who visit, but since it is listed on the historic register, structural alterations to the building are prohibited. Locals are more likely to go to its sister-restaurant, La Choza—same management, same menu, but with a less charming ambience and fewer tourists. This is context for a look at daily communication among the people who work at The Shed.

Patricia "Bibi" Arcos, who has a degree in architecture, came to Santa Fe from her native Bogotá, Colombia, to study intercultural communication at the University of New Mexico. In her architecture classes in Colombia, she studied many iconic buildings in the US, designed by the most famous US architects. But when she arrived Santa Fe, Arcos found that she was in yet another former Spanish colonial town, not so different in layout from towns throughout Colombia and Latin America. In New Mexico she also discovered that here she was "Latina," or "Hispanic," puzzling new identities for her. But puzzlement fed her curiosity about this curious place.

Like so many others, Arcos first visited The Shed to enjoy a meal with friends. Then, intrigued by the setting and interaction, she returned and for more than three months observed the place and the interaction of guests and those working inside. Soon after that, she was hired as a waitress and became an insider, graciously welcoming guests, showing them to their table, taking their orders, and attending to whatever the guests needed. Arcos, who speaks five languages, including her native Spanish, was able to be playful with the Spanish-speaking cooks in the kitchen and gracious with the guests from many parts of the world.

Bibi gained the management's permission and the agreement of everyone with whom she worked for more than a year to do unobtrusive research during work hours, and interview and sometimes take photos during off-hours. Arcos wrote an ethnography of The Shed.[21] What are the systems of relationships and routines that even her friends working there might not be conscious of, the patterns of interaction that make an organization function smoothly in a popular local restaurant?

One of the first things she needed to learn as a waitress was the in-house vocabulary for each of the several rooms in the restaurant, and where and how to lead guests to their table and take their order. The naming of places used exclusively by the wait staff and supervisors is essential for efficient and accurate communication among everyone working there. ["My training] tour . . . included the explanation for the name of each room, the position and number of tables, and the protocol to locate the parties within each room."[22] The front area has a different name for each table. Arcos says this mental map and code can be learned only by walking through the restaurant many times.

When the restaurant was on break between lunch and dinner, she interviewed her co-workers and also photographed them in the places and spaces they knew so well. Miguel Gandert advised her on how to get the kind of photos she wanted when working in spaces that offered few options. Later in her interviews, she showed those pictures to ask each one how they saw themselves in different settings, and also what they thought about how others in those pictures who worked in different spaces might be feeling and thinking. Restaurant work is a highly interdependent, especially in the US where a big part of the income earned by those who meet the guests depends on tips. The waiter relies on the visitors' satisfaction with the presentation and taste of the food served, and also its timely arrival. Management depends on both.

Arcos described interaction among those working in this restaurant not just with respect to the places and spaces where this occurred, but viewed these as *different zones of interaction,* places within the physical, functional spaces where this interaction occurs. These include physical spaces but also a dimension of time that influences relationships, and the kind of communication that characterizes these zones. This involves interpersonal relations, seniority, hierarchies and power relationships, languages spoken, gender, dress, and more, all in combination. She was able to do this through observation, experience, and through interviews aided by photographs she had taken of her co-workers at work and during breaks. Arcos describes *zones* not just as places within a defined physical place that only insiders might recognize if pointed out, but also spaces and places that even those within the system might not be conscious of which, of course, is a theme running through all intercultural work.

Ethnographies are specific, observations about micro-cultures, case studies. The cultural and intercultural dynamics at The Shed have broader applications elsewhere, and not just in restaurants where the cooks and the servers are likely from differing cultural backgrounds and work separately. Though her five-part description of zones was applied to this particular restaurant setting, Arcos presents a template that is applicable in other organizations with a culturally diverse work force.

Space as a Physical and Functional Setting—The first zone that Arcos describes is what a person visiting the restaurant initially sees and feels—the physical and functional setting that actively shapes the communication process within The Shed, and helps frame the experience of being there. Elements include the position and configuration of this area in relation to other parts of the restaurant, the configuration of the area in terms of its scale and proportion, its exposed or enclosed character, and the light and color of the area. The time of day also alters the environment and the mood that affects perceptions by the guests, and also the employees' perceptions of their workplace and their interaction with others working there.

Space as a Narrative Zone—In the second or *narrative zone*, the space is "redefined and appropriated by the different groups of people that need to share the same workspace, beyond their own culture, language or age differences."[23] Arcos describes the appropriation of micro-spaces, with respect to cultural background and language.

In this narrative space we see the beginning of the hidden dimensions of the restaurant, both because the physical dimension permits the organization's members to find and recreate communication and relationships, and also to discover information in a spontaneous way, outside of the official channels. As a consequence, narrative places can be used to relate and understand how members of organizations read and construct a unique and shared memory. Narrative places also shape reality, and are affected and partially defined by the cultural histories of those where this social communication occurs.[24]

As an example, Arcos describes a Friday night after a busy dinner shift. Waitresses find a seat and count their tips. Some thank the others as they leave. Cooks begin to clean the ovens and stands, and the volume of the radio playing "*rancheras mexicanas*" increases. In the maintenance area, the dishwashers prepare to clean the floor with Latin salsas and merengues playing. This is when animated conversations, and lots of jokes (in Spanish) are heard.

"The differences in cultural background play a key role at the moment of differentiating one's and others' territories," Arcos writes. "An attitude of respect for others' workspaces seems to be more important for employees with European (and Anglo) backgrounds, while the ability and viability to talk and make jokes within the work space seems to define territory for employees with Central American backgrounds."[25]

Being able to maintain and actively be able to participate in others' conversations, and be a "*bromista*" (jokester) is highly valued among those working in the kitchen and by those in maintenance." Talking (in Spanish) while sharing a workspace is notable. Arcos describes two cooks "maintaining an animated conversation about marriage. They talked without stopping while reading the orders, doing the dishes, and answering the continuous requests of the waitresses. Nothing seemed to interrupt their conversation at all. It was like they were in the living room of their house talking about something anecdotal and personal," a clear example of Hall's polychronic style.[26]

Space as a Contact Zone and a Place of Dominance—Arcos describes the *contact zone* in a workplace as a place of permanent and ongoing encounters of different cultures that converge into a new culture through transculturation. This process describes how "minorities" create a new culture from the dominating culture that exists within the organization.

Arcos's model defines space as narratives that are socially constructed and recreated, and contact zones where asymmetrical power relations exist. Beyond being places where processes of transferring information occur, at this level they produce, maintain, and reproduce power structures. At different times of the day and when the restaurant is closed, an area that is usually the work space for some of the employees may be used by others, leading to negotiating who can be there, and often indicating the implicit hierarchy. There is no place to go to take a break, nor do the wait staff have breaks. "We have to eat standing up in front of our superior while we continue with our job, without any privacy," said one waitress. One of the cooks complained (in Spanish) "Americans only help each other because each of them is here for themselves." When several people have to work together in the same space, especially at the small bar, and one is not doing his or her share, the others resent it: "You are not here doing your share, get out of my space."

Space as a Place of Resistance and Collaboration—As an answer to the inequality or lack of functionality of a space, new unofficial/ unmarked uses are given to spaces to satisfy the necessities of the community within the workplace, often distortions of what was intended appear. Arcos describes the small, very busy kitchen where the cooks, including those from Mexico and Central America, can ease some of the stresses in their hot, cramped setting by re-creating their space, playing their favorite music, and joking in Spanish about and with others working in the restaurant who are likely to miss *double entendre* humor, and in other ways assert agency. In short, "the use of jokes, compliments, and nonverbal signals are informal tools to differentiate and also to trespass and explore cultural and social boundaries," that help maintain a balance of between those who do not share the same cultural backgrounds, values, and expectations, nor fluency in each other's native language while working together in a very small space.[27]

A Sense of Place

A place is not just a geographical location, a container for the story or information or event therein contained. Places exist in time, and they are where we locate precious memories, even when memories of a place may be at odds with an objective description of that place, whether the place is where we lived or used to live or work or attend classes or play. Keith Basso in his book, *Wisdom Sits in Places,* writes: "As numerous writers have noted, places possess a marked capacity for triggering acts of self-reflection, inspiring thoughts about who one presently is, or memories of who one used to be, or musings on who one might become."[28]

And that is not all. "Place-based thoughts about the self commonly lead to thoughts of other things—other places, other people, other times, whole networks of associations that ramify unaccountably within the expanding spheres of awareness that they themselves engender. The experience of sensing places, then, is thus both thoroughly reciprocal and incorrigibly dynamic. . . .

When places are deeply sensed, the physical landscape becomes rooted in the landscape of the mind, and a ready departure to the roving imagination."

Notes

1. Keith Basso, *Wisdom Sits in Places* (Albuquerque, New Mexico: University of New Mexico Press, 1996).

2. Stein's full quote, in her "cubist" writing style that she shaped in Paris, not Oakland: "What was the use of my having come from Oakland it was not natural to have come from there yes write about if I like or anything if I like but not there, there is no there there." Gertrude Stein, *Everybody's Autobiography*, 1937.

3. British-US born writer and photographer of Nigerian and Ghanaian parentage, Taiye Selasi in a TED Talk, says, "Don't Ask Where I'm From, Ask Where I'm Local," since "from" may be misleading. Where we were born may have little to do with our cultural identity—or identities if our life has included living in many places that make us who we are. Asked where, she would say she is "local," Selasi names Accra, Berlin, New York, and Rome. https://www.ted.com/talks/taiye_selasi_don_t_ask_where_i_m_from_ask_where_i_m_a_local?language=en

4. On November 19, 2021, US Secretary of the Interior, Deb Haaland, the first Indigenous cabinet member to direct the department that oversees Indigenous lands, issued Secretarial Order 3404 that declared the term "squaw" as derogatory and established an inter-agency Derogatory Names Task Force and a process to review and replace derogatory names of sites under federal control.

5. An excellent short video commentary on the titular theme in Keith Basso's *Wisdom Sits in Places* is expressed by a Zuni Pueblo elder: https://www.globalonenessproject.org/library/films/counter-mapping

6. Mildred Reed Hall and Edward T. Hall, *The Fourth Dimension in Architecture: The Impact of Building on Man's Behavior* (Santa Fe, NM: Sunstone Press, 1975).

7. Edward W. Soja, *Thirdspace: Journeys to Los Angeles and Other Real-and-Imagined Places.* Hoboken, New Jersey: Wiley-Blackwell, 1996.

8. Richard Harris, *Paradise: A Cultural Guide* (London: Eastern University Press, 1996). This treatise on how the ideal is conceived across religious traditions calls to mind Mark Twain's remark: "Heaven for climate; Hell for conversations."

9. Richard Harris, "The Cultural Perception of Space: Expanding the Legacy of Edward T. Hall," *Journal of Intercultural Communication & Interactions Research* 2 (1), 2022, 135-150.

10. Rina Swentzell, "Pueblo Space: An Understated Sacredness," in *Telling New Mexico: A New History*, eds. Marta Weigle, Frances Levine, and Louise Stiver (Santa Fe: Museum of New Mexico Press, 2009), 45-48. "An Understated Sacredness" is also the title of a television presentation on KUNM (the Albuquerque PBS station) introduced by V. B. Price, and told by Rina Swentzell. This can be viewed on YouTube: https://www.youtube.com/watch?v=8zHAiOKN6Vo&ab_channel=knmedotorg

11. "The belief in 'races' as natural aspects of human biology, and the structures of inequality (racism) that emerge from such beliefs, are among the most damaging elements in the human experience both today and in the past." This was the statement by the American Association of Physical Anthropologists in 2019.

12. Isabell Wilkerson, *Caste: The Origins of Our Discontents* (New York: Random House, 2020), 116.

13. Gerry Frank Philipsen, "Communication in Teamsterville: A Sociolinguistic study of Speech Behavior in an Urban Neighborhood," (PhD diss., Northwestern University, 1972).

14. Ethel M. Albert, "'Rhetoric,' 'Logic,' and 'Poetics' in Burundi: Culture Patterning of Speech Behavior." *American Anthropologist* (Winter 1964-1965).

15. Daley was once advised to get some coaching about his public speaking from one of my colleagues, Glen Mills. After a few minutes of coaching, Daley said to Mills, "Thanks, Professor, but if I talked the way you tell me to, I'd never get re-elected."

16. The cultural history and sociology of an Irish-American community like Bridgeport in Chicago is documented in a four-part series, "The Irish in America," on PBS and available on YouTube.

17. The "porch" is a cultural as well as a physical construction, as I realized when teaching about this in Japan where a porch in front of a house was a strange conception. Nor are there "blocks" and other categories that in one community is fundamental to the physical design and how we talk about it.

18. This program established by JETRO (Japan External Trade Organization) followed the success of another Japanese government program JET (The Japan Exchange & Teaching Programme) through which college grads who were "native speakers" of English were invited to assist the resident English teacher in public schools in Japan. Later, native speakers of other

foreign languages were added for other positions in municipal or prefectural government offices and as sports coaches. In the late-nineteenth century, during the Meiji era, a dramatic shift from centuries of intentional isolation Japan sent emissaries abroad to learn what today would be called "best practices" in education, law, governance, industry, and transportation.

19. Tomoko Masumoto, "Learning to 'Do Time' in Japan: A Study of US Interns in Japanese Organizations in Japan," *International Journal of Cross-Cultural Management* 4.1 (July 2016).

20. Tomoko Masumoto, "American Interns in Japanese Organizations: Participant Perceptions and Interpretations of Intercultural Communication in the 'US-Japan Industry and Technology Management Program'" (PhD diss., University of New Mexico, 2000).

21. Patricia Bibiana Arcos, "Space and Organizational Communication: A Visual Ethnography of 'The Shed' Restaurant in Santa Fe, New Mexico" (MA thesis, University of New Mexico, 2010). Available on CD Rom through Random Mouse Press.

22. Arcos, 72.

23. Arcos, 100.

24. In her interviews, while showing some of the photos she had taken, many people identified with pictures that showed their workspace: "This is my place," some said. Some idealized others' places: seeing a picture showing the cooks eating their dinner after the restaurant had closed for the night, those who work with the customers said, "It's nice to see these guys sitting down and relaxing."

25. Acros, 105. This is different from another kind of narrative space where a place holds and provokes memories when one returns to the place, and most obvious when inviting others, friend, family, to a place of personal importance that comes with stories, often many stories.

26. Acros, 106.

27. Acros, 108.

28. Basso, *Wisdom Sits in Places*, 107.

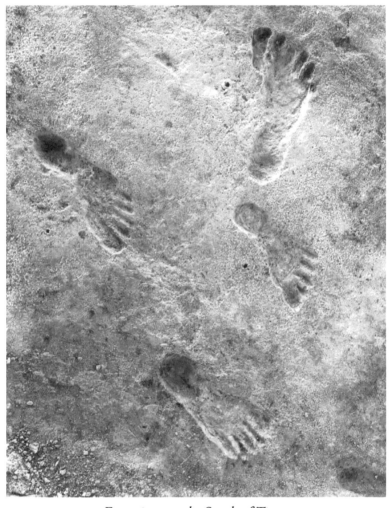

Footprints on the Sands of Time:
Human footprints from 21,000 - 23,000 years ago.
White Sands National Park, New Mexico
Photo by Dan Odess

CHAPTER FOURTEEN

It's About Time

The rush of seconds, hours, years that hurls us toward life then drags us toward nothingness . . . We inhabit time as fish live in water. Our being is being in time. . . In the physics books I read as a university student, [I learned that] time works quite differently from the way it seems to. In those same books I also learned that we still don't know how time actually works. The nature of time is perhaps the greatest remaining mystery.[1]
—*Carlo Rovelli*

The duration of felt experience is between two and three seconds—about as long as it takes . . . for Paul McCartney to sing the words "Hey Jude." Everything before belongs to memory; everything after is anticipation. It's a strange, barely fathomable fact that our lives are lived through this small, moving window.[2]
—*Paul Bloom*

In his lyrical book, *The Order of Time*, theoretical physicist Carlo Rovelli asks: "Do we exist in time or does time exist in us? What does it really mean to say that 'time passes'? What ties time to our nature as persons, to our subjectivity?"[3] The factor of time is foundational in physics and all the natural sciences, beginning with astronomy that seems inseparable from religions everywhere. Rovelli notes that time passes more slowly in the valley than in the mountains, an empirical fact, measurable, as are our bodies' rhythms: circadian, diurnal, ultradian, circalunar, and circannual, measured within a 24-hour time span, or by day and night, or by month or year.

How we experience time, and how we learn to think and talk about time, are also shaped by the cultures which we inhabit and which are habituated in us. The culturally influenced ways we think about time, value time, and how these vary across cultures were a life-long fascination for anthropologist Hall. Because he took special interest in *inter*cultural encounters, he recognized that time, often a basis for judging others—how their interpretations of and performance of time, such as "taking too much time," or being "slow to respond"—could be used as a key to anticipating potential conflicts. And, importantly, a mirror to ourselves: again, "we need others to know who we are."

Many Kinds of Time

Hall begins his book about time, *The Dance of Life: The Other Dimension of Time,* with an overview of some of several kinds of time, some he briefly identifies, and others that he treats in detail.[4] Rather than providing a list, he chose a mandala to "show the relationship of various ideas to each other in a comprehensive, non-linear fashion."[5]

How many kinds of time are there? In his "time mandala" that most readers might call a diagram (Hall called it "a map of time") he identifies eight different kinds of time that he thought included what he "had considered during seventy years of experience and research."

Personal Time—refers to how we experience time, and sometimes describe our feelings about time and pace in places we visit: how "fast" Manhattan feels or how slow—"sleepy" is the cliché—when urbanites venture out to rural spots. A change in "how time feels" is often what vacationers want. Hall mentions the slowing down of heart, respiratory, and breathing rates during meditation, when some say time stands still. A musician friend tells me that when fully in the flow of composing, he is sometimes shocked, but not surprised, by the glimmer of dawn that meets him when he steps out of his studio at the end of a session that began in the early evening. He had no idea how many hours had passed. Mihaly Csikszentmihalyi in his book, *Flow*, describes this phenomenon of how we experience and perceive time.[6] When you're in the flow, consciousness of time can disappear. The expression "being in the moment" suggests something similar. If you are fully present, you don't glance at your watch.

Physical Time—encompasses astronomical observations that centered systems of belief, as our planet and satellite moon revealed consistency, promise, and what Hall mentions in another category: priesthoods, rituals, authority. He writes about the significance of time in the science of physics from Euclid to Einstein. He anticipates, correctly, that our thinking about physical time will continue to change as research and theory evolves. He references the early science fiction writer H. G. Wells's "time machines" as they intrigued readers in previous generations in this context. One constant is that subject or object of "time" has continued to provoke writers in that genre, but perhaps outpaced by physicists and in applications by engineers. Can events, as identified in time, run backwards as well as forwards? Nobel physicist Richard Feynman used to give a lecture on how, at the atomic level, there is no distinguishing between the two directions. Made me think of a question asked of a psychic where the answer precedes the question. Answer: Yes, I can. Question: Can you predict the future?

Of course, the trust in what Hall labeled "physical time" is essential in all aspects of our lives and the technological achievements which, in terms of personal time, we value and celebrate.

Metaphysical Time—a topic that Hall writes little about but believed deserves respect, are those experiences of time that resist rational explanation. Some are in the realm of the occult, in which

Newton showed more than a passing interest, according to Hall. The *déjà vu* experience is at the edge of what he includes as metaphysical time phenomena. Science fiction writing and the increasingly respectability of psychotropic drugs when used in therapy also suggest possibilities of temporal experiences unlike those we know as "normal." In a Catholic faith tradition, an indicator of potential sainthood is a person who witnesses have seen in many different places at the same time. Anthropologists have often described reports of experiences in many other cultural settings that seem inexplicable by Western assumptions about reality. As, too, have writers of science-fiction.

Micro Time—is Hall's term (but not used elsewhere in his writings) for "that system of time that is congruent with and a product of primary culture [what we've acquired and learned as we mature and assume others do as well]," but, he says, "its rules are almost entirely outside of conscious awareness," and this is what people sometimes admire or are irritated by when moving from one cultural time pattern to another.[7]

Sync Time—refers to the interactive synchrony between individuals that begins almost immediately after birth between mother and baby, and when and how we engage in timing, often out of awareness, with others. This is presented in more detail in our discussion of synchrony and rhythm.

Sacred Time—is a time apart, the framing of time that introduces or frames legends, fairy tales, origin tales. *Once upon a time* or *long, long ago* is how folk tales are told, not just to entertain or lull children to sleep. Scheherazade's stories that continued 1001 nights not only delayed her threatened execution, they so charmed the Sultan that he married her. In these tales from the fourteenth century, a golden age of Islamic culture, the use of time as a strategy is a theme of the narratives. Hall notes, "It is not supposed to be like ordinary clock time and everybody knows it isn't."[8]

When participating in religious ceremonies and rituals, the observant one is in the ceremony's time. Unlike the perception of time as flowing like a river—or in many languages segmented in the grammar of past, present, or future, irreversible and unrepeatable (a child might taunt another to "take those words back!" when what is spoken or has happened can't be repeated or reversed)—sacred time, in Hall's categorization, *is* repeatable and reversible. In such a ceremony, even Heraclitus *would be able* to step into the same river and not just twice. The feelings of comfort and security that many say they feel when they attend religious services may be their re-entering a sacred time zone. In discussions about responses to the pain experienced when relocating, by choice or necessity for survival, I've been struck by the many people from many lands and faiths whose "coping mechanism" includes or is centered on the rituals of their faith tradition.

Profane Time—in Hall's typology is not what that name might suggest. In a conventional dialectic, the profane is the contrast to the sacred. Rather, Hall uses the word "profane" as the quotidian: the clock and the calendar, the division of time into weeks and months, fiscal quarters of a corporation, or trimesters of a pregnancy. These divisions in the calendar are all arbitrary, culturally and historically diverse, but known to everyone in the community.

It seems to me Hall's broader use of "profane" misses the social carve-out that cultures give to a time when behavior that would be forbidden at any other time would be allowed, even encouraged. Those are the times that culturally give license to "just do it," like at Carnival, Mardi Gras, the Fat Tuesday that precedes solemn Ash Wednesday, which traditionally begins an austere period in the Christian calendar, leading up to Easter.[9] For some people, midnight at a New Year's Eve party, or at "bachelor" or "bachelorette" parties give license for behavior that in other contexts would be prohibited and risks abuse such as unwanted advances that could bring the offender into a court of law if a complaint were filed. Context, an ever-present touchstone for Hall, is inseparable from what we make of time. The title of an edited book on the anthropology of festivals is well chosen: *Time Out of Time*.[10]

Astrological calculations have been motivated by and guided by the priesthoods of all religions, and likely also led to the discovery or creation of mathematics. The spring and autumn equinoxes have been noted and celebrated across cultures, honored even today among many Indigenous communities where temples and pyramids mark the day and precise hour. At Chichén Itzá in the Mayan Yucatán, on both the spring and autumn equinoxes, the shadow of the plumed serpent appears, ascends, and descends the steps of the pyramid. At Chaco Canyon in New Mexico, the "the sun dagger" strikes the center of concentric circles. The lunar calendar is honored in much of Asia and most famously celebrated in China by a fifth of the world's population. When the "new year" begins depends on which cultural and religious tradition one adheres to, and how the year is enumerated also varies across religious cultures. Though these examples fit Hall's criteria for Profane Time, for most others they would be included in Sacred Time.

Meta Time—is a grab-bag of abstractions of time that Hall called "all those things that philosophers, anthropologists, psychologists and others have written about time: the innumerable theories, discussions and preoccupations concerning the nature of time." *Meta* time is a useful center of Hall's time mandala but less useful to us except as a reminder that what we think and say about the elusive concept of time is not the experience—experiences—that we have learned to talk and think about and try to compress into cultural categories. Visual artists, musicians, even poets working with a common vocabulary may evoke different realms of time. Hall's attention was to where the expectations and actions that arise from and make sense in one context and from one perspective, often make no sense or are at least awkward in another.

How we experience time is at once evolutionary, cultural, personal, and situational, influenced by how we've learned to interpret and communicate meanings that we've encoded in time. In that sense, time shares features of how we experience and attach meanings to space. Asking a friend how far is a place we plan to visit: "about 50 miles," one friend might say, and another: "about an hour's drive—depending on traffic. Or weather. Or the season." More than ever before, time and space and context overlap in how we think and talk. In any digital communication mode, space and time collapse into one. The current network of transport and its speed also dims the association of particular foods with their season of growth and harvest; "fresh" fruits and vegetables can be had in every season.

The Time of Our Life

Historians, journalists and sometimes popular culture figures have given names to eras—"the Gilded Age," "the Roaring Twenties,"—or specific events, and pre- or post-events: the Depression era, the post-War (II) era. A generation conventionally has been a folk measure of time, about twenty years, a rough estimate of the time from when a person is born and when that person might become a parent of a child of the next generation.

In the US, there was the "Silent Generation," children born in the 20 years before the end of WW II, 1945. The name "Silent Generation" was first used in a *Time* magazine article in 1951. Those who returned home from the war famously spoke little about their experience. High school kids of that generation were idealized, two decades later, in the popular television series, "Happy Days." No comment.

That post-war period saw a veritable boom in childbirths. It was an era of optimism and, in the US, a rapidly growing middle class that for many offered greater economic stability. That was the "Baby Boomer" generation (1946-1964), a span of just 18 years. Then came succeeding generations that put "Generation" or "Gen" ahead of the identity, starting with "Generation X," named by a Canadian journalist, spanning just 15 years, 1965-1980. As a new millennium approached, one born during the fifteen years between 1981 and 1996 was part of the "Millennial generation," the first "digital natives" acquiring a competence with cell phones and computers that further distinguishes them from previous generations. Then came "Gen(eration) Z," 1997-2012, an era marked in the US by the Columbine High School massacre in 1999 and "9/11" of 2001. This was the era when "active shooter drills" became routine in US schools as the number of guns purchased soared.

Having reached the end of the Roman alphabet to identify (or impose a name on) those born in a span of fifteen years, we went back to ancient Greek: Generation Alpha, from 2013. What will be the Omega?

"YOLO" (You Only Live Once) became a popular acronym among teens and those in their early 20s around 2012, a safe assumption in many, but not all, cultures and religions, and an implicit encouragement to make the most of it. "Life is not a dress rehearsal." The best time is when one is young and looking ahead, so different from their parents who look back with the conservative worry and warnings that maybe most parents feel, along with a twinge of empathy bordering on envy. YOLO is upbeat, unlike FOMO—Fear of Missing Out—an acronym associated with the previous generation.

Where we are in our arc of life affects how we experience time and imagine what is yet to come. In childhood, one or two months or even moments, as adults count them, are felt as an enormity. Even when we believe we are rational, time-aware adults, we regress in our feelings. The brain hasn't fully developed until about 21 or 22 years, though at 18 many feel fully mature—unless they are with someone much older, say 23, whom those younger look up to. We perceive those we admire as older than their chronological age. When we find ourselves in that descending end of our history's arc, we may hear—say—that "recently . . ." until one in the family or friends, younger and wiser, point out that "recent" actually happened before they were born. (But you don't want to hear my problems.)

Time becomes the measurement and definition of each successive stage in childhood when overt physical changes are most frequent and apparent. Categories differ somewhat across languages and vernaculars, but all show a rich vocabulary to characterize age: "preemie," infant, toddler. The earliest birthdays receive special attention, reassurance for some parents whose babies lived through challenges, real and imagined, to their survival. Parents look ahead, imagining what this little person will evolve into. Children can't wait until they are "older," which, of course, occurs every second. Entering a formal system of education, where the calendar year determines one's place, misleading in any classroom where the youngest thinks and acts more like children in the previous grade, and older children could be comfortable in the subsequent grade. Adolescent, is a term less often used in conversation, sounding more "clinical" than "teenager," invented originally as a marketing category in the early twentieth century, became part of the US vernacular. ("Teenager" is also a "loan word" from US English to other languages/societies, and not always welcomed.) The chronological age varies across regions and nations when the citizen is allowed to vote, drink alcohol, drive a vehicle, marry, be conscripted into the military, and for some facing judgment in a court of law, whether to be tried as child or an adult. Classification by "generations" has become more narrowly characterized; categories are broader, when one becomes "middle aged" and how that affects one so identified, by choice or in the judgment of others; and then becomes "older." In the US, one is politely "older" for many years before one is just "old."

How we talk and name reveals much about our values and our fears. The classic "Western" three-ages (youth, adult, old), is the answer to the riddle of the Sphinx: "What goes on four legs in the morning, two legs in the afternoon, and three legs in the evening?" In Hindu philosophy, there are four stages in a repeated cycle from birth to rebirth, each characterized by expectations and responsibilities, something not prescribed in contemporary western secular or faith traditions.[11]

Advances in medicine and care have greatly extended the life span beyond the "four score and ten," and to be a centenarian is no longer rare. In the US in 2024 there were 101,000 people over the age of 100; it is estimated that by 2054 there may be 422,000. "Old age" is now divided into four quarters, as in a US football game. (The US sports term "sudden death" takes on a new meaning.) As one approaches triple digits, a birthday maybe be regarded as an achievement comparable to the earliest years when a baby took its first steps. When people in their later years reflect on what in life held the most value, they say experiences—for many travel, or intimate events of life such as the birth of a child, falling in love as a teenager, a romance, a special vacation—the occasions that shaped their lives. Not the stuff we buy.

Time Talks

"Time Talks" is the pithy title of a short chapter in *The Silent Language* when Hall introduced one of the topics for which he is best known: how do we enculturate, embody, think, and feel deeply about this always-present, culturally based and interculturally interpreted importance of time? What does it say when a guest invited to dinner arrives early? When an apology arrives too late—or, indeed, what does "early" or "late" mean, and why might we feel and remember those moments?

What distinguishes that which is praised as a skill of "multi-tasking" in one situation, but in another cultural context is seen as "disorganized" if not "chaotic"? How we feel is a part of what meaning we give to any "message" received, irrespective of what was intended, and if, indeed, there was an intention.

The ancient themes of time and space, at once both abstract, hard to define, and yet, the experience that defines our lives, crucial to an understanding of culture (another abstraction) we experience and perform and use to judge others. Time is a foundational construct in the physical sciences, social sciences, in our art, and in the language we internalize. What we have learned to think about time affects how we make sense and how we judge ourselves and others. Ask a friend, "what is time?" the answer might refer to a clock or calendar. That answer Hall might say were examples of "extension transference," where the symbolic representations are taken to be more real than the complexity they represent. Like confusing a map with what it represents, a word for its referent.

Tom Bruneau who contributed much to the cross-cultural study of time, remarked that how long a minute is depends on which side of the bathroom door you are.[12]

Expectations unfulfilled, characteristic of "culture shock," affect our experience and judgment of time. Expect a task to take just 10 minutes but it takes 30, that period of time can feel long and tedious; expect it to take an hour but it's done in half that time, we feel, that was fast! By the clock, the two are the same. By time as experienced, the two are quite different.

Reasoning based on the "before" and "after" of time is a common logical fallacy misleading us when we conclude that because Y came after X, it must be that Y that caused X. This is the *post hoc ergo propter hoc* fallacy in reasoning, among the earliest so identified and the most enduring. But as a factor in scientific research, the sequence of events is important. In serious research, before and after comparisons are essential but insufficient to credit or blame the former for the latter.

A Place in Time

Like each of us, when and where (and how) Hall grew up exerted an impact on his appreciation of perceptions of time. The high desert land includes the geological formations that the Spanish called *"mesas"* (tables) because they appear to be flat on top; in some regions the visible strata of rock of different colors and textures reveal its geological history that may span millions of years. The Indigenous communities, so connected to place, know and feel a different history from those of us who may identify more with where we are going than where our ancestors are from—if we are even encouraged to think of ancestors.

Once when I was planning a field trip seminar that included a visit to the stunning original site of the Pueblo of Acoma (now branded for visitors as "Sky City"), I enjoyed conversations with Nadine, the Acoma woman who welcomed and arranged group visits. Unfortunately, after months of preparation and conversations with her, guests were unable to visit, so I had to cancel the plans. With embarrassment I called to apologize that we wouldn't be coming after all. Nadine was gracious and said, "Don't worry. We've been here for over a thousand years, so whenever you can visit, we will welcome you." It was a response that put my heart at ease, and an expression of pride said with the awareness that the Pueblo sense of time was not the same as that of most of the visitors. For tourists from Athens or Alexandria, Beijing or Osaka, Cholula or Jerusalem, visiting a continuously inhabited community a mere thousand years old, may be less impressed by its age than by its architectural character and its place in the natural environment.

In the US, we see this in a nation where its people are taught to think of its history as beginning in the seventeenth century, ignoring all that came before: a colonialist reckoning of time. A geographical version was in a sign at the major airport at Mozambique's Lorenço Marques (now Maputo) that greeted international arrivals when it was still a Portuguese colony: "Here, too, you are in Portugal." A place in time.

Saving Time

The spread of the novel invention of writing affected the reckoning of time and how it can be saved, memorialized, and made available long after. Walter Ong, in his important book, *Orality and Literacy*, makes that point.[24]

In the oral tradition, memory may more easily adjust to the present; the written record can challenge the received oral history. That is why historians rely on written records and, with that standard, devalue pre- and non-literate cultures. Writing and, more importantly, reading were, like most inventions and innovations, the province of the powerful.

What is written still exerts a kind of power; "as advertised in *The New York Times*" helps sell products. A formal record of the family history is something expected for royalty more than for an ordinary family, where the oral history of the family is what may get passed along. After the death of a relative, there may be increased interest in relationships. As is said, where there's a will, there's a way lot more family concerned.

Time is experienced differently during different mental states. Anyone who has smoked or imbibed cannabis knows that. For some that is part of its appeal, including how it can mess with the sense of time. (And the joke is, "If you remember the 1960s, you weren't really there.") Conditions of stress also change time perception. One bright, clear September morning in the middle of Nebraska on my twenty-first birthday, en route to San Francisco, my car was hit head-on by a truck driven by a farmer who suddenly pulled out of his field and headed toward me in my lane. What I remember most vividly was how, in the seconds when I tried to swerve out of the way but could see the crash about to happen, everything seemed as if in slow-motion: time stretched. I later learned that this was a common perception of time in the immediacy of such a crisis.

Journalist Steven Johnson describes his wife's reactions and her behavior when, with their newborn child in their Manhattan apartment on September 11, 2001, the twin towers were struck, resulting in the loss of more than 3,000 of those trapped within. That terrible day, 9/11, became part of the nation's collective memory and a punctuation point in our reckoning of time. When the news flashed on television, Johnson's wife was nursing their baby. Her journalist husband, as he rushed between watching CNN's televised moment-by-moment coverage of the scene not far away, relaying what he was seeing and hearing, was experiencing time very differently from that of the new mother who remained calm. Not because she was indifferent, but because her new mother's body's reactions were set to a different clock and mood.[13] Always, Hall would remind, we need to honor that each of us is unique in how we think and act.

M-Time, P-Time

In his observations of cultural differences in how time is treated in everyday behavior, Hall observed two different patterns. One he called "monochronic," the other "polychronic." Aware that new four-syllable words that might be impressive in academic cultures can also be off-putting, he used abbreviations: "M-time" and "P-time." The monochronic values doing one thing at a time in some ordered sequence: a schedule, agenda, syllabus, itinerary. Hall identified this as characteristic of Anglo and North European cultures.[14] The value of this is order, predictability. If from childhood we learned to line up, first come first served, we may also have internalized a value of fairness. Cutting into the queue upsets us not just because it breaks the order, but because it is unfair.

The polychronic, "P-time" does not refer to doing many things at once (like so-called "multi-tasking," shown to not really be possible, though it may appear so from the monochronic perspective), but rather the realization that reality doesn't come to us one thing at a time, and we have to deal with the convergence. Hall characterized the monochronic as a line, and polychronic orientation as "a point rather than a ribbon or a road." He even calls this point of convergence to be felt as "sacred," meaning "involvement of people and completing of transactions rather than adherence to pre-set schedules."[15] For those whose world is mostly polychronic, time is rarely considered "wasted" when a day's plan goes astray. "Life is what happens to you when you're busy making other plans," as John Lennon sang.[16]

As always, context is crucial, and the monochronic value risks disregarding context. When we are at home, we are more likely to expect, tolerate, and sometimes even enjoy interruptions in what we routinely do than when we are at work. If while preparing dinner in the kitchen, the phone rings, and then a child comes home with a friend, and maybe minutes later there's a knock at the door from a friend who was "in the neighborhood and thought I'd stop by"—that's a polychronic situation, though that might not be the word one would use just then. A comparable situation at the office might be described as chaotic or "out of control"—a telling idiom about the value ascribed to M-time. It is more often women, especially those who are caring for and responsible to and for children or an elderly parent, who of necessity need to do more than one thing at a time. So it is irritating if a husband or partner returns home at the end of work at the office and asks, "What did you do today?" The late Sir Kenneth Robinson, in remarks at a TED Talk, attributed a neurological difference between men and women, a thicker set of nerves that connects the two halves of the brain, which Robinson said allowed women to multi-task in a way most men cannot:

If my wife is cooking . . . she's talking to the kids, she's dealing
with people on the phone . . . she's painting the ceiling . . . she's
doing open-heart surgery . . . If I'm cooking, the door is shut,
the phone is off the hook, and if she comes in, I get annoyed.
I say, please, can't you see I'm trying to fry an egg in here?[17]

M-time characterizes professionalism in offices and public service
organizations, less so in restaurant kitchens and for the artisan. Work
routines adhere more to schedules of a "one at a time, first things
first" pattern—in part because we imagine that we are a piece of a
larger system that demands each one completes assigned tasks in an
orderly and timely manner. In this context, there is also the relational
power factor: the manager seen talking and laughing with a friend
who stopped by can say, "I'm maintaining important relationships
with our customers (or suppliers or neighbors or even competitors)."
But if someone on the staff does the same, that manager might scold
her or him for wasting time or being "unprofessional." I've heard this
from friends, especially women, who work at a restaurant or bar. "I
hear the boss bullshitting with a friend, and he would say 'it's PR.'
If I do that, I'm told I should be working instead of wasting time."[18]

An M-time-oriented person can feel upset when an otherwise
simple schedule goes astray. Years ago, in Mexico City when taking
a taxi to my destination, the driver stopped to pick up a friend he
spotted. The driver politely asked if I would mind. (Do not generalize
about Mexican taxi drivers from this anecdote.) I was amused then, but
if I were hurrying to an appointment, my reaction might have been
different. Even after the awareness of Hall's M/P time orientations,
I might have felt the tension in my stomach.

Often in conversations, the M-time/P-time distinction may be
helpful categories—what we appreciate and what disappoints, irritates,
upsets. *Just tell me what you want. What's your point? I don't have all
day!* Expecting the relatively straight line that characterizes M-time.

Yet, the asides, and the "you also should know," and "that reminds me" tellings in one context may be our favorite part of conversations among friends, and stories told and retold at reunions, the most remembered by a few students long after they graduated.

Carmen DeNeve, friend and innovate educator, contrasted P-time as more familiar and more often valued in her native Mexico and in "Hispanic" communities than in the dominant cultures in North America. This also fits what multilingual professional intercultural interpreter Edmund Glenn contrasted as culturally rooted reasoning patterns, an important and early offered but less explored avenue of contrasting cultures.[19] A monochronic outlook and engagement may be a reason that many North Americans can seem *cuadrado* (inflexible) to Mexicans. Some Latin Americans are less charitable about P-time in the workplace, though not in the social contexts of being among friends or family. Working internationally across business and NGO organizations, some find the P-time and a more casual treatment of scheduling unprofessional, especially in the business world. That's one reason some say they prefer working where the monochronic pattern is a norm in business.

The M-time orientation is associated with individualism and agency, with "my time" elevated to a cultural value; "our time," not so much. "May I have a few minutes of your time?" we ask; television journalists often conclude interviews with, "Thank you for your time." Joining a company in the US, one signs a contract that specifies expectations regarding hours of work and the increase in compensation for "overtime." When groups must make a decision, do we value each individual vote or strive for consensus, valuing the group even as there is often group pressure at play? Broadly speaking, in the US individualism (less so "individuality") extends to our concepts, like the commodification of time. In much of the world, values center more on cooperation with the relative group, small or large, or groups on whom one's survival depends.

Another way of seeing the M-time/P-time difference is in "task/ social" pairings, a dialectic familiar in the social sciences and in management. In many situations, not just intercultural ones where differences may be acute, but when the occasion involving family and friends is more formalized, a mark that this is special, requiring both social and the task or transactional, the ordinary order may be altered. Is it *business before pleasure,* or do we need a time of not-business, and if not exactly pleasure, at least a time—minutes, hours, years perhaps, before we consider if we even want to do "business"?

I recall a young volunteer with Canada Youth working in Latin America, who was at a conference of International Student Advisors, a cheerful profession that does such important work. Representatives from several schools described their programs that included one or two days of orientation for these students from abroad, including a campus tour, how to use the libraries, and all the services they provide, a talk about academic norms and expectations, and more. That orientation often concluded with an evening dance party. "Why don't you start with the dance?" the Canadian asked. "With enough people who are familiar with the campus, they can make friends so you won't need the orientation."

Time and Context

Should you begin a meeting, a meal, a project at which, say, a dozen people are expected if only half have arrived at the scheduled time? How long should you wait? How many people are "enough"? Context matters: Is this urgent? Is this a routine business meeting? Or a meeting fraught with highly charged emotions? What about the weather or other influences on why many are late? Digital technologies today have altered this scenario, as some ethic or norms of notifying others about unanticipated problems or delays has probably evolved, but the question of the value we place on the plan compared to the social context is always relevant.

Steve Moore was raised in Chile, and his wife Kathryn grew up in Peru, the daughter of US physician who treated patients in the Amazon region. They shared several stories where time was at the heart of the story—in Chile, Peru, and the US. These friends also tell a story recounted by their neighbors, an expat couple in Peru whose families are from England and Spain, all acculturated to Peru. A story worth repeating here.

After this couple fell in love and decided to marry, they had to make a wedding plan that would work for inviting both their local friends as well as their families coming from the UK and elsewhere. They decided to print two wedding invitations so that all the guests would arrive close to the same time: the British side of the family received invitations with the time printed when the couple hoped to start the ceremony; the local, non-British side of the family received invitations announcing a time two hours earlier. Indeed, all the guests arrived close to the same time, thus avoiding family who arrived "on time" stewing until those who have "no regard for punctuality" showed up.[20]

Executive and leadership coach Bego Lozano tells me that regarding weddings in Mexico, if the invitation says 'en punto' it means it starts at that time, but if the invitation says the ceremony begins at 1:00 p.m., guests can assume it will begin closer to 1:30-1:45. She also notes that a Mexican bride arriving at the church will not get out of the car unless a considerable number of people are already in the church. And of course, the later slot is the more coveted one, in case there are guests who hadn't arrived on time.

Guests arriving "too early" can be a similar concern, especially for those who are hosting something in their own home when running late is probably a norm. The whole idea of "hosting a party" with formal invitations is, globally, not part of everyone's experience. In much of the world friends can stop by unannounced. Where formal and informal friendships are blurred can be ambiguous occasions for those new to the culture.[21]

Even for "just a 'party'" in some parts of the world, guests—especially women—may want to arrive early to offer to assist the hosts who can always use help at the last minute. That experience comes as a surprise to North Americans living in Japan, a nation known for its precision—trains really do run on time, down to the minute, and there may be apologies if arriving a few minutes later or even earlier than promised. That generously offered assistance might not be so welcome, especially in M-time situations with the hosts are still fussing to get ready at the last minute. Equally sensitive to the hosts, others arrive after the invited time, to be respectful, not wanting to embarrass if last minute preparing is still underway. I'm still getting ready.

Hall's M-time/P-time contrast, like any abstracted concept, while it may help make sense, in itself it does not always lead to advice. In Tokyo, I was once invited to dinner by the US ambassador. The invitation read: 7:00 p.m. I had to seek advice about what was expected in this situation—right at seven, some appropriate minutes just after seven, and if so, about how many minutes—surely not *before* seven? I was advised that in this situation, seven meant seven. So I arrived, the only guest arriving via taxi, joining a line of chauffeur-driven cars, precisely at seven. Diplomatic culture is a world apart from what students interested in intercultural communication had hoped to learn about if they majored in "International Relations" programs in college.

The reason I was invited may be more interesting than this anecdote about M-time. Previously, at an intercultural conference, I began my talk on cultural values with an introduction that went something like this: "If this were an all-Japanese audience I should begin with an apology. If this were an American audience I should begin with a joke. Since this is a mixed audience, let me apologize for not telling a joke." After the conference proceedings were published, a national newspaper editorial reported those words, and from that time, apparently, other people from the US began using it to begin their speeches to audiences in Japan—including the US Ambassador.

When he learned that the person whose words he had borrowed was still around, he invited, as a courtesy, my wife and myself to dinner at the Ambassador's residence. Later I was told that simple introduction was used so often by speakers that the most prominent English-Japanese interpreter recommended a moratorium on the joke/apology beginning of a speech.

What the Bell Tolled

To the colonized Indigenous peoples in the Americas, the sound of the bell was the sound of oppression. The imported bell and its sound were alien to those subjugated by the colonizers from Spain, a sound that reshaped the day—when to wake up, pray, attend mass, eat, and end the work day. All this contributed to the offences and led to what Puebloan people believe was the first American Revolution: The Pueblo Revolt of 1680. The rallying cry in the Pueblo Revolt (the most successful of several attempts) was "burn the churches, smash the bells":

> The Puebloans particularly loathed the mission bells which were frequent targets of Native fury during the frequent indigenous revolts throughout the Spanish-American empire. Bells held special, albeit very different, meanings to everyone who lived within the range of their peals in Colonial New Spain. . . . Most of the [Indigenous] revolutionaries had lived their entire lives under their sway. When the opportunity to silence their ringing presented itself they seized it with abandon. . . . Throughout the province bells were torn from their towers in the autumn of 1680. . . . [Fragments of bells have been found in post-Revolt [sites]. At Senecú, Alamillo, and Zuni the destruction was elegantly simple: the bells were castrated through the removal of their clappers.[22]

The bells tolled the sound of authority, political and clerical, conjoined in much of world history. A bell in Philadelphia that fell silent after it cracked not long after independence from England became a symbol of "liberty," now enshrined in its own National Historical Park in Philadelphia. Throughout the nineteenth century in Europe's powerful nations and their colonies and former colonies, a clock was installed up where all can see its authority, often with a belfry and great bell that affirmed it acoustically. Big Ben remains an iconic symbol of London and the UK in the same era that saw M. Eiffel's Tower in Paris, and France's gift to the US, the Statue of Liberty that faces back toward England and Europe.

London's clock at the Palace of Westminster, when erected in the mid-nineteenth century, was the largest clock in the world. Its bell tolled the hour not just for the good people of London but across the world as Greenwich, a part of London, was established as the global standard baseline for time from which all other clocks are set. This was in 1884, when the sun never set on the British Empire. GMT, Greenwich Mean Time, became UTC, Coordinated Universal Time, and remains the standard for how we set our clocks. At this peak of the European colonial era, Greenwich became the place that established not only a global standard for time but also for space; it is the Greenwich meridian that divides east and west.

This was also in the era of the employee time-clock, mechanization for line workers needing to work with, while often feeling like they were in conflict with, machines. Later it was assembly lines (Charlie Chaplin's film *Modern Times*), the labor movements where setting boundaries on work time was a big part of what workers fought for, and even the rise of public education and the shape classrooms: rows of desks lined up that many critics see as preparing young people for regimented factory work. Hall writes about the sound of bells in schools, punctuating the day, when classes begin and end.[23]

The authority of the public clock was replicated for the individual in the form of the watch. Today, when so many people use a smart phone to indicate time, watches function more as fashion accessories or, for some, an expression of wealth. But in earlier generations, at retirement the gift of a watch was an expression of appreciation. "To retire," of course, also means to go to bed, maybe now in no need of an alarm clock to rouse one from sleep to start the day and arrive at work "on time." Personally, I don't like the verb "to retire." I prefer the Spanish equivalent, *jubilarse,* to have a jubilee! Functionally, to be retired or a pensioner or a *jubilado* or *jubilada,* probably all evoke similar reactions where they are the words of choice in the vernacular, but as often is the case, words in another language sound more attractive than their translation. But *je ne sais quoi.*

Categories, Idioms, and Metaphors

How we talk reflects our cultural world, the inseparability of culture and communication. "Weekend," a category credited to or blamed on the US influence, has been borrowed as a term and as a concept translated. The standardization of twelve months, a year that begins on the first of January, a "week" of seven days with deference to the sabbath, Saturday or Sunday, "24/7"—not just that form and expression, but the assumption of hours of a day and of seven days in a unit—all these are cultural constructions.

In the US, the "eight-hour day" at work was fought for and legally established in 1916 as a standard. *"Karoshi"* is the Japanese word for "death by overwork," meaning death by pressures to work beyond normal human capacity within a formal frame of time. It is a word that was introduced during the modern era, recognized even by insurance companies in Japan, but not with a specific word elsewhere where workers today die from overwork, including a famous case in China where a worker succumbed to demands at a factory producing iPhones that elsewhere were promoted for their time-saving capacity.

But we also talk about time as a commodity that we can spend or save, invest or waste. "Time is money" is a relatively new perspective, that equation credited to Napoleon and Benjamin Franklin, among others, and very much a part of the post-industrial era, manifest in the "time clock," hourly wages, the concept of "overtime," and the eight-hour day and five-day work week, at this writing on the verge of becoming four ten-hour days. Time is "of the essence," say real estate brokers and day traders and more serious investors in the stock market. The latest, fastest software programs that beat others, can, with a click effect a buy or sell that can bring or lose millions of dollars. So different from the temporal worlds of everyday life.

Most of us talk about and may comprehend time metaphorically. Time is a river, endlessly flowing. Or as I've heard more abroad, in Tanzania and in Japan, *Time flies like an arrow,* which seems to be an English lesson well remembered and more significant that is taught to young students of English. (And, yes, *Fruit flies like a banana*—but that shouldn't be added to a grammar lesson until much later.) One of the most familiar metaphors, at least in "the west," is "time" as beyond our control, a force of nature, or as life's competitor in a race we inevitably will lose: "a race against time," time is "catching up," and may "pass you by!" "But always at my back I hear, time's chariot hurrying near." "Time and tide . . . ," the inevitable, they wait for no one.

Attention to time begins even before we begin our schooling where, studies show, attention to "time" is the beginning of a leitmotif that lasts a lifetime. At school, more than at home, we are taught to respect starting and stopping times, assignments to do and report to classmates, planning for school events. From our first classroom routines and demands, all through what is counted as one's "productive years," schedules, deadlines, quarterly reviews and assessments structure lives. In our younger years we long for when we are "old enough to" do a myriad of things, surely varying across cultures, which might make for an interesting study. These may include "old enough to," in no particular order: drive a car, leave home, get married and start a family, join the military, drink alcohol, vote, etc.

When Time is Running Out

Sharon Waller, a non-denominational hospice chaplain in the San Francisco Bay area for fifteen years, has visited the homes of families from many racial and ethnic backgrounds, faith traditions, and those who are secular. Waller, who also has taught in Latin America and Asia and in the US, says her hospice years have been the most fulfilling and inspiring of her life. Asked about what "time" means to those she has visited, she shares these thoughts:

> For someone who has been given a terminal diagnosis, as well as for their family and loved ones, "time" is most important. The diagnosis instantly raises the questions, "How much time?" "When?" and then, "What if?" with queries about life-prolonging treatments or other interventions. From the instant that a life-threatening diagnosis has been made, there are multiple, complex questions and issues about what might change in what time frame, what else might be done, and ultimately, how to accept—or whether to accept—death.
>
> Events and plans are marked on everyone's calendars. Family members have regular obligations and timetables, and now strategize how to take care of business and yet make a plane reservation to be with a dying relative. A son asks, "Can I wait until the end of the week to come? I have an important meeting. Will it be too late? But I'd like to wait if I can."
>
> The one who is dying also has plans. Now he or she may need to take care of finances, possessions, share wishes about a funeral, deal with unfinished business. Some may need or want to engage in a life review. This may come through thoughts, memories, dreams, and visions that serve to resolve, integrate, restore some piece of the past. They may feel the need to make peace with something from long ago, which may require conversations with someone alive or no longer

alive. Others may not want to do this, or may not be able to, and they have their own end-of-life process, which may or may not bring more anguish. Some want to keep their lives fixed and static as long as possible, and push away any of the end-of-life tasks that social workers or chaplains may encourage them to complete.

In the world of the terminally ill, how long or short, how fast or slow varies immensely, with outcomes that can lead to remorse and regret for family members who arrived "too late," or whose loved ones died "too fast." They may feel guilt about not having arrived in time, or having missed a possible "last conversation." Some family members step out of the room to take a phone call, only to come back and find that their mother or sister or son has just died. The person who is dying may wait to die until a person does go out to the hall or until the whole family walks out of the room to converse.

The question of "when" is particularly poignant when a patient has decided to ingest medication under the End-of-Life Option (available in California and some other states). I spoke with a daughter whose mother took the medication. The daughter was experiencing much anguish that she had not had the "last important conversation." The reality is that there is a window of opportunity for a patient to take the medication by him or herself before it is no longer possible. In this case, the daughter felt her mother could have waited "just a little longer, just so I could see her one more time."

Most family members say that their loved ones died too fast. One time, I visited the home of a man whose wife had just died in hospice care. He was berating himself for having forgotten to wind his wife's cuckoo clock. She had died on the day that clock had stopped. He kept repeating, "If only I had remembered."

Ultimately, the sense of time can radically change for the person who is dying. The present moment and the people in the present may lose significance entirely as deceased friends, relatives, and even pets may appear individually or as a group, and conversations may emerge with them. Some patients say they are waiting to die until a loved one, already dead, appears to them. One patient would not allow me to sit in the one chair by her bed. She said, "No, you can't sit here. All these seats are taken. You see, they've been gathering all day. They are going to take me with them tomorrow." I stood for the visit, and indeed, the next day I learned she had died. Another time, I tried to talk with a patient who kept looking around and past me to the hall. I saw no one there. When I asked what he was seeing, he said, "That is who I've been waiting for. He's looking for me and I need to talk to him." The one who is dying navigates his/her journey according to some indefinable inner directive.

Hall's anthropological perspective in comparing the uses of that abstraction we call "time" has been revelatory and helpful, but he wrote little about "time" across one's lifespan. Rather, he explored the differences in how cultural communities—national, regional, organizational—regard and "perform" time as a key marker of cultural identity. He introduced how we learn to perceive, perform, interpret, and deploy our social awareness of time. His attention was directed to how time is used as a code in our day-to-day communication, which is so enculturated, internalized, that what we say and experience, we take as "common sense." Waller's telling of the meanings of time when "the time has come" reminds us that at the end, in Waller's words, "It is an individual journey."

Notes

1. Carlo Rovelli, *The Order of Time,* translated by Simon Carnell and Erica Segre (New York: Riverhead Books, 2018). Rovelli is an Italian theoretical physicist at Aix-Marseille University.
2. Paul Bloom, "Being in Time: How Much Should We Value the Past, the Present, the Future?" *The New Yorker,* July 9, 2021.
3. Rovelli, *Order of Time,* 3.
4. Edward T. Hall, *The Dance of Life: The Other Dimension of Time* (New York: Anchor Books, 1984).
5. Hall found this form "particularly useful when one is dealing within the paradoxical relationship, dissimilar pairs or clusters of activities which one's intuition indicates are related," but might not have otherwise been combined in some comprehensive system. As throughout his other work, he draws attention to the personal and cultural, the conscious and non-conscious, biological rhythms and micro-rhythms in changing contexts, the distinctions, the fusions, and the confusions experienced in intercultural contexts. His examples and stories are manifold and revealing, leading many readers of *The Dance of Life* to say it's their favorite of Hall's books, long after they've forgotten his mandala.
6. Mihaly Csikszentmihalyi, *Flow: The Psychology of Optimal Experience* (Harper Perennial, 2008).
7. An exemplary example is Hall's distinction between monochronic and polychronic time systems, and assumptions described later in this chapter.
8. We must suspend disbelief when seeing dramas on stage or in movies. As children, we don't need to be asked.
9. In Europe, for centuries, what we now identify as Spring, one of four seasons, was known as Lent, the time between what were the only two named seasons, Winter and Summer. Similarly, Autumn or Fall, a term used mostly in the US that gained popularity after independence from England, when the former colonies introduced several words intended to mark that separation.
10. Alessandro Falassi, *Time Out of Time: Essays on the Festival* (Albuquerque: University of New Mexico Press, 1987).
11. These four stages are *Brahamacharya,* the stage of learning; *Brihastha,* when one begins a new family, with all the work and support that entails; *Vanapreshka,* after all obligations to the family have been fulfilled, a time of solace, seeking deeper knowledge and entering into spiritual practice;

finally, *Saumyasa*, renouncing all material and social needs and seeking freedom from the repeated cycle from birth to re-birth.

12. Thomas Bruneau, "The Time Dimension in Intercultural Communication," *Communication Yearbook 3*, Dan Nimo, ed., New Brunswick, NJ, Transaction Books, 1979.

13. Steven Johnson, *Mind Wide Open: Your Brain and the Neuroscience of Everyday Life* (New York: Scribner, 2004), 106-09.

14. Hall, *Dance of Life*, 46.

15. Hall, *Dance of Life*, 46.

16. Though popularly attributed to Lennon in his last album, with Yoko Ono, a similar line appeared in an article published in 1957 by another Brit, Allen Sanders, that memorialized his late father.

17. https://www.ted.com/talks/sir_ken_robinson_do_schools_kill_creativity?language=en

18. James Spradley and Brenda Mann, *The Cocktail Waitress: Women's Work in a Man's World* (New York: Wiley, 1975).

19. Edmund Glenn, who worked as an interpreter for four US presidents, co-wrote an excellent and, I believe, under-appreciated book on cultural differences in reasoning or patterns of thought: Edmund S. Glenn and Christine G. Glenn, *Man and Mankind: Conflict and Communication Between Cultures* (Norwood, New Jersey: Ablex Publishing, 1981). Another attempt to identify culturally diverse styles of rhetoric was by Robert B. Kaplan, "Cultural Thought Patterns in Inter-cultural Education," *Language Learning* 16, 1 and 2, 1-20.

20. Steve Moore writes: I have grown in my concern that inter-culturalists can be blamed for being too soft and understanding of certain "states of affairs" that some believe need to be confronted boldly. Some lump us all together (or pigeonhole/stereotype us) with those who smile, shrug and dismiss things as merely "cultural," and thus "to-not-be-confronted." In the past twenty years, I have had many people in Peru, Chile, and beyond, ask me not to teach about time as merely a "cultural issue" about which we are to smile, shrug, and do nothing about. They argue that it is a moral issue, because if someone commits to something at a certain time and has no inclination of being there at that time, they are lying, and detrimentally affecting the lives of others. But I am actually hearing this more and more from Chileans, Peruvians, and others as I teach in Central and South America.

21. An invitation to an "Open House" is one such ambiguity for anyone unfamiliar with the concept. Is it a kind of party? Well, not exactly. Should I bring a gift? No, but if you want to bring some food or drink to share, that would be welcome. Oh, is it like what you call a "pot luck?" No, not exactly. An invitation to something intended to seem as informal as possible can be a cause of stress even before arriving. The invitation usually spans several hours, so the question of when to arrive can feel like a challenge. And then when to leave?

22. Matthew Liebmann, *Revolt: An Archaeological History of Pueblo Resistance and Revitalization in 17th Century New Mexico* (Tucson: University of Arizona Press, 2014), 75-76.

23. Many a student who escaped being called upon in class has felt "saved by the bell," the idiom referencing a boxer's relief upon hearing the bell signaling the end of the round when getting beaten up during a boxing match.

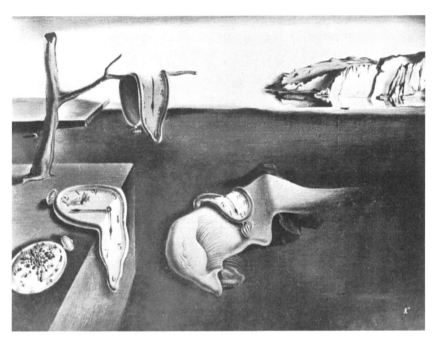

Salvador Dalí, *The Persistence of Memory*, 1931,
Museum of Modern Art, New York

CHAPTER FIFTEEN

Just One Thing After Another

In a letter to advice columnist, Ann Landers, a reader wrote: "Send me your new book. If it's good I'll send you a check." Landers replied, "Send me your check. If it's good, I'll send you my book."

I n Helsinki, a Finn was asked what he thinks when a stranger on the street smiles at him. He answered:

You assume he is drunk.

He is insane.

He's an American.[1]

A European friend asks: "Why do Americans smile so much?" My neighbor asks: "Do we?"

When Walmart opened stores in Germany, the US-designed plan recommended practices for good relations with customers that followed the Walmart way in the US. They soon had to tone down the smiles and cheerful manner "to better suit the sober local mores." Walmart stopped requiring sales clerks to smile at customers, which some male shoppers interpreted as flirting.

Anthropologist Ray Birdwhistell, who pioneered the study of nonverbal behavior, attempted to study smiles in the US at a time when few others were taking "nonverbal behavior" seriously because "communication" was all about the verbal. His research led him to conclude that the frequency and the meanings of a smile are far more complex than they might appear. Birdwhistell then found considerable variation from region to region in the US.[2] "In one part of the country, an unsmiling individual might be queried as to whether he was 'angry about something,' while in another, the smiling individual might be asked, 'What's funny?'" What was puzzling to someone from the US visiting Helsinki could have been anticipated at home by reactions of an old-line Mainer to a cheerful visitor from Iowa.

Nothing means anything by itself, but everywhere meaning depends on when it appears outside of the context of an expected pattern. That smile question may be less about *what,* than about *where* and *when.* Context. A smile, like any expression—word, gesture, pause, frown—offers different meanings depending on the time, place, and timing. That is the ingenuity of human communication, the flexibility of when and where our significant symbols appear affects how we interpret the meaning. In the English language the order of words determines meaning: "Dog bites Man/Man bites Dog." Same words, different order. Striking up a conversation with someone we've just met usually follows a sequence, as does a romance, and even serving a meal. (Who was the cynic who said the problem with marriage was like a poorly served meal, with dessert coming at the beginning?) And some things may happen too soon, while others may be "too little, too late."

Patterns of Sequence

So much of what we do, and what we think we know, is patterned. Much of the work of scientists seeks to identify patterns. These are foundational, the base and the reach for the next. Language is highly patterned, elegantly. Communication as well, as AI has made us all suddenly aware—given enough verbal data, it's possible not just to recognize patterns, but to give them back to us in new, possibly brilliant ways that make sense grammatically and semantically, and in a manner that matches our patterned communication style and fits the context. There are predictable patterns from how we put a sentence together to how we make small talk or negotiate a deal.

There are sequences that form grammar, and also patterns of sequence in the give-and-take of everyday life in any language. When you take an introductory class to learn a conversational competence in a new language, you often practice dialogues, models of everyday conversation. The joke is that after taking five weeks of beginning French at a Berlitz School, you can carry on a short conversation in French with anyone who has also studied French for five weeks at a Berlitz School. (Now I realize that in my high school Latin class, we never had those dialogues. Another reason no one speaks Latin like a native.)

When I lived in Japan, my (ex)wife used to teach English to Japanese children from the neighborhood who came to our house for their lessons. One day, a young boy from her class recognized me when we passed on the street. He paused, and before I could greet him, he eagerly greeted me: "Fine, thank you, and you?"

"Cultural patterns" was one term borrowed from anthropologists to talk about intercultural communication. The patterns provided examples of contrasts, such as in how children are reared, when do praise or stern expectations to do better, the place and cultural significance of apologies. A more complex pattern type that Hall introduced that has been largely overlooked is the interactive pattern. This was taken up in political science and business, in game theory, and in other applications that involve negotiating or bargaining. We recognize this also in the social-sexual sequences of interaction between girls and boys which, in the US, a baseball analogy provided guidance: the first kiss, then getting to first base. Cultural variations and descriptions of patterns, ancient and universal, provide prohibitions and teases for the privileged, and are celebrated in dramas, operas, novels, films. In the US this took the form of "dating" that spread in all its ancient ambiguities through popular culture, especially Hollywood movies. When I moved to Japan at the end of the 1960s, "dating" was a tempting US import, almost as exotic as *sushi* was then in the US.

Adumbration is the foreshadowing of what may follow: behavior that expresses what a person is feeling and, at the same time, may send a message, intentional or not. This might be a facial expression or a sudden shift in body posture, or the quality of eye contact or avoidance, or an unexpected pause in the conversation. Maybe even a puzzling smile. It can alert the other about how to respond. Sometimes a sign of encouragement of what to expect, sometimes a warning. Sensitivity to this is linked to survival.

Related, but distinct, is the concept of *action chains*—sequences of behavior where one action leads to the next, and then the next in turn, until the sequence is complete. This includes everyday behavior: habits. The action chains of greater interest are those between people, which often a third party foresees before those involved: "Don't get them started!"

Adumbration

The ability to anticipate and respond as expected is a pattern that may be part of our evolutionary history, as research indicates that animals show a similar pattern.[3] In the human species, it is more complicated with layers of context, sometimes to be considered in an instant. Hall called this "adumbrative behavior," or "adumbration," the perceived foreshadowing of what response seems appropriate, and what reaction might then follow. The term "adumbration" was borrowed from literature; nothing advances a story better than the reader anticipating what is going to happen next.

> When people communicate they do much more than just toss the conversational ball back and forth. My own studies as well as those of others reveal a series of delicately controlled, culturally conditioned servomechanisms that keeps life on an even keel, much like the automatic pilot on an airplane. All of us are sensitive to subtle changes in the demeanor of the other person as he responds to what we are saying or doing. In most situations people will at first unconsciously and later consciously avoid escalation of what I have termed the adumbrative or foreshadowing part of communication, from the barely perceptible signs of annoyance to open hostility.[4]

As Hall often does, especially in his early work, he alludes to ethology:

> In the animal world, if the adumbrative process is short-circuited or bypassed, vicious fighting is apt to occur. In humans in the international-intercultural sphere of life, many difficulties can be traced to failure to read adumbrations correctly. In such instances, by the time people discover what is going on, they are so deeply involved that they can't back out.[5]

Adumbration is about expectations we have about how we engage and relate with others. It's rarely like a skilled chess player, calculating many steps ahead. It's not game theory and computer programs that predict outcomes, associated with international relations and diplomacy. It's as simple as making eye contact or not, how we greet.[6]

Diplomacy requires being sensitive to the adumbration, and strategically and tactfully responding in ways that at least don't make things worse, and ideally leads to a mutually satisfying result. Self-awareness, at a minimum, is a starting point. Hall says that what is crucial is to act "before 'face' and ego become involved." He says that adumbrations begin at the very high-context end of the scale and become more specific with each step, moving toward what he later called lower-context messages.

Current metaphors for this in the US include "best-case scenario," "worst-case scenario," and become aware of "off-ramps" so an adversary can save face. Adumbration is culture-specific, so projecting what will happen from one's own cultural-experience-based expectations is—in our multicultural workplaces, organizations, and neighborhoods—a matter not just for diplomats.

The shadow part of "foreshadowing" might suggest adumbration refers only to warning signs, like when our usually cheerful pet dog, Pluto, encounters another dog along the path. If he feels threatened, Pluto may first cower in anticipation, stop moving, growl, bare his teeth, and his hair might stand up ("goosebumps" are our residual human reaction). Direct eye contact signals a challenge across many species, including humans: staring daggers. To signal to the other dog that he is not a threat, Pluto will look away, avoiding eye contact.

Most of all adumbration refers to signals, given or perceived, that are instinctive in the moment, and at the same time a signal about what to expect. To the nonverbal behavior we add words, spontaneous or scripted, that may confuse or clarify or just cover as part of that adumbrative behavior—a great euphemism! Maybe every generation, profession, region has its verbal equivalents that lead others to anticipate what might come next.

Action Chains

Action chains, a concept and term originating in studies of animal behavior, was a focus of attention for Hall.[7] He summarizes an action chain as "one action introduces another in a uniform and patterned way" when two parties play different roles that are interdependent: "A invites B who must then respond until the paradigm is played out.

If the chain is broken at any one point it must begin all over again."[8] This is a comprehensive concept that Hall applies even to patterns we might call "habits, like making breakfast, meeting a friend, becoming engaged, buying something in a store, writing a poem or a book." He says these are examples of action chains of varying complexity.[9]

Sometimes we find ourselves caught up in a situation that we soon feel may be more complicated than we anticipated. We may feel that we are unprepared for what is expected, and failing to grasp what is unfolding, we are truly at a loss for words—if words are even called for. This is especially true in intercultural situations of all kinds.

There are many stories, some dire, even tragic, reported in court-rooms and in the news. Here is one delightful, less dramatic experience I'd wondered about for half-a-century.

En route to Tanzania, my very pregnant wife and I stopped off at Kampala, the beautiful capital of Uganda, where we were hosted for a few days at Makerere University. During that visit, I met someone on the staff who kindly invited me to visit him at his *ekibanja,* the small plot of land where he and his family lived and enjoyed the bounty of all that grew there. Of course, I was delighted, all the more so because the invitation was spontaneous—we didn't really know each other.

Shortly after I arrived at his home and was warmly greeted, I was invited to meet his neighbors. We visited a family whose house was nearest my host; the father welcomed me and the children gathered around. As we left, I was given a gift from his garden: a tall stalk of sugarcane. We then walked to another neighbor who was just as welcoming, and I left with another gift. I was becoming more curious about meeting his neighbors, and feeling I should do more than smile and express appreciation. Did they perhaps mistake me for being someone special?

And from there we met another neighbor, and as we moved on, I was introduced to maybe a dozen neighbors, and from each I was given a gift—coffee beans, bananas, there were several eggs, and even a live chicken. Children eagerly joined this improvised parade and carried all of the gifts. It was all quite wonderful but I wondered why I, a stranger just visiting Kampala for a couple of days, was introduced to so many neighbors, and was there anything I might have been expected to do apart from expressing pleasure in meeting them and thanking each for their generosity? I also wondered why this person I had just met, and in a day or two would likely never see again, wanted to introduce me to so many of his neighbors.

Fifty years later, thanks to James Luyirika-Sewagudde, Jr., from Uganda and now emeritus professor at California State University, Chico, and a friend whom I came to know decades after that incident, answered my questions and extended the significance of this kind of incident to other parts of Africa as well. His sister in Uganda, Ruth Sewagudde Stokes, joined in helping to set me straight. In James's words, this is the gist:

> It is important to remember that in the olden days, travelling in Buganda was not very easy or that common. Actually, this condition persists. Therefore, when someone arrived to visit, it was rather an important occasion. In fact, it also meant that the visitor would likely stay for a spell. I believe that when your friend in Kampala introduced you, there was a great deal of pride in showing you off (white, American, young . . . and a professor) as his guest. You were an important person and worth showing off as a friend. But also, there was a degree of pride in letting you know that you were welcomed not only by him, but also by his friends and others. You belonged.
>
> It would therefore have been expected, and good manners, to introduce this guest (*omugenyi*) to the immediate neighbors so that they would not wonder who the foreigner (*omugwira*) might be. But equally as important, the introductions would allow the guest a feeling of belonging and therefore no longer a foreigner.[10]

Some action chains, acquired or learned, are called "scripts," or "routines" by Hall's contemporary, Erving Goffman, who described some of these in his *Presentation of Self in Everyday Life*.[11] Diplomacy and *realpolitik* have their own routines in a realm apart, though not without advice from so-called "pundits," and ordinary folks who have opinions about what should be done as part of the action chains of diplomacy and political theater.[12]

Transactional patterns characterize many action chains: "I owe you lunch." Or it may be just the beginning or characterize what extends and maintains relationships, like family or maybe neighborhood traditions. We mustn't underestimate the importance of these, and what happens when these action chains are abruptly ended, as when the COVID threat and protective defenses kept people apart.

Don't Get Me Started

Action chains are strongly influenced by our cultural upbringing, which is why social scientists like Hall recognize them as so important. What has a cultural explanation of why the progression of action and reaction that in one cultural context is required, may seem to others, petty, cruel, or just baffling. "Spite," "revenge," "payback" are words that come to mind. Feuds are chains that extend across generations; maybe every community, region, can cite examples.

In the US, perhaps the most infamous feud was between the Hatfield and McCoy families whose properties were divided by a creek. How did the feud begin? Like many feuds, who started it is still disputed, but in 1878 one of McCoy's hogs was stolen and the feud ensued, involving generations of two families and their neighbors. There was at least one murder, and even a romantic relationship between young lovers across the divide like the Capulet and Montague families in the tragedy of Romeo and Juliet. The Hatfield-McCoy feud lasted almost 50 years, until the 1920s. And yet . . . .

In Japan, there is a true tale of revenge that is the stuff of legends. It is a story of loyalty and self-sacrifice to avenge an injustice. In the eighteenth century, forty-seven *ronin* (lordless samurai) had served a lord until he was unfairly forced to commit *seppuku* (ritual suicide). These ronin vowed they would avenge his death, announce their complicity, then commit suicide. Today, each December 14, the event is commemorated; the story is part of the national literature of Japan, and has been told and retold in Japan's manifold genres: *kabuki*, *bunraku* (classic puppetry), stage plays, an opera, and in novels, and film. Japanese film director Akira Kurosawa evoked the spirit and values of the 47 ronin in his movie, *The Seven Samurai*, (*Shichinin no Samurai*) that was also inspired by US Western movies, popular at that time.[13]

In 1598, Juan de Oñate led an expedition from *Nueva España* (now, Mexico) to colonize what is now the US state of New Mexico, and also to avenge the death of his nephew who had been killed at the Pueblo of Acoma, about an hour's drive west of present-day Albuquerque. Oñate exacted a punishment on the village, killing hundreds, enslaving others, and infamously, ordering that the right foot of twenty-seven men be cut off. Oñate is among the most reviled by the Pueblo people, along with Christopher Columbus. For many Hispanos today whose families lived in this area when it was a part of *Nueva España*, Oñate was and is recognized as among the first to bring to the region the Spanish language and the Catholic faith. The name Oñate appears in many places in New Mexico where the connection to Spain is honored. On the University of New Mexico campus there is (so far) an Oñate Hall. In 1998, on the 400th anniversary of the arrival of Oñate in the region, a twelve-foot bronze equestrian statue of the colonizer was erected in the village of Alcalde, along the interstate highway between Albuquerque and Santa Fe. Shortly after it had been unveiled, visitors arrived one morning to discover that Oñate's right foot had been severed from the statue. The foot was later reattached.

In the autumn of 2023, there was another skirmish about the Oñate statue, and this time shots were fired and one person died. Fearing future protests, the statue was moved to a less-exposed setting.[14]

Concepts of "honor" that in some cultural environments may "justify" what are, in translation, called honor killings, even killing someone within one's family, are elsewhere unfathomable. Some say that few people in much of world understand the depth of feeling of the concept of "honor" that was the rationale for duels, even in North America, not so long ago. In cities, "gang fights," in the global neighborhood, even "nuclear escalation," could kill almost everyone. Some action chains, Hall noted, are incredibly long, requiring more than a lifetime to be carried out, while others require only a few seconds.[15]

If action chains may be identified universally, each has to be considered in its particular cultural context which, Hall points out, is "high context," meaning any action or word implicates more than seems apparent on the surface. Who, where, when, why, how—but also a history, and probably a community of people unseen, real or imagined, will interpret and judge, a chorus as important as those in the dramas of ancient Greece.

Preventing action disputes from going too far, Hall believed, were safeguards that worked within their cultural context, but because "they are not intellectually understood or made explicit, they seldom function when dealing with outsiders."[16] In some contexts, it may be rule-based or tradition, the observance of which requires checking with some authority that in previous generations would be largely learned through elders and through the experience of participation in commemorative events.

"White Americans, and other low-context people," Hall writes, "particularly those who deal primarily in word systems, do not ordinarily feel as bound to complete obligations regardless of circumstances as some other cultures. They will drop an obligation if they don't like how things are going or if something better comes along."[17] In the

US, we have seen this in an exaggerated manner in the words and actions of former president Donald Trump, for whom everything was "transactional"—I'll do/say this, if you say/do that—without much regard for other people, institutions, and an entire history. His machinations revealed the fragility of the norms and traditions, the assumptions and expectations that define "high context." A nation that prided itself on having a written constitution to guide its politics, in contrast to England where tradition held sway, came to realize that it was "higher context" than realized. For Trump, the notion that if there is nothing in law that says I can't do X, Y, or Z, meant he could take advantage of his position in word and deed, much to the consternation of "the establishment." In 1975, Hall wrote "any society in which commitments are taken lightly or have to be enforced by law is going to have problems with its institutions—a situation that can be unsettling for everyone." Words that later proved prophetic.

Our lives are, in many ways, defined by action chains, integral to one's cultural maturity. Most, Hall noted, never have been studied. Today, our personal data recorded in our digital histories maps our transactions in action chains that shape our romantic, educational, professional, and financial histories. We receive messages suggesting we may want to purchase a brand-new widget we'd never heard of, let alone considered, because marketing departments know that our personal histories fit the pattern of others who after buying (or requesting information about something), were persuaded to order that widget.

A Cautionary Tale

There is a famous story, a fable, that every young person in China knows, and it instructs as any fable must. It is a story that cautions against assuming we can anticipate what will result from any particular incident or action. This wisdom has no counterpart in stories I grew up with, but it is relevant for everyone everywhere today. I asked friend Yuan Fan, from Beijing, currently with her young family in Germany, to tell me about Sai Weng and his horse. "Sai 塞 in ancient times," she says, "generally refers to north of the Great Wall. The word, archaic now, almost always reminds people of the past."

An old man living north of the border (northern China) owned a horse farm. One day one of his horses disappeared. His neighbors were concerned and came to comfort him. But the old man wasn't upset. He said, "How do you know it's not a fortunate thing?"

One year later, the lost horse came back, bringing a handsome colt. The neighbors came to congratulate the old man. However, the old man did not look happy. He said, "Who knows if that's good or bad?"

The colt grew bigger and the old man's son loved the colt and rode him often, but one day, he fell from the colt and broke his leg. The neighbors again came to comfort the old man, who calmly said, "Who knows if that's good or bad?"

Then war broke out and the government needed men to fight. But the old man's son was handicapped because of the fall from the colt, so he was exempt from the draft. As the war went on, many men died, but the old man's son lived on.

The neighbors began to think about what happened to the old man, and then to consider the opposite: if something good happens to him now, maybe something bad is about to happen next. With what seems good now, can we expect bad fortune later?

Yuan Fan provides some historical background to the tale and the values implicit:

This story was originally written in *Huai Nan Zi*, 淮 南子, a philosophy book written by An Liu (179 BCE - 122 BCE) 刘安 and others, blends Daoist, Confucianist and Legalist concepts, which emphasize that nothing is absolute, like yin and yang that coexist. This parable is included in the Humanities Guidelines 人间训, aimed to teach people to adjust their moods and avoid extreme emotions, because things change. Just because something appears "bad" now, doesn't necessarily make it bad in the long run: it might lead to something good later.

She adds, "to those who hoped to be passengers on the fateful voyage of the Titanic but somehow missed their chance, I would quote this parable."

Misinterpretations and Opportunities Missed

Misinterpretations of adumbrative behavior or missed opportunities to act in ways another person expects you to act have been explored in Thomas Kochman's 1981 groundbreaking book, *Black and White Styles in Conflict,*[18] and in *Corporate Tribalism: White Men/White Women and Cultural Diversity at Work,* by Kochman and Jean Mavrelis.[19] Kochman, who is white, recalls a Black colleague's comments:

"So long as I'm talking, you got nothing to worry about. When I stop talking, then you might have something to worry about." This was said by a Black male Dean of Students at my university during the 1970s about the passionate anger he was expressing over some racist event, upon seeing the worried look his colleagues showed in reaction to his emotional expressiveness.

Apart from the ever-present concern that whites have of the possibility of a Black uprising over past and present injustices, the cultural element is also significant. For whites, verbal expressions of anger, or even any form of passionate expressiveness is seen as threatening (potentially violent): the belief and worry being that, if left unchecked, angry words will inexorably lead to violence. Blacks (we're talking about issue-oriented sincere disagreement here) make a clear distinction between angry talk vs. "making a move" on someone, which for Blacks is when a "fight" is seen to really start.

This "words/action" distinction extends beyond the workplace to the street, metaphorically speaking. A nice example can be found in the Jackie Robinson movie, *41*, surrounding the altercation between Jackie and Dixie Walker. Jackie Robinson says, "Watch your hands!" Dixie walker says, "Watch your mouth!"

Mavrelis describes adumbrative examples of missed opportunities between white and Black women in the workplace:

Upon meeting a new co-worker, a white woman may ask, "Where do you live, are you married, do you have any kids?" (One Black woman once said to me, "You got any chips for all that dippin' in my business?") In corporate, Black women get used to white women asking such questions, and they may answer, but if their own home training is that it's rude to ask personal questions, they may not ask back. Now the white woman is left with the impression, "She doesn't want to get to know me—she is a good worker, but 'unapproachable.'"

Another missed opportunity: If a Black woman takes a risk to bring up a difficult conversation in a meeting, a white woman may say nothing in support at that time, and later approach the colleague who spoke up in the hall: "I'm so glad you said something about that." Her Black colleague may ask, "Why didn't you say anything *in there*?"

Mavrelis continues:

I asked myself, "Why do I hear this complaint time and time again from Black women about white women?" As I collected the different messages white women and Black women get from mothers and grandmothers, I believe I found the answer.

Corporate white women said they heard, "Be nice, don't hurt anybody's feelings," while Black women said the messages they heard most often were, "Be strong, be self-reliant." White women learned to give emotional support, not political support! We may not take a risk in the meeting, but we feel compelled to give emotional support afterwards.

There are so many ways white women miss opportunities to be allies because of our expectations. Take, for example, "Gossip Styles." When white women gossip at work, we tend to make ourselves the victim: "I can't believe she did that to me!" Another white woman will likely commiserate, or even join in, "That's horrible, a similar thing happened to me, so I know just how you feel." (If people-pleaser white women had a theme song it would be, "Feelings, nothing more than feelings, alone in my heart.")

Black women make themselves the hero of stories. White woman: "I can't believe she did. . ." Black woman, "Oh no, she did that to me, I'll tell you what I did. . ."

Now the white woman is confused, because she is now feeling "one down" for failing to do anything on her own behalf, when she was looking for commiseration or a matching story.

Another missed opportunity happens when white women minimize Black women's experience of racism in order to make them "feel" better. A group of four white women and one Black woman went to Happy Hour after work. The restaurant was busy. The white woman waitress took their orders, and came back with the four white women's drinks, and not the Black woman's drink. The Black woman said, so the waitress could hear, "That was racist." After the waitress left, one white woman said, "I'm sure it wasn't racist, the same thing happened to me here once." She thought she was making her colleague feel better, but in fact she was saying, "Your experience is invisible to me."

If that same white woman had been with a group of white men, and it was her drink that didn't come, she may have thought it was a gender slight (even from another white woman: "What am I, chopped liver?") It would have at least been a question in her mind, and she wouldn't have appreciated the men telling her she was too sensitive. The Black woman would have appreciated, "That's terrible! Want to leave?" to which she may have said, "No, it is just as likely to happen at another place, but thanks for the support!" Trust is built. In contrast, these unmet expectations certainly build up hard feelings over time (death by a thousand cuts) to keep women across cultures from being more supportive and building on each other's strengths.

These stories are at the edge of the anticipation of Hall's "action chains," but without that foreshadowing of what will or should happen next—at least by the white people involved. And if not as expected or when we don't know what to say or do, we improvise. Hall emphasized the contrasts of cultures, a way to see ourselves reflected in a new light, often highlighting misunderstandings and mistakes in intercultural encounters and efforts. He alerted his readers to cultural contrasts with examples of intercultural contacts gone wrong, but gave little advice that most people seek. Many want "Do's and Don'ts" advice, but the context of who and when and why, and the personal, makes giving general advice impossible.

Mary Catherine Bateson, daughter of Hall's most famous contemporaries, Gregory Bateson and Margaret Mead, home schooled like her mother, welcomes the challenges and rewards that engaging across cultures give us. It is more easily said when the situation is novel, especially across national lines. "Rarely is it possible to study all of the instructions to a game before beginning to play, or memorize the manual before turning on the computer. The excitement of improvisation lives not only in the risk of being involved but in the new ideas, as heady as the adrenaline of performance that seems to come from nowhere."[20]

It may seem to come from nowhere but it must come from everywhere, places and times acquired that we don't know, and informed by what we've learned about people we meet, in another land, or down the street. Being real, heart-felt, expressed in our faces and our whole being, while also conscious of intercultural influences that we experience and express. Hall, an optimist, believed that many intercultural misunderstanding and conflicts were due "more to ignorance than malice."

Notes

1. Olga Khazan, "Why Americans Smile So Much," *The Atlantic,* May 3, 2017.

2. In research in the mid-1960s, Birdwhistell reports, "Middle class individuals from Ohio, Indiana and Illinois, as counted on the street, smiled more often than did New Englanders with a comparable background from Massachusetts, New Hampshire and Maine . . . who smiled with a higher frequency than did western New Yorkers. At the other extreme the highest incidence of smiling was observed in Atlanta, Louisville, Memphis, and Nashville." Ray L. Birdwhistell, *Kinesics and Context: Essays on Body Motion Communication* (Philadelphia: University of Pennsylvania Press, 1970), 29-39.

3. Andrea Ravignani, Laura Verga, Michael D. Greenfield, "Interactive Rhythms Across Species: the Evolutionary Biology of Animal Chorusing and Turn-Taking," *Annals of the New York Academy of Sciences,* Vol. 1453, No. 1, 2019, 12-21.

4. Edward T. Hall, *The Hidden Dimension* (New York: Doubleday, 1966), 5.

5. Edward T. Hall, *Beyond Culture* (New York: Doubleday, 1976), 156.

6. Two psychiatrists pass each other on the street, and one says "hello," and the other thinks, "I wonder what that meant?"

7. Though the concept of "action chains" never caught the public imagination or academic researcher, at least not by that name, it was obviously important to Hall because it appears in three of his books: *The Silent Language, Beyond Culture,* and *The Dance of Life.* In *Beyond Culture,* he devotes two chapters to it.

8. Edward T. Hall, *The Dance of Life: The Other Dimension of Time* (New York: Anchor Books, 1984), 228.

9. Hall, *Beyond Culture,* 141.

10. James Luyirika-Sewagudde, Jr., continues: Let me digress to South Africa, linking the idea of Africanity. The philosophy of Ubuntu: *I am because you are.* In my parents' home, by virtue of my father's position (clergy, headmaster, teacher), the neighbors would be notified of the arrival of so and so. It would be expected, but not demanded, that the neighbors would bring something to present to the guest to show their willingness to share with the guest whatever they had. I distinctly recall returning home with all sorts of things, yes, including chickens, eggs, bananas, sugar canes, and coffee beans, offered to express happiness at seeing and thanking my

father, and also making sure to show their willingness to share with him whatever they had. And since he would not have time to sit with them and enjoy these things, he would take them to enjoy upon his arrival home. On my Fulbright mission to South Africa, we arrived at a woman's tiny house in Soweto. Because we were expected, the entire neighborhood, so it seemed, showed up to welcome us. There was food and drinks and stories and laughter and a sense of belonging. The hostess, whom they called Mama, stood at the bus door step, hugged you (you had no choice), and welcomed you. And before she released you, she assured you that "you will like it here." Welcoming guests *(abagenyi)* and offering whatever you can and making them feel a part of the household, is expressed in various ways across the continent. Chinua Achebe authored *No Longer at Ease* in 1960 to lament the decay of some of the customs which support the Ubuntu philosophy. Indeed, the movement to the cities and the modern economic patterns and practices (survival), many of these valuable and humane customs may not be sustainable for too much longer. The idea of the neighbour not letting you know what is going on is unthinkable because of the way family connections work in the complicated relationships in the villages *(ebyalo)*. Most of the people would be regarded as aunties, uncles, nieces, nephews, or cousins, just because they are of the same clan as your Mum or your Dad. Gifts would be given to visitors especially when they come from afar. People would be so proud telling the whole story of how they welcomed a traveler. (Mind you with a lot of embroidered versions.) Some of it would be just genuinely being kind and generous. Word would go round the neighbouring villages of how kind and generous such a village was. Definitely something the whole village would be proud to be associated with. There was the strange sort of mystic pride people took in being able to tell other people from other villages having a "connection" with a *muzungu* (a white person)! Remember, in this case *muzungu* had nothing to do with colour but about a better person from a faraway land. Not just a poor traveler.

11. Erving Goffman, *The Presentation of Self in Everyday Life* (New York: Anchor Books/Doubleday, 1959), 22-58.

12. *Pundit* is a Sanskrit word ("learned man") first used in English during the colonial raj referring to an Indian in the colonial employ, and in literature as far back as Mark Twain's writing in the nineteenth century. Like the Indian word *guru* (a spiritual guide), *pundit* gained currency in

other former British colonies in the late-twentieth century, primarily in the context of the mass media "talking heads," which the term "*pundit*" replaced as sounding more authoritative.

13. The 1954 movie *Seven Samurai* (*Shichinin no Samurai*), released in the United States initially as *The Magnificent Seven*, was written and directed by Akira Kurosawa. This epic samurai drama takes place in 1586, and is the story of a village of poor farmers who hire seven *rōnin* (masterless samurai) to fight marauding bandits who repeatedly steal their crops. A US adaptation of the Kurosawa film appeared in Antoine Fuqua's 2016 film, *The Magnificent Seven*. The cast featured people of color in leading roles including the Black actor Denzel Washington, Korean actor Lee Byung-hun, and Mexican actor Manuel Garcia-Rulfo. These choices were made by Black director Fuqua, not for the value of diversity but as a multicultural representation faithful to the time and place of the story.

14. Oñate remains controversial in El Paso, Texas, the city he is erroneously said to have named: "the pass of the north." In 2007, El Paso dedicated the world's tallest equestrian statue, rising 36 feet (11 m), in his honor, ten years in the making at a cost of $2,000,000 (US). Local and regional protests led to renaming the statue "The Equestrian," avoiding identifying the man atop the horse. Also problematic, there is no known image of Oñate. Each sculptor or artist must improvise an image of the colonizer. Frank G. Pérez, Professor of Communication at the University of Texas at El Paso, said Oñate has been celebrated as part of the "fantasy heritage" of the Southwest, which Pérez and Carlos F. Ortega write about in their book, *Deconstructing Eurocentric Tourism and Heritage Narratives in Mexican American Communication: Juan de Oñate as a West Texas Icon* (London: Routledge, 2019). Pérez said, "Oñate helped bring Catholicism up through the north but he also killed many indigenous people along the way . . . and took supplies from natives living in what is now New Mexico, leaving them to starve or die from exposure during the particularly cold winter of 1598. Pérez tells me there was another question, where to place the statue. At one point, it was to be installed on the banks of the Río Grande but city leaders feared offending the people of Ciudad Juarez. No one wants a four-story horse's rear end facing their city! In the end, the statue found a home at the El Paso International Airport, allegedly to keep it safe from vandalism. To deface the statue on federal property would incur great criminal penalties. This decision was supposedly driven by fears that

stemmed from the sawing off of an Oñate statue's foot near Alcalde, New Mexico, during the time. Oñate remains controversial in New Mexico and northern Mexico."

15. Edward T. Hall, *Beyond Culture*, 143.

16. Edward T. Hall, *Beyond Culture*, 159.

17. Edward T. Hall, *Beyond Culture*, 147-148.

18. Thomas Kochman, *Black and White Styles in Conflict* (Chicago: University of Chicago Press, 1981).

19. Thomas Kochman and Jean Mavrelis, *Corporate Tribalism: White Men/White Women and Cultural Diversity at Work* (Chicago: University of Chicago Press, 2009).

20. Mary Catherine Bateson, *Peripheral Visions: Learning Along the Way* (New York: Harper-Collins, 1994), 49.

Your turn.

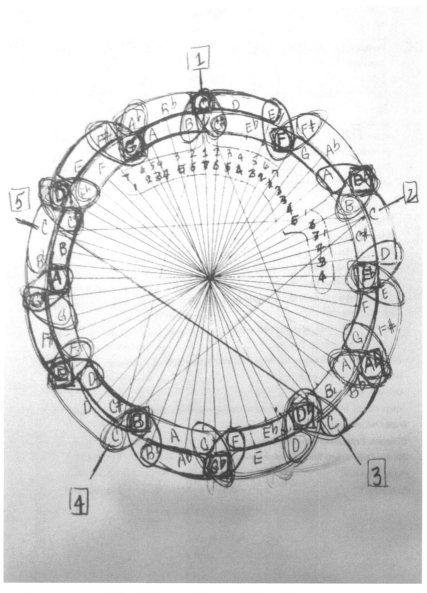

Jazz musician John Coltrane's design of "the Coltrane Progressions,"
a standard advanced harmonic substitution used in jazz improvisation.

CHAPTER SIXTEEN

In Sync, and the Rhythm Takes Over

> To grasp a rhythm it is necessary to have been
> grasped by it; one must let oneself go, give oneself
> over, abandon oneself to its duration.
> —*Henri Lefebvre*

> Everything in the universe has a rhythm, everything dances.
> —*Maya Angelou*

> Music can move us to the heights or depths of emotion
> . . . . But the power of music goes much, much further.
> Indeed, music occupies more areas of our brain than
> language does. Humans are a musical species.
> —*Oliver Sacks*

Down the road from where I live is the Pueblo of Jemez whose people have lived here for a thousand years. The Jemez people speak Towa, and this is the only place where Towa is spoken as a first language. By choice Towa is not written nor, as with other Puebloan languages, is it taught outside of the community. Only outsiders, like me, might use the term "oral tradition," in awe of the enduring vitality of indigenous languages in spite of the previous colonizers' Spanish, and now English as the language of schooling, employment, and the entertainment on television. "Killer English," some linguists call it, like the invasive "salt cedar" (tamarisk) that crowd out native plants along the river. Across the globe, any language that controls the economic and political forces in a region of diverse cultures affects the linguistic ecology.

Yet another inversion is how the technology of writing often gives more economic value than the spoken words it was invented to represent. Hall would say this is an example of extension transference, where a re-presentation or symbol of something comes to be more valued or even taken to be "more real" than that of which it is a representation.

As English is the language that these Indigenous communities use and need in their professional work and in engagement with the larger society, along with the Towa language, it is dance and music that express so much and affirm the identity of a people rooted in place. The land upon which the people dance is inseparable from the meanings felt and expressed by the dancers. Rarely is a winter's snow so intense that it prevents the dancers, bare skin exposed to the elements, from dancing, or the drummers and chanters from sounding the beat. As Miguel Gandert says, the Pueblo people dance not as a performance for others, for it matters not if anyone observes them; they dance because they must. Stories and prayers are danced, sometimes by more than a hundred, adults and young children alike. Those witnessing from the edges of the plaza are fully present, even the youngest reflexively moving their feet to the rhythm of the drums. The rhythm unites. The heartbeat of the people.[1]

A thousand miles away is the metropolis of Los Angeles, so unlike this Puebloan community. Some in the pueblo have lived in southern

California, and not a few have family there. But today's Los Angeles is a place that they came *to*, not *from*. An important distinction for land-based cultures. That's also why many Native Americans don't like Woody Guthrie's WPA-sponsored song that became a kind of national anthem, "*This land is your land, this land is my land . . . .*" This song that raises the issue of "who's land is 'my land,'" a question at the root of many intractable intercultural conflicts everywhere.

Los Angeles is a place of people who bring a richness of cultural histories and identities, languages and foodways, practices and hopes, and where people move to different rhythms. Their convergence creates a region whose strength and beauty are rooted not in common ancestry, but in its diversity of people drawn there by its opportunities, natural beauty, and an imagined future.

Joan Didion, an author most identified with Los Angeles, wrote that what unites this grand and complex community is felt in the rhythms of the freeways:

> The freeway experience . . . is the only secular com-munion Los Angeles has. Mere driving on the freeway is in no way the same as participating in it. Anyone can "drive" on the freeway, and many people with no vocation for it do, hesitating here and resisting there, losing the rhythm of the lane change, thinking about where they came from and where they are going. Actual participation requires total surrender, a concentration so intense as to seem a kind of narcosis, a rapture-of-the-freeway. The mind goes clean. The rhythm takes over.[2]

What is it about rhythm that we feel so deeply? Does it begin with our heartbeat, the pulse we feel, even before birth? Is it a universal birthright rhythm, and our embodiments of rhythms we express and the patterns we perceive that shape our aesthetic sensitivity? Our philosophies and sciences seek patterns. Or maybe it began with those soothing lullabies that mothers hummed and sang as we were held and cradled and rocked to sleep as infants. A National Institutes of Health report by Usha Goswami, begins "All human infants acquire language, but their brains do not know which language/s to prepare for. This observation suggests that there are fundamental components of the speech signal that contribute to building a language system, and fundamental neural processing mechanisms that use these components, which are shared across languages." And what is it that lays down the patterns of the language being acquired? It is not the system of sounds. It is rhythm. "Speech rhythm patterns turn out to be fundamental to both sensory and neural linguistic processing. The rhythmic routines typical of childcare in many cultures, the parental practice of singing lullabies to infants, and the ubiquitous presence of "Baby Talk" (infant-directed speech) all enhance the fundamental [intensity or energy change] components that contribute to building a linguistic brain."[3]

The rhythms of the lullabies that were important in our acquiring our mother tongue are so different from other cultural rhythms we acquire or learn, the rhythms that make us stand up straight, the marches that stir national pride and too often march too many young people into a final sleep, martial rhythms that are so different from the rhythms of the requiems and the dirges that help us mourn. Different still are the sounds of the "jazz funeral" music in New Orleans that begins the trip from the church or funeral home to the cemetery with the slow, heavy sounds of mourning, and then changes into the upbeat jazz sounds of the brass band that celebrates, for all to hear, the life of the one bound for glory.[4]

Daniel Levetin, a neuroscientist who is also a musician, writes about the depth and power of rhythms in his book, *This is Your Brain on Music*.[5] Levetin has performed with Stevie Wonder and Blue Oyster Cult, among others; as a neuroscientist, he traces our sensitivity to rhythms way back through our evolutionary history that is embedded in our brains:

At the neural level playing an instrument requires the orchestration of regions in our primitive, reptilian brain—the cerebellum and the brain stem—as well as higher cognitive systems such as the motor cortex (in the parietal lobe) and the planning regions of our frontal lobes, the most advanced region of the brain.

Our brains require this complex coordination of cells we have no conscious awareness of that affects, literally, what moves us. Rhythm defines music and dance, which preceded language and speech. I suspect it wasn't until writing that dance and music were thought of as separate. In some languages the same word is used for both. In Kiswahili, *ngoma* can mean drum, music, and dance. Western musicians use different vocabularies than dancers when they talk about what they study and the arts they perform. Keith Terry, musician, composer, choreographer, and dancer points out that this is in contrast to much of the world where musicians and dancers share the same vocabulary.

Terry, who trained as a trap drummer, one day realized that what he could express with the drums he could also do using just his body. He entered into the world of academics, trainers, and consultants in intercultural communication out of a desire to see how he might contribute from his internationally known work: bringing together people all over the world who, from childhood, have loved what they never thought of as "body music." It was physical, kinetic, hop-scotch, hambone, clapping rhymes, with mother and grandma, and rap before it was elevated to a genre and performed on stage.

Terry and Linda Akiyama have produced a book and a video, *Rhythm of Math*, for teachers of children from third through fifth grade.[6] "Hear, see, and feel mathematics!" The book encourages kids who hated math and nerdy kids to "get it" together, learning with body and mind, as we all do in our early years, but rarely in school.

As children our first instrument was probably our hands, clapping to the rhythms of nursery rhymes and chanting in sync with the voices (and faces and head movements) of the ones who loved us. In touch, movement, sound in rhythm and in sync—we received our first music lesson even before we could speak. Clapping, stepping, sliding, making sounds from our mouths that are not verbal: no external instrument required. Terry teases us to not forget making armpit sounds, which when we were kids made us laugh. (Terry notes that there is also a traditional style of armpit music from Ethiopia that interests him.) Body music is universal, varied, rich, playful, and also serious. Terry has brought together performers and genres from across the world in the International Body Music festivals hosted in the US, France, Italy, Turkey, Ghana, Brazil, and Bali, giving a stage to traditional and contemporary styles of vernacular music rarely featured. Terry's ensemble invites everyone to *"See the music! Hear the dance!"*

Our body's autonomic systems guide us, entrain us, to get in sync with the rhythms outside of us, be they sounds such as music, the movement of bodies as in watching sports or dance, or even when we are sensitive to the breathing of others as in group meditation and yoga. Listening to music can make our heart race or slow to a relaxing pace. Some find that reggae music is relaxing, as its beat at 60 cycles a minute is just a little slower than the average heartbeat.

The rhythm of the waves that we hear at a sea shore can have a calming effect as it slows our heartbeat. A friend who was a counselor at the University of California, Santa Barbara, sometimes would meet students seeking help at the shoreline of the Pacific Ocean where the sounds of the waves would be calming. I have wondered how listening via earpods to each person's music of choice as they move about might affect their perception of, and response to, the rhythms of the worlds they pass through on their daily routines—while not hearing them.

A Zen master was asked what is most important in the practice of *zazen*, sitting and meditating. He said it was posture and breathing.

And if he had to reduce this to one, it would be posture. Rhythmic breathing—through the nose, not the mouth—induces a state of calm as many practitioners will attest and MRI measurements affirm. Rapid breathing, "hyperventilation," appears in MRI images with other indicators of stress in studies with the same people and conditions. "Breath" translates as both "soul" and "life" in Hebrew and in Greek, historian and commentator, Jon Meacham tells us. Santa Clara Pueblo's Rina Swentzell described the profound significance of the breath in Puebloan cosmology: "Existence is not determined by a physical body or other physical manifestation but by the breath which is symbolized by the movement of the water and wind. It is the breath which flows without distinction between the animate and inanimate existences."[7]

If we accept the view that all behavior communicates to anyone who observes and interprets that behavior, then the rhythms of how we walk, the rhythms of our speech, how we gesture, our sympathetic responses to the environment in which work and move about, are all crucial to understanding the cultures we embody.

Rhythm is the vernacular in speech and movement that characterizes neighborhoods, communities, regions, nations. The rhythms of speech in rural Mississippi are different from rhythms heard in New York City, or even in two big cities separated less by distance than centuries of history, like Tokyo and Kyoto. Within any metropolis in the world, the rhythms of speech, gestures, and walking distinguish one neighborhood from another, and even within those, often rhythms of one generation differ from another.

Across national cultures, contrasting rhythms of everyday life are more apparent. Japanese have sometimes characterized their social conversational style as more like bowling, in contrast to what they liken to tennis when they listen to English speakers. As with everything, it depends on context: a heated argument has a tempo different from sharing philosophical reflections. A pause in responding to another may indicate serious thought or to express respect. In English there is what we call "a pregnant pause"; there is also "a deafening silence." There are judgments—distrust of "a fast talker" and making fun of someone who "isn't up to speed." In a discussion among people whose linguistic cultural norms differ, a person may feel uncomfortable by the pause and so may try to fill what feels awkward with talk, often meaningless talk, just to keep the rhythm going. That effort to "help," doesn't.[8]

The Beat is the Pulse, the Pulse is the Beat

How to describe rhythms? Rhythm is all about patterns of sounds stressed and unstressed or danced the same way. Just saying the word "rhythm" is rhythmic: *rhy*-thm, in the classic *Poetics*, a *"trochee,"* the opposite of Shakespeare's favored *iam*, which favored the unstressed followed by what is given emphasis. Linguists include "rhythm" in the broader category of prosody, along with intonation and stress, that can indicate semantic meaning ("a part," is not "apart"), and also attitude—sarcasm, irony. And for persuasion: in the riveting, so-called "trial of the century," when professional athlete and occasional actor O. J. Simpson was accused of murdering two people, the lead lawyer of his "Dream Team," Johnnie Cochran, presented a glove recovered at the scene of the crime that the prosecution said belonged to Simpson and would prove his guilt. Before asking Simpson to see if he could place the glove on his hand, Cochran told the jury, in a couplet: "If the glove don't fit, you must acquit." Unlikely a white lawyer could say that convincingly. It didn't fit and he was acquitted.

Rhythm and often rhyme are prominent in Black persuasive speech, and central to rap. As with many musical forms, it would be called art by a wide audience of all ages and ethnicities, such as the wide appreciation of a rap version of US history: Lin-Manuel Miranda's *Hamilton*—US history told from a new perspective and genre and cast.

Hall's writing about rhythm in *The Dance of Life* did not make use of a musician's vernacular. While more extensive and specific, as is true in any endeavor and profession, even a rudimentary vocabulary may be useful in describing usual rhythms in speech and behavior heard, seen, and felt today.

Beginning with the rhythm of our lives, the normal heartbeat that we can feel if we put a hand to our wrist or neck and take the pulse of an adult at rest is between 60 and 100 beats per minute. Children's hearts beat a little faster, runners and other athletes' beats per minute are notably slower. Musicians feel and hear the pattern of beats within a particular time frame as a rhythm.[9]

"Classical music" is a category often used to describe the music of Europe and the Americas. Many of today's composers draw inspiration from rhythms of the West African diaspora and from Asia, including Philip Glass, Steve Reich, and John Adams. These include Balinese and Javanese rhythms we might associate with gamelan music that sometimes creates *jam karet*, "rubber time." Terry believes that layered polyrhythms can feel to the listener as if time is being stretched. Imagine, he says, a pyramid of rhythms layered, doubling with each successively smaller instrument, as the pyramid rises. Each smaller instrument adds the beat twice as fast. Or heard in another way, the beat of those successively deeper sounds is twice as slow.

Listeners may experience something like the stretching of time. In a workshop with Terry at the Summer Institute for Intercultural Communication, we asked everyone to set aside their phones, remove their watches, close their eyes, and just listen. The music was by Steve Reich, a composer whom few of the participants had heard of, nor his music. When we stopped the music, we asked the 20 or so people present to estimate how much time had passed. By clock time it was a little over ten minutes, but several guessed three or four minutes and others estimated as much as sixteen. Rubber time. No cannabis was used in this experiment.

Crosspulse and Polyrhythms

Basic is the pulse, whether measured by blood pressure readings taken at a doctor's office or just catching the beat (pulse) to dance. When there are two or more pulses (time signatures, meters) in the same duration of time, that is a "crosspulse," a term not used by all musicians. It is two or more pulses that most listeners hear in its composite or totality as a rhythm. But some musicians and dancers will also hear each rhythm separately, like a 3 over 2, or a 4 over 3, in its rich fusion. A heart beat's "irregular pulse" (arrythmia) is something else, a possible cause for concern.

Except for sociopaths, most people feel stress with inconsistencies, especially in our own lives when what we say or believe conflicts with how we act. Since the 1960s, research credited to psychologist Leon Festinger used the musical term "dissonance" to describe our discomfort in holding two professed beliefs that are contrary to our behavior. "Cognitive dissonance" has entered the popular vocabulary. We expect consistency, harmony, consonance. The same is true in human communication, in voice and movement, individually and with others. But across cultures, communicating with those who move to a different beat—or appreciate a more complex pattern—that expectation is likely to fail.

If communication is likened to a dance, what happens if one comes to waltz and another wants to tango, and someone in authority demands a march? The meeting of two or more rhythms may be dissonant, discordant, but also there is the possibility of a creative fusion where two or more rhythms exist together in harmony. In musical terms, polyrhythms. Western classical music is rich in poly-rhythms. Adding melody ("polyphony"), consider J. S. Bach whose intricate compositions may also sound contemporary, in a way that contemporary design in architecture or art can feel "classic."

Musical composers and other artists have long challenged and persuaded us that what initially seemed dissonant, was a sound of daily life. Igor Stravinsky's *Rite of Spring*, first performed in Paris in 1913, provoked a riot, some in audience throwing chairs. Today it is among the most frequently performed works. My faint hope is that the inclusive and respectful musicians of other rhythms and sounds might be a metaphor for new possibilities in everyday communication in our culturally varied and thus richer world. That the same year, 1913, the famous Armory Show in New York presented Marcel Duchamp's painting, *Nude Descending a Staircase (No. 2)*, a visual artwork that outraged viewers who didn't just didn't like it, thought they were being made fun of, considered it an affront to their religion, and "un-American," as indeed it was. Today, it hangs quietly in a Philadelphia museum.

Wynton Marsalis, in a wonderful lecture and musical series at Harvard, "Music as Metaphor," takes us through a history of cultural fusions of music that is also a cultural history of the US.[10] From West Africa to the Caribbean islands and then to the Americas, by those enslaved and who survived their misery across the middle passage for the profit of the European colonizer, deprived of name and language, the music and its rhythms were kept alive, even when plantation enslavers took away their drums (except where the French colonized, notably in Louisiana). African rhythms would later sound good when joined with the Irish jig brought by "the famine Irish" immigrants. Over time, musical rhythms came together, and still later became part of a national heritage and a gift to the music of the world. In eloquent and telling words, Marsalis and the musicians he assembled created a series that should be part of every school curriculum. Print and talk alone fails. Say it with music.[11]

For me, the realization of polyrhythms—and a word to describe this as a rich harmonious reality in music and dance—is as exciting and hopeful as anything in Hall's insights and vision. I believe he might feel the same. Although "polyrhythm" is not a word that Hall used nor was likely familiar with, as another way of describing intercultural communication it may be more than just a metaphor. To welcome the richness possible when more than one rhythm of expression is present, rather than assuming or without even fully realizing that only one rhythm is acceptable, is comparable to saying only one language or one dialect or dress code and hair style or outlook (and in-put) about life is acceptable. Columbia University linguist and *The New York Times* columnist, John McWhorter, makes that point in an essay, "Blackness and Standard English Can Coexist."[12]

Rhythm Synchronizes the Group

When I was a kid, there were still traveling circuses; literally, the circus came to town and, with them, the roustabouts who pounded long metal stakes in the ground to anchor the main tent: the "Big Top." (I can claim that I once joined the circus; for a few hours one day I carried water for the elephants.) What I remember most vividly were the roustabout teams: four or five strong men encircling a stake and swinging their long-handled sledge hammers in coordination, the sounds ringing in a rapid, rhythmic beat like an ensemble of percussive musicians.

Something very similar happens in Bali when four women rhythmically pound rice with a giant mortar and pestles, and in rural Japan when three or f0ur neighbors wielding heavy wooden mallets pound the glutenous rice into *mochi* for the new year. People everywhere, in all cultural traditions, can add local examples beginning with those whose work rhythms—many rising from the necessity of survival—turn into music and dance.

The musicality of postal workers cancelling stamps at the University of Ghana Post Office is a delight to hear (thank you, Keith).[13] If you listen without knowing who or how or where the sound of the percussion and the whistled tune overlayed, you might think it is jazz ensemble. But these are workers at a post office in Ghana, improvising with a rhythm to make their work go better and bring some joy to what elsewhere might be a boring routine done alone.

A bucket-brigade conveying water to fight a fire, or the turn-taking in New York City of cars converging from two highways to enter the Lincoln Tunnel, is a thing of wonder. Comedian and philosopher Jon Stewart has remarked about this as democracy in action: no one knows the social status of the driver in the car before you or the one that will follow. As Didion said of the drivers on the Los Angeles freeways, the rhythm takes over. Social communication is rhythmic—at the micro- and macro-levels—neither of which may always be apparent to those involved, but often, as in these examples, quite consciously and intentionally utilized by those involved. We see these in the rhythms of work. There is a considerable body of social science research that reviews and analyzes these phenomena, in work and in the rhythms of play, just as we appreciate similar rhythms when presented as art, as in music and dance, but also in architecture and design.[14]

In our daily face-to-face interactions, we are connected in rhythm and synchrony at multiple levels ranging from the moment-by-moment continuity of timed syllables to emergent body and vocal rhythms of pragmatic sense-making. Our human capacity to synchronize with each other may be essential for our survival as social beings. It is not because of some primal force, but our need to maintain a relationship that allows not only for mutual survival but also efficiency in completing a task. It is not so different as the rhythm that arises when any group performs together to complete a task.

Rhythmanalysis

Our lives depend upon rhythms within us; the societies and environments we inhabit also are alive with rhythms. To be aware of our own rhythms is one way to become more aware of and sensitive to the rhythms that we encounter and through which we move. One approach to sensing and interpreting the rhythms of everyday life is *rhythmanalysis* (one word), a philosophy and method that has its origins in Europe in the 1930s.[15] Today, the best-known proponent may be the French Marxist sociologist Henri Lefebvre, author of *Rhythmanalysis: Space, Time and Everyday Life.*[16]

I became aware of this field through Lauren Mark, who trained as a contemporary and contact improvisational dancer before she embarked on doctoral studies. At SUNY, New Paltz, Mark writes: "As someone who has spent over twenty-five years of her life dancing, living and perceiving has always been for me a multisensory, embodied experience more saliently colored by intensity than any other parameter." She explains that rhythmanalysis draws on sensory experience in order to foreground the *pre-cognitive ability* to perceive the nuances of interaction. "The *rhythmanalyst thinks with and through the body* as a tool to measure rhythmic relations and their spatiotemporal interruptions in everyday life, registered as varying intensities of feeling by the body."[17] This way of knowing recognizes the value of what Howard Gardner called "bodily-kinesthetic intelligence," one of five additional "intelligences" he proposes that are often ignored—or even disvalued—while verbal and logical-mathematical competences are rewarded.[18]

Describing rhythmanalysis as perhaps more a suggestion or invitation than a rigorous methodology, Mark mentions a variety of research methods that have been used to study rhythm, "including ethnographies, multi-media approaches—visual recordings, sound diaries—and performance ethnography. To map the functionalities of public life in small city spaces and street performances, some researchers have made use of time-lapse photography to identify rhythms."[19]

Mark describes all this in an account of moving from the US to Taiwan where she lived for seven years. In her essay, "The Acculturative Costs of Rhythmic Belonging," she reflects on the rhythms of Taipei she came to know so well before moving to a place of quite different rhythms, Israel, to be with the Israeli man she would later marry.[20] Here are few of her reflections that give a sense of her perceptions and interpretations of urban rhythms:

My previous experiences of big city life had little relevance in Taipei, despite it being Taiwan's capital. I learned the rhythms of patience, where cyclists slowed to a nearly stationary halt on the sidewalks behind pedestrians strolling at leisurely paces. Pedestrians alike silently acquiesced to fellow walkers who inexplicably stopped in the middle of a walkway to think or pull out their smartphones. As a friend of mine described it: navigating in Taipei is like fording a river whose continuous movement enables a sort of harmony.

I learned in Taiwan that the navigation of shared spaces quickly becomes dimension as well as direction, equally expressive as it is functional, with territorializing repetitions or refrains, taking place through the expression of impulses. I felt the reverberations of a culture's priorities shaped the ways people made room for one another on narrow sidewalks and in overcrowded buses.

Seven years into finding such a home, I packed my bags again. This time for Israel, for the promise of my Israeli partner who I had met in Taiwan. . . . Departures and arrivals have the effect of throwing you into the middle of things and times.

It is that tension between the daily rhythms of life that she encounters in Tel Aviv and in Jerusalem, so different from those she knew in Taipei, that Mark writes most about. Writing before October 2023, she points out how the rhythms of Tel Aviv, said to be Israel's most cosmopolitan city, are very different from with the rhythm of Jerusalem:

While Jerusalem holds revered sites for three of the world's major monotheistic religions . . . the laws of Judaism staunchly govern the city's rhythms. Jerusalem's dedication to tradition generates a distinct atmospheric intensity that distinguishes it from other Israeli locales. The Sabbath siren signals a halt to all official mechanical activity throughout the streets each Friday afternoon, and the few businesses that remain open throughout the weekend are staffed with non-Jewish employees.

... The impact of the political struggles for autonomy between Israelis and Palestinians, as well as those for sovereignty between secular and religious Israeli Jews, fill every corner of its cities with material remnants. At times, protesting bodies obstruct major streets, or wafts of tear gas linger along university campuses. On a regular basis, unrepaired cracks in light rail car windows stare back at passengers. They are fresh scars from rocks thrown out of retaliated frustration against the Israeli government, taken out on transport gliding between Jerusalem's Arab and Jewish neighborhoods. As a non-Jewish sojourner, my experience touches on the year and a half that I spent encountering a vastly different rhythmic atmosphere formed by a confluence of all of these political factors. I do not presume to speak for anyone else.

The political contagion of affect extends well beyond orchestrated protest. Its political nature begins with the seemingly benign, soon to become habitual daily rhythmic practices of how we learn to board buses, cross intersections, or squeeze through narrow sidewalk spaces on foot with cyclists. Repetition after repetition, they gradually shape habituated ways of being in particular places. . . . In the process of becoming attuned to the rhythms of particular situations, we always risk failing. We might think of this in terms of the risk of being a *freier* . . .which loosely translates as being a "sucker" in English. This mentality treats life as a zero-sum game.

She describes an analysis of five-hundred Israeli news articles that mention the term *freier,* and that concludes that "*freier* avoidance" involves "refraining from voluntarily undertaking any activity that would entail an effort not resulting in the actor's own immediate interests or not taking advantage of a situation that presented itself." Further analysis identified five overarching characteristics: "concern for face, disregard for rules, individualism, competition, and machismo."[21]

Mark cites a 1997 *Los Angeles Times* article that described "the aversion toward being a sucker pervades every element of Israeli life, from conducting the most routine task to brokering peace between countries." Prime Minister Benjamin Netanyahu is quoted, "We are not *freiers*. We don't give without receiving." Mark comments, "The de-emphasis on exercising sensitivity and giving without the promise of receiving in routine tasks are cultural elements embedded in the rhythms of local life."

The omnipresence of newly arrived immigrants in the contested contexts of Israel is evident in rhythms so unlike those Mark knew in Taipei or, indeed, unlike those of many other large cities. Lefebvre wrote: "to grasp a rhythm it is necessary to have been grasped by it; one must let oneself go, give oneself over, abandon oneself to its duration." But, Mark adds, "Both Lefebvre and I underestimated a rhythm's power to linger once I gave myself over to certain rhythms."

And she considers the underappreciated, more often unasked questions: "How do we make room for others' rhythms and even incorporate them into our own?" This question, in turn, gave rise to a second question, "What happens when we don't want to be affected by others' rhythms and yet find ourselves inescapably subject to their influence despite our wishes to the contrary?"

Rhythms in Public Speech

We sing in rhythms. A poem has its rhythm. We are conceived in rhythm, and born in rhythms. We also speak in rhythms, distinct across cultures, even within the same city. Oratory, the voice of rhetoric, also deploys rhythm for the rhetor's purpose, one feature that Aristotle didn't mention in his treatise. What audiences respond to in the moment and what is quoted long after, are likely rhythmic.

Today more than ever, it is the professional "sponsored poets," S. I. Hayakawa called them, the advertising copywriters and the political speech writers who write with an ear for rhythm. National Public Radio host, Ari Shapiro, interviewed one of President Barrack Obama's chief speech writers, Jon Favreau, about rhythm and cadence. (Favreau now hosts his own podcast, *Pod Save America*). Favreau described his drafting of Obama's victory speech in January, 2008, after the results of the Iowa caucuses declared him the winner.[22]

> Favreau: That first sentence was, "They said this day would never come."
>
> Shapiro: Eight syllables—poets would say four iambs—a one, a two, a three, a four. And then the second sentence: "They said our sights were set too high." Same pattern—bah dump, bah dump, bah dump, bah dump. A few more lines like that—building and building.
>
> Favreau: And then: "We are one people, and our time for change has come."

About one of Obama's best political speeches, the NPR host comments that rhythm can "get people on their feet, chanting a rhythmic refrain." "In 2011 it was, 'pass this bill;' a couple of years earlier it was, 'yes we can,'" speech writer Favreau affirms. "One of the wonderful things about rhythm is that when you're involved with a rhythm you take on a beat other than your own." Shapiro then reflects on comments by composer and conductor, Rob Kapilow, about how rhythm can create community, as when a crowd chants in unison at a football game, or on the dance floor with everyone moving to the same pulsing beat. Shapiro says, "for a moment we stop being ourselves, and we all become part of a powerful group. . . . we're all looking for that opportunity to step outside of a *me* and become a *we*." He adds, "one of the more surreal moments [was when] rap musician will.i.am had turned that speech into a song."

John McWhorter has written:

> . . . One reason Obama has a different rhythm from other
> presidents has to do with his race. . . . the cadence of African-
> American speech finds its way into Obama's oration . . . it's
> the casual speech of Black American people which goes back
> a very long time, and that's part of the church, that's part of
> the street, that's part of being a real person for most Black
> Americans in the United States.[23]

McWhorter adds:

> The rhythm of a great speech can give people a sense of order in
> a life of chaos. It sets up a pattern that listeners can anticipate
> and follow. . . . The fact that there is rhythm in that way is
> very stirring to any listener, just like we all like music—and
> that's what rhythm does. It gives you that sense of expectation
> which is satisfied. It's very human. It's very primal in its way.
> But it certainly works in a speech.

Many studies of rhythmic synchrony in conversations and physical
movement have been published since Hall's work. Theories including
SAT (Speech Accommodation Theory) and CAT (Communication
Accommodation Theory) demonstrate, using different methods and
different terms, the force of synchrony in our interaction and its effect
on whom we feel attracted to and comfortable with. But for the most
part, these have not looked at intercultural communication when
the appreciation of the poly-rhythms of our speech and movements
have been welcomed, inclusive, and enriching for all, rather than
wanting everyone to march together, be on the same page, get with
the program. . . .

When we hear languages foreign to us, we may try to describe
them by how they sound to us. And such judgments are influenced
by impressions of the places and people who speak that language,

music and maybe movies we've seen, and situations where we've encountered the language. One language sounds musical, another harsh, or repetitive. When I was studying Kiswahili in the 1960s, my classmates and I thought some of it sounded like Japanese, a language none of us knew, but pattern practices included "*siagi haitoshi*" and "*hatutaki samaki*," which translate as "we don't want fish," and "not enough butter." Still sounds Japanese because of that consonant-vowel-consonant-vowel pattern of sounds we knew.

I was surprised to learn from research comparing English and Japanese as perceived in Japan, that for the Japanese, from high school students for whom English language classes are required, to professional interpreters, "rhythmic" was at or near the top of how spoken English was described.[24] Japanese teachers of English are likely to agree. One professor advises his students to practice English as if they are singing Brazilian *bossa nova*. I doubt that most native English speakers think of their mother tongue as particularly rhythmic. In the two generations since this research, the Japanese public has become accustomed to languages heard in music, on television, and even from neighbors, and their experience working abroad and as tourists. But language perceptions are formed early and endure.[25]

Shakespeare wrote in what literary analysts call "iambic" verse—soft sound, stressed sound; soft sound, stressed sound repeated—and in verse, in a five sound/syllable frame, the pentameter. Scholars speculate that this sing-songy rhythm made it easier for the actors to remember their lines.

In mnemonic guides, what we recall more than remember, we use rhythm in stressed syllables, often enhanced by rhyme, like recalling in English how many days are in each month: "*Thir*-ty days hath Sep-*tem*-ber, April, *June*, and No-*vem*-ber . . ." In much of the world that mnemonic is visual or tactile, moving a finger across the knuckles. We have weather wisdom, "Red sky at *night*, sailor's de-*light*; red in the *morn*-ing, sailor take *warn*-ing." Even spelling rules, "*I* before *E*, except after *C* or when *soun*-ded like "A" as in *neigh*-bor and *weigh*." A useful mnemonic, but neglects exceptions such as those in the less rhythmic mnemonic: "Neither the foreigner nor the weird financier seizes leisure at its height." There must be rhythmic mnemonics for every basic in all craft and trade traditions like cooking, sewing, carpentry. Hall was attentive to the impact of standardization of products and procedures that overwhelmed cultural traditions, like the standardized screw-threads on a pipe or hose or the humble screw. But some of us, when we are having trouble trying to insert or attach one thing to another, we may regress to a mnemonic like "righty-tight-y, lefty-loose-y." (If the object is above our head or below, that may complicate things.)

Rhythm is right here always, in how we move and talk, and what shapes our days, our expectations, our lives. Our natural world of days and nights and seasons, the world of the farmer, herder, fisher, soothsayer, and priest who relied on a cosmos and served as a guide for the rhythms we experience, enshrined in holy books and literary arts, has been a guide and precept and promise. The recognition and appreciation of the significance of rhythm now extends beyond musicians and dancers and others to social scientists who consider and can measure and compare daily rhythms—movement, speech—to distinguish cultural enclaves, including urban settings that by other calculations, might seem similar. French scholars may be taking the lead in this. Rhythm has found a place in critical theory.

Synchrony and Entrainment

Serendipity—such a cheerful-sounding word—"is not just an apparent aptitude for making fortuitous discoveries accidentally," writes Steven Strogatz, an award-winning applied mathematics professor at Cornell University and preeminent scholar of synchrony.[26] He distinguishes *synchrony* from *serendipity*. "Serendipitous discoveries are always made by people in a particular frame of mind, people who are focused and alert because they are searching for something. They just happen to find something else." Strogatz's description characterizes some of Hall's insights in his pursuit of something else. It would describe discoveries by other researchers at the time when "nonverbal communication" was just beginning to be taken seriously, when "communication" mostly meant words spoken and in print.

Hall was a relatively late-comer to recognizing synchrony between people, especially when their cultural backgrounds and corresponding cultural behavior and expectations don't match, and maybe more importantly, when we find ourselves in sync with others when our histories would not have anticipated that. Hall became aware of the omnipresence of synchrony in the 1960s, a renaissance era in interpersonal communication research that secured a place in college curricula, with nonverbal and then intercultural communication following. Hall brought synchrony to the attention of those just discovering intercultural communication. This was just ahead of the short-lived pop culture fad of charting one's "bio-rhythms." The late-twentieth century phrase "being in sync," Hall says, originally referred to when movies became "talkies," and the need for the sound and visuals to match. Much later "being in sync" came into popular usage to express feelings of connectedness with another person, if only fleetingly, around the same time that the expression "being in a relationship" referred to a romantic involvement without a formal commitment. It also corresponded to the child's answer to the question, "Have you ever been in love?" "No," the young innocent replied, "but I've been in like."

Sync is both strange and beautiful. It is strange because it seems to defy the laws of physics, though, in fact, it relies on them. It is beautiful because it results in a kind of cosmic ballet that plays out on stages that range from bodies to the universe as a whole. And it is also critically important.[27] It turns out we've always been in sync with others. Like so much in our behavior, we are late in recognizing what has been there all along. Synchrony across the universe of animate species and even more, seems to be universal. Because "being in sync" is omnipresent in all of nature, and not just between animate species, Strogatz suggests it could be considered a law of physics.

Long before the realization of our body's synchronized behavior that emerged in the last half of the past century, synchrony had attracted the attention of scientists. One story in particular tells of the serendipitous discovery by a distinguished Dutch philosopher and scientist, Christiaan Huygens. Huygens is credited with creating the pendulum clock, which he hoped might resolve the challenge that ship captains faced as they navigated toward what Europeans saw as a new world. The leading scientists in that era, including Galileo Galilei and Isaac Newton, tried to devise ways to help the sea captains to know their position at sea. Rewards were even offered by the governments of the colonizing nations for solutions to the clock problem, how to be sure of the precise time, essential to know the ship's location, knowing that if they were lost, they would be prey to lurking pirates. "The challenge was to devise a mechanical clock that never wavered despite the heaving of the ship on violent seas, and despite the assaults of ever-changing humidity, pressure, and temperature, which can rust a clock's gears, expand its springs or thicken its lubricating oil, causing it to speed up, slow down, or stop."[28]

In his bedroom to which an illness confined him, Huygens made a casual experiment that resulted in a most significant discovery. There were two pendulum clocks on the wall in his room. One night, he set the clock pendulums swinging at random, and then went to sleep. When he woke in the morning the pendulums were moving "in sympathy," which Huygens described in a letter to a friend as "miraculous." Strogatz says Huygens had discovered inanimate sync. And although not as famous today as Galileo or Newton, Huygen's discovery is of profound importance three centuries later in our better understanding of how our bodies work and how we engage with each other. Newton called him "*Summus Hugenius*."[29]

A contemporary 2012 demonstration of Huygens's clock experiment is seen in a video filmed at a Toshiba laboratory in Japan in which thirty-two metronomes are, like Huygens's clock pendula, set in random "asynchronous" motion. The experiment, available on YouTube, is mesmerizing. Within three minutes, all thirty-two are in sync.[30] The physicist in us wonders how that happens. The psychologist and sociologist in us, tempted to theorize why we personify these, might think of peer pressures to conform, especially when we see that last metronome holding out. Our attention to the "out of sync" metronome reminds me of a scene in Alfred Hitchcock's film, *Strangers on a Train*, where spectators at a tennis match turn their heads from side-to-side as they watch the players volley back and forth—except for one person whose gaze remains fixed on one player. The man in the stands, out of sync with the crowd; in a Hitchcock film we know this is ominous.

Watching these thirty-two impersonal metronomes, our eyes are fixed on the one that refuses to conform, that last holdout. If we personify the video, it is a kind of Rorschach projective test. Are we annoyed (around the two-minute mark) and just want that deviant to get with the program so that we can move on, or are our sympathies with it? (Pronouns: she/her. Nevertheless, she persisted.) I've watched the metronome video in many classrooms and in workshops and with diverse participants. Some of those who comment on this last out-of-sync metronome say they felt impatient with it, while others hoped it could bravely resist getting with the program. Eventually that last metronome also gets in sync, and some viewers feel their discomfort has been relieved, while others sigh and attach other feelings, some from personal memories, that sometimes you just can't win when everyone around you has conformed.

I find that our feelings about observing synchrony and what is asynchronous or out of sync interesting in itself—that tension is the stuff of drama, as in iconic films like *Twelve Angry Men* or *High Noon*, where one bravely resists group pressure and in the end is heroic. An anthem in tribute to individualism? Maybe, but in the 1970s when karaoke became popular in the inter-dependent-valuing Japanese society, weary *sararīman* at karaoke parties loved the song made famous by Frank Sinatra, "My Way." At work we do it "Our Way." We may cheer the lone hero in song and in the movies, but in daily life our feelings may be quite the opposite—the one holding up traffic, the one standing in the way of progress or justice. Crowds acting in sync are a powerful force, awesome when we are in support of their cause, and frightening if we see them as a threat.[31] But I digress.

What explains why Huygens's clocks and the Toshiba lab metronomes became synchronized? How do these inanimate simple machines communicate with one another? And how is this relevant to the human communication? Huygens's clocks shared a common surface, the wall, and the metronomes shared a common surface on which they were placed, and through these planes, the vibrations were how the "messages" were communicated. Humans and other earthly creatures respond to the vibrations that we sense and make sense of; our very speech and hearing are communicated by delicate vibrations that we decode. Land and sea creatures sense signals of an earthquake and possible tsunami. Other senses, too, are the media through which involuntary reactions at the cellular level become synchronized. The medium may be vibratory, tactile, auditory, visual, or chemical, as research has affirmed frequent reports of the synching of the menstrual cycles of women living in close proximity. Even cardiac pacemakers can synchronize among strangers.

The tendency for people and other creatures to move in sync has intrigued the most curious and creative physicists' minds, including Albert Einstein and Richard Feynman, sometimes considered the past-century's physicist second only to Einstein. But long before, sailors and other travelers to Southeast Asia were astonished to see swarms of fireflies flashing their lights in the night sky in rhythmic synchrony. Their reports were doubted by those at home, but now we can all see video evidence and be astonished once again. This is vividly described in Strogatz's book and in a related TED Talk.[32]

Strogatz points out an unanticipated effect of human synchrony occurred in the year 2000 when London's $27 million/£18.2 million Millennium Bridge opened, a footbridge crossing the Thames from near St. Paul's to the Tate Modern Museum. Like the London bridge in the nursery rhyme, it almost came falling down. It happened because the visitors walking across the bridge panicked when the bridge began to sway, and in an effort to steady it, they rushed *en mass* from side-to-side, which only intensified the oscillation. "Positive feedback" is a dispassionate explanation. The bridge was immediately closed, and, after structural modifications, re-opened two years later.[33]

Personal Synchrony, Intra- and Inter-

Hall's interest in this interpersonal synchrony was influenced by the work of William Condon, no relation that I'm aware of, although we did meet when Hall introduced us in his office when W. Condon visited. Condon's academic background was originally in philosophy, with a concentration in phenomenology, which sometimes seems indistinguishable from social psychology. Indeed, Condon's advanced studies were in psychology, and now he is most often identified as a psychologist. He later also worked with anthropologist and linguistics professor Ray Birdwhistell. Using the technologies available at that time, Condon's empirical research appeared in many publications in the 1960s and 1970s when Hall's work was also reaching a broader public.

William Condon is best known for drawing attention to the significance of communication that demonstrates how our physical movements are also synchronized with our speech. Years later, readers learned of him in Malcolm Gladwell's best-selling book in 2000, *Blink*. I imagine that Condon could have written a long monograph, if not a book, on just that theme of "blink," though as a title "*Blink*" would never have been acceptable for an academic publication.

A blink and a wink are not the same. To be able to wink is an acquired ability, a part of culture—like skipping. A blink is involuntary and, apart from the atmospherics of sudden bright light or dust in the air or problems with contact lenses, it is a physical punctuation of speech. We blink as part of our speech—at beginning of words or between syllables, not randomly. The honored film editor, director, and screen writer, Walter Murch (*American Graffiti, Apocalypse Now, The Godfather Part II, The Talented Mr. Ripley*, and many more films) would make cuts in his editing at the point of a blink to change from one scene to another.[34]

William Condon is credited for his painstaking studies of our behavior observed in micro-seconds. He spent more than a year studying a film documenting an otherwise unremarkable conversation of a family at dinner, taken by anthropologist Gregory Bateson with whom Condon also worked. This was black and white film, and long before video and computers that would have greatly accelerated the recognition of patterns of "micro-momentary movements." Using his improvised hand-cranked movie projector, viewing a 16 mm film for eighteen months, he noted microseconds of every observable movement from broad gestures to, indeed, blinks. After 100,000 viewings, the film was worn out. Condon went on to wear out another 129 copies of the film. Hall later remarked, "There has to be a lot going on at a family dinner to hold someone's attention for a year and a half." He added, "And there is a lot going on, perhaps more than we will ever know."[35]

In his research Condon discovered that our physical movements, broad and barely perceptible, are synchronized. And when we speak, our bodies dance to the rhythm of our speech. He recognized that our coordinated movements, broadly expressed and nearly imperceptible, were synchronized with our brain waves. Hall wrote that "brain rhythms are reliable indicators associated with practically everything that people do; they change in sleep, indicated the kind of sleep that one is having and even whether one is dreaming or not." He credits Condon for establishing that each of the six different brain wave frequencies is linked to specific parts of the self-synchrony spectrum. Brain wave frequencies are associated with speech. Hall wrote that the one-second frequency wave is apparently a basic rhythm of human behavior.[36]

Each body movement, according to Condon, is synchronized to a four-level hierarchical series of rhythms. Condon's calculations were made decades ago with equipment that today is obsolete if not antique—before video, computers, and neurological technologies that allow us to peer at the behavior of the brain. His painstaking research is a testament to his persistence and dedication to establishing the depth and complexity of our body's synchronies.

Condon has said that it took him longer to realize that, in addition to that self-synchrony, we also tend to synchronize with the rhythm of the voice and physical movements when we are with another or others: interactive synchrony. Condon chose to call this "entrainment," our sympathetic, synchronized movement from a source outside of ourselves. He said that he noticed this not when focusing on the scene of the interaction, but rather when one day he glanced at his film from the corner of his eye. Serendipity! Friends who are hunters tell me that it is that it is peripheral vision that gives them their keenest sighting of their prey.

Readers of Hall's books are intrigued by a story he describes in *Beyond Culture*, and re-told in more detail in *The Dance of Life*. "Who would think that widely scattered groups of children in a school playground could be in sync?" Hall asks, and then describes what one of his students discovered in his research observing children at a school playground. He filmed the children at play and watched the film many times at different speeds, as Hall advised his students studying interaction. Hall says the young researcher:

. . . began to notice one very active little girl who seemed to stand out from the rest. She was all over the place. Concentrating on that girl, my student noticed that whenever she was near a cluster of children, the members of that group were in sync not only with each other but with her. Many viewings later, he realized that this girl, with her skipping and dancing and twirling, was actually orchestrating the movements of the entire playground![37]

That brief film segment Condon showed us in Hall's office was seconds of interaction between a male therapist and a female client talking about a problem she presented to the therapist. "So, what are you going to do about it?" the therapist asks, unremarkable when viewed at "normal speed." But at very slow speed, the synchronous behavior—shifting postures, body positions, gestures, and the "micro-kinesic" movements of eye brows and blinks—the body in sync with itself. But the interaction in slow motion, each frame at 1/25 of a second, appears as a choreographed dance. One of Condon's assistants told me that she pointed out to Condon that the movements and his description made it seem like an erotic dance. Condon was shocked, she said, and embarrassed when she pointed that out.

In another study summarized in the publication *Science*, described as "The Dance of the Neonates," Condon and colleague, Louis Sander, showed how even on the first day of life, a newborn responds in synchrony to the mother's voice and movements.[38]

Neither Condon nor Hall, who recognized the value of Condon's research, could realize the depth and extensiveness the role of the synchronous interactions within the body that was discovered decades later. Again, Strogatz helps us appreciate that with this analogy:

. . . [T]he human body is like an enormous orchestra. The musicians are individual cells, all born with a sense of a 24-hour rhythm. The players are grouped into various sections. Instead of strings and woodwinds, we have kidneys and livers, each composed of thousands of cellular oscillators, similar within an organ, different across organs, all keeping a 24-hour biochemical beat but entering and exiting at just the right times. Within each organ suites of genes are active or idle at different times of day ensuring that the organs' characteristic proteins are manufactured on schedule. The conductor for this symphony is the circadian pacemaker, a neural cluster of thousands of clock cells in the brain, themselves synchronized into a coherent unit.[39]

Unaware, we are in sync with others around us, and we are in sync with ourselves and with the cosmos. Synchrony is literally a force of nature. I sync, therefore I am.

Intercultural Implications

As tourists we travel to attractive destinations, anticipating scenes in which we can imagine ourselves taking pictures like those idealized that attracted us. But there are many varieties of tourism today including eco-tourism, medical tourism, heritage or history tourism, "dark tourism," etc. Most tourists expect a welcoming place, and in this multibillion industry, encouragement ("English widely spoken") along with brave teases ("Adventure!"), and consumer teases: images of markets and shops. Or we may say we want to go outside of "our comfort zone," and think of ourselves as "sojourners." But traveling to the "other side" of town or maybe across a state line is something else; we rarely think of ourselves as tourists, but we are, by most definitions.

Traveling across town, we may find ourselves in the parts of a city and among people we rarely visit, meeting people who move to rhythms different from those that we are most familiar with. Martin Luther King said that 11:00 am on Sunday is the most segregated hour in America. Millions of people professing the same faith attending religious services that can be discomfiting to a stranger in the same land.

Traveling abroad, once the privilege of those who enjoyed their visit as a luxury, is not that of those fleeing their homeland in desperation as immigrants and refugees. For millions more who relocate as international students or because of job reassignments, the experience is different still, though there may be that "honeymoon phase" that lasts a few hours or days. But all will likely arrive "out of sync" because their circadian rhythms have been disrupted and it will take a bit of time for the body, even at the cellular level, just to adjust. We feel this most clearly as "jet lag."

If we travel as a group—bringing our group sync and habitual rhythms with us—or if we travel alone, does that make a difference? Is it less stressful being more in sync with the others in the group than if one travels alone? Is the adjustment by a lone traveler likely to occur faster?

A lament I've heard from expat corporate officials, and also from those in government service, is that just when one is "in sync" (metaphorically) with the very people they were sent to connect with, they are likely to be rotated back home. "Good grief, Harry's gone native!" Of course, there is much more involved, but synchronizing with the local rhythms of speech and movement can be part of how trust is shaped, and that can lead to a more critical eye and voice toward the organization that sent you. If "you gotta dance with the one who brung you," time to come home.

The COVID pandemic that began around 2020 disrupted everything all over the world. Work teams and students accustomed to classroom learning were suddenly separated from each other, now linked via Zoom or some comparable digital service. At this writing, the impacts are still being sorted out. Studies indicate the disruptions caused by the pandemic set back childhood education many years.

A study of problem-solving and creativity by pairs of people working together side-by-side, compared with pairs working via Zoom, found that those physically together were more effective. "Synchrony" was not mentioned in the researchers' interpretation, but it was clear that the flat, two-dimensional presence prevented the full range of communication that happens when we are together. Though not expressed in terms of sync, that may be part of the reason that young, creative people want to live in the same place with others, even those who continue to generate the possibilities of digital platforms and media.

Though Hall rarely drew analogies to dance or music, apart from the titular metaphor of his book on "time," *The Dance of Life,* he wrote a lot about rhythm as synchrony in our everyday interaction with others. Without our conscious awareness, our speech and physical movement are synchronized; we are more likely to be aware when we are out of sync with others, and sometimes even with ourselves. Turns out, when we are in good health, emotionally as well as physically, our kinetic expressions—gestures, and other physical movements, even when we blink—are in sync. We dance to the rhythm of our speech.

Notes

1. Those from outside of the community are welcomed as guests (not as spectators) on feast days (Jemez Pueblo has two), and on days important in the Christian calendar. On December 12, the celebration of the Virgin of Guadalupe, Jemez is famous for the *Matachines* dances performed throughout the Americas that reenact, in ritual form, the *mestizaje*—the fusion of European and Indigenous people and cultures with the arrival of the Spanish in what is now Mexico. For others, it reenacts not just the contact, but also the beginning of centuries of colonial influence.

2. Joan Didion, *The White Album* (NY: Simon & Schuster, 1979).

3. As with everything, context matters. The sound of rain at night helps many people fall asleep; there are commercially produced recordings of rain sounds available to encourage sleep. But what if what is keeping people awake is a rain that has continued for days, and there is fear of flooding? I don't know of commercial recordings of the sound of rain ending to produce a sigh of relief and an invitation to sleep.

4. Usha Goswami, "Language Acquisition and Speech Rhythm Patterns: An Auditory Neuroscience Perspective," *Royal Society Open Science* 9, no. 7 (July 27, 2022).

5. Daniel J. Levitin, *This is Your Brain on Music: The Science of a Human Obsession* (New York: Penguin, 2006), 58.

6. Keith Terry and Linda Akiyama, *Rhythm of Math: Teaching Mathematics with Body Music* (Oakland, CA: Crosspulse Media, 2015).

7. Rina Swentzell, "Pueblo Space: An Understated Sacredness," Marta Weigle, ed., *Telling New Mexico* (Albuquerque: University of New Mexico Press, 2009), 45-48. "An Understated Sacredness" is also the title of a television presentation on KUNM, the Albuquerque PBS station, introduced by V. B. Price, and told by Rina Swentzell. This can be viewed on YouTube: https://www.youtube.com/watch?v=8zHAiOKN6Vo&ab_channel=knmedotorg

8. Many of us may have had the experience of trying to engage in a conversation in a language we are still learning, as we try to construct some words we might contribute, the topic has changed: we missed our chance. I recall someone in that situation at a conference in the US who shared his frustration with others in the group when he shared a solution to his challenge. "I realized, all I have to do is say, '*Well . . .*' and everybody stops talking and listens to me."

9. A swing rhythm that many of a certain age will recognize, Terry mentions Henry Mancini's music that introduces the *Pink Panther* movies: *L o n g, short-short, L o n g, short-short.*

10. https://www.youtube.com/watch?v=bkyOFkBAMDg&ab_channel=HarvardUniversity

11. What Marsalis says is "the ground rhythm" walking, "the two-groove beat, that can be played slow or fast." We hear it in popular tunes ("Soldiers' Joy") during colonial times, through "When Johnny Comes Marching Home," among the nation's most famous, to "When the Saints Go Marching In," and the blues, like the "St. Louis Blues." It's the underlying beat onto which other rhythms in the same time frame gave us polyrhythms that became the blues and then jazz.

12. John McWhorter, "Blackness and Standard English Can Co-Exist: Professors Take Notice," *The New York Times,* May 3, 2022.

13. https://www.youtube.com/watch?v=IKXw2QmwJFg&ab_channel=RichardEwards. This was recorded by musicologist James Koetting as part of his fieldwork in Ghana between 1973-1975. The tune that the workers are whistling is traditional in the greater region of Ghana's capital, Accra.

14. Satinder Gill, "Rhythmic Synchrony and Mediated Interaction: Towards A Framework of Rhythm in Embodied Interaction," *AI & Society, Journal for Knowledge, Culture and Communication. Special issue: Witnessed Presence.* Volume 27, Number 1, February 2012.

15. Portuguese philosopher Lúcio Alberto Pinheiro dos Santos is credited with initiating *rhythmanalysis* and coining the term, but it is the French philosopher Gaston Bachelard who elaborated and extended these ideas. Bachelard's name is more familiar to those in the field of communication, including his writings about semantics, and also through his classic study of spaces and places in the home, *La poétique de l'espace*, translated as *The Poetics of Space* (Boston, Beacon Press, 1969). Not surprisingly, apart from musicians and dancers, familiar names of those who have written about rhythms of society span many fields including architects (LeCorbusier) and sociologists (Emile Durkheim, Marcel Mauss).

16. Henri Lefebvre, *Space, Time and Everyday Life* (London: Blackwell, 2004).

17. D. P. McCormack, *Refrains for Moving Bodies: Experience and Experiment in Affective Spaces* (Durham, NC: Duke University Press, 2013).

18. Howard Gardner, *Intelligence Reframed* (New York: Basic Books, 1999).

19. Mark cites T. Edensor, "Walking in Rhythms: Place, Regulation, Style and the Flow of Experience," *Visual Studies*, 2011, 25 (1), 69-79;_T. Hall, B. Lashua, and A. Coffrey, "Sound and the Everyday in Qualitative Research," *Qualitative Inquiry*, 2008, 14 (6), 1019-1040; B. Highmore, "Street Life in London: Towards a Rhythmanalysis of London in the Late Nineteenth Century," *New Formations*, 2002, 47, 171-193.

20. Lauren Mark, "The Acculturative Costs of Rhythmic Belonging," *Capacious: Journal for Emerging Affect Inquiry*, 2019-2020. Vol. 2, No. 1, 60-82.

21. L. R. Bloch, "Who's Afraid of Being a Freier? The Analysis of Communication through a Key Cultural Frame," *Communication Theory*, 2003, 13 (2), 138.

22. https://www.npr.org/2014/06/19/323510652/speechwriters-deliberately-use-rhythm-to-help-make-their-point

23. https://www.npr.org/2014/06/19/323510652/speechwriters-deliberately-use-rhythm-to-help-make-their-point

24 Momoko Nisugi, "Images of Spoken Japanese and Spoken English," in *Intercultural Encounters with Japan*, eds. John Condon and Mitsuko Saito (Tokyo: Simul Press, 1974), 199-204.

25. Japanese, my friend Keisuke Kurata told me, is said to be a great language for ventriloquists because in ordinary conversation speaking Japanese does not require speakers to move their lips far apart or open their mouths widely as do speakers of, say, Spanish or Portuguese.

26. Steven Strogatz, *Sync: How Order Emerges from Chaos in the Universe, Nature, and Daily Life* (New York and Boston: Hachette Books, 2015), 5-6.

27. Strogatz, *Sync*, 5-6.

28. Strogatz, *Sync*, 105. Note: animal fat was often used as a lubricant in clocks that sometimes had the side effect of attracting mice, and thus explaining, in the hickory-dickory-doc rhyme, why a mouse ran up the clock.

29. Strogatz, *Sync*, 108.

30. https://www.theatlantic.com/video/archive/2012/09/watch-32-ticking-metronomes-synch-up-all-by-themselves/467013/

31. While we may thrill to synchrony in ballet, Olympian synchronized swimmers and skaters, we feel frightened by the sight in totalitarian societies of soldiers marching in synchrony or thousands of young people in uniform performing in synchrony as a show of loyalty to the dictator. Einstein, quoted by Strogatz, said, "He who joyfully marches to music rank and

file, has already earned my contempt. He has been given a large brain by mistake, since for him the spinal cord would surely suffice."

32. Strogatz, *Sync*, 11-14. And: https://www.ted.com/talks/steven_strogatz_the_science_of_sync#t-1295045

33. https://www.ted.com/talks/steven_strogatz_the_science_of_sync#t-1295045

34. Walter Murch, *In the Blink of an Eye: A Perspective on Film Editing* (Beverly Hills: Silman-James Press, 1995, 2001).

35. Edward T. Hall, *The Silent Language* (New York: Doubleday, 1959), 180.

36. Edward T. Hall, *The Dance of Life: The Other Dimension of Time* (New York: Anchor Books, 1984), 181.

37. Edward T. Hall, *Dance of Life,* 169.

38. W. S. Condon and L. W. Sander, "Neonate Movement Synchron-ized with Adult Speech: Interactive Participation and Language Acquisition," *Science* Vol. 18, No. 4120, 1974, 99-101.

39. Strogatz, *Sync,* 72.

After Words

The future ain't what it used to be.

—*Yogi Berra*

*W*hat? Still more words in a book called *It Goes **Without** Saying*?
Please indulge me this last chance to revisit Hall's insights
in the context of today's outlook. His life, which spanned most of
the past century, witnessed profound changes that continue today at
an even faster pace. If we view culture *as* communication, it's clear
that what has changed most *is* communication. And so, also, culture.

Consider how our relationship with three areas most identified
with Hall—space, time, and sensing—have changed, largely because
of a fourth: what Hall and Marshall McLuhan called "extensions,"
extending how we perceive, connect with others, and how we sense
and make sense of our place in the world.

Every day we move seamlessly between talking with someone
nearby, as people have for a hundred thousand years, and then, in the
next minute, we are talking with someone half-way around the world
with whom we may feel just as close but have never met in person, nor
ever expect to. The former situation was Hall's domain: our ways of

communicating that had evolved, analog in our nonverbal behavior, and largely outside of our awareness, instinctive. In the latter situation, our communication is via means that was designed and developed within the past few decades: it is digital, mostly intentional, even to the extent that we can review and edit our words and behavior before they are expressed and received.

Space

Hall's proxemics attention was relatively "micro-" social interaction within a shared perceptual field. He also was concerned about the bigger picture, not just between individuals, but also within and between groups. He was especially attentive to the impacts of overcrowding and the loss of agency. His focus was narrow, as within housing "projects" in cities. It was less about the integration of racial communities, or the arrival of immigrants and refugees that followed during what would become, in the US, the most active era of intercultural interaction in a century.

Demographers tell us that our world's population didn't reach one billion people until 1804. Many families can trace their history that far back. Less than a century and a half later, at the onset of World War II, that number had doubled. It took only a dozen more years, around 1960, to hit three billion, and now, at the end of the first quarter of the twenty-first century, we are at eight billion people. Hall probably considered global demographics as outside his field, but I believe that today anyone concerned with intercultural communication needs to take heed of these demographic changes.

In the Americas, Europe, Oceania, Australia, and East Asia, most people now live in cities, not in the rural areas that gave us much of our folk wisdom and idioms. Today over half our world's population lives in Asia, while the fastest growing cities are in Africa, where forty percent of the population is under the age of sixteen. Personal note: in the late 1960s, when I lived in the capital of newly independent

Tanzania, Dar es Salaam, that "Harbor of Peace" was about the size of today's Saskatoon, Saskatchewan, Canada. Now Dar es Salaam is as populous as New York City.

Cities have always been "multicultural" (and multi-everything), a catalyst for cultural diffusion, a collective richness inspired by the confluence of idioms, slang, and borrowed words that offer different perspectives on living. We are enriched by a wealth of music, dance, literature, visual arts, and a banquet of foodways. Communication technologies bring these to people throughout the world, and also invite people everywhere to contribute. Even today, when it is possible to engage and collaborate with others geographically far away, many of our biggest cities—Tokyo, Mexico City, New York, London, Shanghai—remain magnets for young and creative people. Why? People together, engaging all their senses in communication, inspire, affect, and influence each other more than those who meet remotely.

Of still greater importance may be the fact that today we are witness to the largest human migration and diaspora yet known. What drives this change from rural to urban, from one's home to an imagined safer, better place? To flee repression, political or religious, or to escape threats from gangs and poverty conditions with little hope for change: the reasons people have always fled their homelands, seeking refuge and a place where the children might know a better life. And today, more than one hundred million people are on the move, many abandoning the places where their families have always lived, unlikely to return because of the change of climate. For those whose cultural identity is place-based, being forced to leave where the spirits of their ancestors reside is painful in ways that a society which values mobility cannot appreciate. Generations of countless families have grown up in evermore crowded refugee camps, and others seek refuge in densely populated cities.

Greater than the shifting populations are the global forces of our shifting climate. Coastal ports, which for centuries have been places of departures and arrivals that once motivated and defined intercultural communication, are at risk from the rising seas, threatening entire island cultures. Sea life that has sustained human life is itself at risk, largely because of willful human behavior. Nor should we be so arrogant to imagine that humans alone are on the move; there are rapid changes in the biosphere we share with plants, animals, and insects, both friendly and threatening. It is impossible to separate human culture—including where and how we dwell, how we dress, the food that sustains us, and how we work and play—from the natural environment that in myriad ways exerts its influence.

Jane Goodall asked the existential question: *"How is it possible that the most intellectual creature ever to walk the planet Earth is destroying its only home?"*

Time

Hall described the silent languages of time and space, those languages we instinctively have used, which are now combined and compressed, with time the favored dimension. Everyday distance is reckoned by the clock. Someone on the other side of the world is as close as the person next door or elsewhere in the same building. We can have family gatherings and conferences, and can team up to join in a game with strangers—as long as we accommodate the time zones.

When our communication is mediated by digital means, interpersonal distance becomes less relevant. So the language of interpersonal proxemics, moving closer or stepping back, usually out of our awareness, reflecting a change of feeling, may now be expressed through a change in the sound of a voice, a sudden rush of words, a longer pause, and through the time and timing: how long one takes to reply to a message. "Thank you for your time," an interviewer says, as if time were more valued more than the information or opinion given. Bullet-points replace paragraphs. Readers of printed news and opinion sources are advised at the beginning how long it should take to read what follows. Company managers, we are told, spend an average of 27 seconds reading most job applications, and for those who trade stocks, the difference between success and failure may be a delay of a mere 50 milliseconds.

Sensing and Making Sense

"But is it real?" Hall asked his students, challenging their culture-based assumptions of "reality." Sensing to make sense was at the heart of Hall's work. He believed that our body is our "most important instrument for knowing." It's not that what we feel is always accurate, but that our built-in survival instrument should not be ignored in deference to abstractions and measurements. Nor should we ignore what we are feeling by telling ourselves we shouldn't be feeling that way.

As our perceived world and our communication is increasingly mediated electronically, the world we perceive—through sounds and images that we receive digitally from a distance—arrives uncomplicated and often with a limited awareness of relevant contexts. We appear to be entering an era of distrust of what we sense. How this plays out over time is yet to be discovered, but along with the convenience and achievements that artificial intelligence gives us, it is a new cause to doubt what our human history has given us. Confusing the representation of something as "more real" than that which it represents, Hall called "extension transference." Hall's ET may have matured into our AI.

All this recalls a Marxist question. Almost a century ago in the Marx Brothers's comedy *Duck Soup*, Groucho Marx's character walks out of a bedroom, leaving the venerable Margaret Dumont behind. Almost immediately, Groucho's brother, Chico, pops up from under a bed, pretending to be Groucho, who himself was pretending to be someone else (layers of deception). The Dumont character challenges Chico as an imposter. Responds Chico: "Who you gonna believe? *Me*, or your own eyes?" We still can laugh at that line from that 1933 movie, but it also has become a serious question: *"Who we gonna believe?"* What if we can't trust the images and voices of people we are sure we know? And remember, haptics technology is on its way, too, so we may soon have cause to doubt the touch of a hand or feel of an embrace.

Maybe all this concern is alarmist. Another app will take care of that worry—another tech solution for an earlier tech problem. Or maybe we will entrust education to urge greater "awareness," always important but often insufficient. But as more of intercultural communication is remote and mediated, if we distrust what we see and hear . . . then what?

The Paradox of the Inter-

In any system, a change in one part affects changes elsewhere, sometimes everywhere, in the system. That principle is implicit in our talk of culture and communication. "Intercultural communication" now is an even more peculiar enterprise than it used to be: the engagement of behavior of people not fully aware of what or even how *they are communicating*, using even more efficient means to include more people we know even less.

Here lies the paradox of intercultural communication. It can enrich us all through the varieties of diversity, including innovations not previously identified with any cultural history, something new that, in time, will be regarded as tradition. Consider that moment in the mid-1500s when a Venetian chef wondered what might be possible with this strange, red, *pomodoro* from across the ocean.

As we enjoy the convenience and manifold advantages that communication technologies offer, we are also more dependent on these and the vast systems that connect us across the earth. These include those satellites we've placed in the exosphere, that outermost area beyond the stratosphere, that make possible an enormity of our communication of all kinds here on earth. These are as much a part of our culture as anything else we so take for granted that we forget it is part of today's intercultural communication.

However, with our remarkable achievements that can bring people together come two risks. One is a kind of inter-dependence that is new. To a great extent we are dependent on interconnected systems beyond our reach—and for many of us, beyond our understanding. Standardization can offer convenience, predictability, and often economic advantages. But with standardization come risks, including what Kenneth Boulding called a "super culture" with systems of connection and standardization where, if any system fails somewhere, it may affect people everywhere.

Another risk, not unrelated, is the diminishing of the very cultural diversity that has been a resource, strength, and insurance throughout human history. For example, the value of international tourism, seemingly benign, alters the very cultural communities people want to visit: old neighborhoods giving way to more profitable shops selling stereotype trinkets to fit the expectations of the visitors. The same with foods and clothing. Globally, languages spoken by a small population give way to whatever language, with its implicit logic, is dominant. Flight controllers around the world, for example, all use English.

Recall US linguist George Lakoff's plea for the importance of diversity of languages and cultures:

> Just as the gene pool of a species needs to be kept diverse if the species is to survive under a wide variety of conditions, so I believe that diverse ways of comprehending experience are necessary to our survival as a species. I believe that vanishing cultures and languages need to be protected just as vanishing species do. . . . I think we have a lot to learn

from other ways of conceptualizing experience that have evolved around the world.

Mexican poet, Nobelist, and diplomat, Octavio Paz, speaks to this passionately:

What sets worlds in motion is the interplay of differences, their attractions and repulsions.

Life is plurality. Death is uniformity.

By suppressing differences and peculiarities, by eliminating different civilizations and cultures, progress weakens life and favors death.

The ideal of a single civilization for everyone, implicit in the cult of progress and technique, impoverishes and mutilates us.

Every view of the world that becomes extinct, every culture that disappears, diminishes a possibility of life.

Appendixes

What's the Use of Culture?

Matthew Liebmann, PhD

This is part of an exchange of messages in 2017 among the faculty of the Department of Anthropology at Harvard University on the question: "What's the use of culture? And can the culture concept serve as a unifying paradigm for anthropology at Harvard in the 21ˢᵗ century?" Here is how Matthew Liebmann replied. Professor Liebmann, Peabody Professor of American Archaeology and Ethnology, and Chair of the Department of Anthropology at Harvard University, kindly gave permission to share this.

What IS the use of "culture"? The subtext of this question, of course, is: "is culture still useful? Or should we do away with it entirely?" As we're all aware, after serving as the aegis under which anthropology took form in the early 20ᵗʰ century, unease with this concept has waxed and waned over the past 50 years (with more waxing than waning of late). Today, the culture concept is widely critiqued as abstract, essentializing, ahistorical, homogenizing, primordial, bounded, discrete, and totalizing, among other complaints. Our dissatisfaction with the term is signaled by the lexical avoidance behavior that is so prominent in contemporary anthropological writing. Like Aboriginal Australians avoiding our mothers-in-law, we steer clear of the term *culture*, using it only when accompanied by scare quotes, or preferring its adjectival form, "cultural." In its place, a variety of alternatives have been suggested, each more cumbersome than the next. Rather than culture, we use cultural formations, or discursive relations, or habitus, or hegemony, or ethnoscapes, or worldview, or values.

More than 20 years ago, James Clifford famously pronounced that the culture concept had "served its time," an opinion seemingly shared by the likes of Bourdieu, Wolf, Abu-Lughod, Appadurai, and Rosaldo. Far be it from me to tell this crew that they're wrong. Yet to me, reports of culture's death seem a bit exaggerated. It is one of those zombie terms that keeps dragging itself back from the grave. Try as we might to kill it, culture simply won't give up the *geist*.

While some anthropologists may no longer find the culture concept worthwhile, seemingly everyone else does. I for one find this heartening for the future of our discipline. The culture concept opens avenues for discussion between ourselves and non-anthropologists in ways that habitus and discursive formations just can't. Regrettably few other anthropological concepts enjoy such widespread popularity. Notions of culture are regularly employed in business, in law, in politics, in other academic disciplines, and in everyday life. As Marshall Sahlins notes, "people *want* culture, and they often want it in the bounded, reified, essentialized and timeless fashion that most of us do now reject" (Sahlins 1999:403). Indeed, we now live in an era of metaculture, to borrow Greg Urban's term. Culture itself is regularly about culture. As a result, I think that this post-millennial moment is a particularly bad time to disassociate ourselves from the project of culture. To do so not only risks perpetuating the divide between academic life and public life, but it has real-world consequences for the people with whom we work and that are the primary subjects of our research.

Let me take an example from the area that I know best, North American archaeology. The single greatest change to the way archaeology has been practiced in the United States over the past century was brought about by the passage into law of the Native American Graves Protection and Repatriation Act (or NAGPRA) in 1990. This law is built upon the culture concept. NAGPRA codifies culture in what's been called the cornerstone of the law, cultural affiliation, which is legally defined as:

"A relationship of shared group identity which can be reasonably traced between a present-day Indian tribe and an identifiable earlier group." Clearly this definition is based upon a concept of culture that holds that identity can be shared by a group in the past and one in the present.

Critics have argued that NAGPRA perpetuates an essentialized notion of culture, and runs in direct contradiction to the ideas that have been developed in anthropology (and related fields) over the past 30 years. Without getting into an extended discussion of the concept of strategic essentialism here, I would just note that laws such as NAGPRA have been enacted in order to redress the legacy of colonialism that casts its long shadow over anthropology today. If we as anthropologists turn our back on culture as a viable concept now, we support the notion that NAGPRA is untenable because it embraces an outdated notion of culture. (And in fact, this argument has been made by scientists seeking unrestricted access to human remains for academic study—a group not normally known for their penchant to embrace postmodern and constructivist notions of identity. And yet here they do. This shows some of the real danger of not engaging various definitions of culture in the 21st century.) From the Native American perspective, NAGPRA could become yet another example of the rug being pulled out from under their feet. Like so many broken treaties, they were promised a modicum of control over their cultural heritage through NAGPRA, only to have those rights snatched away through an academic slight-of-hand that claims it is impossible to prove that they share a cultural affiliation with their ancestors, because culture actually doesn't exist after all.

So to get back to Gary's original question, what's the use of culture? Well, one particularly important use has been to establish the foundation upon which NAGPRA was built. And this continues to be the best avenue for building bridges between the anthropological and Native American communities that we've had in the past century (in addition to righting some of the wrongs of the colonialist origins of our discipline, at least in part).

So what then do archaeologists make of all the anthropological hand-wringing over the culture concept of the past 30 years? At first glance the answer would seem to be "not much." Unfortunately, we haven't played much of a role in the great Culture Debates thus far. Archaeologists have long been content to play the role of consumers of the culture concepts developed by cultural anthropologists. But this lack of innovation shouldn't be mistaken for a lack of interest. Archaeologists have a long history of debating the relative merits of various definitions of culture for nearly as long as our colleagues have been tweaking them. In the early days of the discipline (the early-twentieth-century), the term "culture" was used by archaeologists mainly to define geographical entities that were assumed to have a semblance of ethnic homogeneity as well—"Olmec culture," "Indus culture," "Sumerian culture," etc. But in the post-WWII era, that began to change, beginning when new calls for an explicitly anthropological archaeology were launched—out of this very department, no less. Phillip Phillips, a Harvard archaeologist, penned the famous phrase that would go on to galvanize new directions for our discipline—"archaeology is anthropology or it is nothing."

At that time, some of the most influential anthropologists of the day, such as Kroeber and Kluckhohn, supported views of culture that were, at their core, essentially idealist. Kroeber wrote in 1948 that "what counts is not the [artifacts]. . . , but the idea of them, their place in life. It is this knowledge, concept, and function that get themselves handed down through the generations, or diffused into other cultures, while the objects themselves are quickly worn out or consumed" (1948:295). The archaeologists of the day struggled to implement notions of culture as a mental phenomenon, most famously embodied in Walter Taylor's "A Study of Archaeology." Many of them rejected the project altogether. But Taylor's call to arms did succeed in opening the floodgates, and archaeologists began to scrutinize their use of the culture concept—and their relationship to cultural anthropology—much more closely.

When explicitly materialist definitions of culture were proffered by neo-evolutionary anthropologists in the 1950s, archaeologists were relieved to turn away from Kroeber and Kluckhohn's idealist notions. Most influential was one definition espoused by Leslie White, who described culture as "man's extrasomatic means of adaptation." This definition was enthusiastically embraced by Lew Binford and multiple generations of processual archaeologists. Binford explicitly rejected idealist notions of culture saying, "We do not have to try to study mental phenomena. In fact, we study material phenomena."

(Now personally, I think that "man's extrasomatic means of adaptation" is a particularly horrible definition of culture. I take exception to virtually every word used: man's, extrasomatic, adaptation . . .) But I digress . . .

Archaeology chugged along through the 60s and 70s, largely ignoring the contributions of symbolic anthropology and sticking with materialist, systems-based models. But in the 1980s a new challenge arose in the form of post-processual critiques, which advocated the investigation of symbolic forms and took its cues from structuralist, and later post-structuralist social theory. While not galvanized by any clear or single notion of culture, post-processual critiques certainly stoked the fires of debate concerning the proper subject of archaeology once again. For the next 20 years, archaeology ping-ponged back and forth in debates over idealist-vs-materialist models of social life.

With the turn of the twenty-first century, these tiresome debates have (finally) begun to subside. And in recent years, some archaeologists (myself included) have advocated for a third way between the Scylla and Charybdis of idealism vs materialism. This anti-Cartesian stance is most clearly evinced in recent discussions of materiality, which espouse not a separation of ideology and material culture, but their mutual constitution. (In other words, the notion that physical objects have the ability to create, mediate, and be shaped by ideology.) Materiality and has drawn interest across the humanities and social sciences of late, and holds some real potential for collaboration among cultural anthropologists and archaeologists. (If, that is, archaeologists begin to attend to the recursive nature of materiality and its implications, rather than merely tossing the term around as a stand-in for "material culture.") This "material turn" builds upon theories of practice and structuration—which is the closest thing we have to a culture concept in contemporary archaeology.

Those of you who are still awake will note that up to this point, I have carefully sidestepped the task of defining culture myself. So now I'll put my neck on the chopping block. Personally, I ascribe to a simplification of Tylor's classic laundry-list definition: culture is that which is socially acquired. While there is much to unpack in this short definition and it is admittedly not without problems, for me the promise it holds comes from a semiotic take on the culture concept, and a focus on the key phrase, "socially acquired." In order for culture to be acquired, it must, by necessity, be externalized in publicly accessible signs. This definition is thus appealing because it accounts for all forms of culture—artifacts, utterances, behaviors, laws, morals, and everything else in that laundry list—all can be thought of as forms of signification. This definition resists being forced into either a materialist or idealist box, and thus appeals to those who recoil at Cartesian dualities. This semiotic take on culture should be particularly appealing to archaeologists, as even the most theoretically averse have to admit that at its most basic level, archaeology consists of interpreting signs of the past. Clearly, there is much in this semiotic take on culture that could bear fruit for discussions among social anthropologists and archaeologists, particularly here at Harvard, which is, after all, Peirce's alma mater.

So, what is the use of culture? If nothing else, it gives anthropologists something to argue about. And I don't mean this flippantly. Is culture a product or a process? Is culture a tool of the colonizer, or can it be used to dismantle the master's house? These are questions I'd like to explore some more. The fact that we can still debate the cornerstone of our discipline after more than a century is something anthropology should embrace and celebrate. Or maybe culture isn't the true cornerstone of anthropology after all—arguing about culture is.

Review of *Understanding Cultural Differences: German, French, American*

Christa Uehlinger, PhD

Christa Uehlinger is an intercultural mentor and trainer, who teaches courses on intercultural communication at universities in Switzer-land. Dr. Uehlinger is also an attorney, author, and TedX Speaker and has worked, lived, and travelled in Europe, the US, Australia, and Asia.

Some general observations

I admit, I am a big fan of Hall—the longer I have studied Hall's work, the more of a fan I have become. His work is visionary and applies today even more in these turbulent times. I particularly love his human, holistic, approach based on observations, not on quantitative (survey) research. After all, intercultural communication is being human. Thus, when I was asked to write a comment, I felt honored and promised not only to look carefully at this book, but I also gave myself permission to look beyond.

Edward T. Hall and Mildred Reed Hall's book, *Understanding Cultural Differences: German, French and Americans*, first published in 1990, offers valuable and still valid information—maybe even too much for the busy businessperson who wants a "quick fix." Written over thirty years ago, we need to remind ourselves that the world, and therefore the context, has changed. The authors use a sensitive, inclusive language, with paragraphs dedicated to women in business who often face different challenges than men.

Still, I was touched to realize that from time-to-time their American cultural perspective emerged. For example, regarding German businesses they wrote that the Germans have yet to learn how to overcome their deeply imbedded compartmentalization. My mind went, but that's German culture. Why should they overcome it? Or regarding the hours when shops are open and which close early, the Halls write: "This may be fair to the small store owner, but it is dreadfully inconvenient for all working people who need weekend and evening shopping hours." The American lenses of being able to shop around the clock made itself apparent.

The Germans

A milestone in German history was the fall of the Berlin wall in 1989 and the reunification of Germany in 1990. That was exactly the year this book was published, meaning the book would have been written just prior to that momentous event. Since then, Berlin became reinstated as the capital of a reunified Germany, one of many historical events that had an impact on German culture. Like in all European countries, which are mostly past-oriented, taking the historical context into consideration is important.

The authors point out that when they use the term German, they refer to those West Germans who inhabit industrialized areas of the north. That is an important aspect, even more so as the integration of West and East Germany still today is a matter of debate. Geographically, Germany is the fourth-biggest country in the EU with the largest population. It is interesting that the Halls describe Germany as a relatively small and intimate market in which everyone will know what you are doing. From a European perspective, or should we say a Swiss perspective, the contrary is true.

Both Germany and the US are monochronic cultures. Based on Hall's model, Germany is very high on the monochronic scale. This shows in punctuality, in sticking to plans, and in defined procedures.

As the Halls mention, procedures are spelled out and remain constant. The same applies to decision making. Once a decision is taken, it will not be altered. The American approach of sometimes changing plans or decisions at the last minute is seen as distracting. This applies not only to German culture, but to other Western European cultures, too. From my own experience, this is extremely important, and frequently a cause of friction.

Hierarchy and understanding of one's position are important in German culture, or as the writers put it: "Power is the name of the game in Germany." The use of titles, such as doctoral degrees, are important: they create status and trust. Status is also reflected in how the office looks or where one parks the car. A friend of mine, also Swiss, who was hired as the CFO by a well-known German company operating globally, told me this story about arriving at the company on his first day at work and parking his car close to the entrance. No sooner had he stepped out of the car, the receptionist came up to him and said: "You can't park here. This is the parking space of a member of the board of directors." My friend smiled to himself and parked his car in another spot suitable for a CFO.

Fascinating in this context are the Halls's comments on the symbolism of the door. Germans tend to keep their doors closed. Formality shows in how German address themselves in a business setting, too. They use last names and the formal *"Sie,"* even after many years of cooperation. A German friend recently told me that she thought it was very strange that Swiss people were becoming comfortable using "familiar" terms of address in the business world, and that she could never call her boss by his first name. The Halls underline this, too, saying that they heard many stories of the damage done by American executives calling their German secretary by their first names which is overly familiar and condescending in the context of German culture—still today. Keep in mind, this not only applies to an interaction with a secretary.

Regarding how German relationships are formed, and when is an acquaintance becomes a friend, the authors emphasize how Germans respect each other's privacy to a degree far beyond anything known in the US. It is their observation that it is possible to live in a German neighborhood for years without forming a close relationship with one's neighbor. This might still be true in some neighborhoods, but generally this has also changed. However, it is accurate to say that it takes a while to make friends, not only in Germany, but also in other Western European countries. If you are called a friend after two minutes, as it is sometimes the case in the US, it is very irritating. The authors say: "German friendships are deeper than anything most Americans have known".

This can also be explained by German-American psychologist Kurt Lewin's well known "U-type" and "G-type" comparison. The Americans, U-type, tend to have much more public than private space, segregated into many specific sections, whereas the Germans, G-type, protect their life spaces. It is harder to enter and one needs the other's permission. Public space is relatively small, while the private spaces are large and diffuse. Therefore, Americans perceive Germans as unfriendly and distant, and Germans regard Americans as superficial.

In terms of verbal communication, the Halls state that from a US perspective it takes a while for a German to get to the point. Yes and no. Yes, as Germans love a good *"Streitgespräch,"* meaning that they tend to question, explain, even lecture, and discuss facts and details. It is important to know that this is the case for an intellectual confrontation, rarely usually a personal one. But also, "no" because in certain contexts Germans can be very direct and frank. But it is true, Germans use a lot of words. Sometimes, this can be tiring—for an American who likes to get to the point quickly and thus might stop listening after a few sentences, but admittedly, for many Swiss, too.

The French

By "the French people" Edward and Mildred Hall mean people who live in Paris and Lyon. Paris is the capital and most populous city of

France with around 2.2 million people today. It has been an important metropole for centuries, both nationally and Europe-wide. One can breathe the air of history, arts, fashion, French cuisine, and science when walking through the streets. Lyon is nowadays the third-largest city of France with a population of 516'000. Lyon was historically an important area for the production and the weaving of silk. Also, it played an essential role in the history of cinema: it is here where Auguste and Louis Lumière invented the cinematograph.

Both cities are living history, as the authors put it. "The French live surrounded by thousands of monuments to their glorious past. Every quarter of Paris has its historically important statues, buildings or fountains." No wonder the historical context plays an important role for the French and they relate their actual events to their origins. One must not forget, however, that Paris and Lyon are only two cities, and France is a very diverse country. This diversity can be seen everywhere but above all in the cities, especially in Paris. Thus, to speak of the French with a focus on Lyon and Paris hardly does the entire country justice.

The Halls mention that the French are Latin and describes that they talk and communicate with their whole body. He adds that their faces are very expressive as are their gestures, all of which reflect the intensity of their involvement with each other. That is an interesting point: I would never have thought of the French as expressive, especially not regarding Parisians. From my perspective, Italians and Spaniards are much more expressive. Additionally, one should not forget that in France there is a German speaking minority (Alsace region) and other non-Latin regional languages, as in Breton that has Celtic roots.

The authors point out that the French culture is highly centralized: "French space is a reflection of French culture and French institutions. Everything is centralized, and spatially the entire country is laid out around centers, with Paris as the most important hub." This is true even nowadays. Centralization is key in France. It runs throughout the history of France. It was most pronounced during the reign of the great French kings, when the royal courts flowered. French courts were renowned for their radiating circles of power, and The French tend to see themselves as the cradle of European civilization and Paris as *"la capitale du monde."* Interestingly enough, they share this mindset of being the center of the world with the Americans. The statement *"L'état c'est moi"* (I am the state), which is attributed to the French Sun King Louis XIV, can be seen as an expression of centralization and absolutism. It is deeply engraved in French culture. If, as an outsider, one is confronted with the pride of the French, it is sometimes said with a wink: *"Oh là là, l'état c'est moi."*

Here is an example of centralization in everyday life. I once took a train to Avignon and I had an issue with the ticket. In Avignon, I went to the counter. The woman checked it and said that there was indeed a mistake and that I would get some money back. However, she needed to send it to Paris, and it took nearly two months until I received my money. In this case, all roads lead to Paris.

Centralization can be seen in bureaucracy, but also in management. Most companies have clear vertical and strongly hierarchical structures. Power is perceived as an authority. "There is one person at the top who makes critical decisions." Thus, French executives tend to go right to the top. Hierarchy and status accompany centralization. It is important to *be* someone.

Additionally, the French move in very restricted circles. Still today, French society is clearly divided into classes. There are elites which have access to elite schools. In the last thirty-plus years since the Halls' book was written, it has not been possible to integrate migrants from former colonies into the elite. Everyone moves in his or her circle and these are hardly permeable.

This shows in language, too. The French prefer to speak French, and they speak mostly in French no matter what. As the English aristocracy spoke French, and English was considered a peasant language, to a very traditional French of maybe aristocratic origin, it might be a challenge to lower himself and to express himself in English. Keep also in mind, that at one time French was the language of most of the courts in Europe and the language of diplomacy around the world, and for many this is true even today.

Once, when I worked in a law office, I had to contact a French lawyer. I told him in French what I needed. Since legal language is difficult, it was even more challenging to explain everything in French. I did my best, but every now and then I stumbled. After thirty minutes the lawyer said: *'Vous pouvez parler allemand. Je le comprends.'* (You may speak in German, I can understand). The Halls point out, that for any foreigner who wishes to function effectively in France, the most important skill is to learn to speak the language well. I could not agree more.

Additionally, French are very high context, and in communi-cation they tend to leave some things to the imagination rather than spell out specific details. They will often talk around the point they wish to make, so one must listen very carefully to get the point. However, the French also admire logic and pragmatism as this is the basis of their thinking.

In relation to the French, you first must position and sell yourself. You need to prove that you are acceptable. "There is a need to get to know another person well enough to be able to predict how that person will behave in a variety of circumstances," the authors say. This cultural aspect led to one of my biggest culture shocks. I was working in an office in Lyon for three months and was lowest in the hierarchy. At the beginning, my co-workers hardly spoke to me, and then, only if they needed to. After some time, we had some exchanges in the office, but each evening everyone disappeared. This went on for three months and I felt quite lonely. Only in the very last week, two of my co-workers approached me and said: "You are actually a nice person and a good worker. Let us invite you to a typical French dinner." It was a lovely evening with a good meal. We had fun. Two days later I left.

When I read their chapter on the French, it seemed to me that Edward T. Hall and Mildred Reed Hall had been infected by the *savoir-vivre* of the French. This chapter contains many more specific aspects of everyday life in France: comments on book markets, food, arts and even the Minitel (the world's first electronic telephone directory) is mentioned. I have a faint suspicion that the culture of the country under study also had influenced the researchers.

The Americans

In the section on their own countrymen, one can tell that Edward Hall in particular has written about this culture several times. When both use the term "Americans," they refer to those people whose forebears came to the US from northern Europe, and thus they refer to "American-European culture." From a European perspective, this is too generalized as there is a huge diversity on the European continent, even in northern Europe. They then state that it is much more difficult to generalize about Americans as the variety is far greater than in Germany or France, and the US spans a whole continent. At this point, one has to respectfully disagree. Yes, the US is much bigger, but this doesn't necessarily mean that it is harder to generalize. On the contrary, the more one digs into cultures, the more one recognizes the finer traits. But this process needs time. So, it may well be that Hall has been so deeply involved studying the Americans that it is more difficult to generalize in this context. But I would argue that something similar would be the case when dealing with other cultures, including Germany and France. In addition, it probably generally true that generalizations are more difficult to make about that which is closer to oneself which one knows better. One grows up in a certain environment and is more aware of the subtleties others would miss.

The authors then characterize the Americans as tending to be ethnocentric, in part because of the great size and the economic power of their country. Moreover, there is the deeply rooted belief that "America is the greatest country in the world", even if it is shaken and challenged, as at the end of the Trump administration when this review is written. This is an attitude that the Americans share with the French, although coming from a different angle. Additionally, the dream of being a country of equal opportunities with no defined class system now seems to contradict itself.

The US is a land of paradoxes or as the Halls put it, "Americans suffer from a tendency to dichotomize, to see things as "all black" or "all white" and therefore are "either 'for' or 'against' something, often without fully examining the alternatives." Coming from a culture in which people deal with each other and find compromises, this has always been an irritation to me. If one thinks only in these two categories, hardly any growth and development is possible, the greys are not seen. However, if one would use both sides, ways could arise which are not visible at first sight.

These constant opposites can be confusing to outsiders. In the book this is explained as follows: "There are a number of paradoxes in the American character that puzzle foreigners. For instance, hand in hand with their individualism, is a competing drive to conform. Despite the surface appearance of easy informality, egalitarianism, and great freedom, there are very strong pressures to conform in certain areas of American culture," a theme the authors urge others to be aware of when dealing with Americans.

What Americans share with the French and the Germans is individualism. However, American individualism is much stronger, as the authors put it, "it's every man for himself." Yet, there although there is high individualism, a fast pace, high mobility and a tendency to superficial relationships, Americans want to be liked and accepted, to be a nice guy. On a deeper level, there is an urge to belong. Many

Americans, the Halls write, suffer from an absence of roots. If one does not have a home within, one probably looks for recognition on the outside. One of my most touching moments in the US was when someone told me: "Please tell the people in Europe that despite the president we have [Donald Trump, at that time] we Americans are still nice people."

Americans as well as Germans and French are monochronic, and time is important. The authors state that schedules are sacred and time commitments are taken very seriously. This is something I have read in many books on American culture, but my practical experiences make me think otherwise. For many years, I coached multicultural teams consisting of Americans and Swiss. Each year, deadlines and appointments are a matter of confusion. In meetings, Americans are frequently five or ten minutes late, whereas Swiss tend to be there around 10 minutes before the meeting starts. Swiss are very strict about sticking to deadlines, whereas Americans are handling them more flexibly. In my observation, Americans manage time more adaptably than some European cultures, based on context. It is often a question of urgency. If they understand the importance, Americans keep the deadlines, and if otherwise they do not. This might also tie into the short-term orientation of Americans. In Europe, most cultures are more long-term oriented, although in business, short-term orientation with attention to quarterly results also has taken-hold.

Regarding business, an important aspect to be aware of are the lines of authority. This is something that Europeans underestimate, because at first glance, the interaction between American employees and superiors seems so informal. At second glance, however, hierarchies become apparent. Depending on the organization, they are sometimes even stronger than in certain cultures in Europe such as in Switzerland, the Scandinavian countries, or the Netherlands, but they are hidden. At meetings, some US companies have a clear hierarchy where the employees defer to the boss. I once met a friend for a drink who worked in a well-known American company. Ten minutes before our appointment, he sent me a text message saying he could not leave the office yet because his boss was still there. An hour later he showed up. His boss had now gone home. I could not understand this behavior at all, as to me our friendship was more important than a boss. The Halls confirms this: "Though Americans seem to have a relaxed and informal working environment, it is important to remember that there are rules and regulations—and lines of authority—even though these rules are seldom spelled out. Even if employees call the boss by her or his first name, the boss has plenty of power—and both employer and employees know it."

Another striking difference is the way of thinking. "Let us agree on the principles and work out the details later. In contrast, Europeans first work out the details. Thus, Americans tend to be inductive (from specific instances into a generalized conclusion) whereas Europeans tend to be more deductive (from generalized principles that are known to be true to a true and thus lead to specific conclusions). These two different approaches create many misunderstandings, and even can block cooperation.

In communication, the authors state that Americans prefer directness. However, from a European perspective—or shall I say a Swiss perspective—Americans are sometimes very indirect in expression, especially when it comes to "political correctness," using a euphemism or circumlocution. Then it is sometimes difficult for an outsider to understand what is actually being said. Furthermore, Americans come to the point quickly and express it briefly, which also can be confusing to Europeans who tend to use longer explanations. I learned that emails that are too long are not answered, and that a maximum of 5 lines are read. So, I started to split my longer emails into several separate ones so that I could receive answers to my questions. It worked.

The positive language, positive politeness, that Americans use such as *Wonderful! Great! Awesome!* can be confusing for Europeans and it sounds exaggerated. Also, feedback might not be understood in Europe when Americans tend to use the "Compliment Sandwich," placing the negative comments between two positive comments. Usually in European cultures people just say what they need to say.

When I reread *Understanding Cultural Differences* I was impressed by many cultural descriptions that are still true today, even though the world moved on. It is full of important observations and wise statements. Everybody who has to work with Germans, French, or Americans will find valuable observations in this book and the encouragement to continue to observe the people work with. "Information," E. T. Hall reminded us, "lies in people, not in your head."

Chronological
E. T. Hall Bibliography

Reprinted from: Steve J. Kulich and John C. Condon, "Toward a Comprehensive Bibliography of Edward T. Hall's Works," *Journal of Intercultural Communication & Interactions Research (JIRIC)*, 2(1), 119-134. Used with permission of Steve Kulich, Chief Editor.

Hall, E. T. (2006). Space speaks. *Journal for the Anthropological Study of Human Movement, 14*(1), 1–14. (Originally a 1959 chapter entitled "Space speaks" in *The silent language*, pp. 162–185.)

Hall, E. T., & Hall, M. R. (2001). Key concepts: Underlying structures of culture. In D. C. Thomas (Ed.), *Readings and cases in international management: A cross-cultural perspective* (pp. 151–162). Sage Publications. (Reprint of 2001 chapter in M. H. Albrecht, Ed.) http://www.csun.edu/sm60012/Intercultural/Key%20Concepts%20 -%20Hall%20and%20Hall%20 -%201.pdf

Hall, E. T., & Hall, M. R. (2001). Key concepts: Underlying structures of culture. In M. H. Albrecht (Ed.), *International HRM: Managing diversity in the workplace* (pp. 24–40). Wiley-Blackwell. (Reprinted 2003 in Readings and cases in interna- tional management, and in other readers.) http://www.csun.edu/~sm60012/Inter- cultural/Key%20Concepts%20-%20Hall%20and%20Hall%20-%201.pdf

Hall, E. T. (2000). Context and meaning. In L. A. Samovar & R. E. Porter (Eds.), *Intercultural communication: A reader* (9th ed., pp. 34–43). Wadsworth. (Reprint of 1984 chapter in *The dance of life*, pp. 44–58.)

Hall, E. T. (2000). Monochronic and polychronic time. In L. A. Samovar & R. E. Porter (Eds.), *Intercultural communication: A reader* (9th ed., pp. 280–286). Wadsworth. (Reprint of chapter in 1984 edition. Original a 1976 chapter in *Beyond culture* entitled "Context and meaning.")

Hall, E. T. (1998). Three domains of culture and the triune brain. In S. Niemeier, C. P. Campbell, & R. Dirven (Eds.), *The cultural context in business communication* (pp. 13–30). John Benjamins. https://doi. org/10.1075/z.87.03hal

Hall, E. T. (1995). Your worst nightmare. *Anthropology News, 36*(3), 2. https:// doi. org/10.1111/an.1995.36.3.2.2

Hall, E. T. (1993). *West of the thirties: Discoveries among the Navajo and Hopi.* Doubleday.

Hall, E. T. (1992). *An anthropology of everyday life.* Doubleday.

Hall, E. T. (1992). Improvisation as an acquired, multilevel process. *Ethno-musicology, 36*(2), pp. 223–235. https://doi.org/10.2307/851915; https:// www.jstor.org/ stable/851915

Hall, E. T. (1991). *Introduction.* In H. L. Newbold (Ed.), *Type A/ type B weight loss book* (pp. xvii). Keats Publishing. https://doi. org/10.1007/978-1-349-21652-9_1

Hall, E. T. (1991). Les langages corporels [Body languages]. In C. Garnier (Ed.), *Le corps rassemblé.* Editions Agence D'Arc.

Hall, E. T., & Hall, M. R. (1990). Guide du comportement dans les affaires internatio- nales: Allemagne, Etats-Unis, France [Guidelines for conduct in international affairs: Germany, United States, France]. Editions Du Seuil.

Hall, E. T., & Hall, M. R. (1990). *Understanding cultural differences: Germans, French and Americans.* Intercultural Press.

Hall, E. T. (1990). Foreword. In C. Patterson-Rudolph, *Petroglyphs and Pueblo myths of the Rio Grande* (pp. i–x). Avanyu Publishing. https://doi. org/10.1016/S0950- 3552(05)80208-1

Hall, E. T. (1990). Unstated features of the cultural context of learning. *The Educational Forum, 54*(1), 21–34. (Kappa Delta Pi) https://doi.org/ 10.1080/00131728909335514

Hall, E. T. (1990). On the shoulders of giants: On Socrates, by way of a book review (of I. F. Stone's *The trial of Socrates.* Little-Brown, 1988). *The Educational Forum, 55*(1), 11–16. (Kappa Delta Pi) https://doi. org/10.1080/00131729009339285 (Originally published May 29, 1988, in *Albuquerque Journal*)

Hall, E. T. (1990). *What Makes a Museum? In Expanding the Exploratorium: A Resource Handbook for Thinking about Institutional Growth.* Exploratorium.

Hall, E. T. (1989). Deaf culture, tacit culture, & ethnic relations. *Sign Language Studies, 1065,* 291–304. (#65. Linstok Press.) https://www.semanticscholar. org/paper/Deaf-Culture%2C-Tacit-Culture-%26-Ethnic-Relations-Hall/ 15abf3a15f772144128eb56d273af53ed69f3bbb

Hall, E. T. (1989). A different way of thinking. *Sign Language Studies*, *62*(1), 63–70. DOI: 10.1353/sls.1989.0004

Hall, E. T. (1989, October 30). Review of *The lore of New Mexico* [1988 book by M. Weigle & P. White, The University of New Mexico Press]. *Albuquerque Journal*, *76*, p. 10 Section G.

Hall, E.T. (1989). Proxemics – A complex cultural language. [Institute for Scientific Information] *Current Contents, Arts & Humanities*, *11*(5), 16. (Cross-referenced in *Current Contents/Social & Behavioral Sciences*, *21*(9), 14.)

Hall, E. T. (1989). Foreword. In Y. Ashihara (Ed.), *The hidden order: Tokyo through the twentieth century*. Kodansha International. https://lib.ugent. be/catalog/ rug01:001283440

Hall, E. T. (1989, February 5). Review of *Deaf in America* [1988 book by C. Padden & T. Humphries]. *Albuquerque Journal*, *62*, p. 8 Section G.

Hall, E. T. (1989, April 9). Review of *New world new mind: Moving toward conscious evolution* [1989 book by R. Ornstein & P. Ehrlich, Doubleday]. *Albuquerque Journal*, *66*, p. 8 Section G.

Hall, E. T. (1988). Le contexte: Pierre angulaire de la communication humaine [The Context: Cornerstone of Human Communication]. [Paper presentation, in Colloquium proceedings]. Exposé devant les Facultes de Sciences Economiques, Politiques et Sociales. Université Catholique de Louvain, Belgium.

Hall, E. T. (1988). The hidden dimensions of time and space in today's world. In F. Poyatos (Ed.), *Cross-cultural perspectives in nonverbal communication* (pp. 145–152). C. J. Hogrefe.

Hall, E. T. (1988, Fall). Gus Foster: Clocking in with Einstein. *Artspace: Southwestern Contemporary Arts*, *12*(4).

Hall, E. T. (1988). Foreword. In T. D. Blakely, *Hemba visual communication and space*. University Press of America.

Hall, E. T. (1988, Winter). Cultural differences: An overview. *International House of Japan*, *8*(1). https://www.i-house.or.jp/eng/programs/publications/ bulletin/ bulletin_list_en/

Hall, E. T., & Hall, M. R. (1987). The sounds of silence. In E. Angeloni (Ed.), *Anthro-pology Connecticut* (pp. 79–84). The Dushkin Publishing Group. (Reprint of 1971 *Playboy* interview.) https://mymission.lamission.edu/ userdata/etherism/docs/ Sounds%20of%20Silence(1).pdf

Hall, E. T., & Hall, M. R. (1987). Hidden differences: Doing business with the Japanese. Doubleday.

Hall, E. T., & Hall, M. R. (1987). Overcoming frictions: Japanese-American business. U.S.A. for Japanese (in Japanese) Japan for Americans (in English and Japanese). Bungei Shunju Ltd. Also published and cited as: Hidden differences: Studies in international communication: Japan for Americans. アメリカのビズネス（主な概念；アメリカ文化；アメリカのビズネス；米国における日本のビズネス）　日本のビズネス（主な概念 – 暗号を読み解く；日本人；日本のビズネス；日本におけるアメリカ企業）

Hall, E. T. (1987). The informatics of high and low context systems. In E. R. Caianiello (Ed.), *Physics of cognitive processes* (pp. 185–208). World Scientific Publishing.

Hall, E. T. (1987). Pensieri sullo sviluppo da un punto di vista mondiale [Thoughts on development from a global point of view]. *Labortorio di scienze dell'uomo*, 3–4.

Hall, E. T. (1987). Visual conventions and conventional vision. *El Palacio (Spring issue)*, 11–15.

Hall, E. T., & Hall, M. R. (1986/1977). Nonverbal communication for educators. *Theory Into Practice (Issue Supp1: Educational perspectives, then and now)*, 26, 364–367. (Reprinted from 1977 *Theory into Practice*, 16(3), 141–144). https://doi. org/10.1080/00405848709543300

Hall, E. T., & Hall, M. R. (1986). (Version in Japanese) *Hidden differences: Studies in international communication – How to communicate with Germans.* Mediahouse. (Original work published 1985)

Hall, E. T. (1986). Unstated features of the cultural context of learning. In A. Thomas & E. W. Ploman (Eds.), *Learning and development: A global perspective* (pp. 157–176). The Ontario Institute for Studies in Education. https://doi.org/10.1080/00131728909335514

Hall, E. T. (1986). Prefazione [Foreword]. In G. Quaranta (Ed.), *L' era dello sviluppo [The Era of Development]*. Franco Angeli.

Hall, E. T. (1986). Foreword. In T. Doi (Ed.), *The anatomy of self: The individual versus society* (pp. 7–10). Kodansha International Ltd.

Hall, E. T. (1986). Introduction. In J. Collier & M. Collier (Eds.), *Visual anthropology: Photography as a research method* (rev. ed.) (pp. xiii–xvii). University of New Mexico Press. Hall, E. T. (1986). Informatics and design: Some experiences in finding appropriate data. In R. Westrum (Ed.), *Organizations, designs, and the future*. Eastern Michigan University Press.

Hall, E. T., Hall, M. R. (1985). *Hidden differences: Studies in international communication--How to communicate with Germans.* Gruner & Jahr/Mediahouse. https:// www.worldcat.org/title/1330269298

Hall, E. T., & Hall, M. R. (1985). Verborgene Signale: Studien zur internationalen Kom- munikation – Über den Umgang mit Japanern [Hidden signals: Study on international communication – On interacting with the Japanese]. Gruner & Jahr.

Hall, E. T. (1985). High performers and low profiles. In G. Vitiello (Ed.), *Pegasus on performance.* Mobil Services.

Hall, E. T., & Hall, M. R. (1984). Verborgene Signale: Studien zur internationalen Kom- munikation – Über den Umgang mit Franzosen [Hidden signals: Study on international communication – On interacting with the French]. Stern/Gruner & Jahr.

Hall, E. T., & Hall, M. R. (1984). Une étude de la communication internationale – comment communiquer avec les Allemands [A Study of International Communication – How to Communicate with Germans]. Gruner & Jahr.

Hall, E. T. (1984). Introduction. In M. Matsumoto (Ed.), *Haragei* (pp. 12–16). Kodansha Ltd. https://doi.org/10.1515/9783110868548.5

Hall, E. T. (1983/1984). *The dance of life: The other dimension of time.* Doubleday. (Some chapters like "Monochronic and polychronic time" (pp. 44–58) reprinted often in Readers.)

Hall, E. T., & Hall, M. R. (1983). Verborgene Signale: Studien zur internationalen Kommunikation – Über den Umgang mit Amerikanern [Hidden signals: Study on international communication – On interacting with Americans]. Gruner & Jahr.

Hall, E. T., & Hall, M. R. (1983). Hidden differences: Studies in international communication – How to communicate with Germans. Gruner & Jahr.

Hall, E. T. (1983). Foreword. In B. Plossu & G. Mora (Eds.), *New Mexico revisited* (pp. vii–viii). University of New Mexico Press.

Hall, E. T. (1983). A metastatement on models. In J. B. Calhoun (Ed.), *Environment and population: Problems of adaptation* (pp. 231–233). Praeger.

Hall, E. T. (1981, March). Epistemiologia e cultura: un modello paradigmatico [Episte- miology and culture: A paradigmatic model]. *Laboratorio di scienze dell'uomo.*

Hall, E. T. (1980). Adumbrative behavior in high and low context situations. In S. Corson *et al.* (Eds.), *Ethnology and nonverbal communication in mental health* (pp. 215–220). Pergamon Press.

Hall, E. T. (1980). Information and feedback as alternative to power confronta-
tions at the grassroots. In R. Fitchen (Ed.), *Special Issue: Communication
and Politics. Communication, 5*(2), 183–204. http://pascal-francis.inist.
fr/vibad/index.php?action= getRecordDetail&idt=PASCAL8110111723

Hall, E. T. (1979). Cultural models in transcultural communication. In A.
Wolfgang (Ed.), *Nonverbal behavior: Applications and cultural implications*
(pp. xi–xvii). Academic Press. (Reprinted from 1976 Condon & Saito
(Eds.), *Communicating across cultures for what?*) https://doi.org/10.1016/
B978-0-12-761350-5.50005-7

Hall, E. T. (1979). Proxemics: The study of man's spatial relations. In N. Klein
(Ed.), *Culture, cures, and contagion: Readings for medical social science* (pp.
22–31). Chandler and Sharp. (Reprinted from I. Galdston, *Man's image
in medicine and anthropology*, 1963, pp. 422–445).

Hall, E. T. (1979). Comment: Anthropology of symbolic healing [and
Comments and Reply]. *Current Anthropology, 20*(1), 59–66 (Comments
continue to p. 80.) https:// doi.org/10.1086/202203

Hall, E. T. (1979). Learning the Arabs' silent language. *Psychology Today, 13*(3),
44–52. Hall, E. T. (1979, January). Let's heat people instead of houses.
Human Nature, 2(1), 45–47.

Hall, E. T., & Hall, M. R. (1978). Nonverbal communication for educators:
Everything communicates – If you can read the messages. *The Education
Digest, 43*(6), 33–41. (Reprinted from 1977 *Theory Into Practice, 16*(3),
141–144. https://doi. org/10.1080/00405847709542689

Hall, E. T. (1978). Prospects for improving human relations overseas. In H. F.
Van Zandt (Ed.), *International business prospects: 1977–1999* (pp. 1–12).
Bobbs-Merrill.

Hall, E. T. (1978). Autonomy and dependence in technological environments:
Review and commentary. In B. D. Ruben (Ed.), *Communication yearbook
II* (pp. 23–28). Transaction Books/Annals of the International Commu-
nication Association. https://doi.org/10.1080/23808985.1978.11923714

Hall, E. T., & Hall, M. R. (1977). Nonverbal communication for educators. *Theory Into Practice (Special Issue: Nonverbal), 16*(3), 141–144.
(Reprinted 1978 in *The Education Digest*, and 1986 in *Theory Into Practice* Special issue: Educational perspectives, then and now.) https://doi.
org/10.1080/00405847709542689

Hall, E. T. (1976). Cultural models in transcultural communication. In J. C. Condon & M. Saito (Eds.), *Communicating across cultures for what?* (pp. 89–102). The Simul Press.

Hall, E. T. (1976, July). How cultures collide: Interview with Edward T. Hall. *Psychology Today*, 66–97.

Hall, E. T. (1976). *Beyond culture*. Doubleday.

Hall, E. T. (1976). Environmental communication. In S. Kaplan & R. Kaplan (Eds.), *Manscape: The human environment*. Duxbury Press. (Reprinted from 1971 Esse, *Behavior and environment*, pp. 247–256.) https://doi.org/10.1007/978-1-4684- 1893-4_18

Hall, E. T., & Hall, M. R. (1975). *The fourth dimension in architecture: The impact of building on man's behavior*. The Sunstone Press. https://www.perlego.com/ book/2697340/the-fourth-dimension-in-architecture-the-impact-of-building-on- behavior-pdf

Hall, E. T. (1974). Meeting man's basic spatial needs in artificial environments. In J. Lang, C. Burnette, W. Moleski, & D. Vachon (Eds.), *Designing for human behavior: Architecture and the behavioral sciences* (pp. 210–220). Dowden, Hutchinson & Ross, Inc.

Hall, E. T. (1974). *Handbook for proxemic research*. Society for the Anthropology of Visual Communication. https://www.worldcat.org/title/1314750

Hall, E. T. (1973). Mental health research and out-of-awareness cultural systems. In L. Nader & T. W Maretzi (Eds.), *Cultural illness and health* (pp. 97–103). American Anthropological Association.

Hall, E. T., & Wekerle, G. (1972). High rise living: Can the same design serve both young and old? *Ekistics, 33*(198), 186–191. https://www.jstor.org/stable/43617942

Hall, E. T. (1972). Art, space, and the human experience. In G. Kepes (Ed.), *Arts of the environment* (pp. 52–59). George Braziller.

Hall, E. T. (1972). Architectural implications of the thermal qualities of the human skin. *Ekistics, 33*(198), 352–354. https://www.jstor.org/stable/43619257

Hall, E. T. (1972). Communication and design. *Man-Environment Systems, 2*(2), 109–112. (Reprinted from 1971, Proxemics and design, *Design & Environment*.)

Hall, E. T. (1972). Silent assumptions in social communication. In J. Laver & S. Hutcheson (Eds.), *Communication in face-to-face interaction* (pp.

274–288). Penguin. (Reprinted from 1964 Rioch & Weinstein, *Disorders of communication*, pp. 41–53.)

Hall, E. T., & Hall, M. R. (1971, June). The sounds of silence. *Playboy*, 138–139, 148, 204, 206. (Reprinted in numerous sociology and anthropology texts.)

Hall, E. T. (1971). Proxemics and design. *D+E: Design & Environment*, 2, 24–25. (Reprinted 1972 in *Man-Environment Systems*.) https://eric. ed.gov/?id=EJ052960

Hall, E. T. (1971). Environmental communication. In A. H. Esse (Ed.), *Behavior and environment: The use of space by animals and men* (Paper presented in 1968) (pp. 247–256). Plenum Press. https://doi. org/10.1007/978-1-4684-1893-4_18

Hall, E. T. (1971). The paradox of culture. In B. Landis & E. S. Tauber (Eds.), *In the name of life* (pp. 218–235). Holt, Rinehart, & Winston. Erich Fromm Document Center download available via Google link through https://opus4.kobv.de/opus4- Fromm/frontdoor/index/index/year/2012/ docId/11372

Hall, E. T. (1971). The influence of space on teacher-student relations. In L. C. Deighton (Ed.), *Encyclopedia of education* (3rd ed.). MacMillan/Free Press. https://www. worldcat.org/title/encyclopedia-of-education/oclc/157490

Hall, E. T. (1970). The anthropology of space: An organizing model. In H. M. Proshansky, W. H. Ittelson, & L. G. Rivlin (Eds.), *Environmental psychology: Man and his physical setting*. Holt, Reinhart, and Winston, Inc.

Hall, E. T. (1970). To each his own: The manpower potential in our ethnic groups. *Bridge: A Center for the Advancement of Intercultural Studies, Occasional Paper No.7*. U.S. Department of Labor, October. (Reprinted from 1967, *Employment Service Review*, 4(10), 24–29.)

Hall, E. T. (1969). Book review of R. G. Barker (1968), *Ecological psychology: Concepts and methods for studying the environment of human behavior*, Stanford University Press. *American Anthropologist*, 71(6), 1184–1186. https://doi.org/10.1525/ aa.1969.71.6.02a00440

Hall, E. T., & Hall, M. R. (1969). The language of personal space. *House & Garden*, 135(4), 108–157. https://doi.org/10.2307/1797332

Hall, E. T. (1969). On proxemic research (Reply to O. M. Watson, Discussion and Criticism section). *Current Anthropology*, 10(2/3), 224. Watson (pp. 222–223): https:// www.journals.uchicago.edu/doi/10.1086/201075; Hall's Reply: https://www. journals.uchicago.edu/doi/10.1086/201076

Hall, E. T. (1969, June 5, 19, 20). *Psychological aspects of foreign policy*. Hearings before the Committee on Foreign Relations, United States Senate, Ninety-first Congress, First Session (pp. 2–43). U.S. Government Printing Office. https://catalog.libraries. psu.edu/catalog/9953252

Hall, E. T. (1969). Listening behavior: Some cultural differences. *Phi Delta Kappan, 50*, 379–380. (Reprinted in numerous in educational development and language arts texts)

Hall, E. T. (1968). Seeing and believing. *Architectural Review, 144*, 117–118.

Hall, E. T. (1968). Proxemics [with Comments and Replies]. *Current Anthropology, 9*(2/3), 83–108. (Reprinted in numerous anthropology and sociology texts) https:// doi.org/10.1086/200975 This special Issue includes Editor-recruited Comments by R. L. Birdwhistell, B. Bock, P. Bohannan, A. R. Diebold, Jr., M. Durbin, M. S. Edmon- son, J. L. Fischer, D. Hymes, S. T. Kimball, W. La Barre, F. Lynch, S. J., J. E. McClellan, D. S. Marshall, G. B. Milner, H. B. Sarles, G. L Trager, and A. P. Vayda. https://www. jstor.org/stable/2740724

Hall, E. T. (1968). Human needs and inhuman cities. In Smithsonian Annals II, *The fitness of man's environment* (pp. 161–172). Smithsonian Institution Press. (Reprinted in several other sources such as 1969, *Ekistics*, 181–185.) https://www.worldcat. org/title/fitness-of-mans-environment/oclc/261655

Hall, E. T. (1967). Quality in architecture: An anthropological view. *AAUW Journal, 60*, 164–166. (Reprinted from 1963, *Journal of the American Institute of Architects, 40*, 44–48.)

Hall, E. T. (1967). To each his own: The manpower potential in our ethnic groups. *Employment Service Review, 4*(10), 24–29. (Reprinted 1970 in *Bridge, Occasional Paper*, No. 7.) https://eric.ed.gov/?id=ED017584

Hall, E. T. (1966). *The hidden dimension*. Doubleday.

Hall, E. T. (1966). Proxemic theory. *Theory of Communication*, 60–67. (Though cited as a Hall original, this is a summary by N. Brown in *CSISS Classics*, uploaded online 2001.) https://escholarship.org/uc/item/4774h1rm#main

Hall, E. T. (1966, September). The anthropology of space. *Architectural Review*, 163– 166.

Hall, E. T. (1966, September). What's too close for comfort. *University of Denver Magazine*.

Hall, E. T. (1965). Territorial needs and limits. *Natural History, 74*(10), 12–19. (Re-printed in several architectural and natural history texts.)

Hall, E. T. (1965). Human adaptability to high density. *Ekistics, 20*(119), 191.

Hall, E. T. (1965). Mechanical and mathematical models. *Ekistics, 20*(119), 206.

Hall, E. T. (1965). Orientation and training in government for work overseas. In D. M. Valdes & D. G. Dean (Eds.), *Sociology in use: Selected readings for the introductory course*. Macmillan. (Reprinted from 1956, *Human Organization, 15*(1), 4–10.) https://doi.org/10.17730/humo.15.1.5183h221g5524x06

Hall, E. T. (1965, July-August). Human behavior and building: An anthropologist's view. *Building Research*.

Hall, E. T. (1964). Adumbration as a feature of intercultural communication [Special issue on: The ethnography of communication]. American Anthropologist, 66(6), 154–163. (Reprinted often.) https://doi.org/10.1525/aa.1964.66.suppl_3.02a00110

Hall, E. T. (1964). What the underdeveloped countries do not want. In G. Hambidge (Ed.), *Dynamics of development: An international reader* (pp. 369–374). Fredrick A. Praeger Press. (Reprinted from 1959 *International Development Review, 1*, 31–36.).

Hall, E. T. (1964). Communication: theoretical and biological studies. Silent assumptions in social communication (paper presented in 1962). In D. M. Rioch & E. A. Wein- stein (Eds.), *Disorders of communication: Proceedings of the Association for Research in Nervous and Mental Disease, 42* (pp. 41–55). Williams and Wilkins. https://pubmed. ncbi.nlm.nih.gov/14265467/ (Reprinted 1972 in Laver & Hutchenson, *Communication in face-to-face interaction.*) https://europepmc.org/article/med/14265467

Hall, E. T. (1963). Man and space: Each controls the other. *The Charette (Pennsylvania Journal of Architecture), 43*(12), 6–9.

Hall, E. T. (1963). A system for the notation of proxemic behavior. *American Anthropologist, 65*(5), 1003–1026. (Reprinted often.) https://doi.org/10.1525/ aa.1963.65.5.02a00020

Hall, E. T. (1963). Quality in architecture: An anthropological view. *Journal of the American Institute of Architects, 40*, 44–48. (Reprinted 1967 in *AAUW Journal.*)

Hall, E. T. (1963). Proxemics: The study of man's spatial relations. In I. Galdston (Ed.), *Man's image in medicine and anthropology (paper presented at 1961 Arden House Conference on Medicine and Anthropology)* (pp. 422–445). International University Press. (Reprinted 1979 in N. Klein, *Culture, cures, and contagion*, pp. 22–31.)

Hall, E. T. (1963). Training and selection. In M. Torre (Ed.), *The selection of personnel for international service [Grant]* (pp. 37–42). The World Federation for Mental Health,

U.S. Committee, Inc. H. Wolff/Canada: National Department of Health and Welfare. Hall, E. T. (1963). Quality in architecture: An anthropological view. *Journal of the American Institute of Architects, 40,* 44–48.

Hall, E. T. (1962). The madding crowd: Space and its organization as a factor in mental health. *Landscape, 12*(1), 26–29.

Hall, E. T. (1962). Sensitivity and empathy at home and abroad: Three Leatherbee lectures.

Harvard University, Graduate School of Business Administration.

Hall, E. T. (1962). Our silent language – "Ocultos" speak louder than words. *Americas, 14*(2), 5–8. (Reprinted in numerous communications and human relations texts.)

Hall, E. T. (1961). The language of space. *Journal of the American Institute of Architects, 35,* 71–75. (Reprinted 1960 from *Landscape, 10*(1), 41–45.)

Hall, E. T., & Whyte, W. F. (1960). Intercultural communication: A guide to men of action. *Human Organization, 19*(1), 5–12. (Reprinted in numerous sociology and anthropology texts. Also in 1963 *Practical Anthropology, 5,* 216–232, and 1967 in *Transcultural Nursing,* 44–62.) https://doi.org/10.1002/tie.5060020407

Hall, E. T. (1960). The language of space. *Landscape, 10*(1), 41–45. (Reprinted 1961 in *Journal of the American Institute of Architects.*)

Hall, E. T. (1960). The silent language in overseas business. *Harvard Business Review, 38*(3), 87–96. https://hbr.org/1960/05/the-silent-language-in-overseas-business

Hall, E. T. (1960). Linguistic models in the analysis of culture [Conference session for Anthropology and African Studies]. In W. M. Austin (Ed.), *Report of the ninth annual roundtable meeting on linguistics and language study* (pp. 157–158). Georgetown University Publications.

Hall, E. T. (1960). A microcultural analysis of time. In A. F. C. Wallace (Ed.), *Men and cultures: Selected papers of the fifth international congress of anthropological and ethnological sciences, 1956* (pp. 118–122). University of Pennsylvania Press. https://doi.org/10.9783/9781512819526-021

Hall, E. T. (1959). *The silent language.* Doubleday.

Hall, E. T. (1959). What the underdeveloped countries do not want. *International Development Review, 1*(1), 31–36. (Reprinted 1964 in G. Hambidge, *Dynamics of development.*)

Hall, E. T., & Oberg, K. (1957). Things to know about culture. *Community Development Review, 7,* 1–4. (International Cooperation Administration: Community Development Division, Office of Public Services.) (Reprinted in 1958 *Ekistics 5*(31), 206–208.) https://www.jstor.org/stable/43613219

Hall, E. T. (1957). Orientation and training in government for work overseas. *Human Organization, 15*(1), 4–10. https://www.jstor.org/stable/44124385 (Reprinted in 1963 Valdes & Dean, *Applied sociology.*)

Hall, E. T. (1956). Orientation and training in government for work overseas. *Human Organization, 15*(1), 4–10. https://doi.org/10.17730/humo.15.1.5183h221g5524x06

Hall, E. T. (1955). The anthropology of manners. *Scientific American, 192*(4), 85–89. https://doi.org/10.1038/scientificamerican0455-84

Trager, G. L., & Hall, E. T. (1954). Culture and communication: A model and an analysis. Explorations: Studies in Communication and Culture (University of Toronto), 3, 137–149.

Hall, E. T., Jr., & Trager, G. L. (1953). *The analysis of culture.* American Council of Learned Societies. https://eric.ed.gov/?id=ED035325

Hall, E. T., & Trager, G. L. (1953). *Human nature at home and abroad.* Foreign Service Institute, Department of State.

Hall, E. T. (1952). *The process of change.* Foreign Service Institute, Department of State. https://www.afsa.org/sites/default/files/fsj-1952-09-september_0.pdf

Hall, E. T., Jr. (1951). Southwestern dated ruins. VI. *Tree-Ring Bulletin, 17*(4), 26–28. https://repository.arizona.edu/handle/10150/255373

Hall, E. T. (1950). Military government on Truk. *Human Organization, 9,* 25–30. https://doi.org/10.17730/humo.9.2.y3355n46jnr616t3

Hall, E. T., Jr. (1950). Ceramic traits and what they indicate as to the nature of culture contact between the Anasazi and Mogollon. In E. K. Reed & D. S. King (Eds.), *For the Dean: Essays in anthropology in honor of Byron Cummings on his eighty-ninth birthday, September 20, 1950 (Chapter 5).* Hohokam Museums Association and Southwest Monuments Association. https://www.jstor.org/stable/664773

Hall, E. T. (1949). The Freudian error as an aid in determining attitudes. *International Journal of Opinion and Attitude Research, 3,* 115.

Hall, E. T. (1949). Race prejudice and negro-white relations in the army. *American Journal of Sociology, 52*(5), 401–409. https://doi.org/10.1086/220032

Hall, E. T., & Pelzer, K. J. (1947/1964). *The economy of the Truk Islands: An anthropological and economic survey.* U.S. Commercial Company Economic Survey of Micronesia. (Field work conducted in Chuuk, March, 1946, included 1964 in New Haven, CN: Yale HRAF files, OR19,17.) http://library.comfsm.fm/webopac/titleinfo?k1=672156&k2=55183

Hall, E. T. (1944). Recent clues to Athapascan prehistory in the Southwest. *American Anthropologist, 46*(1), 98–105. https://doi.org/10.1525/aa.1944.46.1.02a00070

Hall, E. T. (1944). Stone artifacts (pp. 47–52), Dendrochronology (pp. 83–84). In Early stockaded settlements in the Governador New Mexico: A marginal Anasazi development from Basket Maker III to Pueblo I Times. Columbia Studies in Archaeology and Ethnology, Vol. 2. Columbia University Press. https://doi.org/10.7312/hall90930 Hall, E. T. (1942). Notes on preserving and surfacing rotted wood and charcoal. Tree-Ring Bulletin, 12(4), 26–27.

Hall, E. T. (1942). Archaeological survey of Walhalla Glades (Bulletin 20, Museum of Northern Arizona). Northern Arizona Society of Science and Art. http://hdl.han-dle.net/10150/551705

Hall, E. T. (1939). The need for a dendrochronologist as an active member of field expeditions. *American Antiquities, 4*(2), 60.

Hall, E. T. (1939). A method of obtaining a plane surface on charcoal. *Tree-Ring Bulletin, 5*(4), 31. https://repository.arizona.edu/handle/10150/254878

Hall, E. T. (1935). Rainbow Bridge-Monument Valley expedition 1935 report on: An archaeological survey of the Main Tsegi. From the mouth of Betatakin Wash to two miles north of Peach Orchard Spring. *Preliminary bulletins: Archaeological series, No. 3.* National Youth Administration. https://oac.cdlib.org/findaid/ark:/13030/ kt3d5nc397/entire_text/

Bibliography

Allport, Gordon. *The Nature of Prejudice.* New York: Henry Holt, 1954.

Arcos, Patricia Bibiana. "Space and Organizational Communication: A Visual Ethnography of the Restaurant 'The Shed' in Santa Fe, New Mexico." MA thesis, University of New Mexico, 2005.

Azar, Beth, "This is Your Brain on Culture," *Psychology Today*, August 31, 2010, 44.

Bargh, John. *Before You Know It.* New York: Simon and Schuster, 2017.

Barrett, Lisa F. *How Emotions are Made.* New York: Houghton Mifflin Harcourt, 2017.

Basso, Keith H. *Portraits of "the Whiteman": Linguistic Play and Cultural Symbols among the Western Apache.* Cambridge: Cambridge University Press, 1979.

Basso, Keith H. *Wisdom Sits in Places.* Albuquerque, New Mexico: University of New Mexico Press, 1996.

Bateson, Mary Catherine. *Composing a Life.* New York: Harper-Collins, 1991.

Bateson, Mary Catherine. "Improvisation in a Persian Garden." *Peripheral Visions: Learning Along the Way.* New York: Harper/Collins, 1994, 1-14.

Bateson, Mary Catherine. *Peripheral Visions: Learning Along the Way.* New York: Harper-Collins, 1994.

Berger, John. *About Looking.* New York: Vintage, 1992.

Berger, John. *Ways of Seeing.* Harmondsworth, England: Pelican Books, 1972.

Bernstein, Basil. *Class, Codes and Control: Theoretical Studies Towards a Sociology of Language.* New York: Shocken Books, 1975.

Bernstein, Basil. "A Sociolinguistic Approach to Social Learning," in *Class, Codes and Control: Theoretical Studies Towards a Sociology of Language.* New York: Schocken Books, 1971.

Bingmann, Melissa. *Prep School Cowboys: Ranch Schools in the American West.* Albuquerque: University of New Mexico Press, 2015.

Bird, Kai, and Martin Sherwin. *American Prometheus: The Triumph and Tragedy of J. Robert Oppenheimer.* New York: Vintage Books, 2006.

Birdwhistell, Ray L. *Kinesics and Context: Essays on Body Motion Communication.* Philadelphia: University of Pennsylvania Press, 1970.

Bloch, L. R. "Who's Afraid of Being a Freier? The Analysis of Communication through a Key Cultural Frame," *Communication Theory*, May 2003, 13 (2), 125-129.

Bloom, Paul. "Being in Time: How Much Should We Value the Past, the Present, the Future?" *The New Yorker*, July 9, 2021.

Bohannan, Paul, and Mark Glazer, eds., *High Points in Anthropology.* New York: Alfred Knopf, 1973.

Brizendine, Louann. *The Female Brain.* New York: Broadway Books, 2006.

Bruneau, Thomas. "The Time Dimension in Intercultural Communication," *Communication Yearbook 3*, Dan Nimo, ed. New Brunswick, NJ: Transaction Books, 1979.

Bruner, Jerome. *Acts of Meaning.* Cambridge, MA: Harvard University Press, 1990.

Buck, Elizabeth. "English in the Linguistic Transformation of Hawaii: Literacy, Languages, and Discourse," *World Englishes*, 1986, Vol. 5, 2/3, 141-152.

Buck, Elizabeth. *Paradise Remade: The Politics of Culture and History in Hawai'i.* Philadelphia: Temple University Press, 1993.

Burke, Kenneth. *Language as Symbolic Action: Essays on Life, Literature and Method.* Berkeley: University of California Press, 1969.

Carpenter, Edmund. *Oh, What a Blow That Phantom Gave Me!* New York: Holt, Rinehart and Winston, 1973.

Carpenter, Edmund, and Ken Heyman. *They Became What They Beheld.* New York: Ballantine Books/E. P. Dutton, 1970.

Carpenter, Edmund, and Marshall McLuhan, eds. *Explorations in Communication.* Boston, Massachusetts: Beacon Press, 1960.

Carr, Nicolas. *The Shallows: What the Internet is Doing to Our Brains.* New York: W. W. Norton, 2010.

Casey, Mary E., and Shannon Murphy Robinson. *Neuroscience of Inclusion: New Skills for New Times.* Parker, Colorado: Outskirts Press, 2017.

Chapa Cortés, Claudia. "*El service learning internacional como experiencia de transformación en comunidades locales.*" (International service learning as a transformative experience for local communities.) PhD diss., Universidad Marista de Mérida, 2020.

Chapa Cortés, Claudia. "What the Community Learns: International Service-Learning in Yucatán, México." *International Journal of Research on Service-Learning and Community Engagement*. (2019). https://doi.org/10.37333/001c.11493.

Classen, Constance. *The Book of Touch*. Oxfordshire, England: Routledge, 2005.

Classen, Constance. *The Deepest Sense*. Champaign, Illinois: University of Illinois Press, 2012.

Condon, John. "E. T. Hall." In *The Sage Encyclopedia of Intercultural Competence 1*, edited by Janet Bennett, 373-377. Thousand Oaks, California: Sage Publications, 2015.

Condon, John. "Value Dimensions: Kluckhohn and Strodtbeck Value Orientations." In *The Sage Encyclopedia of Intercultural Competence 2*, edited by Janet Bennett, 846-851. Thousand Oaks, California: Sage Publications, 2015.

Condon, John. *With Respect to the Japanese*. Yarmouth, Maine: Intercultural Press, 1984.

Condon, John, and Keisuke Kurata. *In Search of What's Japanese about Japan*. Tokyo: Shufunotomo, 1975.

Condon, John, and Bruce La Brack. "Culture." In *The Sage Encyclopedia of Intercultural Competence 1*, edited by Janet Bennett, 191-195. Thousand Oaks, California: Sage Publications, 2015.

Condon, John, and Tomoko Masumoto. *With Respect to the Japanese II: Going to Work in Japan*. Boston: Intercultural Press, 2011.

Condon, John, and Mitsuko Saito, eds. *Communicating Across Cultures for What? A Symposium on Human Responsibility in Intercultural Communication*. Tokyo: Simul Press, 1976.

Condon, John, and Mitsuko Saito, eds. *Intercultural Encounters with Japan: Communication—Contact and Conflict*. Tokyo: Simul Press, 1974.

Cornell, Ann Weiser. *The Radical Acceptance of Everything: Living a Focusing Life*. Berkeley: Caluna Press, 2005.

Csikszentmihalyi, Mihaly. *Flow: The Psychology of Optimal Experience*. New York: Harper Perennial, 2008.

Cytowic, Richard E. *Synesthesia*. Cambridge, Massachusetts: MIT Press, 2018.

Dale, Edgar. "Clear Only If Known," *ETC.*, XV Summer (1958), 290-293.

Damasio, Antonio. *Feeling and Knowing: Making Minds Conscious*. New York: Vintage Books, 2021.

Damasio, Antonio. *The Strange Order of Things: Life, Feeling, and the Making of Cultures*. New York: Pantheon, 2018.

Davidson, Richard J., and Sharon Begley. *The Emotional Life of Your Brain*. New York: Penguin, 2013.

Deloria, Jr., Vine, and Daniel R. Wildcat. *Power and Place: Indian Education in America*. Golden, CO: Fulcrum Resources, 2001.

Dettering, Richard. "Toward A Psycho-Logics of Human Behavior," *ETC: A Review of General Semantics* Vol. 15, No. 3 (Spring 1958), Institute of General Semantics.

Didion, Joan. *The White Album*. New York: Simon & Schuster, 1979.

Doidge, Norman. *The Brain that Changes Itself*. New York: Penguin, 2007.

Duan, Wen. "Understanding the Challenges of Sharing Humor Across Linguistic and Cultural Boundaries." PhD diss., Cornell University, 2022.

DuBois, G. J., L. B. Potts, and S. J. Kulich. "IC Scholars before Their Time: Rachel Davis-Dubois and the IC Education Movement." In *China Intercultural Communication Annual*, Vol. 2, edited by S. J. Kulich and A. S. English, 54-79. Beijing, China: China Social Sciences Publishing House, 2017.

Edelman, Marcia Warren. "Moving between Identities: Embodied Code-switching," in C. Caldwell & L. B. Leighton, eds., *Oppression and the Body: Roots, Resistance, and Resolutions*, 181-284, North Atlantic Books, 2018.

Epstein, Rebecca, Jamilia J. Blake, and Thalia González. "Girlhood Interrupted: The Erasure of Black Girls' Childhood," https://www.law.georgetown.edu/poverty-inequality-center/wp-content/uploads/sites/14/2017/08/girlhood-interrupted.pdf/

Falassi, Alessandro, ed. *Time Out of Time: Essays on the Festival*. Albuquerque: University of New Mexico Press, 1987.

Fernández-Armesto, F. *A Foot in the River: Why Our Lives Change—and the Limits of Evolution*. Oxford, UK: Oxford University Press, 2015.

Fisher, Walter. *Human Communication as Narration: Toward a Philosophy of Reason, Value, and Action*. Columbia, South Carolina: University of South Carolina Press, 1989

Fuller, Buckminster, with Jerome Angel and Quentin Fiore. *I Seem to Be a Verb*. New York: Bantam Books, 1970.

Galdos, Laia Jorba, and Marcia Warren, "The Body as Cultural Home: Exploring, Embodying, and Navigating the Complexities of Multiple

Identities." *Body, Movement and Dance in Psychotherapy: An International Journal for Theory, Research and Practice* 17:1, 2022.

Galeano, Eduardo, and Mark Fried, trans. *Voices of Time: A Life in Stories.* New York: Picador, 2006.

Gardner, Howard. *Frames of Mind: The Theory of Multiple Intelligences.* New York: Basic Books, 1983.

Gardner, Howard. *Intelligence Reframed.* New York: Basic Books, 1999.

Geertz, Clifford. *Local Knowledge: Further Essays in Interpretive Anthropology.* New York: Basic Books, 2008.

Gill, Satinder. "Rhythmic Synchrony and Mediated Interaction: Towards A Framework of Rhythm in Embodied Interaction." *AI & Society, Journal for Knowledge, Culture and Communication* 27, no. 1 (February 2012).

Gilliam, Walter S., Angela N. Maupin, Chin R. Reyes, Maria Accavitti, and Frederick Shic. "Do Early Educators' Implicit Biases Regarding Sex and Race Relate to Behavior Expectations and Recommendations of Preschool Expulsions and Suspensions?" Yale University Child Study Center, (September 28, 2016).

Glenn, Edmund S., and Christine G. Glenn. *Man and Mankind: Conflict and Communication Between Cultures.* Norwood, New Jersey: Ablex Publishing, 1981.

Goddard, Cliff, and Anna Wierzbicka. "Key Words, Culture and Cognition." *Philosophica* 55 (1995, 1).

Goff, Phillip Atiba, Matthew Christian Jackson, Brooke Allison, Lewis Di Leone, Carmen Marie Culotta, and Natalie Ann DiTomasso. "The Essence of Innocence: Consequences of Dehumanizing Black Children." *Journal of Personality and Social Psychology*, published online February 24, 2014.

Goffman, Erving. *The Presentation of Self in Everyday Life.* New York: Anchor Books/Doubleday, 1959.

Gómez, Myrriah. *Nuclear Nuevo México: Colonialism and the Effects of the Nuclear Industrial Complex.* Tucson: University of Arizona Press, 2023.

Gopnik, Adam. "Feel Me: What the New Science of Touch Says about Ourselves." *The New Yorker,* May 16, 2016.

Goswami, Usha. "Language Acquisition and speech Rhythm Patterns: An Auditory Neuroscience Perspective." *Royal Society Open Science* 9, no. 7 (July 27, 2022).

Grandin, Temple, and Catherine Johnson. *Animals in Translation: Using the Mysteries of Autism to Decode Animal Behavior.* New York: Harcourt, 2005.

Hall, Edward T. *An Anthropology of Everyday Life: An Autobiography.* New York: Doubleday, 1992.

Hall, Edward T. *Beyond Culture.* New York: Doubleday, 1976.

Hall, Edward T. "Cultural Models in Transcultural Communication." In *Communication Across Cultures for What? A Symposium on Humane Responsibility in Intercultural Communication,* edited by John Condon and Mitsuko Saito, 89-102. Tokyo: Simul Press, 1976.

Hall, Edward T. *The Dance of Life: The Other Dimension of Time.* New York: Anchor Books, 1984.

Hall, Edward T. "The Drive to Learn." *Santa Fe Magazine,* Spring, 1988.

Hall, Edward T. *Handbook for Proxemic Research: Studies in the Anthropology of Visual Communication.* Society for the Anthropology for Visual Communication, 1974.

Hall, Edward T. *The Hidden Dimension.* New York: Doubleday, 1966.

Hall, Edward T. "Race, Prejudice, and Negro-White Relations in the Army," *American Journal of Sociology* LII, no. 5 (March 1947): 401-409.

Hall, Edward T. *The Silent Language.* New York: Doubleday, 1959.

Hall, Edward T. "Visual Conventions and Conventional Vision." In *Poetics of Space*, edited by Steve Yates. Albuquerque: University of New Mexico Press, 1995.

Hall, Edward T. *West of the Thirties: Discoveries among the Navajo and Hopi.* New York: Doubleday, 1993.

Hall, Mildred Reed, and Edward T. Hall. *The Fourth Dimension in Architecture: The Impact of Building on Man's Behavior.* Santa Fe, NM: Sunstone Press, 1975.

Hall, Edward T., and Mildred Reed Hall. *Guide du comportement dans les affaires internationales: Allemagne, Etats-Unis, France [Guidelines for conduct in international affairs: Germany, United States, France].* Editions Du Seuil, 1990.

Hall, Edward T., and Mildred Reed Hall. *Une étude de la communication internationale – comment communiquer avec les Allemands [A Study of International Communication – How to Communicate with Germans].* Gruner & Jahr, 1984.

Hall, Edward T., and Mildred Reed Hall. *Verborgene Signale: Studien zur internationalen Kommunikation – Über den Umgang mit Amerikanern [Hidden signals: Study on international communication – On interacting with Americans].* Gruner & Jahr, 1983.

Hall, Edward T., and Mildred Reed Hall. *Verborgene Signale: Studien zur internationalen Kommunikation – Über den Umgang mit Franzosen [Hidden signals: Study on international communication – On interacting with the French]*. Stern/Gruner & Jahr, 1984.

Harris, Richard. "The Cultural Perception of Space: Expanding the Legacy of Edward T. Hall." *Journal of Intercultural Communication & Interactions Research* 2 (1), 2022, 135-150.

Harris, Richard. *Paradise: A Cultural Guide*. London: Eastern University Press, 1996.

Harrison, Roger, and Richard Hopkins. "The Design of Cross-Cultural Training: An Alternative to the University Model." *The Journal of Applied Behavioral Science* 3, no. 4 (December 1967).

Hayashi, A. M. "When to Trust Your Gut." *Harvard Business Review* 79(2), March 2001, 58-65.

Hirsch, Jr., E. D. *Cultural Literacy: What Every American Needs to Know*. New York: Vintage, 1988.

Hofer, M. K., H. K. Collins, A. V. Whillans, and F. S. Chen. "Olfactory Cues from Romantic Partners and Strangers Influence Women's Responses to Stress." *Journal of Personality and Social Psychology,* 114(1), (2018): 1–9.

Hoffman, Kelly M., Sophie Trawalter, Jordan R. Axt, and M. Norman Oliver. "Racial Bias in Pain Assessment and Treatment Recommendations, and False Beliefs about Biological Differences between Blacks and Whites." *Proceedings of the National Academy of Sciences of the United States of America* (April 19, 2016), 113 (16) 4296-4301.

Hofstede, Geert. *Culture's Consequences: International Differences in Work-Related Values*. Thousand Oaks, California: SAGE Publications, 1984.

Holl, Steven, Juhani Pallasman, and Alberto Pérez-Gómez. *Questions of Perception: Phenomenology of Architecture*. Tokyo: Architecture and Urbanism, 1994.

Jackson, John Brinckerhoff. *Discovering the Vernacular Landscape*. New Haven and London: Yale University Press, 1984.

Jarvis, Brooke. "What Can COVID-19 Teach Us About the Mysteries of Smell?" *The New York Times,* Jan 28, 2021.

Jenks, Chris. *Culture*. London and New York: Routledge, 1993.

Jennings, Francis. *The Invasion of America: Indians, Colonialism, and the Cant of Conquest*. New York: W. W. Norton, 1976.

Johnson, Steven. *Mind Wide Open: Your Brain and the Neuroscience of Everyday Life*. New York: Scribner, 2004.

Jones, Lynette A. *Haptics*. Cambridge, Massachusetts: MIT Press, 2018.

Khazan, Olga. "Why Americans Smile So Much." *The Atlantic,* May 3, 2017.

Kluckhohn, Florence, and Fred Strodtbeck. *Variations in Value Orientations*. Evanston, IL: Row, Peterson, 1961.

Kochman, Thomas. *Black and White Styles in Conflict*. Chicago: University of Chicago Press, 1981.

Kochman, Thomas, and Jean Mavrelis. *Corporate Tribalism: White Men/White Women and Cultural Diversity at Work*. Chicago: University of Chicago Press, 2009.

Koestler, Arthur. *The Act of Creation*. New York: Macmillan, 1964.

Kroeber, A. L. and Clyde Kluckhohn. *Culture: A Critical Review of Concepts and Definitions*. Cambridge: Peabody Museum Press, 1952.

Kulich, S. J. "Reviewing Intercultural Study Roots: From Reviving Histories Toward Reassessing the Status of the Field (Section 1 Intro)." In *China Intercultural Communication Annual, Vol. 2*, edited by S. J. Kulich and A. S. English, 33-53. Beijing, China: China Social Sciences Publishing House, 2017.

Kulich, Seven J., and John C. Condon. "Toward a Comprehensive Bibliography of Edward T. Hall's Works." *Journal of Intercultural Communication & Interactions Research* 2, no. 1 (2023): 119-134(16)

Kulich, S. J., L. P. Weng, R. T. Tong, and G. DuBois. "Interdisciplinary History of Intercultural Communication Studies: From Roots to Research and Praxis." In *Cambridge Handbook of Intercultural Training*, 4th ed., edited by D. Landis and D. P. S. Bhawuk, 60-163. London, UK: Cambridge University Press, 2020.

Lakoff, George. *Women, Fire, and Dangerous Things: What Categories Reveal about the Mind*. Chicago: University of Chicago Press, 1987.

Lee, Dorothy. *Freedom and Culture*. Englewood Cliffs, NJ: Prentice-Hall, 1959.

Leeds-Hurwitz, Wendy. "Notes on the History of Intercultural Communication: The Foreign Service Institute and the Mandate for Intercultural Communication Training." *Quarterly Journal of Speech* 76, no. 3 (August 1990): 262-281.

Lefebvre, Henri. *Space, Time and Everyday Life*. London: Blackwell, 2004.

Leki, R., and S. J. Kulich. "Conceptualization of Culture for Intercultural Communication Training: A Classic Interview with Edward T. Hall."

Journal of Intercultural Communication & Interactions Research (JIRIC) 2, no. 1 (2022): 101-118. https://doi.org/10.3726/jicir.2022.1.0006

Levine, Robert A., and Donald T. Campbell. *Ethnocentrism: Theories of Conflict, Ethnic Attitudes, and Group Behavior.* New York: John Wiley and Sons, 1972.

Levinson, Paul. "Five Views of St. Marshall." *Wired*, July/August, 1993.

Levitin, Daniel J. *This is Your Brain on Music: The Science of a Human Obsession.* New York: Penguin, 2006.

Levitin, Daniel J. *The World in Six Songs: How the Musical Brain Created Human Nature.* New York: Plume, 2009.

Liebmann, Matthew. *Revolt: An Archaeological History of Pueblo Resistance and Revitalization in 17th Century New Mexico.* Tucson: University of Arizona Press, 2014.

Lippman, Walter. *Public Policy.* New York: Harcourt, Brace and Co., 1922.

Linden, David. *The Accidental Mind: How Brain Evolution Has Given Us Love, Memory, Dreams, and God.* Cambridge, MA: Belknap Press of Harvard University Press, 2008.

Linden, David. "Can a Neuroscientist Fight Cancer with Mere Thought?" *The New York Times*, March 18, 2023.

Linden, David. "A Neuroscientist Prepares for Death: Lessons my terminal cancer has taught me about the mind." *The Atlantic*, December 30, 2021.

Liu, Eric. "What Every American Should Know: Defining Common Cultural Literacy for an Increasingly Diverse Nation." *The Atlantic,* July 3, 2015.

Lynch, Kevin. *What Time is This Place?* Cambridge, Massachusetts and London: MIT Press, 1972.

Manteuffel, Rachel. "The Context Behind the Fatal Punchline that Obscured the Lincoln Assassination." *The Washington Post*, April 13, 2021.

Mark, Lauren. "The Acculturative Costs of Rhythmic Belonging." *Capacious: Journal for Emerging Affect Inquiry* 2, no. 1 (2019-2020).

Masumoto, Tomoko. "American Interns in Japanese Organizations: Participant Perceptions and Interpretations of Intercultural Communication in the 'US-Japan Industry and Technology Management Program'." PhD diss., University of New Mexico, 2000.

Masumoto, Tomoko. "Learning How to Learn: Preparing Expatriate Interns to Work in a Japanese Organization." *International Journal of Humanities and Social Sciences* 2, no. 18 (October 2012): 77-84.

Masumoto, Tomoko. "Learning to 'Do Time' in Japan: A Study of US Interns in Japanese Organizations in Japan." *International Journal of Cross-Cultural Management* 4, no. 1 (April 2004): 19-37.

Masumoto, Tomoko. "The Semantic Dimensions of an International Story: The Ehime Maru Incident." *ETC: A Review of General Semantics*, 68, no. 2 (April 2011): 204-213.

McCormack, D. P. *Refrains for Moving Bodies: Experience and Experiment in Affective Spaces.* Durham, North Carolina: Duke University Press, 2013.

McGilchrist, Iain. *The Master and His Emissary: The Divided Brain and the Making of the Western World.* New Haven, Connecticut: Yale University Press, 2009.

McKeller, Peter. *Experience and Behavior.* Harmondsworth, England: Pelican Books, 1968.

McLuhan, Marshall. *Understanding Media: The Extensions of Man.* New York: McGraw-Hill, 1964.

McLuhan, Marshall, and Edmund Carpenter, eds., *Explorations in Communication: An Anthology.* Boston: Beacon Press, 1968.

McLuhan, Marshall, and Quentin Fiore. *The Medium is the Massage: An Inventory of Effects.* Berkeley: Gingko Press, 1967.

McWhorter, John. "Blackness and Standard English Can Co-Exist: Professors Take Notice." *The New York Times,* May 3, 2022.

Miller, Greg. "Axel, Buck Share Award for Deciphering How the Nose Knows." *Science* 306 (October 8, 2004): 207.

Milton, John R., ed., *Conversations with Frank Waters.* Chicago: Swallow Press, 1971.

Montanari, Massimo. *Food is Culture.* Translated by Albert Sonnenfeld. New York: Columbia University Press, 2006.

Murch, Walter. *In the Blink of an Eye: A Perspective on Film Editing, Second Edition.* Beverly Hills: Silman-James Press, 2001.

Nabokov, Peter. *A Forest of Time: American Indian Ways of History.* Cambridge, UK: Cambridge University Press, 2002.

Nisugi, Momoko. "Images of Spoken Japanese and Spoken English." In *Intercultural Encounters with Japan*, edited by John Condon and Mitsuko Saito. Tokyo: Simul Press, 1974.

Ong, Walter. *Orality and Literacy: The Technologizing of the Word.* London: Methuen & Co. Ltd., 1982.

Pagel, Mark. *Wired for Culture: Origins of the Human Social Mind*. New York: W.W. Norton, 2012.

Pérez, Frank G., and Carlos F. Ortega. *Deconstructing Eurocentric Tourism and Heritage Narratives in Mexican American Communication: Juan de Oñate as a West Texas Icon*. London: Routledge, 2019.

Philipsen, Gerry. "Communication in Teamsterville: A Sociolinguistic study of Speech Behavior in an Urban Neighborhood." PhD diss., Northwestern University, 1972.

Philipsen, Gerry. "Places for Speaking in Teamsterville." *Quarterly Journal of Speech* 62 (February 1976): 15-25.

Philipsen, Gerry. "Speaking 'Like a Man' in Teamsterville: Culture Patterns of Role Enactment in an Urban Neighborhood." *Quarterly Journal of Speech* 61, no. 1 (1975): 13–22.

Pooley, Jefferson. "How to Become a Famous Media Scholar: The Case of Marshall McLuhan." *Los Angeles Review of Books*, December 20, 2016.

Porges, S. W. *The Pocket Guide to the Polyvagal Theory: The Transformative Power of Feeling Safe*. New York: W. W. Norton & Company, 2017.

Ravignani, Andrea, Laura Verga, and Michael D. Greenfield. "Interactive Rhythms Across Species: The Evolutionary Biology of Animal Chorusing and Turn-Taking," *Annals of the New York Academy of Sciences* 1453, no. 1 (2019): 12-21.

Richie, Donald. *Ozu*. Berkeley: University of California Press, 1974.

Roberts, Monty. *The Man Who Listens to Horses*. Arrow, 1997.

Roeser, Sabine. "Intuitions, Emotions and Gut Reactions in Decisions about Risks: Towards a Different Interpretation of 'Neuroethics.'" *Journal of Risk Research* 13, no. 2 (2010).

Rogers, Everett. "The Extensions of Men: The Correspondence of Marshall McLuhan and Edward T. Hall." *Mass Communication and Society 3, no. 1 (Winter 2000): 117-135.*

Roose, Kevin. "A Conversation with Bing's Chatbot Left Me Deeply Unsettled." *The New York Times,* February 16, 2023.

Roose, Kevin. "We Need to Talk About How Good A.I. Is Getting." *The New York Times,* August 24, 2022.

Rothenberg, Jerome, and Diane Rothenberg. *Symposium of the Whole: A Range of Discourse Toward an Ethnopoetics*. Berkeley and Los Angeles: University of California Press, 1983.

Rovelli, Carlo. *The Order of Time*. New York: Riverhead Books, 2018.

Sacks, Oliver. *Musicophilia: Tales of Music and the Brain.* New York: Alfred A. Knopf, 2007.

Sando, Joe S. *Nee Hemish: A History of the Jemez Pueblo.* Albuquerque, NM: University of New Mexico Press, 1982.

Sekimoto, Sachi, and Christopher Brown. *Race and the Senses: The Felt Politics of Racial Embodiment.* London and New York: Routledge, 2020.

Shachtman, Noah. "Honoring *Wired's* Patron Saint." *Wired*, May 13, 2002.

Shaules, Joseph. "Edward Hall Ahead of His Time: Deep Cultural, Intercultural Understanding, and Embodied Cognition." *Intercultural Communication Education* 2, no. 1 (2019): 1-19.

Shlain, Leonard. *The Alphabet Versus the Goddess: The Conflict Between Word and Image.* Viking Penguin, 1998.

Singer, P. W., and Emerson T. Brooking. *Like War: The Weaponization of Social Media.* Boston, New York: Houghton Mifflin Harcourt, 2018.

Soja, Edward W. *Thirdspace: Journeys to Los Angeles and Other Real-and-Imagined Places.* Hoboken, New Jersey: Wiley-Blackwell, 1996.

Soloman, Andrew. *Far From the Tree: Parents, Children, and the Search for Identity.* New York: Scribner, 2012.

Sorrells, Kathryn. "Gifts of Wisdom: An Interview with Dr. Edward T. Hall." *The Edge: The E-Journal of Intercultural Relations* 1, no. 3 (Summer 1998). https://people.umass.edu/~leda/comm494r/The Edge Interview Hall.htm

Sorrells, Kathryn. *Intercultural Communication: Globalization and Social Justice, Third Edition.* Thousand Oaks, California: Sage Publications, 2021.

Spencer, Katherine B., Amanda K. Charbonneau, and Jack Glaser. "Implicit Bias and Policing." *Social and Personality Psychology Compass* 10, no. 1 (2016): 50–63, 10.1111/spc3.12210 University of California, Berkeley.

Spradley, James, and Brenda Mann. *The Cocktail Waitress: Women's Work in a Man's World.* New York: Wiley, 1975.

Steppat, M., and S. J. Kulich. "Concepts of Culture: Histories and Genealogies." *Journal of Intercultural Communication & Interactions Research (JIRIC)* 2, no. 1 (2022): 7-36. https://doi.org/10.3726/jicir.2022.1.0003

Stilgoe, John R. *Outside Lies Magic: Regaining History and Awareness in Everyday Places.* New York: Walker and Company, 1998.

Stille, Alexander. "Marshall McLuhan is Back from the Dustbin of History: With the Internet, His Ideas Again Seem Ahead of Their Time." *The New York Times*, October 1, 2018.

Strogatz, Steven. *Sync: How Order Emerges from Chaos in the Universe, Nature, and Daily Life.* New York: Hachette, 2015.

Suina, Joseph. "And Then I Went to School: Memories of a Pueblo Childhood." *Rethinking Schools* 5, 4 (1991): 1-4.

Suina, Joseph H. "Pueblo Secrecy: Result of Intrusions." *New Mexico Magazine,* January, 1992.

Swentzell, Rina. "Pueblo Space: An Understated Sacredness." In *Telling New Mexico: A New History,* edited by Marta Weigle, Frances Levine, and Louise Stiver. Santa Fe: Museum of New Mexico Press, 2009.

Tannen, Deborah. *Gender and Discourse.* New York: Oxford University Press, 1996.

Tannen, Deborah. *You Just Don't Understand: Women and Men in Conversation.* New York: William Morrow Paperbacks, 2007.

Tannen, Deborah. *Talking from 9 to 5, Women and Men at Work: Language, Sex and Power.* London: Virago Press, 1994.

Terry, Keith, and Linda Akiyama. *Rhythm of Math: Teaching Mathematics with Body Music.* Oakland: Crosspulse Media, 2015.

Torgan, Carol. "Humans Can Identify More than One Trillian Smells." *NIH Research Matters,* March 31, 2014.

Tsunoda, Tadanobu. *The Japanese Brain.* Translated by Yoshinori Oiwa. Tokyo: Taishukan, 1985.

Tuan, Yi-Fu. *Humanist Geography: An Individual's Search for Meaning.* Staunton, Virginia: George F. Thompson Publishing, 2012.

Tuan, *Yi-Fu. Space and Place: The Perspective of Experience.* Minneapolis: University of Minnesota Press, 1977.

Tuan, Yi-Fu. *Topophilia: A Study of Environmental Perception, Attitudes, and Values.* Englewood Cliffs, New Jersey, 1974.

Turkle, Sherry. *Alone Together: Why We Expect More from Technology and Less from Each Other.* New York: Basic Books, 2011.

van Vogt, A. E. *The Players of Null-A.* New York: Berkley Books, 1974.

van der Kolk, Bessel. *The Body Keeps the Score: Brain, Mind, and Body in the Healing of Trauma.* Viking, 2014.

Vande Berg, Michael, R. Michael Paige, and Kris Hemming Lou. *Student Learning Abroad: What Our Students Are Learning, What They're Not, and What We Can Do About It.* Sterling, Virginia: Stylus, 2012.

Vogt, Evan, and Ethel Albert, eds. *The People of Rimrock: A Study of Values in Five Cultures.* Cambridge, Massachusetts: Harvard University Press, 1966.

Wade, Nicholas. *Before the Dawn: Recovering the Lost History of Our Ancestors.* New York: Penguin Books, 2006.

Warren, Marcia Bonato. *Movement and Identity: Multiculturalism, Somatic Awareness and Embodied Code-Switching*. London: Singing Dragon, 2025.

Watzlawick, Paul, Janet Helmick Beavin, and Don D. Jackson. *Pragmatics of Human Communication: A Study of Interactional Patterns, Pathologies and Paradoxes.* New York: W.W. Norton, 1967.

Weschler, Lawrence. *Seeing is Forgetting the Name of the Thing One Sees: A Life of Contemporary Artist Robert Irwin.* Los Angeles and Berkeley: University of California Press, 1982.

Whorf, Benjamin Lee, John B. Carroll, ed. *Language Thought and Reality: Selected Writings of Benjamin Lee Whorf.* Boston, Massachusetts: MIT Press, 1956.

Wiener, Norbert. *The Human Use of Human Beings: Cybernetics and Society.* Boston: Houghton Mifflin, 1950.

Wierzbicka, Anna. *Imprisoned in English: The Hazards of English as a Default Language.* Oxford University Press, 2013.

Wilson, Chris. *The Myth of Santa Fe: Creating a Modern Regional Tradition.* Albuquerque: University of New Mexico Press, 1997.

Wilkerson, Louise. *Caste: The Origins of Our Discontents.* Random House, 2020.

Witherspoon, Gary. *Language and Art in the Navajo Universe.* Ann Arbor, Michigan: University of Michigan Press, 1977.

Wirth, John D., and Linda Harvey Aldrich. *Los Alamos: The Ranch School Years, 1917-1943.* Albuquerque: University of New Mexico Press, 2003.

Yardley, Jim "Land for Los Alamos Lab Taken Unfairly, Heirs Say." *The New York Times*, August 27, 2001.

Yeats, W. B. "Among School Children." *The Collected Poems of W. B. Yeats.* Stansted, UK: Wordsworth Editions, 1994.

Zeman, Adam. *A Portrait of the Brain.* New Haven: Yale University Press, 2008.

People Quoted at the Beginnings of Chapters

Muhammad Ali, US, heavyweight boxing champion; civil rights activist opposing US involvement in the war in Viet Nam.

Maya Angelou, US, poet, prolific author, playwright, performer, and civil rights activist; poet for the first inauguration of US Pres. Bill Clinton.

Sir David Attenborough, UK, author, biologist, naturalist historian, spokesperson on many media about the natural environment and the human impact on it.

Keith Basso, US, anthropologist at Yale Univ. and Univ. of New Mexico, author, with emphasis on US indigenous cultures and white/Native American communication.

Adrian Belew, US, progressive guitarist with Frank Zappa, David Bowie, Talking Heads, and others.

Paul Bloom, Canadian-US, professor of psychology at Yale University and the University of Toronto, known for the child's and adult's perception of the world.

Paul Bohannan, US, anthropologist, specialist in African cultures, and Professor at Princeton University, Northwestern Univ., and Univ. of California, Santa Barbara.

Christopher Brown, US, professor of Communication and Founding Dean of the College of Humanities and Social Sciences, Minnesota State University, Mankato.

Holloway Brown, US, journalism professor, Director of the Public Information Office at International Christian University in Mitaka, Japan, and for two decades, editorial writer for *The Japan Times*.

Julian Jaynes, US, psychology professor at Yale University and Princeton University, and author, best known for his research on consciousness.

Ann Landers, US, pen-name for Ruth Crowley, syndicated newspaper "advice columnist" for 56 years.

Henri Lefebvre, France, Marxist sociologist and philosopher, known as critic of everyday life, and the study of social space.

David Linden, US, neuroscientist at Johns Hopkins Univ. and award-winning author known for his ability to explain, with clarity and wit, neurology to the non-specialist.

Marshall McLuhan, Canadian, prolific and influential author on media's impact on culture; first director of the Centre for Culture and Technology at the University of Toronto.

C. Wright Mills, US, sociology professor at Columbia University, critic of US policy in Viet Nam and Cuba.

Azar Nafisi, Iranian-US American, author. Her best-selling book *Reading Lolita in Tehran: A Memoir in Books,* won the 2004 Non-Fiction Book of the Year award.

Jack Parsons, award-winning US photographer and cinematographer; grandson of anthropologist Louise Parsons.

Marcel Proust, French, early twentieth century writer, best known for his seven-volume novel, *À la rechche du temps puerdu (In Search of Lost Time).*

Will Rogers, Cherokee Nation, Native American performer on stage and in film, and often quoted "homespun philosopher" in the early part of the twentieth century.

Carlo Rovelli, Italian, theoretical physicist, philosopher, author, based in Centre de Phyique de Luminy, Marseille.

Oliver Sacks, British-born, US resident, physician, neurologist, historian of science, and prolific author.

Sachi Sekimoto, Japanese-born, US resident, Professor of Communication, theorist of culture and embodiment, University of Minnesota-Mankato.

Erwin Schrödinger, Austrian born, naturalized Irish, theoretical physicist and quantum mechanics, and recipient of the Nobel Prize in physics.

Yi-Fu Tuan, Taiwanese-born, founded the field of humanistic geography, professor at several US universities, and prolific writer.

Benjamin Lee Whorf, US, chemical engineer whose avocation was linguistics and considered among the most influential and controversial linguists of his time.

E. O. Wilson, US, biologist, entomologist, naturist and sociobiologist, a field he is credited with creating, and twice recipient of the Pulitzer Prize.

Image Credits

S pecial thanks to Ricardo Caté, Native American syndicated cartoonist (Kewa Pueblo, New Mexico), for permission to use his cartoon on the front cover of the book; to Anna-Maria Hass of Hamburg, Germany, for the photo taken at the Summer Institute for Intercultural Communication, Portland, Oregon, that appears on the back cover; to graphic designer Lina Biel of Vilnius, Lithuania, for the cover design; and to Ghislain Viau of Creative Publishing Book Design for layout and formatting.

I am most grateful to Robert Caslin for the front door sketch introducing Chapter One; to Miguel Gandert for the photo of Professor Hall introducing Chapter Two, and to the Los Alamos Historical Society Archives, for permission to reprint the photos in Chapter Two; to Amy Jones for her calligraphy introducing Chapter Three; to Yurchanka Siarhei for the photo introducing Chapter Four; to Dave Coverly for permission to reprint his cartoon in Chapter Seven; to Alex Jones for the photo introducing Chapter Twelve; to Peter Barber, *The Map Book*, for the photo introducing Chapter Thirteen; to Dan Odess for the photo introducing Chapter Fourteen; to Tijanap for the photo introducing Chapter Fifteen; and special thanks to Ted Greer for his photographic enhancement of the graphics, artwork, and photos throughout the book.

For granting permission to reprint "A Map of Culture," my thanks to the E. T. Hall Estate.

Index

Made in United States
Troutdale, OR
12/01/2024